Reformation,
Absolutism:
1450–1650

The Structure of European History
studies and interpretations

◆§§◆

NORMAN F. CANTOR and MICHAEL S. WERTHMAN, Editors

Volume I
ANCIENT CIVILIZATION:
4000 B.C.–400 A.D.

Volume II
MEDIEVAL SOCIETY:
400–1450

Volume III
RENAISSANCE, REFORMATION, AND ABSOLUTISM:
1450–1650

Volume IV
THE FULFILLMENT AND COLLAPSE OF THE OLD REGIME:
1650–1815

Volume V
THE MAKING OF THE MODERN WORLD:
1815–1914

Volume VI
THE TWENTIETH CENTURY:
1914 to the Present

Renaissance, Reformation, and Absolutism: 1450–1650

Second Edition

edited by NORMAN F. CANTOR

State University of New York at Binghamton

and MICHAEL S. WERTHMAN

Thomas Y. Crowell Company   *New York*

ESTABLISHED 1834

ACKNOWLEDGMENTS: The editors wish to express their gratitude to the following publishers and individuals for permission to quote selections from the works designated:

Jacob Burckhardt, *The Civilisation of the Renaissance in Italy*, translated by S. G. C. Middlemore. Reprinted by permission of George Allen & Unwin Ltd.

Herbert Butterfield, *The Origins of Modern Science: 1300–1800*. Reprinted by permission of G. Bell & Sons, Ltd. and the author.

Sir George Clark, *Early Modern Europe from about 1450 to about 1720*. Reprinted by permission of The Clarendon Press, Oxford.

J. H. Elliott, *Imperial Spain*. Reprinted by permission of St. Martin's Press, Inc. and Edward Arnold (Publishers) Ltd., London.

Joseph Lortz, *The Reformation in Germany*, Volume I, translated by Ronald Walls. Reprinted by permission of Herder and Herder, New York.

J. H. Parry, *The Age of Reconnaissance: Discovery, Exploration and Settlement 1450 to 1650*. Copyright © 1963 in London, England, by J. H. Parry. Reprinted by permission of Weidenfeld (Publishers) Ltd., London and Praeger Publishers, Inc., New York.

Hans Rosenberg, *Bureaucracy, Aristocracy and Autocracy: The Prussian Experience, 1660–1815*. Copyright 1958 by the President and Fellows of Harvard College. Reprinted by the permission of Harvard University Press.

H. R. Trevor-Roper, "The General Crisis of the Seventeenth Century," from *The Crisis of the Seventeenth Century: Religion, the Reformation and Social Change*. Copyright © 1959 by H. R. Trevor-Roper. Originally published in England by Macmillan and Company Limited under the title *Religion, the Reformation and Social Change*. Reprinted by permission of Harper & Row, Publishers, Inc., The Macmillan Company of Canada, and Macmillan, London and Basingstoke.

Preface

~§~ *The Structure of European History* is a six-volume anthology series whose purpose is to present to the undergraduate and lay reader leading interpretations of fundamental political, economic, social, and intellectual change in European history from the advent of civilization to the present day. The six volumes are devoted to the following eras of European history:

I. Ancient Civilization: 4000 B.C.–400 A.D.
II. Medieval Society: 400–1450
III. Renaissance, Reformation, and Absolutism: 1450–1650
IV. The Fulfillment and Collapse of the Old Regime: 1650–1815
V. The Making of the Modern World: 1815–1914
VI. The Twentieth Century: 1914 to the Present

Every volume consists of eight relatively long selections, each of which is preceded by an editors' introduction that outlines the problem, identifies the author, defines his methods and assumptions, and establishes his interpretation within the historiography of the subject. A brief list of additional important books in the same subject or on related subjects follows each selection. Each volume contains a brief introduction to the period as a whole that delineates the leading themes by which modern scholarship has illuminated the era.

Almost all of the forty-eight selections in the six volumes were written in the past forty years and the majority since 1940. In recent decades historians of Europe have sought to extrapolate broad movements of historical change from the vast amount of data that modern research has built up. There has been a general tendency in modern scholarship to bridge the conventional compartmentalization of political, economic, social, and intellectual history and to analyze a movement or event which falls primarily in one of these categories within the context of a total view of social and cultural change. Historians more and more attempt to present a picture of the past as rich, as complex, and as full of human experience itself. The intertwining and mutual involvement of many kinds of aspirations and achievements are now seen to be the basic existential facts shaping previous societies just as they shape social conditions in our own time.

We have sought in these six volumes to present to the student and lay reader examples of this comprehensive and total approach to the understanding of European history. In making our selections we have been governed by the criterion of choosing interpretations which view critical movements and trends in the history of Western civilization in as broad and as many-faceted a context as possible. We have also aimed to make selections which are distinguished by a clear and forceful style and which can be easily comprehended by students in a freshman survey course and by the college-educated lay reader.

Most of the selections in each of the six volumes of this series are the original, seminal theses presented by distinguished scholars after many years of research and reflection. In a few instances the criterion of comprehension by the novice student and lay reader has led us to take an extract from a work of synthesis and high vulgarization which in turn is based on very important monographic studies.

N.F.C.
M.S.W.

Contents

Introduction

During the 1920's and 30's there was a widespread belief among historians that the structure of European history between 1450 and 1650 was founded upon the interaction of capitalism and Protestantism. Scholars were fascinated by what appeared to be the rapid upsurge of commercial and industrial capitalism in Protestant Holland, England, and northern Germany, while Catholic southern Europe was held to have slid into a precipitous economic decline marked by the Italian cities' failure to maintain their leadership in finance and trade and by the catastrophic inability of the Spaniards to take advantage of their imperial American wealth.

Subsequent research has severely weakened this clear-cut contrast between the aggressive northern Protestants advancing into the modern world with bourgeois thrift and enterprise and the Mediterranean peoples sinking into stagnation and poverty under the dead weight of medieval Catholicism. This interpretation of sixteenth-century economic history was a favorite liberal Victorian myth but does not quite fit the facts; twentieth-century scholars who felt impelled to establish a direct relationship between Protestantism and capitalism too easily accepted the Victorian assumptions at face value. The weight of empirical evidence strongly supports those critics who have dissented from the facile association of Protestantism and capitalism. The Flemish cities remained loyal to traditional Catholicism while continuing to enjoy substantial commercial and financial prosperity, and the supposedly steep economic

1

decline of Spain and Italy in the sixteenth century has been called into question by the results of recent detailed research. At the end of the sixteenth century the Mediterranean world, for all its devotion to the Council of Trent, the Inquisition, and the Jesuit order, was still a thriving economic unit. The economic decline of Spain and Italy is largely a seventeenth-century phenomenon to which strictly political problems made important contributions.

Nor is it so clear that Protestant fervor necessarily implied capitalist enterprise. Fanatically Calvinist Scotland remained an intensely rural and backward economic area until the eighteenth century, while the Scandinavian countries, after their acceptance of Lutheranism, slowly retreated from their medieval involvement in international commerce and by the end of the seventeenth century, at least in the case of Norway and Sweden, had become the underdeveloped areas they were to remain, for all their Protestant piety, until the twentieth century. Nor does the economic development of even Holland or England in the sixteenth and seventeenth centuries represent the steady and unmitigated advancement of capitalist enterprise. The Dutch burghers flourished in commerce and banking in the late sixteenth and first three-quarters of the seventeenth centuries, but they proved totally incapable of effecting the industrialization which would have allowed them to maintain their leading place in European economic life; the hegemony of the merchant oligarchy of Holland proved as transient a phenomenon as the prominence in international finance and trade once enjoyed by the Florentines and Venetians. Nor did the break with Rome and even the spread of Calvinism in England prevent severe difficulties for English commerce and industry, periodic depressions, and a great slowing down of the pace of economic growth in the late sixteenth and early seventeenth centuries. It would not be too farfetched to draw from recent scholarship the ironic conclusion that the more devoutly Protestant the English became from 1560 to 1640, the less successful were they in business.

Because of arguments like these there has been in the last two decades a general, though by no means unanimous, retreat from the interpretations of early modern

Europe as the product of the interaction of Protestantism and capitalism. A more complex structure of European history in the period 1450 to 1650 has been slowly emerging in recent historiography, and the eight themes illustrated by the selections in this book are among those which have been most carefully analyzed.

With certain reservations, the idea of Italian Renaissance civilization propounded by Jacob Burckhardt a century ago still holds the field in the interpretation of late fifteenth-century intellectual history. Modern research, however, must be credited with illuminating the significance of the fifteenth-, sixteenth-, and seventeenth-century voyages of discovery and exploration. Recent work has described the impact on European politics, society, and even the consciousness of that age. Likewise, interpretation of the Reformation has undergone radical change; religious inspiration has been given the central place in this movement while ecclesiastical, national, and social factors have come to be viewed as critical preconditions that gave faith and fervor the fertile ground needed for universal expression. The so-called Wars of Religion, that protracted period of European conflict that traditionally appeared to be caused by confessional oppositions and religious fanaticism, are now understood to have been the result of a complex of motivations—reasons of state, class, and dynastic pride—always driven by a desire for power and mastery.

Against this background of almost constant warfare, the Scientific Revolution stands as a monument to human ingenuity and determination. The great breakthrough in scientific thought, which in the older historiography received only peripheral attention, has been viewed as the most important intellectual movement of the late sixteenth and seventeenth centuries and its enormous social consequences are now appreciated. In recent scholarship much closer attention has also been given to the mechanics of statecraft and the institutions of government in the early modern era. There is a growing conviction among historians of the period that the destiny of certain states and the development of political institutions were more important than economic change in shaping the direction of European society during the sixteenth and early seventeenth cen-

turies. Fresh and illuminating discussion has been generated about the causes of the decline of Spain; a spirited
and remarkably informative debate has burned over the
concept of a general crisis brought about in the seventeenth
century by the inability of monarchical bureaucratic governments to implement their policies owing to the limitations of their administrative machinery and because of the
opposition—often violent and revolutionary—of their subjects. Especially provocative implications have been found
in the institutional foundations of the French absolutist
monarchy's rise to European hegemony and in Prussian
absolutism's thorough-going regimentation and exploitation
of the resources of the state.

JACOB BURCKHARDT

The Discovery of the World and of Man

Jacob Burckhardt's *The Civilisation of the Renaissance in Italy* was published in 1860. The most remarkable tribute to the quality of this work is the astonishing fact that of all the ambitious and imposing historical studies published by writers of Burckhardt's generation, this is the only one that still remains in print and is still read, not primarily because it serves as an exemplar of nineteenth-century historiography, but because the author's idea—in this case, Burckhardt's view of Renaissance culture—is still largely accepted by historians and still dominates our view of the structure of early modern Europe.

The distinctive quality of the author's mind is reflected in every page of Burckhardt's work. He was a scion of the Basel aristocracy, a German-Swiss scholar and gentleman, an elegant and at the same time deeply serious man. Burckhardt prized individuality, the free development and expression of the human mind above all other values. Like his contemporaries Alexis de Tocqueville, John Stuart Mill, and Matthew Arnold, he feared the consequences of the growth of democracy, the striking out to power of an irrational and ignorant mob that would desire to pull everyone down to its own vulgar level. Before his death in 1897 Burckhardt foretold with remarkable accuracy the coming of the idols of the mob, "the terrible simplifiers," who would submerge all individuality in the mass and harness

FROM Jacob Burckhardt, *The Civilisation of the Renaissance in Italy*, 4th ed. rev. (London: Phaidon Press Ltd., 1951), pp. 81–93, 104–120, 171–191, 211–216.

every mind and body to the service of an egalitarian military state.

Already in the 1850's and 60's, his period of literary productivity, Burckhardt's detestation of the growing proletarianization of culture drove him to long visits in his beloved Italy and to the study of the classical and Renaissance past in which, he believed, the human spirit had achieved its greatest flowering of individuality. *Die Kultur der Renaissance in Italien* is the second half of a dual study, the first part of which, *The Age of Constantine the Great* (1853), depicted the crushing of the free classical spirit of antiquity in the fourth century by a state church set up by a cynical and self-seeking dictator. The *Renaissance* aimed to show how by 1500 the leaders of the Italian city-state, having developed "a social world . . . which felt the want of culture and the leisure and the means to obtain it," found kindred spirits in the men of antiquity, the products of a similar civic life; how they sensed in ancient civilization a guide "to knowledge of the physical and intellectual world," with the result that they cast off the "fantastic" and "childish" medieval world view and "rediscovered man and the world."

This thesis Burckhardt expounded with a carefully thought-out and highly self-conscious methodology. He assumed that the history of humanity can be strictly set off into well-defined periods. Within each of these eras, the historian can discern a coherent complex of thought and action which gives unity to the era. This is the "culture" of the age. Burckhardt further assumed that every people possesses a distinctive *Volksgeist* or communal spirit which the historian can determine. Both the *Volksgeist* and the culture, which in the case of the fifteenth century were synonymous, come to fullest expression in certain superior individuals who are the embodiment of the civilization and the people's spirit. He also assumed that the art and belletristic literature of an era are the finest expressions of its cultural form.

From his own lifetime until about 1920, Burckhardt's view of fifteenth-century history enjoyed the unanimous assent of academic scholarship. Furthermore, although Burckhardt himself confined his portrayal of the Renais-

sance to Italy and was cautious and vague on the question
of whether European culture north of the Alps in the same
period could be characterized in the same way, his admirers
exhibited no reticence in this regard. It thus became fashionable to define the fourteenth and fifteenth centuries as
"the Renaissance era" and to depict the discovery of the
world and of man as the primary theme of general European history in the two centuries before 1500.

After 1920 a reaction against the Renaissance idea began
slowly to set in, and by the 1940's Burckhardt's interpretations and methods were being subjected to severe, and
frequently savage, criticism. This historical revision was
inaugurated by the brilliant Dutch scholar Johan Huizinga,
who found that social life in the Low Countries in the
fifteenth century was marked by manifestations of decay-
ing medieval culture rather than the new dawn of the
Renaissance (see Volume II, Selection 8 in this series).
Medieval historians, angered by Burckhardt's disparage-
ment of the civilization they studied and admired, raised a
number of highly plausible objections to his thesis. They
pointed out that the rediscovery of classical thought was as
much—if not more—the work of scholastic thinkers of the
twelfth and thirteenth centuries as of Burckhardt's favored
Italian humanists. It was claimed that the new individualism made its appearance in France and northern Italy in
the late eleventh and twelfth centuries, and also that England and France in the thirteenth century were led by
governments which exhibited the qualities of modern statecraft and bureaucracy as much as those of the fifteenth-
century Italian city-states. Doubt furthermore was cast on
the scientific contribution of the Renaissance humanists;
and late thirteenth- and fourteenth-century scholastics,
rather than the Italian scholars of the fifteenth century,
were seen as the precursors of modern scientific thought.
In addition to these circumstantial objections, Burckhardt's
methods and assumptions were dismissed as representative
of outmoded nineteenth-century organic and nationalist
theories.

By the 1950's, at the point when Burckhardt's study was
on the verge of losing academic respectability, further consideration of fifteenth-century intellectual and social his-

tory and changes in historiographical methods restored much of his earlier reputation. We can no longer speak without extensive qualification of a Renaissance era, but it is apparent that there did occur in Italy in the fourteenth and fifteenth centuries a self-consciously revolutionary intellectual movement which had a profound effect on literature, art, government, and the style of life of the aristocracy and high bourgeoisie, and this impact was spreading to northern Europe in 1500. Perhaps this movement was narrowly elitist. It was shrilly self-important and undoubtedly it exaggerated its cultural achievements and the sharpness of its separation from the medieval past. But Europe in 1500 was still an elitist society in which the ideas and conduct of a few princes, courtiers, and intellectuals did have great consequence. The fact that the Italian humanists thought of themselves as different from, and superior to, the scholastic culture of the thirteenth century, even if these feelings were not altogether well founded in historical fact, is important for the world of the fifteenth century, because it allowed the thinkers of the period to break away from some of the assumptions of medieval thought and to move out in new directions. The Renaissance, we might conclude, was a highly influential intellectual movement which played a role in its environment similar to that of the rebellious Romantics of the early nineteenth century and of the nonconformist intellectuals of the early twentieth century.

Burckhardt's method of cultural history has also appeared, on second thought, to have much to recommend it. Removing the facade of nineteenth-century organic and racist terminology, we can see that Burckhardt was engaged in model-building in the manner of twentieth-century sociological historians like Marc Block (see Volume II, Selection 2 in this series). He created an hypostatized, idealized, social type which could be examined as a distinctive mode of thought and feeling. He defined for us the nature of Renaissance culture; we do not have to agree with him that this model was fully operative in fifteenth-century Italy to acknowledge that such an abstract model does give us an effective conceptualization of at least one important aspect of the Europe of 1500. Whatever the detailed objections to Burckhardt's thesis, the fact remains that something of great consequence was occurring in fifteenth-century Italian intellectual life that he persuasively defined in a meaningful, holistic interpretation. And in the century since Burckhardt wrote, no other model of late fifteenth-century culture has replaced his synthetic view.

   In the character of these States, whether republics or despotisms, lies, not the only, but the chief reason for the early development of the Italian. To this it is due that he was the firstborn among the sons of modern Europe.

   In the Middle Ages both sides of human consciousness—that which was turned within as that which was turned without—lay dreaming or half awake beneath a common veil. The veil was woven of faith, illusion, and childish prepossession, through which the world and history were seen clad in strange hues. Man was conscious of himself only as a member of a race, people, party, family, or corporation—only through some general category. In Italy this veil first melted into air; an *objective* treatment and consideration of the State and of all the things of this world became possible. The *subjective* side at the same time asserted itself with corresponding emphasis; man became a spiritual *individual*, and recognized himself as such. In the same way the Greek had once distinguished himself from the barbarian, and the Arab had felt himself an individual at a time when other Asiatics knew themselves only as members of a race. It will not be difficult to show that this result was due above all to the political circumstances of Italy.

   In far earlier times we can here and there detect a development of free personality which in Northern Europe either did not occur at all, or could not display itself in the same manner. The band of audacious wrongdoers in the tenth century described to us by Liudprand, some of the contemporaries of Gregory VII (for example, Benzo of Alba), and a few of the opponents of the first Hohenstaufen, show us characters of this kind. But at the close of the thirteenth century Italy began to swarm with individuality; the ban laid upon human personality was dissolved; and a thousand figures meet us each in its own special shape and dress. Dante's great poem would have been impossible in any other country of Europe, if only for the reason that they all still lay under the spell of race. For Italy the august poet, through the wealth of individuality which he set forth, was the most national herald of his time.

But this unfolding of the treasures of human nature in literature and art . . . this fact appears in the most decisive and unmistakable form. The Italians of the fourteenth century knew little of false modesty or of hypocrisy in any shape; not one of them was afraid of singularity, of being and seeming unlike his neighbours.

Despotism . . . fostered in the highest degree the individuality not only of the tyrant or Condottiere himself, but also of the men whom he protected or used as his tools—the secretary, minister, poet, and companion. These people were forced to know all the inward resources of their own nature, passing or permanent; and their enjoyment of life was enhanced and concentrated by the desire to obtain the greatest satisfaction from a possibly very brief period of power and influence.

But even the subjects whom they ruled over were not free from the same impulse. Leaving out of account those who wasted their lives in secret opposition and conspiracies, we speak of the majority who were content with a strictly private station, like most of the urban population of the Byzantine empire and the Mohammedan States. No doubt it was often hard for the subjects of a Visconti to maintain the dignity of their persons and families, and multitudes must have lost in moral character through the servitude they lived under. But this was not the case with regard to individuality; for political impotence does not hinder the different tendencies and manifestations of private life from thriving in the fullest vigour and variety. Wealth and culture, so far as display and rivalry were not forbidden to them, a municipal freedom which did not cease to be considerable, and a Church which, unlike that of the Byzantine or of the Mohammedan world, was not identical with the State—all these conditions undoubtedly favoured the growth of individual thought, for which the necessary leisure was furnished by the cessation of party conflicts. The private man, indifferent to politics, and busied partly with serious pursuits, partly with the interests of a *dilettante*, seems to have been first fully formed in these despotisms of the fourteenth century. Documentary evidence cannot, of course, be required on such a point. The novelists, from whom we might expect information, describe to us oddities in plenty, but only from one point of view and in so far as the needs of the story demand. Their scene, too, lies chiefly in the republican cities.

In the latter, circumstances were also, but in another way, favourable to the growth of individual character. The more frequently the governing party was changed, the more the individual was led to make the utmost of the exercise and enjoyment of power. The statesmen and popular leaders, especially in Florentine history, acquired so marked a personal character that we can scarcely find, even exceptionally, a parallel to them in contemporary history, hardly even in Jacob van Arteveldt.

The members of the defeated parties, on the other hand, often came into a position like that of the subjects of the despotic States, with the difference that the freedom or power already enjoyed, and in some cases the hope of recovering them, gave a higher energy to their individuality. Among these men of involuntary leisure we find, for instance, an Agnolo Pandolfini (d. 1446), whose work on domestic economy is the first complete programme of a developed private life. His estimate of the duties of the individual as against the dangers and thanklessness of public life is in its way a true monument of the age.

Banishment, too, has this effect above all, that it either wears the exile out or develops whatever is greatest in him. 'In all our more populous cities,' says Gioviano Pontano, 'we see a crowd of people who have left their homes of their own free will; but a man takes his virtues with him wherever he goes.' And, in fact, they were by no means only men who had been actually exiled, but thousands left their native place voluntarily, because they found its political or economic condition intolerable. The Florentine emigrants at Ferrara and the Lucchese in Venice formed whole colonies by themselves.

The cosmopolitanism which grew up in the most gifted circles is in itself a high stage of individualism. Dante, as we have already said, finds a new home in the language and culture of Italy, but goes beyond even this in the words, 'My country is the whole world'. And when his recall to Florence was offered him on unworthy conditions, he wrote back: 'Can I not everywhere behold the light of the sun and the stars; everywhere meditate on the noblest truths, without appearing ingloriously and shamefully before the city and the people? Even my bread will not fail me'. The artists exult no less defiantly in their freedom from the constraints of fixed residence. 'Only he who has learned everything,' says Ghiberti, 'is nowhere a stranger; robbed of his fortune and without friends, he is yet the citizen of every country, and can fearlessly despise the changes of fortune.' In the same strain an exiled humanist writes: 'Wherever a learned man fixes his seat, there is home'.

An acute and practised eye might be able to trace, step by step, the increase in the number of complete men during the fifteenth century. Whether they had before them as a conscious object the harmonious development of their spiritual and material existence, is hard to say; but several of them attained it, so far as is consistent with the imper-

fection of all that is earthly. It may be better to renounce the attempt
at an estimate of the share which fortune, character, and talent had
in the life of Lorenzo il Magnifico. But look at a personality like that of
Ariosto, especially as shown in his satires. In what harmony are there
expressed the pride of the man and the poet, the irony with which he
treats his own enjoyments, the most delicate satire, and the deepest
goodwill!

When this impulse to the highest individual development was combined with a powerful and varied nature, which had mastered all the
elements of the culture of the age, then arose the 'all-sided man'—
'l'uomo universale'—who belonged to Italy alone. Men there were of
encyclopædic knowledge in many countries during the Middle Ages,
for this knowledge was confined within narrow limits; and even in the
twelfth century there were universal artists, but the problems of architecture were comparatively simple and uniform, and in sculpture and
painting the matter was of more importance than the form. But in Italy
at the time of the Renaissance, we find artists who in every branch
created new and perfect works, and who also made the greatest
impression as men. Others, outside the arts they practised, were
masters of a vast circle of spiritual interests.

Dante, who, even in his lifetime, was called by some a poet, by
others a philosopher, by others a theologian, pours forth in all his
writings a stream of personal force by which the reader, apart from
the interest of the subject, feels himself carried away. What power of
will must the steady, unbroken elaboration of the *Divine Comedy*
have required! And if we look at the matter of the poem, we find that
in the whole spiritual or physical world there is hardly an important
subject which the poet has not fathomed, and on which his utterances
—often only a few words—are not the most weighty of his time. For
the visual arts he is of the first importance, and this for better reasons
than the few references to contemporary artists—he soon became himself the source of inspiration.

The fifteenth century is, above all, that of the many-sided men.
There is no biography which does not, besides the chief work of its
hero, speak of other pursuits all passing beyond the limits of dilet-
tantism. The Florentine merchant and statesman was often learned in
both the classical languages; the most famous humanists read the
Ethics and Politics of Aristotle to him and his sons; even the daughters
of the house were highly educated. It is in these circles that private
education was first treated seriously. The humanist, on his side, was
compelled to the most varied attainments, since his philological learn-

ing was not limited, as it is now, to the theoretical knowledge of classical antiquity, but had to serve the practical needs of daily life. While studying Pliny, he made collections of natural history; the geography of the ancients was his guide in treating of modern geography, their history was his pattern in writing contemporary chronicles, even when composed in Italian; he not only translated the comedies of Plautus, but acted as manager when they were put on the stage; every effective form of ancient literature down to the dialogues of Lucian he did his best to imitate; and besides all this, he acted as magistrate, secretary and diplomatist—not always to his own advantage.

But among these many-sided men, some, who may truly be called all-sided, tower above the rest. Before analysing the general phases of life and culture of this period, we may here, on the threshold of the fifteenth century, consider for a moment the figure of one of these giants—Leon Battista Alberti (b. 1404, d. 1472). His biography, which is only a fragment, speaks of him but little as an artist, and makes no mention at all of his great significance in the history of architecture. We shall now see what he was, apart from these special claims to distinction.

In all by which praise is won, Leon Battista was from his childhood the first. Of his various gymnastic feats and exercises we read with astonishment how, with his feet together, he could spring over a man's head; how, in the cathedral, he threw a coin in the air till it was heard to ring against the distant roof; how the wildest horses trembled under him. In three things he desired to appear faultless to others, in walking, in riding, and in speaking. He learned music without a master, and yet his compositions were admired by professional judges. Under the pressure of poverty, he studied both civil and canonical law for many years, till exhaustion brought on a severe illness. In his twenty-fourth year, finding his memory for words weakened, but his sense of facts unimpaired, he set to work at physics and mathematics. And all the while he acquired every sort of accomplishment and dexterity, cross-examining artists, scholars and artisans of all descriptions, down to the cobblers, about the secrets and peculiarities of their craft. Painting and modelling he practised by the way, and especially excelled in admirable likenesses from memory. Great admiration was excited by his mysterious 'camera obscura', in which he showed at one time the stars and the moon rising over rocky hills, at another wide landscapes with mountains and gulfs receding into dim perspective, and with fleets advancing on the waters in shade or sunshine. And that which others created he welcomed joyfully, and held every human achievement which followed the laws of beauty for something almost divine. To all this must be added his literary works, first of all those on art, which are landmarks and authorities of the first order for the Renaissance of Form, especially in architecture; then his Latin prose writings—novels and other works—of which some have been taken for productions of antiquity; his elegies, eclogues, and humorous dinner-speeches. He also wrote an Italian treatise on domestic life in four books; and even a funeral oration on his dog. His serious and witty sayings were thought worth collecting, and specimens of them, many columns long, are quoted in his biography. And all that he had and knew he imparted, as rich natures always do, without the least reserve, giving away his chief discoveries for nothing. But the deepest spring of his nature has yet to be spoken of—the sympathetic intensity with which he entered into the whole life around him. At the sight of noble trees and waving cornfields he shed tears; handsome and dignified old men he honoured as 'a delight of nature', and could never look at them enough. Perfectly formed animals won his goodwill as being specially favoured by nature; and more than once, when he was ill, the sight of a beautiful landscape cured him. No wonder that those who saw him in this close and mysterious communion with the world ascribed to him the gift of prophecy. He was said to have foretold a bloody catastrophe in the family of Este, the fate of Florence and that of the Popes many years beforehand, and to be able to read in the countenances and the hearts of men. It need not be added that an iron will pervaded and sustained his whole personality; like all the great men of the Renaissance, he said, 'Men can do all things if they will'.

And Leonardo da Vinci was to Alberti as the finisher to the beginner, as the master to the *dilettante*. Would only that Vasari's work were here supplemented by a description like that of Alberti! The colossal outlines of Leonardo's nature can never be more than dimly and distantly conceived.

To this inward development of the individual corresponds a new sort of outward distinction—the modern form of glory.

In the other countries of Europe the different classes of society lived apart, each with its own medieval caste sense of honour. The poetical fame of the Troubadours and Minnesänger was peculiar to the knightly order. But in Italy social equality had appeared before the time of the tyrannies or the democracies. We there find early traces of a general society, having, as will be shown more fully later on, a common ground in Latin and Italian literature; and such a ground was needed for this new element in life to grow in. To this must be added that the Roman

authors, who were now zealously studied, are filled and saturated with
the conception of fame, and that their subject itself—the universal
empire of Rome—stood as a permanent ideal before the minds of
Italians. From henceforth all the aspirations and achievements of the
people were governed by a moral postulate, which was still unknown
elsewhere in Europe.

Here, again, as in all essential points, the first witness to be called is
Dante. He strove for the poet's garland with all the power of his soul.
As publicist and man of letters, he laid stress on the fact that what he
did was new, and that he wished not only to be, but to be esteemed
the first in his own walks. But in his prose writings he touches also on
the inconveniences of fame; he knows how often personal acquaintance
with famous men is disappointing, and explains how this is due partly
to the childish fancy of men, partly to envy, and partly to the imper-
fections of the hero himself. And in his great poem he firmly maintains
the emptiness of fame, although in a manner which betrays that his
heart was not free from the longing for it. In Paradise the sphere of
Mercury is the seat of such blessed ones as on earth strove after glory
and thereby dimmed 'the beams of true love'. It is characteristic that
the lost souls in hell beg of Dante to keep alive for them their memory
and fame on earth, while those in Purgatory only entreat his prayers
and those of others for their deliverance. And in a famous passage, the
passion for fame—'lo gran disio dell'eccellenza' (the great desire of
excelling)—is reproved for the reason that intellectual glory is not absolute, but relative to the times, and may be surpassed and eclipsed
by greater successors.

The new race of poet-scholars which arose soon after Dante quickly
made themselves masters of this fresh tendency. They did so in a double
sense, being themselves the most acknowledged celebrities of Italy, and
at the same time, as poets and historians, consciously disposing of the
reputation of others. An outward symbol of this sort of fame was the
coronation of the poets, of which we shall speak later on.

A contemporary of Dante, Albertinus Musattus or Mussatus,
crowned poet at Padua by the bishop and rector, enjoyed a fame which
fell little short of deification. Every Christmas Day the doctors and
students of both colleges at the University came in solemn procession
before his house with trumpets and, it seems, with burning tapers, to
salute him and bring him presents. His reputation lasted till, in 1318,
he fell into disgrace with the ruling tyrant of the House of Carrara.

This new incense, which once was offered only to saints and heroes,
was given in clouds to Petrarch, who persuaded himself in his later

years that it was but a foolish and troublesome thing. His letter 'To Posterity' is the confession of an old and famous man, who is forced to gratify the public curiosity. He admits that he wishes for fame in the times to come, but would rather be without it in his own day. In his dialogue on fortune and misfortune, the interlocutor, who maintains the futility of glory, has the best of the contest. But, at the same time, Petrarch is pleased that the autocrat of Byzantium knows him as well by his writings as Charles IV knows him. And in fact, even in his lifetime, his fame extended far beyond Italy. And the emotion which he felt was natural when his friends, on the occasion of a visit to his native Arezzo (1350), took him to the house where he was born, and told him how the city had provided that no change should be made in it. In former times the dwellings of certain great saints were preserved and revered in this way, like the cell of St. Thomas Aquinas in the Dominican convent at Naples, and the Portiuncula of St. Francis near Assisi; and one or two great jurists also enjoyed the half-mythical reputation which led to this honour. Towards the close of the fourteenth century the people at Bagnolo, near Florence, called an old building the 'Studio of Accursius' (died in 1260), but, nevertheless, suffered it to be destroyed. It is probable that the great incomes and the political influence which some jurists obtained as consulting lawyers made a lasting impression on the popular imagination.

To the cult of the birthplaces of famous men must be added that of their graves, and, in the case of Petrarch, of the spot where he died. In memory of him Arquà became a favourite resort of the Paduans, and was dotted with graceful little villas. At this time there were no 'classic spots' in Northern Europe, and pilgrimages were only made to pictures and relics. It was a point of honour for the different cities to possess the bones of their own and foreign celebrities; and it is most remarkable how seriously the Florentines, even in the fourteenth century— long before the building of Santa Croce—laboured to make their cathedral a Pantheon. Accorso, Dante, Petrarch, Boccaccio, and the jurist Zanobi della Strada were to have had magnificent tombs there erected to them. Late in the fifteenth century, Lorenzo il Magnifico applied in person to the Spoletans, asking them to give up the corpse of the painter Fra Filippo Lippi for the cathedral, and received the answer that they had none too many ornaments to the city, especially in the shape of distinguished people, for which reason they begged him to spare them; and, in fact, he had to be content with erecting a cenotaph. And even Dante, in spite of all the applications to which Boccaccio urged the Florentines with bitter emphasis, remained sleeping tranquilly in San Francesco at Ravenna, 'among ancient tombs of emperors and vaults of saints, in more honourable company than thou, O Florence, couldst offer him'. It even happened that a man once took away unpunished the lights from the altar on which the crucifix stood, and set them by the grave, with the words, 'Take them; thou art more worthy of them than He, the Crucified One!' (Franco Sacchetti, Novella 121.)

And now the Italian cities began again to remember their ancient citizens and inhabitants. Naples, perhaps, had never forgotten its tomb of Virgil, since a kind of mythical halo had become attached to the name.

The Paduans, even in the sixteenth century, firmly believed that they possessed not only the genuine bones of their founder, Antenor, but also those of the historian Livy. 'Sulmona,' says Boccaccio, 'bewails that Ovid lies buried far away in exile; and Parma rejoices that Cassius sleeps within its walls.' The Mantuans coined a medal in 1257 with the bust of Virgil, and raised a statue to represent him. In a fit of aristocratic insolence, the guardian of the young Gonzaga, Carlo Malatesta, caused it to be pulled down in 1392, and was afterwards forced, when he found the fame of the old poet too strong for him, to set it up again. Even then, perhaps, the grotto, a couple of miles from the town, where Virgil was said to have meditated, was shown to strangers, like the 'Scuola di Virgilio' at Naples. Como claimed both the Plinys for its own, and at the end of the fifteenth century erected statues in their honour, sitting under graceful baldachins on the façade of the cathedral.

History and the new topography were now careful to leave no local celebrity unnoticed. At the same period the northern chronicles only here and there, among the list of popes, emperors, earthquakes, and comets, put in the remark, that at such a time this or that famous man 'flourished'. We shall elsewhere have to show how, mainly under the influence of this idea of fame, an admirable biographical literature was developed. We must here limit ourselves to the local patriotism of the topographers who recorded the claims of their native cities to distinction.

In the Middle Ages, the cities were proud of their saints and of the bones and relics in their churches. With these the panegyrist of Padua in 1450, Michele Savonarola, begins his list; from them he passes to 'the famous men who were no saints, but who, by their great intellect and force (*virtus*) deserve to be added (*adnecti*) to the saints'—just as in classical antiquity the distinguished man came close upon the hero. The further enumeration is most characteristic of the time. First

comes Antenor, the brother of Priam, who founded Padua with a band
of Trojan fugitives; King Dardanus, who defeated Attila in the Euga-
nean hills, followed him in pursuit, and struck him dead at Rimini with
a chessboard; the Emperor Henry IV, who built the cathedral; a King
Marcus, whose head was preserved in Monselice; then a couple of
cardinals and prelates as founders of colleges, churches, and so forth;
the famous Augustinian theologian, Fra Alberto; a string of philosophers beginning with Paolo Veneto and the celebrated Pietro of
Abano; the jurist Paolo Padovano; then Livy and the poets Petrarch,
Mussato, Lovato. If there is any want of military celebrities in the
list, the poet consoles himself for it by the abundance of learned men
whom he has to show, and by the more durable character of intellectual glory, while the fame of the soldier is buried with his body, or, if
it lasts, owes its permanence only to the scholar. It is nevertheless
honourable to the city that foreign warriors lie buried here by their
own wish, like Pietro de' Rossi of Parma, Filippo Arcelli of Piacenza,
and especially Gattemelata of Narni (d. 1443), whose brazen equestrian
statue, 'like a Cæsar in triumph', already stood by the church of the
Santo. The author then names a crowd of jurists and physicians, nobles
'who had not only, like so many others, received, but deserved, the
honour of knighthood'. Then follows a list of famous mechanicians,
painters, and musicians, and in conclusion the name of a fencing-master
Michele Rosso, who, as the most distinguished man in his profession,
was to be seen painted in many places.

By the side of these local temples of fame, which myth, legend, popular admiration, and literary tradition combined to create, the poet-
scholars built up a great Pantheon of world-wide celebrity. They made
collections of famous men and famous women, often in direct imitation of Cornelius Nepos, the pseudo-Suetonius, Valerius Maximus,
Plutarch (*Mulierum virtutes*), Jerome (*De viris illustribus*), and others:
or they wrote of imaginary triumphal processions and Olympian assemblies, as was done by Petrarch in his 'Trionfo della Fama', and
Boccaccio in the 'Amorosa Visione', with hundreds of names, of which
three-fourths at least belong to antiquity and the rest to the Middle
Ages. By and by this new and comparatively modern element was
treated with greater emphasis; the historians began to insert descriptions of character, and collections arose of the biographies of distinguished contemporaries, like those of Filippo Villani, Vespasiano
Fiorentino, Bartolommeo Fazio, and lastly of Paolo Giovio.

The North of Europe, until Italian influence began to tell upon its
writers—for instance, on Trithemius, the first German who wrote the

lives of famous men—possessed only either legends of the saints, or descriptions of princes and churchmen partaking largely of the character of legends and showing no traces of the idea of fame, that is, of distinction won by a man's personal efforts. Poetical glory was still confined to certain classes of society, and the names of northern artists are only known to us at this period in so far as they were members of certain guilds or corporations.

The poet-scholar in Italy had, as we have already said, the fullest consciousness that he was the giver of fame and immortality, or, if he chose, of oblivion. Boccaccio complains of a fair one to whom he had done homage, and who remained hard-hearted in order that he might go on praising her and making her famous, and he gives her a hint that he will try the effect of a little blame. Sannazaro, in two magnificent sonnets, threatens Alfonso of Naples with eternal obscurity on account of his cowardly flight before Charles VIII. Angelo Poliziano seriously exhorts (1491) King John of Portugal to think betimes of his immortality in reference to the new discoveries in Africa, and to send him materials to Florence, there to be put into shape (*operosius excolenda*), otherwise it would befall him as it had befallen all the others whose deeds, unsupported by the help of the learned, 'lie hidden in the vast heap of human frailty'. The king, or his humanistic chancellor, agreed to this, and promised that at least the Portuguese chronicles of African affairs should be translated into Italian, and sent to Florence to be done into Latin. Whether the promise was kept is not known. These pretensions are by no means so groundless as they may appear at first sight; for the form in which events, even the greatest, are told to the living and to posterity is anything but a matter of indifference. The Italian humanists, with their mode of exposition and their Latin style, had long the complete control of the reading world of Europe, and till last century the Italian poets were more widely known and studied than those of any other nation. The baptismal name of the Florentine Amerigo Vespucci was given, on account of his book of travels, to a new quarter of the globe, and if Paolo Giovio, with all his superficiality and graceful caprice, promised himself immortality, his expectation has not altogether been disappointed.

Amid all these preparations outwardly to win and secure fame, the curtain is now and then drawn aside, and we see with frightful evidence a boundless ambition and thirst after greatness, regardless of all means and consequences. Thus, in the preface to Machiavelli's Florentine history, in which he blames his predecessors Leonardo, Aretino and Poggio for their too considerate reticence with regard to the politi-

cal parties in the city: 'They erred greatly and showed that they understood little the ambition of men and the desire to perpetuate a name.
How many who could distinguish themselves by nothing praiseworthy,
strove to do so by infamous deeds!' Those writers did not consider
that actions which are great in themselves, as is the case with the
actions of rulers and of States, always seem to bring more glory than
blame, of whatever kind they are and whatever the result of them may
be. In more than one remarkable and dreadful undertaking the motive
assigned by serious writers is the burning desire to achieve something
great and memorable. This motive is not a mere extreme case of ordinary vanity, but something dæmonic, involving a surrender of the will,
the use of any means, however atrocious, and even an indifference to
success itself. In this sense, for example, Machiavelli conceives the
character of Stefano Porcari; of the murderers of Galeazzo Maria
Sforza (1476), the documents tell us about the same; and the assassination of Duke Alessandro of Florence (1537) is ascribed by Varchi
himself to the thirst for fame which tormented the murderer Lorenzino
Medici. Still more stress is laid on this motive by Paolo Giovio. Lorenzino, according to him, pilloried by a pamphlet of Molza, broods over
a deed whose novelty shall make his disgrace forgotten, and ends
by murdering his kinsman and prince. These are characteristic features
of this age of overstrained and despairing passions and forces, and remind us of the burning of the temple of Diana at Ephesus in the time
of Philip of Macedon.

*   *   *   *   *

Now that this point in our historical view of Italian civilization has
been reached, it is time to speak of the influence of antiquity, the 'new
birth' of which has been one-sidedly chosen as the name to sum up the
whole period. The conditions which have been hitherto described
would have sufficed, apart from antiquity, to upturn and to mature the
national mind; and most of the intellectual tendencies which yet remain
to be noticed would be conceivable without it. But both what has gone
before and what we have still to discuss are coloured in a thousand
ways by the influence of the ancient world; and though the essence
of the phenomena might still have been the same without the classical
revival, it is only with and through this revival that they are actually
manifested to us. The Renaissance would not have been the process of
world-wide significance which it is, if its elements could be so easily
separated from one another. We must insist upon it, as one of the chief
propositions of this book, that it was not the revival of antiquity alone,

but its union with the genius of the Italian people, which achieved the conquest of the western world. The amount of independence which the national spirit maintained in this union varied according to circumstances. In the modern Latin literature of the period, it is very small, while in the visual arts, as well as in other spheres, it is remarkably great; and hence the alliance between two distant epochs in the civilization of the same people, because concluded on equal terms, proved justifiable and fruitful. The rest of Europe was free either to repel or else partly or wholly to accept the mighty impulse which came forth from Italy. Where the latter was the case we may as well be spared the complaints over the early decay of mediæval faith and civilization. Had these been strong enough to hold their ground, they would be alive to this day. If those elegiac natures which long to see them return could pass but one hour in the midst of them, they would gasp to be back in modern air. That in a great historical process of this kind flowers of exquisite beauty may perish, without being made immortal in poetry or tradition, is undoubtedly true; nevertheless, we cannot wish the process undone. The general result of it consists in this—that by the side of the Church which had hitherto held the countries of the West together (though it was unable to do so much longer) there arose a new spiritual influence which, spreading itself abroad from Italy, became the breath of life for all the more instructed minds in Europe. The worst that can be said of the movement is, that it was anti-popular, that through it Europe became for the first time sharply divided into the cultivated and uncultivated classes. The reproach will appear groundless when we reflect that even now the fact, though clearly recognized, cannot be altered. The separation, too, is by no means so cruel and absolute in Italy as elsewhere. The most artistic of her poets, Tasso, is in the hands of even the poorest.

The civilization of Greece and Rome, which, ever since the fourteenth century, obtained so powerful a hold on Italian life, as the source and basis of culture, as the object and ideal of existence, partly also as an avowed reaction against preceding tendencies—this civilization had long been exerting a partial influence on mediæval Europe, even beyond the boundaries of Italy. The culture of which Charlemagne was a representative was, in face of the barbarism of the seventh and eighth centuries, essentially a Renaissance, and could appear under no other form. Just as in the Romanesque architecture of the North, beside the general outlines inherited from antiquity, remarkable direct imitations of the antique also occur, so too monastic scholarship had not only gradually absorbed an immense mass of materials from Roman writers, but the style of it, from the days of Einhard onwards, shows traces of conscious imitation.

But the resuscitation of antiquity took a different form in Italy from that which it assumed in the North. The wave of barbarism had scarcely gone by before the people, in whom the former life was but half effaced, showed a consciousness of its past and a wish to reproduce it. Elsewhere in Europe men deliberately and with reflection borrowed this or the other element of classical civilization; in Italy the sympathies both of the learned and of the people were naturally engaged on the side of antiquity as a whole, which stood to them as a symbol of past greatness. The Latin language, too, was easy to an Italian, and the numerous monuments and documents in which the country abounded facilitated a return to the past. With this tendency other elements—the popular character which time had now greatly modified, the political institutions imported by the Lombards from Germany, chivalry and other northern forms of civilization, and the influence of religion and the Church—combined to produce the modern Italian spirit, which was destined to serve as the model and ideal for the whole western world.

How antiquity influenced the visual arts, as soon as the flood of barbarism had subsided, is clearly shown in the Tuscan buildings of the twelfth and in the sculptures of the thirteenth centuries. In poetry, too, there will appear no want of similar analogies to those who hold that the greatest Latin poet of the twelfth century, the writer who struck the keynote of a whole class of Latin poems, was an Italian. We mean the author of the best pieces in the so-called 'Carmina Burana'. A frank enjoyment of life and its pleasures, as whose patrons the gods of heathendom are invoked, while Catos and Scipios hold the place of the saints and heroes of Christianity, flows in full current through the rhymed verses. Reading them through at a stretch, we can scarcely help coming to the conclusion that an Italian, probably a Lombard, is speaking; in fact, there are positive grounds for thinking so. To a certain degree these Latin poems of the 'Clerici vagantes' of the twelfth century, with all their remarkable frivolity, are, doubtless, a product in which the whole of Europe had a share; but the writer of the song 'De Phyllide et Flora' and the 'Æstuans Interius' can have been a northerner as little as the polished Epicurean observer to whom we owe 'Dum Dianæ vitrea sero lampas oritur'. Here, in truth, is a reproduction of the whole ancient view of life, which is all the more striking from the mediæval form of the verse in which it is set forth. There are many works of this and the following centuries, in which a careful imitation of the antique appears both in the hexameter and pentameter of the metre and in the classical, often mythological, character of the subject, and which yet have not anything like the same spirit of antiquity about them. In the hexametric chronicles and other works of Guglielmus Apuliensis and his successors (from about 1100), we find frequent traces of a diligent study of Virgil, Ovid, Lucan, Statius, and Claudian; but this classical form is, after all, a mere matter of archæology, as is the classical subject in compilers like Vincent of Beauvais, or in the mythological and allegorical writer, Alanus ab Insulis. The Renaissance, however, is not a fragmentary imitation or compilation, but a new birth; and the signs of this are visible in the poems of the unknown 'Clericus' of the twelfth century.

But the great and general enthusiasm of the Italians for classical antiquity did not display itself before the fourteenth century. For this a development of civic life was required, which took place only in Italy, and there not till then. It was needful that noble and burgher should first learn to dwell together on equal terms, and that a social world should arise which felt the want of culture, and had the leisure and the means to obtain it. But culture, as soon as it freed itself from the fantastic bonds of the Middle Ages, could not at once and without help find its way to the understanding of the physical and intellectual world. It needed a guide, and found one in the ancient civilization, with its wealth of truth and knowledge in every spiritual interest. Both the form and the substance of this civilization were adopted with admiring gratitude; it became the chief part of the culture of the age. The general condition of the country was favourable to this transformation. The mediæval empire, since the fall of the Hohenstaufen, had either renounced, or was unable to make good, its claims on Italy. The Popes had migrated to Avignon. Most of the political powers actually existing owed their origin to violent and illegitimate means. The spirit of the people, now awakened to self-consciousness, sought for some new and stable ideal on which to rest. And thus the vision of the world-wide empire of Italy and Rome so possessed the popular mind that Cola di Rienzi could actually attempt to put it in practice. The conception he formed of his task, particularly when tribune for the first time, could only end in some extravagant comedy; nevertheless, the memory of ancient Rome was no slight support to the national sentiment. Armed afresh with its culture, the Italian soon felt himself in truth citizen of the most advanced nation in the world.

It is now our task to sketch this spiritual movement, not indeed in all its fullness, but in its most salient features, and especially in its first beginnings.

Rome itself, the city of ruins, now became the object of a wholly different sort of piety from that of the time when the 'Mirabilia Romæ' and the collection of William of Malmesbury were composed. The imaginations of the devout pilgrim, or of the seeker after marvels and treasures, are supplanted in contemporary records by the interests of the patriot and the historian. In this sense we must understand Dante's words, that the stones of the walls of Rome reserve reverence, and that the ground on which the city is built is more worthy than men say. The jubilees, incessant as they were, have scarcely left a single devout record in literature properly so called. The best thing that Giovanni Villani brought back from the jubilee of the year 1300 was the resolution to write his history which had been awakened in him by the sight of the ruins of Rome. Petrarch gives evidence of a taste divided between classical and Christian antiquity. He tells us how often with Giovanni Colonna he ascended the mighty vaults of the Baths of Diocletian, and there in the transparent air, amid the wide silence with the broad panorama stretching far around them, they spoke, not of business or political affairs, but of the history which the ruins beneath their feet suggested, Petrarch appearing in these dialogues as the partisan of classical, Giovanni of Christian antiquity; then they would discourse of philosophy and of the inventors of the arts. How often since that time, down to the days of Gibbon and Niebuhr, have the same ruins stirred men's minds to the same reflections!

This double current of feeling is also recognizable in the 'Dittamondo' of Fazio degli Uberti, composed about the year 1360—a description of visionary travels, in which the author is accompanied by the old geographer Solinus, as Dante was by Virgil. They visit Bari in memory of St. Nicholas, and Monte Gargano of the archangel Michael, and in Rome the legends of Aracoeli and of Santa Maria in Trastevere are mentioned. Still, the pagan splendour of ancient Rome unmistakably exercises a greater charm upon them. A venerable matron in torn garments—Rome herself is meant—tells them of the glorious past, and gives them a minute description of the old triumphs; she then leads the strangers through the city, and points out to them the seven hills and many of the chief ruins—'che comprender potrai, quanto fui bella'.

Unfortunately this Rome of the schismatic and Avignonese popes was no longer, in respect of classical remains, what it had been some generations earlier. The destruction of 140 fortified houses of the

Roman nobles by the senator Brancaleone in 1257 must have wholly altered the character of the most important buildings then standing: for the nobles had no doubt ensconced themselves in the loftiest and best-preserved of the ruins. Nevertheless, far more was left than we now find, and probably many of the remains had still their marble incrustation, their pillared entrances, and their other ornaments, where we now see nothing but the skeleton of brickwork. In this state of things, the first beginnings of a topographical study of the old city were made.

In Poggio's walks through Rome the study of the remains themselves is for the first time more intimately combined with that of the ancient authors and inscriptions—the latter he sought out from among all the vegetation in which they were imbedded—the writer's imagination is severely restrained, and the memories of Christian Rome carefully excluded. The only pity is that Poggio's work was not fuller and was not illustrated with sketches. Far more was left in his time than was found by Raphael eighty years later. He saw the tomb of Cæcilia Metella and the columns in front of one of the temples on the slope of the Capitol, first in full preservation, and then afterwards half destroyed, owing to that unfortunate quality which marble possesses of being easily burnt into lime. A vast colonnade near the Minerva fell piecemeal a victim to the same fate. A witness in the year 1443 tells us that this manufacture of lime still went on: 'which is a shame, for the new buildings are pitiful, and the beauty of Rome is in its ruins'. The inhabitants of that day, in their peasant's cloaks and boots, looked to foreigners like cowherds; and in fact the cattle were pastured in the city up to the Banchi. The only social gatherings were the services at church, on which occasion it was possible also to get a sight of the beautiful women.

In the last years of Eugenius IV (d. 1447) Blondus of Forli wrote his 'Roman Instaurata', making use of Frontinus and of the old 'Libri Regionali', as well as, it seems, of Anastasius. His object is not only the description of what existed, but still more the recovery of what was lost. In accordance with the dedication to the Pope, he consoles himself for the general ruin by the thought of the precious relics of the saints in which Rome was so rich.

With Nicholas V (1447–1455) that new monumental spirit which was distinctive of the age of the Renaissance appeared on the papal throne. The new passion for embellishing the city brought with it on the one hand a fresh danger for the ruins, on the other a respect for them, as forming one of Rome's claims to distinction. Pius II was

wholly possessed by antiquarian enthusiasm, and if he speaks little of
the antiquities of Rome, he closely studied those of all other parts
of Italy, and was the first to know and describe accurately the remains
which abounded in the districts for miles around the capital. It is true
that, both as priest and cosmographer, he was interested alike in classical and Christian monuments and in the marvels of nature. Or was he
doing violence to himself when he wrote that Nola was more highly
honoured by the memory of St. Paulinus than by all its classical reminiscences and by the heroic struggle of Marcellus? Not, indeed, that his
faith in relics was assumed; but his mind was evidently rather disposed to an inquiring interest in nature and antiquity, to a zeal for
monumental works, to a keen and delicate observation of human life.
In the last years of his Papacy, afflicted with the gout and yet in the
most cheerful mood, he was borne in his litter over hill and dale to
Tusculum, Alba, Tibur, Ostia, Falerii, and Otriculum, and whatever
he saw he noted down. He followed the Roman roads and aqueducts,
and tried to fix the boundaries of the old tribes which had dwelt round
the city. On an excursion to Tivoli with the great Federigo of Urbino
the time was happily spent in talk on the military system of the ancients, and particularly on the Trojan war. Even on his journey to the
Congress of Mantua (1459) he searched, though unsuccessfully, for
the labyrinth of Clusium mentioned by Pliny, and visited the so-called
villa of Virgil on the Mincio. That such a Pope should demand a
classical Latin style from his abbreviators, is no more than might be
expected. It was he who, in the war with Naples, granted an amnesty
to the men of Arpinum, as countrymen of Cicero and Marius, after
whom many of them were named. It was to him alone, as both judge
and patron, that Blondus could dedicate his 'Roma Triumphans', the
first great attempt at a complete exposition of Roman antiquity.

Nor was the enthusiasm for the classical past of Italy confined at this
period to the capital. Boccaccio had already called the vast ruins of
Baiæ 'old walls, yet new for modern spirits'; and since his time they
were held to be the most interesting sight near Naples. Collections of
antiquities of all sorts now became common. Ciriaco of Ancona (d.
1457) travelled not only through Italy, but through other countries of
the old Orbis terrarum, and brought back countless inscriptions and
sketches. When asked why he took all this trouble, he replied, 'To
wake the dead'. The histories of the various cities of Italy had from
the earliest times laid claim to some true or imagined connection with
Rome, had alleged some settlement or colonization which started from
the capital; and the obliging manufacturers of pedigrees seem con-

stantly to have derived various families from the oldest and most famous blood of Rome. So highly was the distinction valued, that men clung to it even in the light of the dawning criticism of the fifteenth century. When Pius II was at Viterbo he said frankly to the Roman deputies who begged him to return, 'Rome is as much my home as Siena, for my House, the Piccolomini, came in early times from the capital to Siena, as is proved by the constant use of the names Æneas and Sylvius in my family'. He would probably have had no objection to be held a descendant of the Julii. Paul II, a Barbo of Venice, found his vanity flattered by deducing his House, notwithstanding an adverse pedigree, according to which it came from Germany, from the Roman Ahenobarbus, who had led a colony to Parma, and whose successors had been driven by party conflicts to migrate to Venice. That the Massimi claimed descent from Q. Fabius Maximus, and the Cornaro from the Cornelii, cannot surprise us. On the other hand, it is a strikingly exceptional fact for the sixteenth century that the novelist Bandello tried to connect his blood with a noble family of Ostrogoths.

To return to Rome. The inhabitants, 'who then called themselves Romans', accepted greedily the homage which was offered them by the rest of Italy. Under Paul II, Sixtus IV and Alexander VI, magnificent processions formed part of the Carnival, representing the scene most attractive to the imagination of the time—the triumph of the Roman Imperator. The sentiment of the people expressed itself naturally in this shape and others like it. In this mood of public feeling, a report arose on April 18, 1485, that the corpse of a young Roman lady of the classical period—wonderfully beautiful and in perfect preservation—had been discovered. Some Lombard masons digging out an ancient tomb on an estate of the convent of Santa Maria Nuova, on the Appian Way, beyond the tomb of Cæcilia Metella, were said to have found a marble sarcophagus with the inscription, 'Julia, daughter of Claudius'. On this basis the following story was built. The Lombards disappeared with the jewels and treasure which were found with the corpse in the sarcophagus. The body had been coated with an antiseptic essence, and was as fresh and flexible as that of a girl of fifteen the hour after death. It was said that she still kept the colours of life, with eyes and mouth half open. She was taken to the palace of the 'Conservatori' on the Capitol; and then a pilgrimage to see her began. Among the crowd were many who came to paint her; 'for she was more beautiful than can be said or written, and, were it said or written, it would not be believed by those who had not seen her'. By order of Innocent VIII she was secretly buried one night outside the Pincian Gate; the empty sarcophagus remained in the court of the 'Conservatori'. Probably a coloured mask of wax or some other material was modelled in the classical style on the face of the corpse, with which the gilded hair of which we read would harmonize admirably. The touching point in the story is not the fact itself, but the firm belief that an ancient body, which was now thought to be at last really before men's eyes, must of necessity be far more beautiful than anything of modern date.

Meanwhile the material knowledge of old Rome was increased by excavations. Under Alexander VI the so-called 'Grotesques', that is, the mural decorations of the ancients, were discovered, and the Apollo of the Belvedere was found at Porto d'Anzio. Under Julius II followed the memorable discoveries of the Laocoön, of the Venus of the Vatican, of the Torso of the Cleopatra. The palaces of the nobles and the cardinals began to be filled with ancient statues and fragments. Raphael undertook for Leo X that ideal restoration of the whole ancient city which his (or Castiglione's) celebrated letter (1518 or 1519) speaks of. After a bitter complaint over the devastations which had not even then ceased, and which had been particularly frequent under Julius II, he beseeches the Pope to protect the few relics which were left to testify to the power and greatness of that divine soul of antiquity whose memory was inspiration to all who were capable of higher things. He then goes on with penetrating judgment to lay the foundations of a comparative history of art, and concludes by giving the definition of an architectural survey which has been accepted since his time; he requires the ground plan, section and elevation separately of every building that remained. How archæology devoted itself after his day to the study of the venerated city and grew into a special science, and how the Vitruvian Academy at all events proposed to itself great aims, cannot here be related. Let us rather pause at the days of Leo X, under whom the enjoyment of antiquity combined with all other pleasures to give to Roman life a unique stamp and consecration. The Vatican resounded with song and music, and their echoes were heard through the city as a call to joy and gladness, though Leo did not succeed thereby in banishing care and pain from his own life, and his deliberate calculation to prolong his days by cheerfulness was frustrated by an early death. The Rome of Leo, as described by Paolo Giovio, forms a picture too splendid to turn away from, unmistakable as are also its darker aspects—the slavery of those who were struggling to rise; the secret misery of the prelates, who, notwithstanding heavy debts, were forced to live in a style befitting their rank; the system of literary patronage, which drove men to be parasites or adventurers; and, lastly, the scandalous maladministration of the finances of the State. Yet the same Ariosto who knew and ridiculed all this so well, gives in the sixth satire a longing picture of his expected intercourse with the accomplished poets who would conduct him through the city of ruins, of the learned counsel which he would there find for his own literary efforts, and of the treasures of the Vatican library. These, he says, and not the long-abandoned hope of Medicean protection, were the baits which really attracted him, if he were again asked to go as Ferrarese ambassador to Rome.

But the ruins within and outside Rome awakened not only archæological zeal and patriotic enthusiasm, but an elegiac or sentimental melancholy. In Petrarch and Boccaccio we find touches of this feeling. Poggio Bracciolini often visited the temple of Venus and Roma, in the belief that it was that of Castor and Pollux, where the senate used so often to meet, and would lose himself in memories of the great orators Crassus, Hortensius, Cicero. The language of Pius II, especially in describing Tivoli, has a thoroughly sentimental ring, and soon afterwards (1467) appeared the first pictures of ruins, with a commentary by Polifilo. Ruins of mighty arches and colonnades, half hid in plane-trees, laurels, cypresses and brushwood, figure in his pages. In the sacred legends it became the custom, we can hardly say how, to lay the scene of the birth of Christ in the ruins of a magnificent palace. That artificial ruins became afterwards a necessity of landscape gardening is only a practical consequence of this feeling.

But the literary bequests of antiquity, Greek as well as Latin, were of far more importance than the architectural, and indeed than all the artistic remains which it had left. They were held in the most absolute sense to be the springs of all knowledge. The literary conditions of that age of great discoveries have often been set forth; no more can here be attempted than to point out a few less-known features of the picture.

Great as was the influence of the old writers on the Italian mind in the fourteenth century and before, yet that influence was due rather to the wide diffusion of what had long been known than to the discovery of much that was new. The most popular Latin poets, historians, orators and letter-writers, together with a number of Latin translations of single works of Aristotle, Plutarch, and a few other Greek authors, constituted the treasure from which a few favoured individuals in the time of Petrarch and Boccaccio drew their inspiration. The former, as is well known, owned and kept with religious care a Greek Homer, which he was unable to read. A complete Latin translation of the Iliad

and Odyssey, though a very bad one, was made at Petrarch's suggestion, and with Boccaccio's help, by a Calabrian Greek, Leonzio Pilato.
But with the fifteenth century began the long list of new discoveries,
the systematic creation of libraries by means of copies, and the rapid
multiplication of translations from the Greek.

Had it not been for the enthusiasm of a few collectors of that age,
who shrank from no effort or privation in their researches, we should
certainly possess only a small part of the literature, especially that of
the Greeks, which is now in our hands. Pope Nicholas V, when only a
simple monk, ran deeply into debt through buying manuscripts or
having them copied. Even then he made no secret of his passion for the
two great interests of the Renaissance, books and buildings. As Pope
he kept his word. Copyists wrote and spies searched for him through
half the world. Perotto received 500 ducats for the Latin translation of
Polybius; Guarino, 1,000 gold florins for that of Strabo, and he would
have been paid 500 more but for the death of the Pope. Filelfo was to
have received 10,000 gold florins for a metrical translation of Homer,
and was only prevented by the Pope's death from coming from Milan
to Rome. Nicholas left a collection of 5,000 or, according to another
way of calculating, of 9,000 volumes, for the use of the members of
the Curia, which became the foundation of the library of the Vatican.
It was to be preserved in the palace itself, as its noblest ornament, like
the library of Ptolemy Philadelphus at Alexandria. When the plague
(1450) drove him and his court to Fabriano, whence then, as now, the
best paper was procured, he took his translators and compilers with
him, that he might run no risk of losing them.

The Florentine Niccolò Niccoli, a member of that accomplished circle
of friends which surrounded the elder Cosimo de' Medici, spent his
whole fortune in buying books. At last, when his money was all gone,
the Medici put their purse at his disposal for any sum which his purpose might require. We owe to him the later books of Ammianus
Marcellinus, the 'De Oratore' of Cicero, and other works; he persuaded
Cosimo to buy the best manuscript of Pliny from a monastery at
Lübeck. With noble confidence he lent his books to those who asked
for them, allowed all comers to study them in his own house, and was
ready to converse with the students on what they had read. His collection of 800 volumes, valued at 6,000 gold florins, passed after his
death, through Cosimo's intervention, to the monastery of San Marco,
on the condition that it should be accessible to the public.

Of the two great book-finders, Guarino and Poggio, the latter, on the
occasion of the Council of Constance and acting partly as the agent of

Niccoli, searched industriously among the abbeys of South Germany. He there discovered six orations of Cicero, and the first complete Quintilian, that of St. Gallen, now at Zürich; in thirty-two days he is said to have copied the whole of it in a beautiful handwriting. He was able to make important additions to Silius Italicus, Manilius, Lucretius, Valerius Flaccus, Asconius Pedianus, Columella, Celsus, Aulus Gellius, Statius, and others; and with the help of Leonardo Aretino he unearthed the last twelve comedies of Plautus, as well as the Verrine orations.

The famous Greek, Cardinal Bessarion, in whom patriotism was mingled with a zeal for letters, collected, at a great sacrifice, 600 manuscripts of pagan and Christian authors. He then looked round for some receptacle where they could safely lie until his unhappy country, if she ever regained her freedom, could reclaim her lost literature. The Venetian government declared itself ready to erect a suitable building, and to this day the Biblioteca Marciana retains a part of these treasures.

The formation of the celebrated Medicean library has a history of its own, into which we cannot here enter. The chief collector for Lorenzo il Magnifico was Johannes Lascaris. It is well known that the collection, after the plundering in the year 1494, had to be recovered piecemeal by the Cardinal Giovanni Medici, afterwards Leo X.

The library of Urbino, now in the Vatican, was wholly the work of the great Federigo of Montefeltro. As a boy he had begun to collect; in after years he kept thirty or forty 'scrittori' employed in various places, and spent in the course of time no less than 30,000 ducats on the collection. It was systematically extended and completed, chiefly by the help of Vespasiano, and his account of it forms an ideal picture of a library of the Renaissance. At Urbino there were catalogues of the libraries of the Vatican, of St. Mark at Florence, of the Visconti at Pavia, and even of the library at Oxford. It was noted with pride that in richness and completeness none could rival Urbino. Theology and the Middle Ages were perhaps most fully represented. There was a complete Thomas Aquinas, a complete Albertus Magnus, a complete Bonaventura. The collection, however, was a many-sided one, and included every work on medicine which was then to be had. Among the 'moderns' the great writers of the fourteenth century—Dante and Boccaccio, with their complete works—occupied the first place. Then followed twenty-five select humanists, invariably with both their Latin and Italian writings and with all their translations. Among the Greek manuscripts the Fathers of the Church far outnumbered the rest; yet in the list of the classics we find all the works of Sophocles, all of

Pindar, and all of Menander. The last codex must have quickly disappeared from Urbino, else the philologists would have soon edited it.

We have, further, a good deal of information as to the way in which manuscripts and libraries were multiplied. The purchase of an ancient manuscript, which contained a rare, or the only complete, or the only existing text of an old writer, was naturally a lucky accident of which we need take no further account. Among the professional copyists those who understood Greek took the highest place, and it was they especially who bore the honourable name of 'scrittori'. Their number was always limited, and the pay they received very large. The rest, simply called 'copisti', were partly mere clerks who made their living by such work, partly schoolmasters and needy men of learning, who desired an addition to their income. The copyists at Rome in the time of Nicholas V were mostly Germans or Frenchmen—'barbarians' as the Italian humanists called them, probably men who were in search of favours at the papal court, and who kept themselves alive meanwhile by this means. When Cosimo de' Medici was in a hurry to form a library for his favourite foundation, the Badia below Fiesole, he sent for Vespasiano, and received from him the advice to give up all thoughts of purchasing books, since those which were worth getting could not be had easily, but rather to make use of the copyists; whereupon Cosimo bargained to pay him so much a day, and Vespasiano, with forty-five writers under him, delivered 200 volumes in twenty-two months. The catalogue of the works to be copied was sent to Cosimo by Nicholas V, who wrote it with his own hand. Ecclesiastical literature and the books needed for the choral services naturally held the chief place in the list.

The handwriting was that beautiful modern Italian which was already in use in the preceding century, and which makes the sight of one of the books of that time a pleasure. Pope Nicholas V, Poggio, Gianozzo Manetti, Niccolò Niccoli, and other distinguished scholars, themselves wrote a beautiful hand, and desired and tolerated none other. The decorative adjuncts, even when miniatures formed no part of them, were full of taste, as may be seen especially in the Laurentian manuscripts, with the light and graceful scrolls which begin and end the lines. The material used to write on, when the work was ordered by great or wealthy people, was always parchment; the binding, both in the Vatican and at Urbino, was a uniform crimson velvet with silver clasps. Where there was so much care to show honour to the contents of a book by the beauty of its outward form, it is intelligible that the sudden appearance of printed books was greeted at first with anything but favour. Federigo of Urbino 'would have been ashamed to own a printed book'.

But the weary copyists—not those who lived by the trade, but the many who were forced to copy a book in order to have it—rejoiced at the German invention. It was soon applied in Italy to the multiplication first of the Latin and then of the Greek authors, and for a long period nowhere but in Italy, yet it spread with by no means the rapidity which might have been expected from the general enthusiasm for these works. After a while the modern relation between author and publisher began to develop itself, and under Alexander VI, when it was no longer easy to destroy a book, as Cosimo could make Filelfo promise to do, the prohibitive censorship made its appearance.

The growth of textual criticism which accompanied the advancing study of languages and antiquity belongs as little to the subject of this book as the history of scholarship in general. We are here occupied, not with the learning of the Italians in itself, but with the reproduction of antiquity in literature and life. One word more on the studies themselves may still be permissible.

Greek scholarship was chiefly confined to Florence and to the fifteenth and the beginning of the sixteenth centuries. The impulse which had proceeded from Petrarch and Boccaccio, superficial as was their own acquaintance with Greek, was powerful, but did not tell immediately on their contemporaries, except a few; on the other hand, the study of Greek literature died out about the year 1520 with the last of the colony of learned Greek exiles, and it was a singular piece of fortune that northerners like Erasmus, the Stephani, and Budæus had meanwhile made themselves masters of the language. That colony had begun with Manuel Chrysoloras and his relation John, and with George of Trebizond. Then followed, about and after the time of the conquest of Constantinople, John Argyropulos, Theodore Gaza, Demetrios Chalcondylas, who brought up his sons Theophilos and Basilios to be excellent Hellenists, Andronikos Kallistos, Marcos Musuros and the family of the Lascaris, not to mention others. But after the subjection of Greece by the Turks was completed, the succession of scholars was maintained only by the sons of the fugitives and perhaps here and there by some Candian or Cyprian refugee. That the decay of Hellenistic studies began about the time of the death of Leo X was due partly to a general change of intellectual attitude, and to a certain satiety of classical influences which now made itself felt; but its coincidence with the death of the Greek fugitives was not wholly a matter of accident. The study of Greek among the Italians appears, if we take the year 1500 as our standard, to have been pursued with extraordinary zeal. Many of those who then learned the language could still speak it half a century later, in their old age, like the Popes Paul III and Paul IV. But this sort of mastery of the study presupposes intercourse with native Greeks.

Besides Florence, Rome and Padua nearly always maintained paid teachers of Greek, and Verona, Ferrara, Venice, Perugia, Pavia and other cities occasional teachers. Hellenistic studies owed a priceless debt to the press of Aldo Manuzio at Venice, where the most important and voluminous writers were for the first time printed in the original. Aldo ventured his all in the enterprise; he was an editor and publisher whose like the world has rarely seen.

Along with this classical revival, Oriental studies now assumed considerable proportions. The controversial writings of the great Florentine statesman and scholar, Gianozzo Manetti (d. 1459), against the Jews afford an early instance of a complete mastery of their language and science. His son Agnolo was from his childhood instructed in Latin, Greek and Hebrew. The father, at the bidding of Nicholas V, translated the whole Bible afresh, as the philologists of the time insisted on giving up the 'Vulgata'.

Many other humanists devoted themselves before Reuchlin to the study of Hebrew, among them Pico della Mirandola, who was not satisfied with a knowledge of the Hebrew grammar and Scriptures, but penetrated into the Jewish Cabbalah and even made himself as familiar with the literature of the Talmud as any Rabbi.

Among the Oriental languages, Arabic was studied as well as Hebrew. The science of medicine, no longer satisfied with the older Latin translations of the great Arab physicians, had constant recourse to the originals, to which an easy access was offered by the Venetian consulates in the East, where Italian doctors were regularly kept. Hieronimo Ramusio, a Venetian physician, translated a great part of Avicenna from the Arabic and died at Damascus in 1486. Andrea Mongaio of Belluno lived long at Damascus for the purpose of studying Avicenna, learnt Arabic, and emended the author's text. The Venetian government afterwards appointed him professor of this subject at Padua.

We must here linger for a moment over Pico della Mirandola, before passing on to the general effects of humanism. He was the only man who loudly and vigorously defended the truth and science of all ages against the one-sided worship of classical antiquity. He knew how to value not only Averroës and the Jewish investigators, but also the scholastic writers of the Middle Ages, according to the matter of their writings. In one of his writings he makes them say, 'We shall live for ever, not in the schools of word-catchers, but in the circle of the wise, where they talk not of the mother of Andromache or of the sons of Niobe, but of the deeper causes of things human and divine; he who looks closely will see that even the barbarians had intelligence (*mercurium*), not on the tongue but in the breast'. Himself writing a vigorous and not inelegant Latin, and a master of clear exposition, he despised the purism of pedants and the current over-estimate of borrowed forms, especially when joined, as they often are, with one-sidedness, and involving indifference to the wider truth of the things themselves. Looking at Pico, we can guess at the lofty flight which Italian philosophy would have taken had not the counter-reformation annihilated the higher spiritual life of the people.

*   *   *   *   *

Freed from the countless bonds which elsewhere in Europe checked progress, having reached a high degree of individual development and been schooled by the teachings of antiquity, the Italian mind now turned to the discovery of the outward universe, and to the representation of it in speech and form.

On the journeys of the Italians to distant parts of the world, we can here make but a few general observations. The Crusades had opened unknown distances to the European mind, and awakened in all the passion for travel and adventure. It may be hard to indicate precisely the point where this passion allied itself with, or became the servant of, the thirst for knowledge; but it was in Italy that this was first and most completely the case. Even in the Crusades the interest of the Italians was wider than that of other nations, since they already were a naval power and had commercial relations with the East. From time immemorial the Mediterranean Sea had given to the nations that dwelt on its shores mental impulses different from those which governed the peoples of the North; and never, from the very structure of their character, could the Italians be adventurers in the sense which the word bore among the Teutons. After they were once at home in all the eastern harbours of the Mediterranean, it was natural that the most enterprising among them should be led to join that vast international movement of the Mohammedans which there found its outlet. A new half of the world lay, as it were, freshly discovered before them. Or, like Polo of Venice, they were caught in the current of the Mongolian peoples, and carried on to the steps of the throne of the Great Khan. At an early period, we find Italians sharing in the discoveries made in the Atlantic Ocean; it was the Genoese who, in the thirteenth century, found the Canary Islands. In the same year, 1291, when Ptolemais, the last remnant of the Christian East, was lost, it was again the Genoese who made the first known attempt to find a sea-passage to the East Indies. Columbus himself is but the greatest of a long list of Italians who, in the service of the western nations, sailed into distant seas. The true discoverer, however, is not the man who first chances to stumble upon anything, but the man who finds what he has sought. Such a one alone stands in a link with the thoughts and interests of his predecessors, and this relationship will also determine the account he gives of his search. For which reason the Italians, although their claim to be the first comers on this or that shore may be disputed, will yet retain their title to be pre-eminently the nation of discoverers for the whole latter part of the Middle Ages. The fuller proof of this assertion belongs to the special history of discoveries. Yet ever and again we turn with admiration to the august figure of the great Genoese, by whom a new continent beyond the ocean was demanded, sought and found; and who was the first to be able to say: 'il mondo è poco'—the world is not so large as men have thought. At the time when Spain gave Alexander VI to the Italians, Italy gave Columbus to the Spaniards. Only a few weeks before the death of that pope Columbus wrote from Jamaica his noble letter (July 7, 1503) to the thankless Catholic kings, which the ages to come can never read without profound emotion. In a codicil to his will, dated Valladolid, May 4, 1506, he bequeathed to 'his beloved home, the Republic of Genoa, the prayer-book which Pope Alexander had given him, and which in prison, in conflict, and in every kind of adversity, had been to him the greatest of comforts'. It seems as if these words cast upon the abhorred name of Borgia one last gleam of grace and mercy.

The development of geographical and allied sciences among the Italians must, like the history of their voyages, be touched upon but very briefly. A superficial comparison of their achievements with those of other nations shows an early and striking superiority on their part. Where, in the middle of the fifteenth century, could be found, anywhere but in Italy, such a union of geographical, statistical, and historical knowledge as was found in Æneas Sylvius? Not only in his great geographical work, but in his letters and commentaries, he describes with equal mastery landscapes, cities, manners, industries and products, political conditions and constitutions, wherever he can use his own observation or the evidence of eye-witnesses. What he takes from books is naturally of less moment. Even the short sketch of that valley in the Tyrolese Alps where Frederick III had given him a benefice, and still more his description of Scotland, leaves untouched none of the relations of human life, and displays a power and method of unbiased observation and comparison impossible in any but a countryman of Columbus, trained in the school of the ancients. Thousands saw and, in part, knew what he did, but they felt no impulse to draw a picture of it, and were unconscious that the world desired such pictures.

In geography as in other matters, it is vain to attempt to distinguish how much is to be attributed to the study of the ancients, and how much to the special genius of the Italians. They saw and treated the things of this world from an objective point of view, even before they were familiar with ancient literature, partly because they were themselves a half-ancient people, and partly because their political circumstances predisposed them to it; but they would not so rapidly have attained to such perfection had not the old geographers shown them the way. The influence of the existing Italian geographies on the spirit and tendencies of the travellers and discoverers was also inestimable. Even the simple 'dilettante' of a science—if in the present case we should assign to Æneas Sylvius so low a rank—can diffuse just that sort of general interest in the subject which prepares for new pioneers the indispensable groundwork of a favourable predisposition in the public mind. True discoverers in any science know well what they owe to such mediation.

For the position of the Italians in the sphere of the natural sciences, we must refer the reader to the special treatises on the subject, of which the only one with which we are familiar is the superficial and depreciatory work of Libri. The dispute as to the priority of particular discoveries concerns us all the less, since we hold that, at any time, and among any civilized people, a man may appear who, starting with very scanty preparation, is driven by an irresistible impulse into the path of scientific investigation, and through his native gifts achieves the most astonishing success. Such men were Gerbert of Rheims and Roger Bacon. That they were masters of the whole knowledge of the age in their several departments was a natural consequence of the spirit in which they worked. When once the veil of illusion was torn asunder, when once the dread of nature and the slavery to books and tradition were overcome, countless problems lay before them for solution. It is another matter when a whole people takes a natural delight in the study and investigation of nature, at a time when other nations are indifferent, that is to say, when the discoverer is not threatened or wholly ignored, but can count on the friendly support of congenial spirits. That this was the case in Italy is unquestionable. The Italian students of nature trace with pride in the 'Divine Comedy' the hints and proofs of Dante's scientific interest in nature. On his claim to priority in this or that discovery or reference, we must leave the men of science to decide; but every layman must be struck by the wealth of his observations on the external world, shown merely in his picture and comparisons. He, more than any other modern poet, takes them from reality, whether in nature or human life, and uses them never as mere ornament, but in order to give the reader the fullest and most adequate sense of his meaning. It is in astronomy that he appears chiefly as a scientific specialist, though it must not be forgotten that many astronomical allusions in his great poem, which now appear to us learned, must then have been intelligible to the general reader. Dante, learning apart, appeals to a popular knowledge of the heavens, which the Italians of his day, from the mere fact that they were a nautical people, had in common with the ancients. This knowledge of the rising and setting of the constellations has been rendered superfluous to the modern world by calendars and clocks, and with it has gone whatever interest in astronomy the people may once have had. Nowadays, with our schools and handbooks, every child knows—what Dante did not know—that the earth moves round the sun; but the interest once taken in the subject itself has given place, except in the case of astronomical specialists, to the most absolute indifference.

The pseudo-science which dealt with the stars proves nothing against the inductive spirit of the Italians of that day. That spirit was but crossed, and at times overcome, by the passionate desire to penetrate the future. We shall recur to the subject of astrology when we come to speak of the moral and religious character of the people.

The Church treated this and other pseudo-sciences nearly always with toleration; and showed itself actually hostile even to genuine science only when a charge of heresy together with necromancy was also in question—which certainly was often the case. A point which it would be interesting to decide is this: whether and in what cases the Dominican (and also the Franciscan) Inquisitors in Italy were conscious of the falsehood of the charges, and yet condemned the accused, either to oblige some enemy of the prisoner or from hatred to natural science, and particularly to experiments. The latter doubtless occurred, but it is not easy to prove the fact. What helped to cause such persecutions in the North, namely, the opposition made to the innovators by the upholders of the received official, scholastic system of nature, was of little

or no weight in Italy. Pietro of Abano, at the beginning of the fourteenth century, is well known to have fallen a victim to the envy of
another physician, who accused him before the Inquisition of heresy
and magic; and something of the same kind may have happened in the
case of his Paduan contemporary, Giovannino Sanguinacci, who was
known as an innovator in medical practice. He escaped, however, with
banishment. Nor must it be forgotten that the inquisitorial power of
the Dominicans was exercised less uniformly in Italy than in the North.
Tyrants and free cities in the fourteenth century treated the clergy at
times with such sovereign contempt that very different matters from
natural science went unpunished. But when, with the fifteenth century,
antiquity became the leading power in Italy, the breach it made in the
old system was turned to account by every branch of secular science.
Humanism, nevertheless, attracted to itself the best strength of the
nation, and thereby, no doubt, did injury to the inductive investigation
of nature. Here and there the Inquisition suddenly started into life,
and punished or burned physicians as blasphemers or magicians. In
such cases it is hard to discover what was the true motive underlying
the condemnation. But even so, Italy, at the close of the fifteenth
century, with Paolo Toscanelli, Luca Pacioli and Leonardo da Vinci,
held incomparably the highest place among European nations in mathematics and the natural sciences, and the learned men of every country,
even Regiomontanus and Copernicus, confessed themselves its pupils.
This glory survived the Counter-reformation, and even today the
Italians would occupy the first place in this respect if circumstances
had not made it impossible for the greatest minds to devote themselves
to tranquil research.

A significant proof of the widespread interest in natural history is
found in the zeal which showed itself at an early period for the collection and comparative study of plants and animals. Italy claims to be
the first creator of botanical gardens, though possibly they may have
served a chiefly practical end, and the claim to priority may be itself
disputed. It is of far greater importance that princes and wealthy men,
in laying out their pleasure-gardens, instinctively made a point of
collecting the greatest possible number of different plants in all their
species and varieties. Thus in the fifteenth century the noble grounds
of the Medicean Villa Careggi appear from the descriptions we have of
them to have been almost a botanical garden, with countless specimens
of different trees and shrubs. Of the same kind was a villa of the
Cardinal Trivulzio, at the beginning of the sixteenth century, in the
Roman Campagna towards Tivoli, with hedges made up of various

species of roses, with trees of every description—the fruit-trees especially showing an astonishing variety—with twenty different sorts of
vines and a large kitchen-garden. This is evidently something very
different from the score or two of familiar medicinal plants which were
to be found in the garden of any castle or monastery in Western
Europe. Along with a careful cultivation of fruit for the purposes of the
table, we find an interest in the plant for its own sake, on account of
the pleasure it gives to the eye. We learn from the history of art at how
late a period this passion for botanical collections was laid aside, and
gave place to what was considered the picturesque style of landscape-
gardening.

The collections, too, of foreign animals not only gratified curiosity,
but served also the higher purposes of observation. The facility of
transport from the southern and eastern harbours of the Mediterranean, and the mildness of the Italian climate, made it practicable to
buy the largest animals of the south, or to accept them as presents
from the Sultans. The cities and princes were especially anxious to
keep live lions, even where a lion was not, as in Florence, the emblem
of the State. The lions' den was generally in or near the government
palace, as in Perugia and Florence; in Rome, it lay on the slope of the
Capitol. The beasts sometimes served as executioners of political judgements, and no doubt, apart from this, they kept alive a certain terror
in the popular mind. Their condition was also held to be ominous of
good or evil. Their fertility, especially, was considered a sign of public
prosperity, and no less a man than Giovanni Villani thought it worth
recording that he was present at the delivery of a lioness. The cubs
were often given to allied States and princes, or to Condottieri as a
reward of their valour. In addition to the lions, the Florentines began
very early to keep leopards, for which a special keeper was appointed.
Borso of Ferrara used to set his lion to fight with bulls, bears, and wild
boars.

By the end of the fifteenth century, however, true menageries (ser-
ragli), now reckoned part of the suitable appointments of a court, were
kept by many of the princes. 'It belongs to the position of the great,'
says Matarazzo, 'to keep horses, dogs, mules, falcons, and other birds,
court-jesters, singers, and foreign animals.' The menagerie at Naples, in
the time of Ferrante, contained even a giraffe and a zebra, presented, it
seems, by the ruler of Baghdad. Filippo Maria Visconti possessed not
only horses which cost him each 500 or 1,000 pieces of gold, and
valuable English dogs, but a number of leopards brought from all parts
of the East; the expense of his hunting-birds, which were collected
from the countries of Northern Europe, amounted to 3,000 pieces of

gold a month. King Emanuel the Great of Portugal knew well what he was about when he presented Leo X with an elephant and a rhinoceros. It was under such circumstances that the foundations of a scientific zoology and botany were laid.

A practical fruit of these zoological studies was the establishment of studs, of which the Mantuan, under Francesco Gonzaga, was esteemed the first in Europe. All interest in, and knowledge of the different breeds of horses is as old, no doubt, as riding itself, and the crossing of the European with the Asiatic must have been common from the time of the Crusades. In Italy, a special inducement to perfect the breed was offered by the prizes at the horse-races held in every considerable town in the peninsula. In the Mantuan stables were found the infallible winners in these contests, as well as the best military chargers, and the horses best suited by their stately appearance for presents to great people. Gonzaga kept stallions and mares from Spain, Ireland, Africa, Thrace, and Cilicia, and for the sake of the last he cultivated the friendship of the Sultans. All possible experiments were here tried, in order to produce the most perfect animals.

Even human menageries were not wanting. The famous Cardinal Ippolito Medici, bastard of Giuliano, Duke of Nemours, kept at his strange court a troop of barbarians who talked no less than twenty different languages, and who were all of them perfect specimens of their races. Among them were incomparable *voltigeurs* of the best blood of the North African Moors, Tartar bowmen, Negro wrestlers, Indian divers, and Turks, who generally accompanied the Cardinal on his hunting expeditions. When he was overtaken by an early death (1535), this motley band carried the corpse on their shoulders from Itri to Rome, and mingled with the general mourning for the open-handed Cardinal their medley of tongues and violent gesticulations.

These scattered notices of the relations of the Italians to natural science, and their interest in the wealth and variety of the products of nature, are only fragments of a great subject. No one is more conscious than the author of the defects in this knowledge on this point. Of the multitude of special works in which the subject is adequately treated, even the names are but imperfectly known to him.

But outside the sphere of scientific investigation, there is another way to draw near to nature. The Italians are the first among modern peoples by whom the outward world was seen and felt as something beautiful.

The power to do so is always the result of a long and complicated development, and its origin is not easily detected, since a dim feeling of this kind may exist long before it shows itself in poetry and painting and thereby becomes conscious of itself. Among the ancients, for example, art and poetry had gone through the whole circle of human interests, before they turned to the representation of nature, and even then the latter filled always a limited and subordinate place. And yet, from the time of Homer downwards, the powerful impression made by nature upon man is shown by countless verses and chance expressions. The Germanic races, which founded their States on the ruins of the Roman Empire, were thoroughly and specially fitted to understand the spirit of natural scenery; and though Christianity compelled them for a while to see in the springs and mountains, in the lakes and woods, which they had till then revered, the working of evil demons, yet this transitional conception was soon outgrown. By the year 1200, at the height of the Middle Ages, a genuine, hearty enjoyment of the external world was again in existence, and found lively expression in the minstrelsy of different nations, which gives evidence of the sympathy felt with all the simple phenomena of nature—spring with its flowers, the green fields and the woods. But these pictures are all foreground without perspective. Even the crusaders, who travelled so far and saw so much, are not recognizable as such in their poems. The epic poetry, which describes armour and costumes so fully, does not attempt more than a sketch of outward nature; and even the great Wolfram von Eschenbach scarcely anywhere gives us an adequate picture of the scene on which his heroes move. From these poems it would never be guessed that their noble authors in all countries inhabited or visited lofty castles, commanding distant prospects. Even in the Latin poems of the wandering clerks, we find no traces of a distant view—of landscape properly so called—but what lies near is sometimes described with a glow and splendour which none of the knightly minstrels can surpass. What picture of the Grove of Love can equal that of the Italian poet—for such we take him to be—of the twelfth century?

> 'Immortalis fieret
> Ibi manens homo;
> Arbor ibi quaelibet
> Suo gaudet pomo;
> Viae myrrha, cinnamo
> Fragrant, et amomo—
> Conjectari poterat
> Dominus ex domo' etc.

To the Italian mind, at all events, nature had by this time lost its taint of sin, and had shaken off all trace of demoniacal powers. Saint Francis of Assisi, in his Hymn to the Sun, frankly praises the Lord for creating the heavenly bodies and the four elements.

But the unmistakable proofs of a deepening effect of nature on the human spirit begin with Dante. Not only does he awaken in us by a few vigorous lines the sense of the morning air and the trembling light on the distant ocean, or of the grandeur of the storm-beaten forest, but he makes the ascent of lofty peaks, with the only possible object of enjoying the view—the first man, perhaps, since the days of antiquity who did so. In Boccaccio we can do little more than infer how country scenery affected him; yet his pastoral romances show his imagination to have been filled with it. But the significance of nature for a receptive spirit is fully and clearly displayed by Petrarch—one of the first truly modern men. That clear soul—who first collected from the literature of all countries evidence of the origin and progress of the sense of natural beauty, and himself, in his 'Aspects of Nature', achieved the noblest masterpiece of description—Alexander von Humboldt has not done full justice to Petrarch; and following in the steps of the great reaper, we may still hope to glean a few ears of interest and value.

Petrarch was not only a distinguished geographer—the first map of Italy is said to have been drawn by his direction—and not only a reproducer of the sayings of the ancients, but felt himself the influence of natural beauty. The enjoyment of nature is, for him, the favourite accompaniment of intellectual pursuits; it was to combine the two that he lived in learned retirement at Vaucluse and elsewhere, that he from time to time fled from the world and from his age. We should do him wrong by inferring from his weak and undeveloped power of describing natural scenery that he did not feel it deeply. His picture, for instance, of the lovely Gulf of Spezia and Porto Venere, which he inserts at the end of the sixth book of the 'Africa', for the reason that none of the ancients or moderns had sung of it, is no more than a simple enumeration, but Petrarch is also conscious of the beauty of rock scenery, and is perfectly able to distinguish the picturesqueness from the utility of nature. During his stay among the woods of Reggio, the sudden sight of an impressive landscape so affected him that he resumed a poem which he had long laid aside. But the deepest impression of all was made upon him by the ascent of Mont Ventoux, near Avignon. An indefinable longing for a distant panorama grew stronger and stronger in him, till at length the accidental sight of a passage in Livy, where King Philip, the enemy of Rome, ascends the Hæmus, decided him. He thought that what was not blamed in a grey-headed

monarch, might well be *excused* in a young man of private station. The
ascent of a mountain for its own sake was unheard of, and there
could be no thought of the companionship of friends or acquaintances.
Petrarch took with him only his younger brother and two country people from the last place where he halted. At the foot of the mountain
an old herdsman besought him to turn back, saying that he himself had
attempted to climb it fifty years before, and had brought home nothing
but repentance, broken bones, and torn clothes, and that neither before nor after had anyone ventured to do the same. Nevertheless, they
struggled forward and upward, till the clouds lay beneath their feet,
and at last they reached the top. A description of the view from the
summit would be looked for in vain, not because the poet was in-
sensible to it, but, on the contrary, because the impression was too
overwhelming. His whole past life, with all its follies, rose before his
mind; he remembered that ten years ago that day he had quitted
Bologna a young man, and turned a longing gaze towards his native
country; he opened a book which then was his constant companion, the
'Confessions' of St. Augustine, and his eye fell on the passage in the
tenth chapter, 'and men go forth, and admire lofty mountains and
broad seas, and roaring torrents, and the ocean, and the course of the
stars, and forget their own selves while doing so'. His brother, to whom
he read these words, could not understand why he closed the book
and said no more.

Some decades later, about 1360, Fazio degli Uberti describes, in his
rhyming geography, the wide panorama from the mountains of
Auvergne, with the interest, it is true, of the geographer and antiquarian only, but still showing clearly that he himself had seen it. He must,
however, have ascended far higher peaks, since he is familiar with
facts which only occur at a height of 10,000 feet or more above the
sea—mountain-sickness and its accompaniments—of which his imaginary comrade Solinus tries to cure him with a sponge dipped in an
essence. The ascents of Parnassus and Olympus, of which he speaks,
are perhaps only fictions.

In the fifteenth century, the great masters of the Flemish school,
Hubert and Jan van Eyck, suddenly lifted the veil from nature. Their
landscapes are not merely the fruit of an endeavour to reflect the real
world in art, but have, even if expressed conventionally, a certain
poetical meaning—in short, a soul. Their influence on the whole art of
the West is undeniable, and extended to the landscape-painting of the
Italians, but without preventing the characteristic interest of the Italian
eye for nature from finding its own expression.

On this point, as in the scientific description of nature, Æneas Sylvius is again one of the most weighty voices of his time. Even if we grant the justice of all that has been said against his character, we must nevertheless admit that in few other men was the picture of the age and its culture so fully reflected, and that few came nearer to the normal type of the men of the early Renaissance. It may be added parenthetically, that even in respect to his moral character he will not be fairly judged, if we listen solely to the complaints of the German Church, which his fickleness helped to baulk of the Council it so ardently desired.

He here claims our attention as the first who not only enjoyed the magnificence of the Italian landscape, but described it with enthusiasm down to its minutest details. The ecclesiastical State and the south of Tuscany—his native home—he knew thoroughly, and after he became Pope he spent his leisure during the favourable season chiefly in excursions to the country. Then at last the gouty man was rich enough to have himself carried in a litter across the mountains and valleys; and when we compare his enjoyments with those of the Popes who succeeded him, Pius, whose chief delight was in nature, antiquity, and simple, but noble, architecture, appears almost a saint. In the elegant and flowing Latin of his 'Commentaries' he freely tells us of his happiness.

His eye seems as keen and practised as that of any modern observer. He enjoys with rapture the panoramic splendour of the view from the summit of the Alban Hills—from the Monte Cavo—whence he could see the shores of St. Peter from Terracina and the promontory of Circe as far as Monte Argentaro, and the wide expanse of country round about, with the ruined cities of the past, and with the mountain-chains of Central Italy beyond; and then his eye would turn to the green woods in the hollows beneath and the mountain-lakes among them. He feels the beauty of the position of Todi, crowning the vineyards and olive-clad slopes, looking down upon distant woods and upon the valley of the Tiber, where towns and castles rise above the winding river. The lovely hills about Siena, with villas and monasteries on every height, are his own home, and his descriptions of them are touched with a peculiar feeling. Single picturesque glimpses charm him too, like the little promontory of Capo di Monte that stretches out into the Lake of Bolsena. 'Rocky steps,' we read, 'shaded by vines, descend to the water's edge, where the evergreen oaks stand between the cliffs, alive with the song of thrushes.' On the path round the Lake of Nemi, beneath the chestnuts and fruit-trees, he feels that here, if anywhere, a poet's soul must awake—here in the hiding-place of Diana! He often held consistories or received ambassadors under huge old chestnut-trees, or beneath the olives on the greensward by some gurgling spring. A view like that of a narrowing gorge, with a bridge arched boldly over it, awakens at once his artistic sense. Even the smallest details give him delight through something beautiful, or perfect, or characteristic in them—the blue fields of waving flax, the yellow gorse which covers the hills, even tangled thickets, or single trees, or springs, which seem to him like wonders of nature.

The height of his enthusiasm for natural beauty was reached during his stay on Monte Amiata, in the summer of 1462, when plague and heat made the lowlands uninhabitable. Half-way up the mountain, in the old Lombard monastery of San Salvatore, he and his court took up their quarters. There, between the chestnuts which clothe the steep declivity, the eye may wander over all Southern Tuscany, with the towers of Siena in the distance. The ascent of the highest peak he left to his companions, who were joined by the Venetian envoy; they found at the top two vast blocks of stone one upon the other—perhaps the sacrificial altar of a prehistoric people—and fancied that in the far distance they saw Corsica and Sardinia rising above the sea. In the cool air of the hills, among the old oaks and chestnuts, on the green meadows where there were no thorns to wound the feet, and no snakes or insects to hurt or to annoy, the Pope passed days of unclouded happiness. For the 'Segnatura', which took place on certain days of the week, he selected on each occasion some new shady retreat 'novos in convallibus fontes et novas inveniens umbras, quæ dubiam facerent electionem'. At such times the dogs would perhaps start a great stag from his lair, who, after defending himself a while with hoofs and antlers, would fly at last up the mountain. In the evening the Pope was accustomed to sit before the monastery on the spot from which the whole valley of the Paglia was visible, holding lively conversations with the cardinals. The courtiers, who ventured down from the heights on their hunting expeditions, found the heat below intolerable, and the scorched plains like a very hell, while the monastery, with its cool, shady woods, seemed like an abode of the blessed.

All this is genuine modern enjoyment, not a reflection of antiquity. As surely as the ancients themselves felt in the same manner, so surely, nevertheless, were the scanty expressions of the writers whom Pius knew insufficient to awaken in him such enthusiasm.

The second great age of Italian poetry, which now followed at the end of the fifteenth and the beginning of the sixteenth centuries, as well as the Latin poetry of the same period, is rich in proofs of the powerful effect of nature on the human mind. The first glance at the lyric poets of that time will suffice to convince us. Elaborate descriptions of natural scenery, it is true, are very rare, for the reason that, in this energetic age, the novels, and the lyric or epic poetry had something else to deal with. Boiardo and Ariosto paint nature vigorously, but as briefly as possible, and with no effort to appeal by their descriptions to the feelings of the reader, which they endeavour to reach solely by their narrative and characters. Letter-writers and the authors of philosophical dialogues are, in fact, better evidence of the growing love of nature than the poets. The novelist Bandello, for example, observes rigorously the rules of his department of literature; he gives us in his novels themselves not a word more than is necessary on the natural scenery amid which the action of his tales takes place, but in the dedications which always precede them we meet with charming descriptions of nature as the setting for his dialogues and social pictures. Among letter-writers, Aretino unfortunately must be named as the first who has fully painted in words the splendid effect of light and shadow in an Italian sunset.

We sometimes find the feeling of the poets, also, attaching itself with tenderness to graceful scenes of country life. Tito Strozzi, about the year 1480, describes in a Latin elegy the dwelling of his mistress. We are shown an old ivy-clad house, half hidden in trees, and adorned with weather-stained frescoes of the saints, and near it a chapel much damaged by the violence of the River Po, which flowed hard by; not far off, the priest ploughs his few barren roods with borrowed cattle. This is no reminiscence of the Roman elegists, but true modern sentiment; and the parallel to it—a sincere, unartificial description of country life in general—will be found at the end of this part of our work.

It may be objected that the German painters at the beginning of the sixteenth century succeeded in representing with perfect mastery these scenes of country life, as, for instance, Albrecht Dürer, in his engraving of the Prodigal Son. But it is one thing if a painter, brought up in a school of realism, introduces such scenes, and quite another thing if a poet, accustomed to an ideal or mythological framework, is driven by inward impulse into realism. Besides which, priority in point of time is here, as in the descriptions of country life, on the side of the Italian poets.

To the discovery of the outward world the Renaissance added a still greater achievement, by first discerning and bringing to light the full, whole nature of man.

This period, as we have seen, first gave the highest development to individuality, and then led the individual to the most zealous and thorough study of himself in all forms and under all conditions. Indeed, the development of personality is essentially involved in the recognition of it in oneself and in others. Between these two great processes our narrative has placed the influence of ancient literature because the mode of conceiving and representing both the individual and human nature in general was defined and coloured by that influence. But the power of conception and representation lay in the age and in the people.

The facts which we shall quote in evidence of our thesis will be few in number. Here, if anywhere in the course of this discussion, the author is conscious that he is treading on the perilous ground of conjecture, and that what seems to him a clear, if delicate and gradual, transition in the intellectual movement of the fourteenth and fifteenth centuries, may not be equally plain to others. The gradual awakening of the soul of a people is a phenomenon which may produce a different impression on each spectator. Time will judge which impression is the most faithful.

Happily the study of the intellectual side of human nature began, not with the search after a theoretical psychology—for that, Aristotle still sufficed—but with the endeavour to observe and to describe. The indispensable ballast of theory was limited to the popular doctrine of the four temperaments, in its then habitual union with the belief in the influence of the planets. Such conceptions may remain ineradicable in the minds of individuals, without hindering the general progress of the age. It certainly makes on us a singular impression, when we meet them at a time when human nature in its deepest essence and in all its characteristic expressions was not only known by exact observation, but represented by an immortal poetry and art. It sounds almost ludicrous when an otherwise competent observer considers Clement VII to be of a melancholy temperament, but defers his judgement to that of the physicians, who declare the Pope of a sanguine-choleric nature; or when we read that the same Gaston de Foix, the victor of Ravenna, whom Giorgione painted and Bambaia carved, and whom all the historians describe, had the saturnine temperament. No doubt those who use these expressions mean something by them; but the terms in which they tell us their meaning are strangely out of date in the Italy of the sixteenth century.

As examples of the free delineation of the human spirit, we shall first speak of the great poets of the fourteenth century.

If we were to collect the pearls from the courtly and knightly poetry of all the countries of the West during the two preceding centuries, we should have a mass of wonderful divinations and single pictures of the inward life, which at first sight would seem to rival the poetry of the Italians. Leaving lyrical poetry out of account, Godfrey of Strassburg gives us, in 'Tristram and Isolt', a representation of human passion, some features of which are immortal. But these pearls lie scattered in the ocean of artificial convention, and they are altogether something very different from a complete objective picture of the inward man and his spiritual wealth.

Italy, too, in the thirteenth century had, through the 'Trovatori', its share in the poetry of the courts and of chivalry. To them is mainly due the 'Canzone', whose construction is as difficult and artificial as that of the songs of any northern minstrel. Their subject and mode of thought represents simply the conventional tone of the courts, be the poet a burgher or a scholar.

But two new paths at length showed themselves, along which Italian poetry could advance to another and a characteristic future. They are not the less important for being concerned only with the formal and external side of the art.

To the same Brunetto Latini—the teacher of Dante—who, in his 'Canzoni', adopts the customary manner of the 'Trovatori', we owe the first-known 'versi sciolti', or blank hendecasyllabic verses, and in his apparent absence of form, a true and genuine passion suddenly showed itself. The same voluntary renunciation of outward effect, through confidence in the power of the inward conception, can be observed some years later in fresco-painting, and later still in painting of all kinds, which began to cease to rely on colour for its effect, using simply a lighter or darker shade. For an age which laid so much stress on artificial form in poetry, these verses of Brunetto mark the beginning of a new epoch.

About the same time, or even in the first half of the thirteenth century, one of the many strictly balanced forms of metre, in which Europe was then so fruitful, became a normal and recognized form in Italy—the sonnet. The order of rhymes and even the number of lines varied for a whole century, till Petrarch fixed them permanently. In this form all higher lyrical and meditative subjects, and at a later time subjects of every possible description, were treated, and the madrigals, the sestine, and even the 'Canzoni' were reduced to a subordinate place.

Later Italian writers complain, half jestingly, half resentfully, of this inevitable mould, this Procrustean bed, to which they were compelled to make their thoughts and feelings fit. Others were, and still are, quite satisfied with this particular form of verse, which they freely use to express any personal reminiscence or idle sing-song without necessity or serious purpose. For which reason there are many more bad or insignificant sonnets than good ones.

Nevertheless, the sonnet must be held to have been an unspeakable blessing for Italian poetry. The clearness and beauty of its structure, the invitation it gave to elevate the thought in the second and more rapidly moving half, and the ease with which it could be learned by heart, made it valued even by the greatest masters. In fact, they would not have kept it in use down to our own century had they not been penetrated with a sense of its singular worth. These masters could have given us the same thoughts in other and wholly different forms. But when once they had made the sonnet the normal type of lyrical poetry, many other writers of great, if not the highest, gifts, who otherwise would have lost themselves in a sea of diffusiveness, were forced to concentrate their feelings. The sonnet became for Italian literature a condenser of thoughts and emotions such as was possessed by the poetry of no other modern people.

Thus the world of Italian sentiment comes before us in a series of pictures, clear, concise, and most effective in their brevity. Had other nations possessed a form of expression of the same kind, we should perhaps have known more of their inward life; we might have had a number of pictures of inward and outward situations—reflexions of the national character and temper—and should not be dependent for such knowledge on the so-called lyrical poets of the fourteenth and fifteenth centuries, who can hardly ever be read with any serious enjoyment. In Italy we can trace an undoubted progress from the time when the sonnet came into existence. In the second half of the thirteenth century the 'Trovatori della transizione', as they have been recently named, mark the passage from the Troubadours to the poets —that is, to those who wrote under the influence of antiquity. The simplicity and strength of their feeling, the vigorous delineation of fact, the precise expression and rounding off of their sonnets and other poems, herald the coming of a Dante. Some political sonnets of the Guelphs and Ghibellines (1260–1270) have about them the ring of his passion, and others remind us of his sweetest lyrical notes.

Of his own theoretical view of the sonnet, we are unfortunately ignorant, since the last books of his work, 'De vulgari eloquentia', in

which he proposed to treat of ballads and sonnets, either remained un-
written or have been lost. But, as a matter of fact, he has left us in his
Sonnets and 'Canzoni' a treasure of inward experience. And in what a
framework he has set them! The prose of the 'Vita Nuova', in which
he gives an account of the origin of each poem, is as wonderful as the
verses themselves, and forms with them a uniform whole, inspired with
the deepest glow of passion. With unflinching frankness and sincerity
he lays bare every shade of his joy and his sorrow, and moulds it reso-
lutely into the strictest forms of art. Reading attentively these Sonnets
and 'Canzoni' and the marvellous fragments of the diary of his youth
which lie between them, we fancy that throughout the Middle Ages
the poets have been purposely fleeing from themselves, and that he
was the first to seek his own soul. Before his time we meet with many
an artistic verse; but he is the first artist in the full sense of the word
—the first who consciously cast immortal matter into an immortal form.
Subjective feeling has here a full objective truth and greatness, and
most of it is so set forth that all ages and peoples can make it their
own. Where he writes in a thoroughly objective spirit, and lets the
force of his sentiment be guessed at only by some outward fact, as
in the magnificent sonnets 'Tanto gentile', etc., and 'Vede perfetta-
mente', etc., he seems to feel the need of excusing himself. The most
beautiful of these poems really belongs to this class—the 'Deh pere-
grini che pensosi andate'. ('Oh, pilgrims, walking deep in thoughts',
from *Vita Nuova*.) Even apart from the 'Divine Comedy', Dante would
have marked by these youthful poems the boundary between medi-
ævalism and modern times. The human spirit had taken a mighty step
towards the consciousness of its own secret life.

The revelations in this matter which are contained in the 'Divine
Comedy' itself are simply immeasurable; and it would be necessary
to go through the whole poem, one canto after another, in order to
do justice to its value from this point of view. Happily we have no
need to do this, as it has long been a daily food of all the countries of
the West. Its plan, and the ideas on which it is based, belong to the
Middle Ages, and appeal to our interest only historically; but it is
nevertheless the beginning of all modern poetry, through the power
and richness shown in the description of human nature in every shape
and attitude.

From this time forward poetry may have experienced unequal fortunes, and may show, for half a century together, a so-called relapse.
But its nobler and more vital principle was saved for ever; and whenever in the fourteenth, fifteenth, and in the beginning of the sixteenth

centuries, an original mind devotes himself to it, he represents a more advanced stage than any poet out of Italy, given—what is certainly not always easy to settle satisfactorily—an equality of natural gifts to start with.

Here, as in other things in Italy, culture—to which poetry belongs —precedes the visual arts and, in fact, gives them their chief impulse. More than a century elapsed before the spiritual element in painting and sculpture attained a power of expression in any way analogous to that of the 'Divine Comedy'. How far the same rule holds good for the artistic development of other nations, and of what importance the whole question may be, does not concern us here. For Italian civilization it is of decisive weight.

The position to be assigned to Petrarch in this respect must be settled by the many readers of the poet. Those who come to him in the spirit of a cross-examiner, and busy themselves in detecting the contradictions between the poet and the man, his infidelities in love, and the other weak sides of his character, may perhaps, after sufficient effort, end by losing all taste for his poetry. In place, then, of artistic enjoyment, we may acquire a knowledge of the man in his 'totality'. What a pity that Petrarch's letters from Avignon contain so little gossip to take hold of, and that the letters of his acquaintances and of the friends of these acquaintances have either been lost or never existed! Instead of Heaven being thanked when we are not forced to inquire how and through what struggles a poet has rescued something immortal from his own poor life and lot, a biography has been stitched together for Petrarch out of these so-called 'remains', which reads like an indictment. But the poet may take comfort. If the printing and editing of the correspondence of celebrated people goes on for another half-century as it has begun in England and Germany, he will have illustrious company enough sitting with him on the stool of repentance.

Without shutting our eyes to much that is forced and artificial in his poetry, where the writer is merely imitating himself and singing on in the old strain, we cannot fail to admire the marvellous abundance of pictures of the inmost soul—descriptions of moments of joy and sorrow which must have been thoroughly his own, since no one before him gives us anything of the kind, and on which his significance rests for his country and for the world. His verse is not in all places equally transparent; by the side of his most beautiful thoughts stands at times some allegorical conceit or some sophisticated trick of logic, altogether foreign to our present taste. But the balance is on the side of excellence.

Boccaccio, too, in his imperfectly-known Sonnets, succeeds sometimes in giving a most powerful and effective picture of his feeling. The return to a spot consecrated by love (Son. 22), the melancholy of spring (Son. 33), the sadness of the poet who feels himself growing old (Son. 65), are admirably treated by him. And in the 'Ameto' he has described the ennobling and transfiguring power of love in a manner which would hardly be expected from the author of the 'Decameron'. In the 'Fiammetta' we have another great and minutely-painted picture of the human soul, full of the keenest observation, though executed with anything but uniform power, and in parts marred by the passion for high-sounding language and by an unlucky mixture of mythological allusions and learned quotations. The 'Fiammetta', if we are not mistaken, is a sort of feminine counterpart to the 'Vita Nuova' of Dante, or at any rate owes its origin to it.

That the ancient poets, particularly the elegists, and Virgil, in the fourth book of the Æneid, were not without influence on the Italians of this and the following generation is beyond a doubt; but the spring of sentiment within the latter was nevertheless powerful and original. If we compare them in this respect with their contemporaries in other countries, we shall find in them the earliest complete expression of modern European feeling. The question, be it remembered, is not to know whether eminent men of other nations did not feel as deeply and as nobly, but who first gave documentary proof of the widest knowledge of the movements of the human heart.

Why did the Italians of the Renaissance do nothing above the second rank in tragedy? That was the field on which to display human character, intellect, and passion, in the thousand forms of their growth, their struggles, and their decline. In other words: why did Italy produce no Shakespeare? For with the stage of other northern countries besides England the Italians of the sixteenth and seventeenth centuries had no reason to fear a comparison; and with the Spaniards they could not enter into competition, since Italy had long lost all traces of religious fanaticism, treated the chivalrous code of honour only as a form, and was both too proud and too intelligent to bow down before its tyrannical and illegitimate master. We have therefore only to consider the English stage in the period of its brief splendour.

It is an obvious reply that all Europe produced but one Shakespeare, and that such a mind is the rarest of Heaven's gifts. It is further

possible that the Italian stage was on the way to something great when
the Counter-reformation broke in upon it, and, aided by the Spanish
rule over Naples and Milan, and indirectly over almost the whole
peninsula, withered the best flowers of the Italian spirit. It would be
hard to conceive of Shakespeare himself under a Spanish viceroy, or in
the neighbourhood of the Holy Inquisition at Rome, or even in his own
country a few decades later, at the time of the English Revolution. The
stage, which in its perfection is a late product of every civilization,
must wait for its own time and fortune.

Among the new discoveries made with regard to man, we must
reckon, in conclusion, the interest taken in descriptions of the daily
course of human life.

The comical and satirical literature of the Middle Ages could not
dispense with pictures of everyday events. But it is another thing, when
the Italians of the Renaissance dwelt on this picture for its own sake
—for its inherent interest—and because it forms part of that great,
universal life of the world whose magic breath they felt everywhere
around them. Instead of and together with the satirical comedy, which
wanders through houses, villages, and streets, seeking food for its
derision in parson, peasant, and burgher, we now see in literature the
beginnings of a true *genre*, long before it found any expression in
painting. That *genre* and satire are often met with in union, does not
prevent them from being wholly different things.

How much of earthly business must Dante have watched with atten-
tive interest, before he was able to make us see with our own eyes all
that happened in his spiritual world. The famous pictures of the busy
movement in the arsenal at Venice, of the blind men laid side by side
before the church door, and the like, are by no means the only instances of this kind: for the art, in which he is a master, of expressing
the inmost soul by the outward gesture, cannot exist without a close
and incessant study of human life. (Cf. Inferno xxi, 1–6, Purgatorio
xiii, 61–66.) The poets who followed rarely came near him in this
respect, and the novelists were forbidden by the first laws of their
literary style to linger over details. Their prefaces and narratives might
be as long as they pleased, but what we understand by *genre* was outside their province. The taste for this class of description was not fully
awakened till the time of the revival of antiquity.

And here we are again met by the man who had a heart for everything—Æneas Sylvius. Not only natural beauty, not only that which
has an antiquarian or a geographical interest, finds a place in his descriptions, but any living scene of daily life. Among the numerous

passages in his memoirs in which scenes are described which hardly one of his contemporaries would have thought worth a line of notice, we will here only mention the boat-race on the Lake of Bolsena. We are not able to detect from what old letter-writer or story-teller the impulse was derived to which we owe such lifelike pictures. Indeed, the whole spiritual communion between antiquity and the Renaissance is full of delicacy and of mystery.

To this class belong those descriptive Latin poems of which we have already spoken—hunting-scenes, journeys, ceremonies, and so forth. In Italian we also find something of the same kind, as, for example, the descriptions of the famous Medicean tournament by Politian and Luca Pulci. The true epic poets, Luigi Pulci, Boiardo, and Ariosto, are carried on more rapidly by the stream of their narrative; yet in all of them we must recognize the lightness and precision of their descriptive touch as one of the chief elements of their greatness. Franco Sacchetti amuses himself with repeating the short speeches of a troop of pretty women caught in the woods by a shower of rain.

Other scenes of moving life are to be looked for in the military historians. In a lengthy poem, dating from an earlier period, we find a faithful picture of a combat of mercenary soldiers in the fourteenth century, chiefly in the shape of the orders, cries of battle, and dialogue with which it is accompanied.

But the most remarkable productions of this kind are the realistic descriptions of country life, which are found most abundantly in Lorenzo il Magnifico and the poets of his circle.

Since the time of Petrarch, an unreal and conventional style of bucolic poetry had been in vogue, which, whether written in Latin or Italian, was essentially a copy of Virgil. Parallel to this, we find the pastoral novel of Boccaccio and other works of the same kind down to the 'Arcadia' of Sannazaro, and later still, the pastoral comedy of Tasso and Guarini. They are works whose style, whether poetry or prose, is admirably finished and perfect, but in which pastoral life is only an ideal dress for sentiments which belong to a wholly different sphere of culture.

But by the side of all this there appeared in Italian poetry, towards the close of the fifteenth century, signs of a more realistic treatment of rustic life. This was not possible out of Italy; for here only did the peasant, whether labourer or proprietor, possess human dignity, personal freedom, and the right of settlement, hard as his lot might sometimes be in other respects. The difference between town and country is far from being so marked here as in northern countries. Many of the smaller towns are peopled almost exclusively by peasants who, on coming home at nightfall from their work, are transformed into townfolk. The masons of Como wandered over nearly all Italy; the child Giotto was free to leave his sheep and join a guild at Florence; everywhere there was a human stream flowing from the country into the cities, and some mountain populations seemed born to supply this current. It is true that the pride and local conceit supplied poets and novelists with abundant motives for making game of the 'villano', and what they left undone was taken charge of by the comic improvisers. But nowhere do we find a trace of that brutal and contemptuous class-hatred against the 'vilains' which inspired the aristocratic poets of Provence, and often, too, the French chroniclers. On the contrary, Italian authors of every sort gladly recognize and accentuate what is great or remarkable in the life of the peasant. Gioviano Pontano mentions with admiration instances of the fortitude of the savage inhabitants of the Abruzzi, in the biographical collections and in the novelists we meet with the figure of the heroic peasant-maiden who hazards her life to defend her family and her honour.

Such conditions made the poetical treatment of country life possible. The first instance we shall mention is that of Battista Mantovano, whose eclogues, once much read and still worth reading, appeared among his earliest works about 1480. They are a mixture of real and conventional rusticity, but the former tends to prevail. They represent the mode of thought of a well-meaning village clergyman, not without a certain leaning to liberal ideas. As Carmelite monk, the writer may have had occasion to mix freely with the peasantry.

But it is with a power of a wholly different kind that Lorenzo il Magnifico transports himself into the peasant's world. His 'Nencia di Barberino' reads like a crowd of genuine extracts from the popular songs of the Florentine country, fused into a great stream of octaves. The objectivity of the writer is such that we are in doubt whether the speaker—the young peasant Vallera, who declares his love to Nencia —awakens his sympathy or ridicule. The deliberate contrast to the conventional eclogue is unmistakable. Lorenzo surrenders himself purposely to the realism of simple, rough country life, and yet his work makes upon us the impression of true poetry.

The 'Beca da Dicomano' of Luigi Pulci is an admitted counterpart to the 'Nencia' of Lorenzo. But the deeper purpose is wanting. The 'Beca' is written not so much from the inward need to give a picture of popular life, as from the desire to win the approbation of the educated Florentine world by a successful poem. Hence the greater and more deliberate coarseness of the scenes, and the indecent jokes. Nevertheless, the point of view of the rustic lover is admirably maintained.

Third in this company of poets comes Angelo Poliziano, with his 'Rusticus' in Latin hexameters. Keeping clear of all imitation of Virgil's Georgics, he describes the year of the Tuscan peasant, beginning with the late autumn, when the countryman gets ready his new plough and prepares the seed for the winter. The picture of the meadows in spring is full and beautiful, and the 'Summer' has fine passages; but the vintage-feast in autumn is one of the gems of modern Latin poetry. Politian wrote poems in Italian as well as Latin, from which we may infer that in Lorenzo's circle it was possible to give a realistic picture of the passionate life of the lower classes. His gipsy's love-song is one of the earliest products of that wholly modern tendency to put oneself with poetic consciousness into the position of another class. This had probably been attempted for ages with a view to satire, and the opportunity for it was offered in Florence at every carnival by the songs of the maskers. But the sympathetic understanding of the feeling of another class was new; and with it the 'Nencia' and this 'Canzone zingaresca' mark a new starting-point in the history of poetry.

Here, too, we must briefly indicate how culture prepared the way for artistic development. From the time of the 'Nencia', a period of eighty years elapses to the rustic genre-painting of Jacopo Bassano and his school.

. . . Differences of birth had lost their significance in Italy. Much of this was doubtless owing to the fact that men and mankind were here first thoroughly and profoundly understood. This one single result of the Renaissance is enough to fill us with everlasting thankfulness. The logical notion of humanity was old enough—but here the notion became a fact.

The loftiest conceptions on this subject were uttered by Pico della Mirandola in his Speech on the Dignity of Man, which may justly be called one of the noblest of that great age. God, he tells us, made man at the close of the creation, to know the laws of the universe, to love its beauty, to admire its greatness. He bound him to no fixed place, to no prescribed form of work, and by no iron necessity, but gave him freedom to will and to love. 'I have set thee,' says the Creator to Adam, 'in the midst of the world, that thou mayst the more easily behold and see all that is therein. I created thee a being neither heavenly nor earthly, neither mortal nor immortal only, that thou mightest be free to shape and to overcome thyself. Thou mayst sink into a beast, and be born anew to the divine likeness. The brutes bring from their

mother's body what they will carry with them as long as they live; the
higher spirits are from the beginning, or soon after, what they will be
forever. To thee alone is given a growth and a development depending
on thine own free will. Thou bearest in thee the germs of a universal
life.'

Suggestions for Further Reading

BARON, HANS, *The Crisis of the Early Italian Renaissance.* Princeton, N.J.:
    Princeton University Press, 1955.
BECKER, MARVIN, *Florence in Transition.* Baltimore, Md.: Johns Hopkins
    Press, 1967.
BRUCKER, GENE A., *Renaissance Florence.* New York: John Wiley & Sons,
    1969.
CHABOD, F., *Machiavelli and the Renaissance.* London: Bowes & Bowes,
    1958.
FERGUSON, W. K., *The Renaissance in Historical Thought.* Boston: Hough-
    ton Mifflin Company, 1948.
GILMORE, M. P., *The World of Humanism, 1453–1517.* New York: Harper
    and Brothers, 1952.
KRISTELLER, P. O., *The Classics and Renaissance Thought.* Cambridge,
    Mass.: Published for Oberlin College by Harvard University Press,
    1955.
KRISTELLER, P. O., E. CASSIRER, ET AL., *The Renaissance Philosophy of
    Man.* Chicago: University of Chicago Press, 1963.
MARTINES, LAURO, *The Social World of the Florentine Humanists.* Prince-
    ton, N.J.: Princeton University Press, 1963.
SYMONDS, J. A., *The Renaissance in Italy,* 6 vols. London: Smith, Elder,
    1898.

J. H. PARRY

The Spirit of the Age of Reconnaissance

◆§◈ The development that historians—with Western chauvinist assumptions—used to call the Expansion of Europe, and which we would now call more correctly The First Age of European Imperialism, 1450–1650, had a profound impact on several critical aspects of European life. First, the drawing into Europe of vast wealth from overseas produced the great inflation and substantially inspired the commercial expansion of the sixteenth century, and these developments in turn had enormous consequences for European economy and social structure. Second, two agricultural products transplanted from the Americas—maize and the potato—provided a new staple of animal fodder and a new nourishing staple for the common man, thereby improving health and life expectancy and serving as an important foundation for the population boom of the eighteenth century. Third, the establishment of overseas empires and their exploitation powerfully affected the relative strength of the Western states. The rise of Hapsburg power in the sixteenth century was directly, if not exclusively, attributable to Spain's American resources, which were funneled into support of the awesome Hapsburg mercenary armies.

Finally, by the late seventeenth century the overseas experience of European man was beginning to affect his con-

FROM J. H. Parry, *The Age of Reconnaissance* (New York: Praeger Publishers, Inc., 1969), pp. 1–5, 15–16, 19–37, 321–327.

sciousness of himself and his world. Europeans discovered
that there were different ways of organizing society, a variety of cultures, religions, and life styles, and they began
to see that the structure of their own civilization was not
the only possible one. This relativist attitude fostered the
new critical approach to political and social institutions
which is a central ingredient of the Enlightenment and
the democratic movement of the eighteenth century.

What did the native Americans and Asians among whom
the Europeans established their trading centers, colonies,
and imperial governments receive in return for these benefits that Europeans derived from their overseas ventures?
In the long run, it might be said that they got European
technology, medicine, and political and economic institutions—but in most instances they would have gained these
things anyway without experiencing conquest and subju-
gation. Japan, never conquered by a western power until
1945, had become the most westernized of Asian nations
in terms of science, technology, and industry. And even
such benefits as resulted from European expansion were
a long time in coming, and very partial in their dissemina-
tion.

As far as the sixteenth and seventeenth centuries are
concerned, what the non-Europeans received from Europeans was pillage, massacre, exploitation, robbery, and/or
enslavement—and, in some instances, conversion to Christianity. What a price to pay for the Catholic or Protestant
(usually Catholic) heaven! Even venereal disease, "the
French disease," that historians used to think the Europeans
picked up from the Amerindians, we now know to have
existed in Europe at least since Roman times—this, too,
was a European gift to the native people of the New
World.

What inspired the Europeans at the end of the fifteenth
century to break out of their geographic and intellectual
shell and accept the challenges of vast oceans and uncharted
continents? This important question is answered, in subtle
and penetrating fashion, by J. H. Parry of Harvard, a leading authority on what he calls the Age of Reconnaissance.

Between the middle of the fifteenth century and the late seventeenth, Europeans learned to think of the world as a whole and of all seas as one. Their lessons were those of experience and eye-witness report. During those two and a half centuries European explorers actually visited most of the habitable regions of the globe; nearly all those, in fact, which were accessible by sea. They found vast territories formerly unknown to them, and drew the rough outlines of the world which we know. The period, especially the earlier half of it, is commonly called the Age of Discovery, and with reason. Geographical exploration, however, is only one of many kinds of discovery. The age saw not only the most rapid extension of geographical knowledge in the whole of European history; it saw also the first major victories of empirical inquiry over authority, the beginnings of that close association of pure science, technology, and everyday work which is an essential characteristic of the modern western world. During this period, especially the latter half of it, European scientists sketched the outline of the physical universe which, broadly speaking, is that accepted by the ordinary educated man today, and formulated the laws they deduced from the movement and interaction of its parts. All forms of discovery, all forms of original thought, are connected in some way, however distant: and it is natural to see a connection between these particular forms. The seaman, exploring uncharted seas, needed the help of learned men, especially men learned in mathematics, astronomy, and physical science; also, though this came later, in medical science. The student of science, seeing the achievements of geographical exploration (most empirical of all forms of inquiry, and most destructive of purely *a priori* reasoning) was naturally stimulated to further exploration in his chosen field. Both kinds of discovery further stimulated, and were stimulated by, the work of philosophers, poets and pamphleteers.

Connection there undoubtedly was; but its precise nature was both complex and elusive. The modern historian, accustomed to finding as the result of seeking, to discovery as the product of research, is tempted both to exaggerate and to anticipate. It is confidently expected today that every decade will produce new and important additions to the mounting sum of human knowledge. In the fifteenth and sixteenth centuries people—even educated people—had no such confident expectation. The intellectual temper of the sixteenth century, particularly, was conservative, respectful of authority. Even with evidence before their eyes that seamen were in fact finding lands formerly unknown and unsuspected, learned men were slow to draw analogies in other fields of inquiry. The idea that there was an America of learning and understanding beyond the horizon of the classics, ancient philosophy and the teachings of religion, was still in those years new and strange —the vision of comparatively few men. Students of science were concerned less with research than with attempts to provide neat and consistent explanations of known phenomena. It is significant that Copernicus—perhaps the most original figure in sixteenth-century science —reached his momentous conclusions by a mixture of reasoning and intuition, and made little or no attempt to check his hypotheses by actual observation. The first major European astronomical research to be based upon careful detailed observation over a long span of years was undertaken in the late sixteenth century and the early seventeenth by that perverse and unmanageable enthusiast, Tycho Brahe, and by Kepler, the mathematical genius into whose hands Tycho's mass of raw data providentially fell. Until towards the end of our period, certainly until the time of Tycho and Kepler, scientific inquiry in general tended to remain hypothetical and tentative, more given to broad speculation than to precise observation and experiment. Scientists had still, moreover, to be a little wary of charges of heresy; a danger which they commonly avoided by framing as hypotheses conclusions which in some instances they really regarded as proven fact. Galileo's difficulties with the ecclesiastical authorities arose chiefly from his neglect of this elementary precaution. In these circumstances, it was only by very slow degrees that science and technology, intuition and experience, experiment and everyday skill, could be brought together freely to illuminate one another.

It is commonly assumed today, at least among educated people, not only that knowledge can be indefinitely extended, but that all extensions are potentially useful—that all new knowledge will somehow or other, sooner or later, be turned to practical account. Conversely, it is fairly generally accepted that a technological approach need not inhibit pure inquiry; on the contrary, it can prove fruitful in giving rise to problems of a purely theoretical kind. It can help the inquirer, whether in the natural or the social sciences, in the fundamental task of selecting problems; and it imposes a discipline upon his speculative inclinations, by forcing him to submit his theories to definite standards of clarity and testability. These ideas and assumptions were also foreign to the intellectual temper of the period we are discussing. Science was then very far from being harnessed to technology, as it is sometimes said to be today; or as some say it should be. Possibly it gained in originality and intuitive strength by this very fact; but its immediate usefulness was limited, and less was expected of it by practical men. Scientific discoveries of obvious practical value were incidental, often fortuitous. The system of mutual check and stimulation between pure science and technology—the regular submission of theories to standards of clarity and testability—operated only in very limited fields. Geographical exploration, with its associated skills of navigation and cartography, was not merely the principal field of human endeavour in which scientific discovery and everyday technique became closely associated before the middle of the seventeenth century; except for the arts of war and of military engineering and (to a very limited extent) medical practice, it was almost the only field; hence its immense significance in the history of science and of thought. Even in this field, association was slow and hard to establish. The sailors and explorers received only meagre crumbs from the table of the philosophers and scientists. The elementary processes of arithmetic were naturally among the first to be seized and accepted. Arithmetic, which freed men from dependence upon the abacus, was made practicable by Hindu numerals, first introduced into Europe by Leonardo of Pisa's book of arithmetic at the beginning of the thirteenth century. Leonardo was exceptional, a well-travelled man, of merchant stock, who kept the needs of practical men in mind. His book took the reader as far as the Rule of Three. He wrote helpfully also on geometry and its application to measurement. Later came the trigonometry of the plane right-angled triangle, a simple and essential tool of dead-reckoning navigation, but slow to find application in regular use. The influence of astronomy came much later still. At first and for long, only the simplest celestial phenomena—the apparent immobility of the pole star and the movement of the sun relative to the earth—were seen to have any practical significance for the ocean traveller; and not until the fifteenth century was a technique evolved for making use even of these. Long after that, great discoveries continued to be confined to the learned world. The influence of Copernicus upon the development of astronomy was tremendous. His influence on the development of navigation was negligible. Galileo made great indirect contributions to navigation, but not—at least in our period—by his astronomical reasoning and observation. It was his work in the field of optics which, by facilitating the making of instruments, eventually made the task of the navigator easier and more precise. That the invention of the telescope, by making possible an estimation of the relative distances of heavenly bodies, also revolutionized the study of astronomy, was, from the point of view of contemporary seamen, irrelevant. Similarly, navigators were scarcely, and only indirectly, affected by Kepler's resounding declaration, in the introduction to the *New Astronomy*, that the earth 'is round, circumhabited by antipodes, of a most insignificant smallness, and a swift wanderer among the stars.'

If the discoveries and the hypotheses of the scientists were only occasionally and fortuitously helpful to seamen, most seamen—even sometimes sea-going explorers and compilers of navigation manuals—tended for their part to be sceptical and unreceptive of scientific ideas. Seamen were then, much more than now, a race apart, practical, conservative, employing traditional skills, relying on accumulated experience. To say this is not to belittle the skill or the experience. Hydrography and pilotage developed steadily in the later Middle Ages. Practical use had given the sailor, well before the fifteenth century, charts and sailing directions of good working accuracy for the known trade routes of the Mediterranean, the Black Sea, and the coasts of western Europe, and instruments—straight-edge and dividers, compass and lead-line—accurate enough to lay off and follow courses on those charts. The charts, the rutters and the instruments, however, were adequate only for the limited area and the relatively short passages of the regular trade routes. Information about the world outside that area, guidance on how to navigate on long ocean passages, could come only from books; and sailors, traditionally suspicious of book-learning, absorbed it very slowly. Even arithmetic, the elementary arithmetic of Leonardo of Pisa, to take a simple instance, made very slow headway. For short, familiar passages it was unnecessary. Well into the sixteenth century, accounts of ships' stores, records of mileages run, were still often kept in Roman figures. Most sailors, moreover, had naturally little wish to leave the familiar trade routes where their living lay, unless they could see a clear advantage in doing so. Even the great discoverers of the fifteenth and sixteenth centuries were not primarily interested in discovery for its own sake. Their main interest, the main task entrusted to them by the rulers and investors who sent them out, was to link Europe, or particular European countries, with other areas known or believed to be of economic importance. The discovery of distant, unknown islands and continents, like much scientific discovery, was incidental, often fortuitous. Sometimes it was positively unwelcome. In the fifteenth and sixteenth centuries an immense body of geographical knowledge was accumulated by this somewhat haphazard process; but this knowledge, despite (or because of) its vast extent, was still rough and sketchy. For the most part it revealed only coast-lines, roughly explored, and harbours. It lacked precision and unity; it left many gaps and perpetuated some long-lived myths. In the story of discovery in the broadest sense, then, our period was a time of tentative, though splendid, beginnings. 'The Age of Reconnaissance' seems the most appropriate name by which to describe it.

*   *   *   *   *

But how did Reconnaissance begin? Information about the world outside Europe, available to Europeans in the first half of the fifteenth century, was all . . . misleading to a greater or less degree. It was either purely theoretical and academic, ignoring practical experience; or out-of-date; or merely fanciful, compounded of myth and guess-work. Technical knowledge of means of communication with African or Asian coasts outside the Mediterranean by sea—the only practicable way, in view of Turkish power, save on the Turks' own terms—was even more inadequate. The political situation, on the face of it, could hardly have been less propitious. The most recently acquired information, from newly discovered ancient sources, was interesting and valuable, but on the whole very discouraging—Ptolemy's land-locked Indian Ocean, for example. What other factors operated, to make this unpropitious half-century the beginning of a movement of world-wide exploration?

The initial steps in expansion were modest indeed: the rash seizure by a Portuguese force of a fortress [Ceuta] in Morocco; the tentative extension of fishing and, a little later, trading, along the Atlantic coast of North Africa; the prosaic settlement by vine and sugar cultivators, by log-cutters and sheep-farmers, of certain islands in the eastern Atlantic. There was little, in these early- and mid-fifteenth-century ventures, to suggest world-wide expansion. In the later fifteenth century, however, new advances in the arts of navigation and cartography, made by a new combination of academic knowledge and nautical experience, enabled the explorers for the first time to observe and record the position—or at least the latitude—of a point on an unknown coast; and even, in favourable circumstances, of a ship at sea. New methods in the design of ships, consequent upon a marriage of European with oriental traditions, made it possible for sailors not only to make long voyages of discovery, but to repeat them, and so to establish regular communication with newly discovered lands. New developments in gunnery and the making of guns, particularly in ship-borne artillery, gave European explorers a great advantage over the inhabitants of even the most civilized countries to which they sailed; enabled them to de-

fend themselves, upon arrival, sometimes against overwhelming numbers; and encouraged them to establish trading posts even in places
where they were clearly unwelcome. This vital technical superiority in
ships and guns ensured the continuous development of the Reconnaissance and the permanence of its results. By the end of our period
European explorers had not only sketched the rough outlines of most
of the continents of the world; they had established, in every continent
except Australasia and Antarctica, European outposts—trading factories, settlements, or lordships, according to the nature of the area—
small, scattered, diverse, but permanent. In so doing, they not only derived help from physical scientists and stimulated the further development of physical science—though tentatively and indirectly at first . . . ;
they also called attention to new and far-reaching problems in the social
sciences, in economics, in anthropology, and in the arts of government.
In these fields also there was a tentative but widespread Reconnaissance, a wide but uneven series of additions to knowledge, with momentous consequences for Europe and the world as a whole. In all
branches of science, as the Reconnaissance proceeded and became less
tentative, as the European picture of the world became fuller and more
detailed, so the idea of continually expanding knowledge became more
familiar and the links between science and practical life became closer.
A technological attitude to knowledge, an extreme readiness to apply
science in immediately practical ways, eventually became one of the
principal characteristics which distinguish western civilization, the civilization originally of Europe, from other great civilized societies. The
unprecedented power which it produced eventually led Europe from
Reconnaissance to world-wide conquest, and so created the world of
yesterday, much of which was governed by Europeans, and the world
of today, almost all of which has accepted European technology and
European techniques of government, even if only to escape from actual
European rule.

* * * * *

ATTITUDES AND MOTIVES

Among the many and complex motives which impelled Europeans,
and especially the peoples of the Iberian peninsula, to venture overseas
in the fifteenth and sixteenth centuries, two were obvious, universal,
and admitted: acquisitiveness and religious zeal. Many of the great
explorers and conquerors proclaimed these two purposes in unequivocal
terms. Vasco da Gama, on arrival at Calicut, explained to his reluctant
Indian hosts that he had come in search of Christians and spices. Bernal

Díaz, frankest of *conquistadores*, wrote that he and his like went to the Indies 'to serve God and His Majesty, to give light to those who were in darkness, and to grow rich, as all men desire to do.'

Land, and the labour of those who worked it, were the principal sources of wealth. The quickest, most obvious, and socially most attractive way of becoming rich was to seize, and to hold as a fief, land already occupied by a diligent and docile peasantry. Spanish knights and noblemen in particular had long been accustomed to this process, for which successful war against the Muslim states in Spain had offered occasion and excuse. In most parts of Europe, during the constant disorders of the fourteenth and early fifteenth centuries, such acquisitions of land had also often been made by means of private war. In the later fifteenth century, however, rulers were again becoming strong enough to discourage private war; and even in Spain, the territory still open to acquisition by lawful force of arms was narrowly limited, and protected by its feudal relations with the Crown of Castile. Further opportunities were unlikely to arise unless the rulers of Granada denounced their vassalage, and so gave the Castilians occasion for a formal campaign of conquest. Even if that campaign were successful, kings and great noblemen would get the lion's share of the booty. For lesser men, the best chances of acquiring land by fighting for it lay outside Europe.

A second possibility was the seizure and exploitation of new land—land either unoccupied, or occupied by useless or intractable peoples who could be killed or driven away. New land could be colonized by adventurous farmers or by small owners of flocks and herds. Such men often wished to be their own masters, to avoid the increasingly irksome obligations imposed by feudal tenure and by the corporate privileges of transhumant graziers, particularly in Castile. This was a less attractive, but still promising alternative, which also could most readily be pursued outside Europe. Madeira and parts of the Canaries were occupied in this way in the fifteenth century, respectively by Portuguese and Spanish settlers, comparatively humble people, who borrowed capital from princely or noble promoters in return for relatively light obligations. The settlements were economically successful. They brought in revenue to the princes and noblemen—notably Prince Henry of Portugal—who financed them; and set a fashion for islands which lasted more than two hundred years. Rumours of further islands and mainlands to be discovered in the Atlantic all helped to encourage interest in this type of oversea adventure.

A less sure, and in most places socially less attractive way to wealth, was by investment in trade, especially long-distance trade. The most sought-after trades were in commodities of high value and small bulk, most of them either of eastern origin—spices, silk, ivory, precious stones and the like—or Mediterranean in origin but in demand in the East, such as coral and some high-quality textiles. These rich trades almost all passed through the Mediterranean and were conducted chiefly by the merchants of the Italian maritime cities, in particular Venetians and Genoese. Some Atlantic maritime peoples were already looking enviously at the rich trades. Portugal in particular possessed a long ocean seaboard, good harbours, a considerable fishing and sea-faring population and a commercial class largely emancipated from feudal interference. Portuguese shippers were able and eager to gradu-ate from an Atlantic coastal trade in wine, fish and salt, to more wide-spread and lucrative ventures in gold, spices and sugar. They had little hope of breaking into the Mediterranean trades, which were guarded by the Italian monopolists with formidable naval force; with unrivalled knowledge of the East derived from many generations of merchants and travellers; and with an assiduous diplomacy which reached across the ancient dividing line between Christendom and Islam. Merchant capi-talists in Portugal and western Spain therefore had strong motives for seeking by sea alternative sources of gold, ivory and pepper; and ac-cording to information current in Morocco, such sources existed. It is highly likely that in undertaking West African voyages, the Portuguese were encouraged by information about the gold mines of the Guinea kingdoms, obtained through their conquest at Ceuta and not available to the rest of Europe. At least, the voyages quickly demonstrated that sailing in the Tropics was easier and less dangerous than pessimists had supposed. If, as was hinted in some of the travel literature of the time, it were even possible to penetrate by sea to the oriental sources of silk and spice, that would provide a still stronger incentive for sea-borne exploration.

Failing the rich trades, there was one commodity which the Portu-guese thoroughly understood and which always commanded a sale everywhere in Europe: fish. Long before Columbus reached America, or the sea route to India became a possibility, the demands of the salt-fish trade were encouraging Portuguese deep-sea fishermen to venture further and further into the Atlantic. Fishing took them to Icelandic waters, well on the way to America; and fishing was one of the principal reasons for their interest in the north-west coast of Africa.

Precious commodities—indeed, most marketable commodities— might be secured not only by trade, but by more direct methods; by plunder, if they should be found in the possession of people whose religion, or lack of religion, could be made an excuse for attacking them;

or by direct exploitation, if sources of supply were discovered in lands either uninhabited, or inhabited only by ignorant savages. Here again, rumour and imaginative travel literature suggest the possibility of hitherto unknown mines, gold-bearing streams, or pearl fisheries. Casual unforeseen treasures also occasionally came the way of adventurous sailors: the unexpected lump of ambergris upon a deserted beach, or the narwhal's potent horn.

All these economic considerations, these imaginative dreams of quick adventurous gain, were heavily reinforced by the promptings of religious zeal. The discoverers and *conquistadores* were devout men for the most part, whose devotion took forms at once orthodox and practical. Of the many possible forms of religious zeal, two in particular appealed to them, and to the rulers and investors who sent them out. One was the desire to convert—to appeal to the minds and hearts of individual unbelievers by preaching, reasoning, or force of example, by any means of persuasion short of force or threat, and so to bring unbelievers into the community of belief. The other was the more simple-minded desire to ensure by military and political means the safety and independence of one's own religious community and, better still, its predominance over others; to defend the believer against interference and attack; to kill, humiliate, or subdue the unbeliever. Of course, these two possible lines of action might be confused or combined. It might appear politic, for example, to subdue unbelievers in order to convert them. In general, however, two expressions of religious devotion in action were kept distinct in men's minds. The first called for intense effort, with little likelihood of immediate material gain. The second, the politico-military expression, provided an excuse for conquest and plunder on a grand scale. It was an aspect of religious zeal with which Europe had long been familiar, since for several centuries it had supplied one of the principal motives for the crusades.

The fifteenth-century voyages of discovery have often been described as a continuation of the crusades. Certainly the menacing proximity of Islam was always in the minds of fifteenth-century kings, especially in eastern and southern Europe. Nevertheless, those kings were realists enough, for the most part, to see that a crusade of the traditional pattern—a direct campaign against Muslim rulers in the eastern Mediterranean lands, with the object of capturing the Holy Places and establishing Christian principalities on the shores of the Levant—was no longer even a remote possibility. Crusades of this type in earlier centuries had been, in the long run, costly failures. The wide mixture of motives among the crusaders—religious zeal, personal love of adventure, hope of gain, desire for reputation—and jealousy and suspicion among the rulers concerned, had always been powerful factors preventing effective unity. The European nations had never embarked on crusades as organized States. Even those armies led by kings or by the Emperor in person had been bound together only by feudal and personal ties. No medieval European kingdom had possessed an organization capable of administering distant possessions; only the knightly Orders had the organization, and their resources were inadequate. Conquests, such as the Latin States established after the first crusade, were made possible only by disunity among the local Arab principalities, and could not survive the counter-attack of a capable and unifying Muslim ruler. In the long run, the political effect of the crusades was to reduce the Byzantine Empire, the leading Christian State of eastern Europe, to a fragment of Greek territory, and to enable the Venetians to extort commercial privileges in Constantinople. From the thirteenth century onwards the great feudal monarchies of northern Europe lost interest in crusading, and left the war against Islam to those who had Muslim neighbours: to the Byzantine emperors and the neighbouring Balkan kings, and to the Christian kings of the Iberian peninsula.

These war-hardened rulers, left to themselves, achieved considerable successes. The Greek Empire, employing a supple diplomacy as well as military tenacity, showed a remarkable capacity for survival. It was still a formidable naval power. It recovered much territory in the fourteenth century. Weakened though it was, it could normally hold its own, in stable conditions, against a variety of settled and relatively orderly Muslim states, who had no more unity among themselves than had the Christian kingdoms. The chief danger to the empire came from newly-Islamized barbarian hordes who from time to time migrated from their homes in central Asia, broke into the lands of the 'fertile crescent', overthrew the established Muslim States, created new and unified military sultanates and embarked on holy war against the Christian unbeliever. If successfully resisted, a horde might settle down and become, in its turn, an organized and stationary kingdom; but the Greek power of resistance, under successive blows, was becoming less and less reliable. The most dangerous of these invasions, from a European point of view, was that of the Ottoman Turks in the fourteenth century.

At the other end of the Mediterranean these great waves of assault were felt at first only as attenuated ripples. The aggression of the Iberian kingdoms against Islam was a long-term, ding-dong local affair which in the later Middle Ages had steadily gained ground. At the beginning of the fifteenth century the only Muslim State surviving in

Europe was the ancient and highly civilized kingdom of Granada; and, rich and powerful though this kingdom had been, it now paid tribute to Castile, and the rulers of Castile could look forward, with good hope of success, to its eventual incorporation in their own dominions. The rulers of Portugal no longer had a land frontier with Muslim neighbours and were beginning to contemplate a sea-borne assault on the rich Arab-Berber principalities of North Africa.

The end of the fourteenth and beginning of the fifteenth centuries brought a brief respite to the beleaguered Greeks. Two great Muslim States confronted one another in the Levant. One was the Mamluk kingdom of Egypt and Syria, firmly established a century and a quarter before by that great Sultan Baybars who had chased the remaining Franks out of Syria and had also defeated the grandson of Chingis Khan. The other was the more recently founded Ottoman kingdom in Asia Minor, which was restless, aggressive, and a constant danger to its neighbours, both Christian and Muslim. The Turks had crossed the Dardanelles in 1353 and in 1357 occupied Adrianople, so almost surrounding the Byzantine Empire. To some extent, Byzantine survival depended on Mamluk power in the Ottomans' rear. At the very end of the fourteenth century, both these Muslim States were over-run by the cavalry of the last great nomad Mongol Khan, Timur the Lame. In 1400 Timur sacked both Aleppo and Damascus; in 1402, he defeated the Ottoman army at Ankara, sacked Smyrna, and took the Sultan Bayezid I prisoner. The Christian rulers naturally regarded this most savage of conquerors as a deliverer. The Byzantine Emperor offered him tribute. Even the Castilians sent him an embassy, which, however, arrived in Samarcand to find him already dead. The Christian respite was thus very brief. Timur died in 1405. His heirs fell to quarrelling and his exploits were never repeated. In the long run, and indirectly, the Mongol incursion worked to the disadvantage of Byzantium and so of Christian Europe. The Ottomans had been less severely mauled, and recovered more quickly from their defeat, than their Mamluk rivals. Their military organization and equipment was by far the best among the Muslim states. Their civil administration bore comparatively lightly upon conquered subjects, and made them not entirely unwelcome conquerors to an over-taxed peasantry. The immediate question was where their formidable strength would first be exerted: against the Mamluks, against the heretic Safawid kingdom in Persia, or against the Byzantine Empire. All three were overthrown eventually; but the Byzantine Empire, the weakest of the three, received the first blows. Constantinople was besieged in 1422. Rebellions in Asia Minor and counter-attacks from Hungary against the Turks prolonged Greek resistance; but the great city finally fell to Muhammad II in 1453.

The fall of Constantinople had been so long expected, and so long delayed, that much of its psychological effect in Europe was dissipated. In Italy, it is true, the news of the fall provided a powerful motive for a general, if uneasy, pacification among the major states—the Most Holy League; but there was no effective call to arms, and despite much talk, no general crusade. If Europe was a beleaguered fortress, its garrison was not so small nor so closely invested that its members felt any special need for unity among themselves. Nevertheless, the event clearly marked the emergence of the Ottoman Empire as the most powerful State of the Near East, a State beside which most European kingdoms were petty principalities; a State, moreover, bent on military expansion. The kingdoms of the Balkans and the Danube basin immediately received the impact of Turkish aggression. They were thrown upon a desperate defensive, retreating step by step, until the middle of the sixteenth century, when Sulaiman the Magnificent unsuccessfully besieged Vienna. Even more serious from a European point of view, the Turks became almost overnight the most formidable of the Mediterranean powers. They had hitherto been horsemen rather than sailors. In Muhammad I's day they had been decisively defeated at sea by the Venetians. The capture of Constantinople, however, made them the heirs to the naval power of Byzantium. The Venetians, fearing for their trading privileges, hastened to make their peace, and succeeded in retaining most of their business contacts and some of their colonies, notably Crete. They could not, however, prevent the loss of the Morea and other territorial possessions, or deter the Turks from further Mediterranean aggression. In 1480, Muhammad II actually invaded Italy, took Otranto and established there a flourishing market in Christian slaves. Possibly a sustained campaign of conquest was prevented only by the Sultan's death in the following year. Naval power made the eventual defeat of the Mamluks and the extension of Turkish rule round the shores of the Levant certain. It also rendered any direct seaborne attack by a western force against the centres of Muslim power in the Levant quite out of the question. By the middle of the fifteenth century the mantle of the crusaders had fallen upon the Iberian kingdoms. Alone among European States, they were still in a position to inflict damage upon Islam. Their activities were necessarily, in the circumstances, local and limited; but the effects even of local successes might be widely felt throughout Islam, if vigorously exploited. It is against the background of disastrous European defeats in the Levant that Castilian campaigns against Granada and Portuguese expeditions to north-west Africa must be considered.

Both in Castile and in Portugal the idea of a crusade still had power to fire the imagination of men of gentle birth and adventurous impulses; though Iberian crusading fervour in the later Middle Ages was more sophisticated and more complex than the headstrong ransom-gambling adventurousness of the earlier crusades. Nor had it much in common with the Christian apostolate which had converted northern Europe in still older times. Nobody supposed that any serious impression could be made upon Islam by preaching or by rational disputation. Muslims were not only powerful and well-organized; they were also—though diabolically misguided—clever, self-confident and civilized. A missionary friar would have had no more chance of making converts in Granada or Damascus than would a mullah in Rome or Burgos. He would have been considered at best an interesting curiosity, at worst a spy or a dangerous lunatic. A duty to attempt conversion was recognized, of course. Individual captives, especially if captured in youth, were brought up in the faith of their captors. Naturally, also, considerable numbers of Muslims under Christian rule—or Christians under Muslim rule—adopted the religion of their rulers, either from conviction or as a matter of political or commercial prudence. Christian conquerors might sometimes attempt the forcible mass conversion of entire Muslim populations; but conversions achieved in this way were generally understood to be insincere and often temporary. No Christian ruler possessed, or attempted to create, any body of men comparable with the Turkish Janissaries. Genuine conversion on a wide scale was generally assumed to be an impracticable ideal. It might, moreover, be financially unprofitable, since both Christian and Muslim rulers often levied special taxes from subjects of different religion from their own; a practice which encouraged wars of conquest but discouraged attempts to convert the conquered. Nor—despite loud talk about smiting the infidel—was a crude policy of extermination ever seriously considered as either practicable or desirable.

Contact with the Arab world in the Middle Ages had formed part of the education of a rough and primitive Europe. European art and industry owe much to the Arabs. Greek science and learning found their way to medieval Europe—in so far as they were known at all—largely through Arabic translations. Even the elaborate conventions of late medieval chivalry were to some extent imitated from Arab customs and Arab romances. The Iberian peninsula was the principal channel of contact between the two cultures; and the more intelligent among the Christian rulers there understood the value and the importance of their intermediary function. Archbishop Raymond of Toledo in the twelfth century had founded schools where Arab, Jewish and Christian scholars collaborated in a series of works which, when communicated to the learned centres in Europe, opened a new era in medieval science. Alfonso X of Castile also gathered into his court the learned of three religions, for he was as eager to sift the wisdom of the East as of the West. He was the first European king to show a systematic interest in secularizing culture. His oriental works were translated into French, and influenced Dante. His astronomical tables were studied in Europe for centuries, and were read and annotated by Copernicus himself. Though exceptional, he was by no means unique in tolerance and wisdom. The greatest of all the monarchs of the Reconquest, Fernando III, King and Saint, is proclaimed by his epitaph to have been a king who tolerated infidel cults in mosque and synagogue.

Within the Iberian peninsula, then, Christian and Muslim kingdoms had existed side by side for centuries and had perforce, when not actually fighting one another, maintained some kind of relations, however perfunctory. Occasionally, Christian rulers had allied with Muslims against Christians, and vice versa. Similarly, within particular kingdoms, Christian and Muslim populations had lived side by side, and while often feeling for one another little respect and no affection, had grown accustomed to one another's ways. Where conversions occurred, there were mixed marriages and mixed blood. Inevitably, Spanish culture, except in the very north, was profoundly affected. Arab influence made itself evident in the immense and varied vocabulary of the Spanish language, in social habits such as the seclusion of women, in architecture and the lay-out of towns, in commercial practices, and in a great range of practical devices: irrigation and water-lifting appliances; the design and rig of boats and ships; saddlery and harness. Moorish influence was less obvious in Portugal than in Spain. By the fifteenth century crusading in Portuguese territory was little more than a distant memory; hence the somewhat bookish and romantic crusading notions of, for example, Prince Henry 'the Navigator', contrasted with the much more practical attitude of his Spanish contemporaries. In their varying degrees, however, both Spain and Portugal were homes of mixed societies, and probably that very fact equipped Spaniards and Portuguese, better than other Europeans, to understand and to deal with the still more exotic cultures they were to encounter when they embarked upon a career of oversea adventure.

By the fifteenth century, European civilization had developed to a point where it no longer depended upon the Arab world for inspiration and instruction, and in Spain Africanizing fashions tended to become a somewhat sterile affectation. At the hedonistic and disorderly court of Henry IV of Castile [1454–1474], this affectation was pushed to extremes in which the Christian religion was derided, Moorish customs openly adopted, and the war against Islam forgotten or deliberately postponed. The Succession War and the accession of Isabella brought a sharp reversal. Isabella, inspired not only by intense religious conviction, but also by apprehension of the danger threatening from the East, was determined to press ahead immediately with preparations against Granada (whose rulers, emboldened by the Succession War, had withheld tribute in 1476) and if possible eventually to carry the war into the enemy's territory in Africa, as the Portuguese had already done at Ceuta in 1415. Systematic operations for the conquest of the Moorish kingdom, village by village, began in 1482. Spaniards embarked on this last European crusade with a complex mixture of attitudes towards the Muslim enemy. The mixture included intense religious exaltation; abhorrence of unbelief, modified (on the part of feudal superiors) by concessions to economic expediency; acquisitiveness, in the sense not only of hope of plunder, but of determination to exploit the Moors as vassals; social dislike, modified by long familiarity; economic envy (for the Moors were usually better farmers and craftsmen, and often sharper traders, than their Spanish rivals); and finally acute political fear— fear not of Granada, but of the powerful support which might reach Granada if that kingdom were not brought under Christian control. As for Granada, isolated and divided within itself, the issue was never in serious doubt. The capital city fell in 1492. All Spain, for the first time in many centuries, was ruled by Christian sovereigns. The territory of Granada was duly divided in fiefs among the leaders in the campaign.

The conquest did not relieve Spain of the fear of Islam; nor did the Spanish invasion of North Africa, which began with the capture of Melilla in 1492, prevent the advance of the Turks. Early in the sixteenth century they conquered Syria and Egypt and extended their suzerainty along the whole north African coast. The immense power of the Ottoman Empire could then be summoned to defend the Muslim rulers of the coast, and possibly even to support rebellion among disaffected Moors in Spain. It was a power too strong to be challenged, as yet, by the forces of the Spanish kingdoms. Meanwhile, the enthusiasms and ambitions generated by the war against Granada persisted, only partially satisfied by victory. An outlet for this pent-up martial energy was suggested, only a year after the fall of Granada, by Columbus' report of islands in the western Atlantic, and by his insistence that those islands might be used as stepping-stones to China. Within a generation, the feelings which had rallied Spaniards against Granada developed into a bold and methodical imperialism which, casting about for new provinces to conquer, found its opportunity overseas. While Portuguese imperialism in West Africa sought, among other objects, a back door through which to attack the Arab and the Turk, Spanish imperialism, by chance discovery, was led to operate in a new world.

Granada was to the Spaniards what Constantinople, in its last enfeebled years, had been to the Turks: the culmination of one series of conquests, and the beginning of another. There was a curious parallel between the role of the Turks in the Byzantine Empire and that of the Castilians in Muslim Spain. The Turks had been nomads; they had entered the Near East as highly mobile mounted bands operating against a long-established agricultural or city-dwelling society. They settled down as overlords, living by the labour of a conquered peasantry, and recruiting their subordinate officials and their technical experts from the literate among their new subjects; but never themselves entirely losing their character as horsemen. The Castilians had never been parasitic upon the horse in the same degree as the Turks, but they too, in Andalusia and elsewhere, employed mobile and largely mounted forces against sedentary communities. Among them, in the arid uplands of Castile, pastoral pursuits, the grazing of semi-nomadic flocks and herds, had long been preferred to arable farming. The preference was social and military as well as economic; it was the legacy of centuries of intermittent fighting, of constantly shifting frontiers. The man on horseback, the master of flocks and herds, was best adapted to such conditions; the peasant, conversely, was economically vulnerable and socially despised. As the work of conquest proceeded, the Castilians, or the upper classes, the fighting classes, among them, retained their pastoral interests and possessions, their mobility and military effectiveness, and their respect for the man on horseback. Like the Turks, as far as possible they lived by the labour and employed the skill of vassal peoples as well as of their own peasants and craftsmen. These social habits produced a class of fighting men well fitted for the conquest, and the subsequent organization, of the settled peoples of the New World, who were prosperous arable farmers or docile town-dwellers, and who had never before even seen horses and horned cattle. Small bands of mounted Spaniards could achieve remarkable victories, and could then settle as quasi-feudal overlords, retaining their own pastoral interests and avocations, relying on conquered peasants to grow grain for them, as both they and the Turks had done in the Old World; their mobility as horsemen enabling them to suppress revolts with a minimum of effort. In this respect also, reconquest in Spain was an appropriate training for imperial expansion in America.

Isabella, however, advised by the uncompromising ecclesiastics who surrounded her, was little disposed to allow the Moors of Granada to settle down peacefully as Muslim vassals of Christian overlords. Religious zeal, for her, must find expression not only in conquest and suzerainty, but in conversion. After the capture of Granada she inaugurated a new policy of vigorous proselytizing. This policy, initially confined to preaching and persuasion, met with very limited success, despite the devotion of the Observant Franciscans to whom it was entrusted. The impatience of the Queen and her minister Cisneros soon insisted upon sterner measures: systematic persecution and a drastic stiffening of ecclesiastical discipline. The expulsion of the Jews, the violent baptism of the Moors of Granada, the extraordinary powers entrusted to the new Inquisition, were all radical departures from medieval tradition in Spain. All three were, on the whole, publicly approved, as they would not have been a hundred years before; and in Castile (though not in Aragon) they were vigorously enforced. They represented both a reaction against the intensified Muslim pressure on Christendom since the fall of Constantinople, and an intensification of religious fervour, and so of religious intolerance, in Spain. This intensification of zeal, this new enthusiasm for conversion, quickly travelled to the New World, where it was to find new and more effective forms of expression.

Humanist learning, apostolic fervour, and discipline, were the principal features of the reform of the Church in Spain undertaken by Cardinal Ximénez de Cisneros in the late fifteenth and early sixteenth centuries. The regular Orders included in their ranks many men who were exalted by a spiritual unrest closely akin to that which was to break out in Reformation in northern Europe. Cisneros' reforms appealed to this unrest, and rendered it effective. He sought above all to purify the clergy by strengthening the austerity and the preaching mission of the mendicant Orders. Among the Orders he favoured his own Franciscans, and among Franciscans the strict Observants, who in Spain and Portugal elected to preach their simple and austere Christianity among poor and neglected rural folk, and among infidels, as their papal privileges expressly commanded them to do. Internal reform movements similar to the Franciscan Observance occurred about the turn of the century in other Orders also, particularly among Dominicans and Jeronymites. A remarkable increase in the reformed mendicant population occurred in Cisneros' lifetime. From it emerged a spiritual *élite* of evangelical tendency, which was to sympathize with Erasmus and to come under suspicion of Lutheranism later in the century. From it emerged, also, a spiritual militia, recruited from disciplined, highly-trained religious radicals, available for employment in the New World. The Amerindian peoples encountered by Spaniards in Cisneros' own day were weak, primitive, and few in number; but from the second decade of the sixteenth century Spaniards came into contact with the settled city-building peoples of Mexico and Central America, and in dealing with them, missionary policy became an issue of burning importance. They were numerous and well-organized. They possessed a material culture which, despite crucial technical weaknesses, impressed and attracted the Spanish invaders. They had no knowledge of Christianity, a deficiency for which they clearly could not be blamed or punished; and on the credit side they were uncontaminated by Islam. Their own religion included rites of horrifying savagery; but individually they appeared to be gentle and docile people for the most part; and their agrarian collectivism seemed to provide an ideal basis on which to build Christian communities. Neither Crown nor Church in Spain could ignore the opportunity and the duty of bringing such people into the Christian fold, or could contemplate leaving matters to the consciences of the *conquistadores*. The Crown early decided to entrust the American mission to the mendicant Orders. For a time, at least, it gave masterful support to the mendicant vows of renunciation, the Christian doctrine of a compassionate deity, and the institutional authority of the sacraments. Such a missionary policy, with its logical consequences in terms of control over the native population, inevitably conflicted with the economic interests of the leading colonists, and led to long and acrimonious disputes; but the friars commanded the respect and sympathy of many of the *conquistadores*, including Cortés, who himself petitioned for a Franciscan mission to Mexico. The feeling of 'bringing light to those who were in darkness' was general even among the humbler soldiers, and helps to explain their conviction that, however unsanctified their own lives might be, the Saints fought on their side. This is not to suggest an unsophisticated credulity. The stories of the actual appearance of St James in battle were invented by chroniclers, not by *conquistadores*; Bernal Díaz treats these 'miracles' with ironic contempt. Nevertheless, the *conquistadores* prayed to St Peter and St James before their battles, and the feeling of divine support was strong among them. In somewhat

lesser degree, and in very different circumstances, the same was true
of the Portuguese in India. Missionary zeal, the desire to bring genuine
conversion to millions of pagan souls, must be placed high among the
motives of the Reconnaissance.

Acquisitiveness and religious zeal, however, even taken together,
are not the whole story. The unprecedented harshness with which
Isabella treated the Moors of Granada was more than an expression of
religious intolerance and political hostility. It represented a deliberate rejection on the Queen's part of the African element in Spanish
culture. It was accompanied by an equally deliberate affirmation of
Spain's community with the rest of Christian Europe. The Queen's
iron will and keen intelligence worked to end the intellectual isolation
of Spain, not by a timid and defensive obscurantism, but by a vigorous and self-confident encouragement of European learning. Her reign
was a golden age for universities. The famous foundations of Alcalá,
Salamanca and Valladolid date from this time. (The founding impulse was soon carried to the New World, for both Mexico and Peru
were to have universities within a generation or so of their conquest.)
Many printing presses were set up in Spain in Isabella's reign. Foreign
scholars and foreign books, Italian, French, German and Flemish,
were welcomed and encouraged. Ideas and literary conventions characteristic of the Italian Renaissance spread throughout Spain, albeit
in forms modified by Spanish sobriety and conservatism, and without
the superficial paganism of much Italian writing. Classical scholars
such as Alfonso de Palencia and Antonio de Lebrija (who had been
educated in Italy) worked in the direct tradition of Lorenzo Valla.
The great Polyglot Bible is one of the chief glories of Renaissance
scholarship. In more popular literary forms also, Italian influence
pervaded Spain. The *Orlando Furioso* of Ariosto was quickly translated
and widely read in Spanish. Epics and romances of all kinds enjoyed
a great vogue in Spain in the early sixteenth century. Bernal Díaz,
writing of his first breathtaking sight of the city of Mexico, remarked
quite naturally that it put him in mind of the Amadis romances.

With Renaissance literary conventions, Spaniards absorbed Renaissance attitudes of mind: the cult of the individual, the passion for personal reputation. This passion was vital in the mental make-up of the
conquistadores, and goes far to explain their prickly pride, their dislike of discipline and regimentation, their insistence on being con-
sulted about every decision. On the other hand, it also helps to explain
their extravagant daring and their indifference to wounds and fatigue.
They conducted themselves, and their chroniclers wrote, with the high

seriousness of men conscious of taking part in great deeds; men who
saw themselves not as imitators, but as rivals, of the heroes of antiquity and of romance. Cortés—most eloquent of *conquistadores*, one
most sensitive to the mood of his men, and himself a product of Renaissance Salamanca—returned again and again in his speeches and
letters to this theme. He alluded sometimes to the riches that lay ahead,
and sometimes to the glory of winning pagan souls; but most frequently
to the prospect of human fame. In endeavouring, for example, to persuade his men on the beach at Vera Cruz to burn the boats in which
they had come from Cuba, he gave them 'many comparisons with
brave deeds done by heroes among the Romans'. When his more
cautious companions complained that Alexander had attempted nothing
so foolhardy as the taking of Mexico with four hundred men, he told
them that history would relate greater things of them than of the ancient captains. There were darker comparisons, of course. Cortés could
not have missed the analogy between Cuauhtémoc and Vercingetorix;
vae victis [woe to the vanquished]. But Cortés, like Caesar, cultivated
in general a reputation for gallant and politic clemency, and he ran
considerable risks to stop his Indian allies butchering the defeated
Aztecs. Bernal Díaz—every historian of the *conquista* must return to
that scrupulous old soldier—boasted no nobility save that of having
fought in a hundred and nineteen battles—more than twice those of
Julius Caesar; and like the great Roman he wished—as he explains—
to record his own deeds, along with those of Cortés, "in the manner
of the writings and reports of . . . illustrious men who served in wars
in time past; in order that my children, grandchildren and descendants
can say "my father came to discover and conquer these lands . . . and
was one of the foremost in the conquest".' This passionate care for
reputation was not, of course, confined to Spaniards. It was common
to most of the pioneers of the Reconnaissance, of whatever nation.
Sir Humphrey Gilbert's serene (and avoidable) death [1583] on board
the *Squirrel* was a late instance of it. Such men sought not only riches
'such as all men desire', not only merit in the eyes of God, but also
fame among their own people and in posterity.

With a new attitude towards the individual, the Renaissance fostered
a new attitude towards the State, also Italian in origin. A sensitive
alertness, a studied, objective attention to the most effective and most
elegant means of achieving desired ends, tended to supplant the older
notion of the State as a network of fixed, traditional rights and duties,
over which the monarch presided as a judge of disputes. It was becoming recognized that a government might use force, whether against

subjects or against neighbouring princes, in pursuit of rational interests as well as in support of legal claims. Like many Italian rulers, Isabella of Castile owed her throne to a mixture of war and diplomacy. A masterful restoration of public order and discipline was one of her major achievements, and contributed greatly to the growth of authoritarian feeling in Castile. Machiavelli's principles of statecraft had no more successful exemplars than Ferdinand of Aragon and John II of Portugal. It is true that this more flexible attitude towards sovereignty and statecraft, this cult of governmental expediency, was restrained, particularly in Spain, by legalistic conservatism as well as by individual obstinacy. Nevertheless, it helped to prepare men's minds for the immense task of political and administrative improvisation which was to confront Spanish government in the New World.

The fifteenth century was remarkable for the spontaneous growth, among a few gifted and highly-placed men, of a genuine disinterested curiosity. Like the passion for classical learning (and, of course, associated with it) this spirit of curiosity was among the leading characteristics of the Renaissance. It can hardly, at first, be called scientific, for it was undisciplined and quite unsystematic. The men of the Renaissance were concerned to absorb knowledge rather than to digest it, to amass rather than to select. Their curiosity was far stronger in inquiry than in arrangement; but it was omnivorous, lively, uninhibited; and while it corroded and gradually weakened the accepted medieval systems of knowledge, it collected, with avid and apparently random enthusiasm, the materials of which new systems would eventually be constructed. It was shared not only by scholars, but by princes and by men of action in their *entourage*, especially in Italy, but also in Portugal and Spain. Geography and cosmography were prominent among the objects upon which it seized, but it had many others. The attention paid to medical research at the time, especially to anatomy, is well known. Less obvious, but also important in the growth of the idea of discovery, is a new and more observant attitude towards natural history. How far explorers and promoters of exploration were directly and consciously moved by scientific curiosity, is impossible to say on the scanty evidence which remains; but the explorers' attitude towards what they saw, and the reception of their reports by the public at home, were both profoundly affected by the new spirit. Bernal Díaz, for example, was greatly impressed, but not particularly surprised, by the extensive collections of plants and wild animals kept in Montezuma's compound; botanical gardens and menageries were common among the hobbies of Renaissance princes, and it seemed to him perfectly natural that Montezuma should have similar interests. Alvarado, who climbed to the crater of Popocatépetl, partly to get sulphur to make gunpower, partly out of bravado, but also partly out of curiosity, was emulating—consciously or not—the celebrated exploit of Petrarch on Mont Ventoux in an age when mountain climbing was unheard of. One of the earliest books about America, written by an eye-witness—Oviedo's *General History of the Indies*—admirably illustrates this Renaissance interest by the clarity and detail of its account of animals and plants. Of geographical curiosity—the disinterested desire to know what lay beyond the horizon—the outstanding fifteenth-century expression was the *De Orbe Novo* of Peter Martyr, significantly written by a cultivated Italian who found a congenial home in Spain.

Technical inventions in the fifteenth century, not immediately connected with the use of the sea, served to widen and popularize this growing curiosity. The most important of these was, of course, printing. Printing not only made possible a far wider diffusion of sailing directions, navigational manuals, and other aids to literate sailors, and not only spread the news of discoveries far more quickly than manuscripts could do; it contributed to a rapid increase in the numbers of the reading public, and in so doing created a great demand for comparatively light reading—reading intended for literate, educated people who were not professional scholars. This demand was met partly by romances, but also very largely by accounts of travels, both real and fictitious. Mandeville's *Travels*, for example, circulated widely in manuscript in the fifteenth century, among people who could not be sure whether or not the voyages it described were genuine; but it circulated more widely still later, in printed editions, and enjoyed its greatest vogue in the second half of the sixteenth century, when it was already suspected of being a fraud and was read mainly for entertainment. Many serious books—Peter Martyr's *De Orbe Novo*, Montalboddo's *Paesi novamente retrovati*, Sebastian Münster's *Cosmographia universalis*, all 'best-sellers' through many editions—were widely read in the same spirit; and later still, no gentleman's library was complete without the stately folios of De Bry's *Grands Voyages*. These are but a few of the most famous among hundreds of well-known titles. The popularity of travel books, and of references to remote lands in plays and allegories, was a striking feature of the literary life of the sixteenth century, and contributed greatly to the steady growth of interest in exploration and discovery.

The explorers, the promoters who sent them out, the public who applauded their deeds and profited by their discoveries, were impelled, then, by a complex mixture of motives and feelings. Generations of historians have endeavoured to sort out the mixture, to identify the elements in it which can be labelled 'medieval', 'Renaissance', 'modern', and so forth; but the mixture remains. The Renaissance, in the most commonly accepted use of the term, was primarily a Mediterranean achievement, the Reconnaissance primarily an Atlantic one. It is tempting to describe the Iberian peninsula, from which most of the early discoverers sailed, as the meeting ground where Mediterranean knowledge, curiosity and inventiveness met, and inspired, Atlantic courage and skill. The thesis has much truth in it; but it is not a complete explanation, and in linking Renaissance and Reconnaissance we must take care not to anticipate. Portuguese captains were sailing on tentative voyages of Atlantic discovery long before the Italian Renaissance had seriously affected Iberian culture. Most of these early voyages—at least those of which record remains—were undertaken by the command, or with the encouragement, of Prince Henry of Portugal [1394–1460], the 'Navigator', most famous of the precursors and inspirers of the Reconnaissance. The waters between Cape St Vincent, the Canaries, and the north-west coast of Morocco, were already known in his day to adventurous Portuguese fishermen. Prince Henry placed gentlemen of his own household in command of the ships, and set them definite geographical objects to be reached and passed. Thus from the habit of making fishing and casual trading voyages along a relatively short stretch of coast, there developed a programme of progressive, though intermittent, exploration much further south. Prince Henry did not, of course, go to sea himself, except as a military commander against the Moorish kingdom of Fez; late medieval conventions of propriety would have prevented a royal prince from participating—even had he wished—in long voyages of discovery in small vessels ill-provided for his state. His function was to provide the ships, the backing, the organization and the encouragement; and it may be presumed that his personal wishes dictated at least the official aims. Zurara, the contemporary chronicler of Prince Henry's achievements, lists the motives which impelled the Prince to undertake the exploration of the West African coast, and states that the first was a desire to know what lay beyond the Canaries and Cape Bojador. There is no suggestion, however, of a scientific or disinterested curiosity; the purpose was practical. Diogo Gomes, one of Prince Henry's captains, was specific on this point. In his account of his own voyages of 1444 and 1463, he states that the Prince desired to find the countries whence came the gold which reached Morocco by the desert routes, 'in order to trade with them and so maintain the gentlemen of his household'.

Again the familiar formula: serve God and grow rich. Zurara gives as Prince Henry's second reason a desire to open profitable new trades, but insists that trade must only be with Christian peoples, whom the explorers hoped to encounter beyond the country of the Moors. This was standard medieval doctrine. Although some purists considered *all* trade to be incompatible with knighthood, it was thought legitimate by many to deprive the infidel of resources for making war by indirect means if direct means failed. The third, fourth and fifth objects mentioned by Zurara were all conventional crusading aims: to investigate the extent of Moorish power, to convert pagans to Christianity, and to seek alliance with any Christian rulers who might be found. The long-lived Prester John legend, fed no doubt by rumours of the Coptic kingdom of Abyssinia, was by this time localized in Africa; and the hope of contact with some such ruler connected African exploration with the older Mediterranean crusade.

The sixth, and according to Zurara the strongest motive, was the Prince's desire to fulfil the predictions of his horoscope, which bound him 'to engage in great and noble conquests, and above all . . . to attempt the discovery of things which were hidden from other men'. This, too, was a conventional late medieval attitude, and a reminder that in Prince Henry's day astronomical knowledge was still more commonly applied to fortune-telling than to navigation. Prince Henry's own personality remains an enigma for the historian; but the picture which emerges from the chronicle is that of a conservative, staunchly medieval figure. The characteristics most stressed by contemporaries who knew him—by Zurara, by Diogo Gomes, and by the Venetian merchant venturer Cadamosto—were his rigid piety, his personal asceticism, and his obsession with the idea of the Crusade. Zurara, it is true, wrote as a panegyrist in Henry's lifetime; but that is all the more reason for supposing that he emphasized traits in which Henry himself took pride. As for Cadamosto, he clearly admired the Prince, but was not his dependent and had no reason to be other than truthful. About Henry's crusading obsession there can be no doubt. Despite his perpetual need of money —a need which the revenues of the Order of Christ [of which Henry was General] only partly relieved—he reconciled himself only late in his career, and then reluctantly, to the trade which his captains initiated —for lack of Christian princes in West Africa—with pagan peoples. He was always ready to drop the indirect crusade of the African voyage in favour of direct military assaults upon Morocco, whenever his royal relatives could be persuaded to mount these costly and fruitless adventures. The memorial which he wrote in 1436 urging an attack on Tangier, and his own gallant but inflexible conduct in command of the enterprise, both recall the pages of Froissart. All this was far from the Renaissance, with its bright, lively curiosity, its clear, hard sense of expediency, its passion for human fame, its love of learning and the arts. The evidence of Henry's support of learning is far from clear. He was not particularly learned himself, and unlike his royal brothers, left no writings. Though he was a generous patron of sailors and cartographers, the story of a school of astronomy and mathematics at Sagres is pure invention. Certainly this pious and chivalrous ascetic was no Renaissance humanist.

The concept of Renaissance itself is elusive and hard to define. An eminent scholar has recently reminded us that the Renaissance, in some of its aspects, was more 'medieval' than many historians have supposed. However Renaissance be defined, the Reconnaissance, the early process of discovery, began independently, with medieval motives and assumptions. Prince Henry and his captains were, in the main, men of the Middle Ages. Even Columbus . . . embarked on his famous enterprise with an intellectual equipment which was mainly medieval and traditional. In the course of the later fifteenth century, the movement gained speed and power from a series of vital technical improvements and inventions. Towards the end of the fifteenth, and in the early sixteenth century, it was further accelerated and profoundly modified by ideas associated with the Renaissance in Italy and imported from there into the Iberian peninsula.

*   *   *   *   *

CONCLUSION

By the middle of the seventeenth century the main geographical impetus of the Reconnaissance was spent; the first tentative charting of the size, shape and disposition of the continents had been in large measure completed. There were still, it is true, large gaps in European knowledge, even of coastlines. The Pacific coast of North America, north of Lower California, was almost unknown, and the longitudinal extent of the continent was the subject of wild and widely differing guesses. The Pacific coast of Asia was little better known, though a few Chinese and Japanese ports had been visited by European ships and there were flourishing European settlements in the Philippines. Of the thousands of islands scattered in the vast expanse of the Pacific, few had been sighted; and for all men knew, there might be whole continents there, still undiscovered. One such continent, indeed, was known to exist; the west coast of Australia had been sketched in rough outline by Dutch navigators who had learned to fear its dangers. It clearly belonged to a great land mass, whose dimensions were unknown, but which was generally supposed to include New Guinea. *Terra Australis Incognita*, the old southern continent of Ptolemy, also lingered in men's minds. The west coast of New Zealand, which Tasman had sighted, might be part of it; and Tasman himself—not a very careful explorer—had assumed Cook Strait to be a mere inlet. No man had seen the coast of the real Antarctic continent.

The main coastlines of the rest of the world—the Atlantic coasts of the Americas and the Pacific coast of South America; the whole outline of Africa; the southern coasts of Asia, and the Asian archipelagos; all these were known in varying degrees of detail to European navigators, and through maps to the reading public. Here and there European knowledge went behind the coastlines. Spaniards had explored by land most of Mexico and Central America, considerable areas of South America, and, very sketchily, parts of what are now the United States. In eastern North America, French explorers had travelled great distances in canoes, and acquired some knowledge of the great labyrinth of lakes and rivers used by Indian traders. In the Old World, on the other hand, there had been little inland penetration, and the interior of Asia was hardly better known to Europe in the seventeenth century than it had been in the thirteenth. A few Europeans had travelled inland in mainland Asia as ambassadors or adventurers, but they had stuck for the most part to the ancient roads regularly used by pilgrims, merchants and officials. Interior Africa, still more, was unknown save for a few visits to Egypt and Abyssinia. In general, the world outside Europe, as known to Europeans, was a world of coastlines, roughly charted, of scattered harbours connected by a network of seaborne communication.

Seaborne skill and strength had enabled Europeans to exploit their geographical knowledge and to settle here and there in all the known continents except Australia. The nature of their settlements varied greatly, but all alike depended upon metropolitan countries in Europe. None was fully self-supporting; none yet aspired to independence of the founding State, though some colonies had changed hands as the result of European wars and many more were to change hands later in the century. The hold of the European nations upon many of their outposts was still weak. Only a few relatively small areas could be said to be Europeanized, and the most potent factor in determining the nature of a European colony was the character of the native race among whom it was planted.

In some places Europeans had settled as a permanent resident aristocracy among more primitive, but settled peoples, living by their labour
and to a limited extent intermarrying with them. This was the situation
in Spanish and Portuguese America; though the areas under effective
European government still covered only a small part of the immense
areas claimed by Portugal and Spain, and no province was without its
Indian frontier. In the West Indies also, Europeans formed a resident
aristocracy, though the primitive labour force there was not native but
imported.

In other regions, where the native population was too sparse or too
intractable to furnish an adequate labour force, and where settlers did
not want, or could not afford to buy, imported slaves, Europeans had
cleared land and formed purely European communities, living largely
by their own labour as farmers, fishermen or traders. A thin fringe of
settlements of this type stretched along the Atlantic seaboard of North
America; settlements with small harbour towns looking towards Europe,
with a dangerous forest frontier not far inland. English and French
America lagged far behind Spanish America in population, wealth and
cultural attainments, but was growing rapidly in assertiveness and
strength.

In the Old World, Europeans had concentrated their efforts upon regions known to produce articles of value, and seaborne commerce rather
than empire had been their principal object. In West Africa, source of
gold, ivory and slaves, the climate and the forest, no less than the hostility of the inhabitants, had deterred them from settling. In the East
they had encountered numerous and civilized peoples, organized and
well-armed States. Here there could be no question of invading, of settling as a resident aristocracy. They came as armed traders, sometimes
as pirates, constantly quarrelling among themselves as pirates commonly do. Their impact upon the great empires of Asia had been very
slight. The government of China, with its highly organized, deeply cultivated official hierarchy, barely condescended to notice the uncouth foreign hucksters in the Canton river. In the territories subject to the
Mughal Empire [in India], various European groups had secured foot-
holds, as merchants residing on sufferance, as vassals, as allies and
somewhat unreliable mercenaries, in a few places as minor territorial
rulers, nowhere as overlords. With Persia they had little direct contact,
save through the Dutch factory at Bandar Abbas. The Ottoman Empire,
with conquests thrust far into eastern Europe, was obliged to pay serious attention to Europeans, for it faced them continuously on two
fronts. In the Mediterranean and the Balkans they were traders and

profitable customers in peace, military enemies in war. In the Indian Ocean, the Red Sea and the Persian Gulf, they were well-established armed interlopers, intercepting and diverting a great part of the commerce which had formerly been in Arab hands. As yet, however, the Turk was little influenced and not seriously threatened by European power. Among the smaller principalities on the southern fringe of Asia, European invaders had asserted themselves more effectively; but even here, except for a few small areas in south India and in the East Indian islands, actual European possessions were still confined to forts and trading factories.

Nevertheless, considering the relatively small size and loose organization of most European States, the achievements of two centuries of reconnaissance were remarkable. The objects with which the early discoverers set out had been in great measure achieved. The Turk had been taken in the rear, and his power, though great, no longer seemed overwhelming. Europe was connected by regular sea passages with the sources of most of the goods which Europeans most desired, and many of these goods were being shipped from European factories abroad, in European ships. The colonies which Europeans had established in places suited for European habitation seemed likely to endure and to develop. Moreover, wherever conquerors, planters or merchants had settled, churches had been founded, and there were Christian communities in every inhabited continent.

The success of the Reconnaissance, by its very magnitude, produced in the later seventeenth century a dulling of geographical curiosity. Men no longer expected to find Atlantis. Few still seriously hoped to penetrate by a northern route to Cathay. Though many thousands of miles of coast remained uncharted, and whole continents still awaited the explorer, these little-known places appeared to offer little prospect of immediate gain. The business corporations which, in the seventeenth century, controlled most long-distance voyaging, would not dissipate their shareholders' capital in the profitless pursuit of knowledge. There is a striking contrast between the intense, expectant curiosity of a Magellan, a Sebastian Cabot, a Henry Hudson, and the perfunctory attention which Dutch navigators, a little later, gave to the coasts of Australia and New Zealand. The exploring freelance buccaneer—such as Dampier, for example—was an increasingly rare exception. On the whole, the seventeenth century, by contrast with the sixteenth, was an age of consolidation overseas, of trading and planting exploitation, rather than of original exploration.

Seventeenth-century concentration on distant trade and planting was accompanied by a fierce competitive pugnacity, to be expected in a mercantilist age which regarded foreign trade as another form of war. In their incessant fighting over trade and territory, most European governments, lacking adequate naval force, made free use of buccaneers and pirates. In both East and West Indies, any gang of cut-throats whose predatory activities could be made to serve an immediate national advantage, could secure letters of marque and could be sure of the support and countenance of one or another colonial governor. The result was the creation of great areas of savage, unorganized conflict, through which only the very well-armed or the very inconspicuous could move with any confidence. The indiscriminate employment of buccaneers, it is true, was a temporary phase. These ruffians soon became so serious a nuisance to peaceful traders among their own countrymen that even French and English colonial governors were in time induced to co-operate with naval forces in their suppression; though naval officers themselves were not above occasional piracy. In the later seventeenth century a series of treaties between colonial powers formally repudiated the old convention of 'no peace beyond the Line', and the practice of egging on pirates to attack other nations' harbours and shipping ceased to be regarded as a respectable expedient of international conduct, even in the West Indies. The gradual suppression of buccaneering, however, did not mean an end of fighting in the Tropics. It merely confined major hostilities to periods of formal war; and wars were frequent. Throughout the last decades of the seventeenth century and the whole of the eighteenth, tropical possessions were among the principal bones of contention in every major war, and among the principal prizes in every major treaty. It was a sign of the growing importance of tropical colonies and trade in the estimation of the western world, that the age of the buccaneers should be followed by the age of the admirals.

Seventeenth-century expansion overseas, increasingly concentrated upon commercial ends, savagely competitive, became also increasingly independent of religious motives. In the colonies of the Catholic powers in the sixteenth century the period of crusading war and plunder had been succeeded by a period of deep and thoughtful missionary fervour. In Spanish America especially, the Church had striven not only to convert but to teach the Indians, and to recruit and train an educated native priesthood. By the end of the sixteenth century the attitude of Spanish missionaries, and still more the attitude of the secular clergy, towards the Christian Indian had become less optimistic. The ideal of a native priesthood was in large measure abandoned, partly through conviction of its hopelessness, partly through social opposition from secular sources. The principle upon which Las Casas [Dominican missionary, 1474–1566] had insisted, that the Indian was potentially the spiritual and intellectual equal of the European, was less emphatically urged in the seventeenth century, both by theologians and by those who professed to know the Indian. The work of spreading the Faith went on, it is true, in hundreds of Franciscan and Jesuit missions, penetrating into remote regions of the Americas far beyond the limits of ordinary white settlement. In French America, Jesuit explorer-missionaries performed miracles of endurance and devotion, though often to little apparent effect. In the Portuguese East, also, the work of Jesuit missionaries went on steadily, though often discredited by the piracies which their countrymen committed. In Europe, the establishment in 1622 of the Propaganda—the Congregation for the propagation of the Faith— evinced the direct concern of the Papacy in colonial missions, in the training of missionaries, and once again in the creation of native priesthoods.

In the later seventeenth century, despite the efforts of the Propaganda, missionary enterprise began perceptibly to slacken. The growing weakness of Spanish and Portuguese colonial government and French preoccupation with European affairs together caused a loss of effective support. The general intellectual temper of Europe, also, grew less favourable to missions. The seventeenth century was a time of profound religious conflict, often expressed in war and persecution. It was also a time of deep and original religious thought; for the Church had to face not only the challenge of schism and dissent, not only the challenge of growing national absolutism, but also the intellectual challenge presented by mathematics and physical science. This last challenge was, as yet, only latent; but the intellectual and spiritual energies of European Christendom were more and more directed to its own internal problems, less and less to the problem of how best to spread a simple, agreed version of the Faith among supposedly simple pagan peoples. Moreover, the main initiative in expansion was passing from the Catholic to the Protestant nations of Europe; and though many Dutchmen and Englishmen carried abroad religious convictions of an uncompromising kind, they showed considerably less skill and enthusiasm than their Catholic rivals in missionary enterprise. They showed also, on the whole, correspondingly less care for the material well-being of peoples who came under their influence. It was not to be expected, in particular, that commercial concerns should spend much money or thought upon missionary work or upon the work of general welfare which commonly accompanies evangelization.

*   *   *   *   *

Apart from economic enterprise, there were two characteristics of the Reconnaissance which commanded respect and which, together with high courage, gave a certain nobility to the whole movement, despite the plunder and the savagery. One was intellectual curiosity, disinterested zeal for the increase of knowledge; the other a sense of responsibility, of obligation, towards men of other races. Both were in eclipse, in the field of oversea exploration, in the later seventeenth century. Both were to revive in different and more effective forms later.

The prodigious advances made by Galileo and Newton in astronomy, in optics and in mechanics, and the increasing skill of craftsmen in applying scientific knowledge, were to place in the hands of navigators and explorers instruments of a range and accuracy formerly undreamed of, and so to lay the foundations of a new age of discovery. When geographical curiosity reasserted itself, as it did in the mid-eighteenth century, in the hands of Cook and his successors and the scientists associated with them, it took the form, not of a search for particular places of interest or value, but of a systematic and precise charting of the earth's surface in the interests of science. Eighteenth-century exploration, moreover, was backed not merely by individuals or trading companies, but by the power and resources of governments.

Science and technology not only sharpened the perceptions and improved the techniques of explorers; they also conferred upon European peoples ever-increasing military and naval advantages over the rest of the world. These reinforced the truculent and cynical greed with which European States in the eighteenth century often embarked on wars of colonial aggression. But just as the brutalities of the Spanish conquest in America had produced anxious searchings of conscience and movements for reform among Spanish theologians and officials, so in the late eighteenth and early nineteenth centuries the destructiveness of European imperialism was met by the revival of a feeling of responsibility. Chief among the symptoms of this revival were the growth of the great Protestant missionary societies, with their emphasis upon educational and medical work as well as upon evangelization; the profound revulsion against slavery and the trade in slaves; the repeated emphasis laid upon the creation—in India, for example—of an accessible and uncorrupt judiciary. Later still, this feeling of responsibility has shown itself in the development of the idea of trusteeship, and in deliberate attempts to build up, among subject peoples, workable modern systems of government and welfare. Inevitably the development of western education among dependent peoples has proved, from the imperial point of view, to be a Trojan horse; but it has rarely been discouraged for that reason. In recent years an enlightened realism about the political aspirations of such peoples has led to many more or less voluntary withdrawals of imperial control and the establishment, on friendly terms, of independent states. None of the ideas which prompted these acts were entirely new. All were suggested, in one form or another, in the days of Las Casas and Vitoria [sixteenth-century Dominican jurist]. The sense of responsibility which lay behind them, though intermittent and imperfect, was an essential characteristic of the Reconnaissance, and must have its place in the story along with the curiosity, the ingenuity, the vanity, the courage and the greed.

Suggestions for Further Reading

BAKER, J. N. L., *The History of Geographical Discovery and Exploration,* rev. ed. New York: Barnes & Noble, 1963.

CIPOLLA, C. M., *Guns, Sails, and Empires.* New York: Funk and Wagnalls, 1967.

ELLIOTT, J. H., *The Old World and the New, 1492–1650.* New York: Cambridge University Press, 1970.

HANKE, LEWIS, *The Spanish Struggle for Justice in the Conquest of America.* Boston: Little, Brown, 1966.

MORRISON, SAMUEL E., *Admiral of the Ocean Sea,* 2 vols. Boston: Little, Brown, 1942.

MORRISON, SAMUEL E., *The European Discovery of America.* New York: Oxford University Press, 1971.

PENROSE, B., *Travel and Discovery in the Renaissance.* Cambridge, Mass.: Harvard University Press, 1955.

REYNOLDS, ROBERT L., *Europe Emerges.* Madison, Wisc.: University of Wisconsin Press, 1961.

SANFORD, C. L., *The Quest for Paradise.* Urbana, Illinois: University of Illinois Press, 1961.

THORNTON, A. P., *Doctrines of Imperialism.* New York: John Wiley & Sons, 1965.

JOSEPH LORTZ

Luther and the Reformation

ঙ§ই The most creative and vital movement in Christianity in the past three decades has been the liberal and reforming wing of Catholicism, which received its most effective expression in the Second Vatican Council of 1962–1965.
Nineteenth-century Catholicism tended to reject modern
thought in fearful and obscurantist fashion, but the leading Catholic thinkers of recent decades have entered into
a great effort to renew and modernize the Church, and to
reformulate Catholic doctrine in the light of twentieth-
century culture and social experience. The main thrust of
liberal Catholic thought has come from Germany, and
Joseph Lortz has been in the forefront of this Catholic intellectual upheaval.

The recent and contemporary movement of Catholic revival has felt an affinity with the reformers of the sixteenth
century, and partly as a way of understanding how the
modern Church took shape and also as a way of fully
understanding themselves, the liberal Catholic thinkers
have turned back to reexamine the Lutheran Revolution
and to establish its significance and evaluate its meaning.
While traditionally Catholic scholarship approached the
Lutheran Reformation in a spirit of what Lortz condemns
as "bilateral confessionalism"—from an antagonistic and

FROM Joseph Lortz, *The Reformation in Germany*, Vol.
I, trans. Ronald Walls (New York: Herder and Herder; London:
Darton, Longman & Todd, 1968), pp. 3–4, 5, 7–21, 167–175,
219–232.

adversary position, Lortz has tried to understand the Reformation experience in its own terms, and while also free from the sentimental and uncritical praise of Luther that has characterized so much of Protestant writing on the subject, to arrive at an unbiased and dispassionate judgment.

Lortz regards the Reformation as the direct consequence of the ecclesiastical and social situation of the later Middle Ages. He regards the Church on the eve of the Reformation as a sick, disorganized, and ineffective institution, no longer adequately serving the needs of society. He severely censures "curial fiscalism," the papal curia's materialism, reckless greed, and sloppy and dysfunctional centralizing proclivities. He sees Europe ripe for a lay revolt against the Church hierarchy at the beginning of the sixteenth century, and attributes the outbreak of this revolt in Germany specifically, to frustrations arising from the German failure to develop the national political institutions that had emerged in several other parts of Europe.

Lortz has a very clear-headed and perceptive understanding of Luther, whom he regards as a man of overpowering feeling, a passionate cultivator of experience, rather than as a careful, critical thinker. At bottom, according to Lortz, Luther was "a non-Catholic Occamist"—a disciple of the fourteenth-century radical English Franciscan theologian who made an absolute separation between an omnipotent, transcendent God and humanity, while the main thrust of Catholicism was to integrate divinity and humanity through the institutional Church.

It is in connection with this latter thesis on Luther that one comment on Lortz's argument may be made. In medieval Catholicism there was a continual tension from the twelfth century (if not indeed from the time of St Augustine) between a tendency to integrate God's power and human capacity and an urge to separate God from man. Luther, in taking the latter position, was not "non-Catholic"; he merely emphasized one of the two extremes in medieval religious thought. Another observation on Lortz's interpretation of the Reformation is that he does not allow for the pressures arising from economic change. The penetration into European life of capitalist institutions created the opportunity for social mobility in ambitious merchants and aggressive petty nobles alike. It also widened the road to power for great aristocrats who could accustom themselves to a rational, calculating kind of behavior. It is not true that the Reformation simply arose from the ideology and desires of the bourgeoisie, although this was a contributing factor; but it does appear that Luther's theology, and the possibilities opened by his revolt against Rome, were immediately attractive to the upwardly mobile and extraordinarily ambitious people of several social groups in the early sixteenth century.

THE CAUSES OF THE REFORMATION

Christianity divided is a self-contradiction. This, however, has been the state of Christianity since the Reformation. Quite apart from the eastern schism, for the past four hundred years a fundamental split has persisted in a Christianity that formerly was one. During this space of time a far greater number of Christians—a far greater number of non-Catholic Christians indeed—have lived than during the whole of the first fifteen Christian centuries.

From this fact emerges the real question which a Christian must put to the Reformation historian: What was the meaning and the historical purpose of the Reformation?

To answer this question we require knowledge not only of the course but also of the foundation of the Reformation. Without this knowledge the course itself remains incomprehensible. Enquiry into *the causes of the Reformation* is thus essential to a study of the history of the Reformation.

What we have in mind is not primarily the answering of questions about how particular developments led up to the Reformation, but rather the answer to the preliminary question as to how any Church revolution such as was accomplished in the sixteenth century could have been possible at all, and how it was, in a deeper sense, necessary. That the Reformation should have occurred is by no means self-evident. On the contrary: to arrive at a deeper understanding of what it was, we must first become quite clear as to how it was possible for it to happen; we must try to relive the strange, the colossal, trial of strength which called in question the absolutely fixed norm of Christian faith and government that directed with divine authority the entire life of individuals and communities.

*   *   *   *   *

The age of the Reformation was marked by a complexity and diversity of life hitherto unknown. In a measure likewise unknown until then, personalities of second and third stature appeared on the stage of history and drew the masses into the course of events. The great precondition of all modern history: numbers, numbers of individuals, that is, caught up in the historical process, and in turn reacting upon it in some way or other, and upon each other in a variety of ways, is indeed a characteristic of Reformation history. The history of the preaching friars, of theology, of the mercenaries, of the peasants' wars, provides an indication of this factor. An even better indication lies in the fact that this period was the first to be decisively touched by that power which first made possible any sort of real public opinion, any spiritual mass-movement—the art of printing.

The full significance of this appears when we recognise that the Reformation period was heir to the close of the fifteenth century—a period of countless interwoven antitheses. These antitheses for their part were the result of centuries-old dissolutions and rebuildings, and as such not only characterise or even dominate the image of life at that time but also make this whole life an antithesis from its very foundations upwards.

*   *   *   *   *

No century is merely a termination or a transition. The concrete variety of life in every era contradicts such a conception; the late Middle Ages were more than just autumn or just early spring. They had an intrinsic meaning of their own. Whoever wishes to give a complete description of any period must above all comprehend it as it is at its centre, without antecedent consideration of its precedents and its consequences.

But every period is also a transition to another; and many parts of history are so strongly marked by this character that we may describe them as typical periods of transition. One of such periods is the later and concluding Middle Ages, that is, the period from about 1300 until the end of the fifteenth century. All serious quarrel over this conception disappears if one considers the late Middle Ages in their relation to the period of the Reformation and to the Reformation itself. For the late Middle Ages are, in general, the cause of the Reformation, and it is evident that an extraordinary number of powerful forces at work in that period can be easily classed together under that designation.

The mighty change which the Reformation effected in the total life of Europe—ecclesiastical, religious, scientific, political and economic—was one half the result of a change and disintegration which set in around 1300. The other half was Luther.

If we define 'causes' as 'presuppositions', there is indeed a summary, but penetrating and most illuminating formula which answers our question. The Reformation was caused by the disintegration of the basic principles and basic forms upon which the Middle Ages were built.

The principal question is that of the disruption of the unity of the Middle Ages; for the Reformation was without doubt essentially the break-up of this unity, or, better, the revolutionary consummation of this break-up.

The shortest formula for the empirical situation in so far as it appears as a preparation for the Reformation goes something like this: the unity of western Christianity had gone; the *una civitas christiana* [unified Christian sovereignty] had already vanished. This meant that the unity of dogma and of Church life—still manifestly present—had surrendered in essence the substratum which supported their existence. The separation of the individual components of Europe and of the Roman Catholic Church (the rise of nations, in fact) had advanced so far that the lever could be applied with good prospect of achieving disruption. This state of affairs was brought to light by Luther, and he, indeed, was the first to allow it to lead right into schism.

Evidence for the pre-Reformation break-up of Christian unity or for the threat of its imminent disappearance is not difficult to produce. (*a*) Avignon (the pope, formerly truly a universal figure, now very nearly became a French court bishop); the schism of the west (split of the entire western Church into two camps mutually excommunicating each other); the nationally conceived reform councils based upon a radically separatist idea of a council; the Renaissance popes as Italian princes. In contrast to the cohesion of medieval universalism these phenomena present a series of logically increasing expressions of religious nationalism.
(*b*) The national-political division of Europe, the rise of great national monarchies in the west, the emergence therein of national Churches, and, in Germany, the gradual tendency towards the erection of territorial Churches.
(*c*) The refusal of the west to respond to the papal call to war against the enemy of Christendom; the inevitable hardening of this refusal on

account of the political relations of both popes with the Turks (Innocent VIII as paid gaoler of the captive brother of the Turkish sultan, and Alexander VI). The fall of Constantinople in 1453 was the expression of a Europe become disunited: it no longer mobilised its united strength towards a common end.

(d) The expulsion of heretical Bohemia from the common Christian heritage.

The beginnings of a new sense of unity which European humanism brought were powerless against the disappearance of western, Christian unity; they hastened it, in fact, for on the whole humanism moved towards secularisation, that is, the dissolution of the more spiritual Middle Ages.

*   *   *   *   *

This disruptive process was making room for a reconstruction, for the evolution of something that was both new and of value. This development was deliberately fostered by the Church itself in the great work of educating the nations of Europe, the result of which was bound to be the maturity of these nations, and their accepting adult responsibility. The achieving of this aim necessarily brought about an alteration in the relationship of attachment to the Church that had grown up in the early Middle Ages. The decisive question was: Would the transition result in people, hitherto accustomed only to being led, entering into a relationship of free co-operation; or would the changed conditions result in animosity and schism?

We know the answer. But why was the result animosity and schism?

The growth of the European nations was burdened, among other things, by a dangerous unevenness. The foundation was the linking together of religion and political-social life to become a single whole. With the co-operation and leadership of the Church in the course of many centuries secular society fought doggedly and consistently towards ever greater independence. This was in accordance with natural necessity and, as we have said, with the purpose of all true education. But the Church, although she had established and fostered this independence, was not entirely happy about it. By the Church we mean the socially and economically privileged priestly estate, the bishops, the church courts, the great religious orders, living and exercising their care of souls in the cities, and the Roman curia. Two classes within the same vital social organism grew at quite a different tempo and, to some extent, in different directions: a spiritual breach was easy, if not inevita-

ble. On the other hand, the Church tolerated a carelessness in the expression of religious opinions, which gave too much latitude to freedom,
and became a dangerous temptation. We must take account of certain
dominant humanist views which were at work in this process.

The line of development is evident: the Reformation is an expression
of Europe's attainment of intellectual and religious independence. It is
the revolutionary declaration of the coming of age of the Christian people of Europe. As early as 1300 polemical writings on Church politics
were full of the revolt of the laity in every form, and so basic that they
simply could not be overlooked.

Not only did the basic mental and religious attitudes which characterised the Middle Ages change but so did the forms of expression they
had known in the Church and the world. Medieval institutions were
passing away. Concerning the Church, we think of everything that
comes under the heading of the disintegration of its concept as an
apostolic, religious entity, and under the heading of ecclesiastical abuses
in the widest sense of the word. Concerning the world, we think of the
colossal reorganisation in the social, cultural and political spheres. (Political: the impotence of the empire and the emperor, its diminution as a
result of the loss of large frontier areas; the separation and enmity between countless emergent territories and regions.)

In the battle against this disorder and reorganisation in world and
Church there arose those power currents which governed German history in the period of confessional division. But these did not arise
merely from this battle. They arose essentially from their own roots. It
was this latter fact alone which made the Reformation no mere episode,
but an epoch in German history. The violence of its convulsion in the religious sphere even made it an epoch in world history.

In fact at the beginning of the sixteenth century this disintegration
of medieval principles in every area of national-political, ecclesiastical,
religious and scientific life had gone so far, reaching the Church and
striking against her, that in broad outline the framework of the Reformation seemed to have been prepared. Seen as a religious and ecclesiastical event the Reformation is the denial of the visible Church,
rooted and grounded in the objective teaching authority and in the
sacramental priesthood; and it is the acceptance of a religion of conscience erected upon the judgment of the individual with regard to the
biblical word. That is to say: along these two lines of its development,
the Reformation replaced the basic medieval attitudes of objectivism,
traditionalism and clericalism by those of subjectivism, spiritualism and

laicism. This was a development, therefore, which took up, united, and carried on with surprising intensity tendencies of the late medieval interplay of forces. The Reformation was a revolutionary revolt against the papal Church by a theological lay movement. Everything which prepared the enmity of the laity against papacy and Church belongs to the causes of the Reformation.

In the intellectual sphere the most far-reaching effect was produced by that slowly emerging force which we like to call the subjectivist tendency, although it was still centuries removed from modern subjectivism. This development had begun in the moment when the western mind began to adopt its own independent attitude towards the Christian message, to pose bold questions and to give answers unheard of before. This happened at first within, but soon outside, the Church. The two epoch-making figures, both belonging to the high Middle Ages, are Bernard of Clairvaux and Peter Waldo.

An historical analysis of the intellectual, ecclesiastical, political and social situation at the turn of the sixteenth century yields, further, the precise reflection of this disintegration: a very strong, widespread and dangerous dissatisfaction with prevailing conditions and, moreover, strong agitation and a corresponding demand for reform that had already become violent. In reality the Lutheran Reformation, which grew into a denunciation of the former way of life, became an outlet for all this. But at the decisive point, namely, opposition to the Church as the supporting power of the Middle Ages, the demand for reform was expressed with extraordinary sharpness, and here it developed an unusually explosive power, which in its turn reverberated to unusual lengths.

The tension expressed vis-à-vis the Church possessed such great explosive power because a thorough reform had been due for three hundred years; indeed, Innocent III had made reform the theme of the fourth Lateran council [1215]. Furthermore, in spite of the manifestly great achievements and persons (in the papacy, episcopacy, clergy, monasticism, civil life, in piety, theology and art) a consistent decadence had set in within this development and, in spite of all the excellence, it could not be concealed or smoothed over. No matter how one may extol the value of fourteenth-century mysticism; no matter how we now concede many Christian features to the Renaissance, the sequence Avignon-schism-Renaissance is, seen as a whole, a development of religious debilitation, a dangerous disintegration of Christian and priestly life, a perilous eclipse of the Catholic idea. Indeed, when the Church was in danger of its life, in the two-, and then three-headed papacy, had not the self-seeking of the highest senate of the Church and of some of the popes prevented the initiation of the long-overdue reform? Certainly one can concede to Möhler that 'by rebuilding upon the existent foundations (of the Church), according to the laws of continuity, a new and better time' could have been ushered in; but, in virtue of the inner consistency of the concrete situation at the beginning of the sixteenth century, there was not much prospect of this possibility becoming a reality. Conversely, the many, vain, centuries-old attempts at reform and the countless, frequently successful revolts against the Church's authority made things ripe for a radical break-through. People had had more than enough. They wanted to make an end of it. A radical revolution was bound to find many enthusiastic adherents.

The distribution of forces is seen even more in the fact that the absolute necessity of reform was a profound conviction in all trends and circles within the Church, all of whom were possessed by an intense longing for some sort of renewal.

The call for a reformation in head and members was, to be sure, vastly different from a merely polemical antipapal or anti-Church movement. It was first of all the positive expression of the conviction which penetrated to the very roots of western consciousness that the profoundest order of the Church had become distorted, and which imperiously demanded a transformation; there was also the conviction that this transformation would come through a tremendous revolution —an apocalyptic chastisement willed by God. This expectation was characterised by both longing and fear. From the most diverse quarters, in all spheres of life, this revolutionary mood had grown as a wish, a fear, a plan, as a prophecy, as an already living movement. Conditions were intolerable; a fundamental change had to come. The tyranny had to be broken. In a time of famine, with great frankness in his cathedral pulpit Geiler von Kayserberg (d. 1510) incited the people of Strasburg to take grain from the rich by force. It was this same, truly Catholic and deeply devout Geiler who knew that 'Christianity was distorted from top to bottom, from the pope to the sacristan, from the emperor to the shepherd'.

No revolution could be too radical to prevent many from finding at once, in this longing and fear, a proof of its justification. Luther, at first intensely earnest, then bold and obstinate, then reckless, in attack, found here an unusually well-prepared soil.

And yet, despite all we have said, the onset of the Reformation had not become self-evident. Its appearance and the world-historical shattering of Christianity which it precipitated, remain primarily a mystery. But we make a mystery no more accessible to understanding by hushing up whatever constitutes its incomprehensibility. It is better to emphasise the enigma which it conceals. By going beyond the quite inadequate forms of explanation hitherto provided, and realistically investigating the origin of the Reformation we are now, it is true, progressively illuminating its tragic genesis; but at the same time too much stress has been laid on one angle. It is time now to do justice to irrational factors. The complex of causes of the Reformation had so thoroughly come to a head that the breaking of a storm became almost an absolute necessity. But in spite of this, much of the undiluted essence of the Church, much of the heroic spirit of Christianity remained. It is false to describe the process as though the disintegration took place without any opposition, and even falser to trace back such a dissolution simply to an act of malice. The Reformation was a battle for the authentic form of Christianity; its emergence was not a self-evident fact; less still was it self-evident that the struggle was to be resolved by the greater part of western Christendom turning against the Church.

One of the indispensable preconditions of reaching an understanding of the development of the Reformation, and of assessing its value, is that we clarify the magnitude of the cleavage represented by the Reformation, in terms of these two problems. Only then will sufficient light be cast on Luther's responsibility for the Reformation schism.

[One of the] fundamental preconditions for the possibility of the Reformation [was] that the question be asked, whether the existent and ruling papal Church, believed to be of divine right, were in fact the true representation of Christianity.

We can sense at once the colossal development which was necessary before there could be any question of the Reformation. That is to say, doubt had to be raised not simply over this or that aspect of the ecclesiastical system: the whole presentation of the faith had to be rejected, and a fresh total conception of Christianity produced, capable of capturing the mind—almost overnight—of the majority of the members of the Church. For things to have reached such a state it was necessary that there should have been a prior, interior decadence in the religious and ecclesiastical heritage of the nations of Europe. Even the compelling power of Luther's oratory could not have found such an echo, had the beginnings of his views not somehow been familiar for a long time to the European mind.

It was, therefore, in the nature of things that this radical questioning should grow but slowly. Above all, before it had clearly emerged into consciousness, before it had been formulated, or grasped in its full import, it lay for long inarticulate within the secret, inner trend of the thoughts and deeds which determined the movement of history. From the awakening of the strongly personal piety within the Church in the twelfth-century the way led through the destructive struggle of the Church with the 'enlightened' Frederick II [1215–1250] to the antipapal disintegration of the late Middle Ages. Ever more consciously, the contrast became expressed between the Roman Church and Christendom, between curia and papacy, between papal church and early Christian Church. To this one can add the name of Philip IV of France [1285–1314], the poverty controversy, nominalism, Occam, *Defensor Pacis*, conciliar ideas, the Waldensians, the Cathars, Wycliffe, Huss, Hussites. What a vast, many-sided movement away from the Church then becomes visible.

And this movement of defection can be traced back to roots lying much further in the past.

Thus, for example, the whole tragic interconnection of justification, duty and fate in the course of the history of the world and of the Church had already become manifest in that great movement which the Church had been conducting—since the time of Gregory VII [1073–1085]—for the liberation of its religious and spiritual principle from secular control. For this mighty process developed, at the same time, into a clericalisation of the Church, that is, to an exclusion of the laity from active participation in the government of the Church (strained relations with the ruling priestly caste arose and then changed to enmity), and to a de-sacralisation of the secular-political sphere. This process of secularisation contained also a bitter and self-perpetuating opposition between the Germanic and the papal, ultimately between Rome and Germany. From then on the interests even of the German Church were very often no longer those of the papacy. Pure faith, in terms of which it was possible to make a sharp division between papal politics and the papal, Catholic religion, provided a means of softening that opposition; but in real life this faith was not strong enough to keep friction permanently away from vital interests. Even at that time the great flight of churchmen and their concept of the Church into a 'purely ecclesiastical' sphere (beyond real life in the actual political realm) was not particularly good for the Church.

The investiture controversy, in its broadest sense, inaugurated the rise of the medieval Church. Without it the great achievements of the Church in the high Middle Ages could scarcely have been realised. But, by the law of original sin, even the constructive elements in history are doomed to contain within themselves the seeds of their own corruption, which leads to new burdens, new trials and to new decisions. And so here too the investiture controversy became the cause of the decline of the Church, in the sense of a severe and lasting weakening of things papal and ecclesiastical.

This happened in a roundabout way through the concept of power which Gregory VII had introduced into the papal programme, but which so many of his successors had not succeeded in keeping on the high plane of heroic, religious devotion. Out of human weakness and egotism, by means of politics, law and greed they brought about that secularisation that led even further away from true Christianity, and which we know as the exaggerated curialism of the late Middle Ages, with its completely exaggerated views of direct papal jurisdiction over the temporal goods and laws of the Church and world.

In the meantime, the behaviour of the higher clergy had led the political rulers to turn a dangerous opinion into an axiom: the Church, that is its papal and episcopal incumbents, were to be fought like any other political, judicial and financial power. The battle against the pope, so often reckless in tone and in practical dealings (the pope figuring as 'Antichrist', 'son of wickedness', 'blood sucker', 'oppressor'), prepared the ground. As soon as this battle became allied with dogmatically false propositions people could easily, or at least more easily, find justification for false dogma in the long-familiar legitimacy of the battle. One cannot see, for example, how in 1412 in Prague [center of Hussitism] the papal bulls could have been consigned to the flames if people had not long been accustomed to that grim battle. The inner distortion (or emptiness) of the meaning of ecclesiastical institutions made independence from them easy, in spite of the fact that dogma was considered just as binding as ever. However, that this one-sided bond could never have developed and sustained sufficient strength to save the essential supreme authority of the Church, is taught by daily experience and proved extensively by history. This acceptance of dogma, and loyalty to the externals of the Church tend to be the last things to go, but once they do begin to go, their decline is very rapid. Suddenly they seem to lose their meaning. One day staunch Catholicism is there and is being emphatically lauded; the next day it is gone.

And hence it came about, that that fundamental doubt which had grown so slowly, spread out still more slowly into the masses. But in reality, as already indicated, in every sphere of life the ties with the Church became slacker and less absolute. That is to say, the impossibility of seriously calling the Church in question progressively dissolved, and the possibility of a radical transformation became more evident.

At the beginning of modern times the dissolution or obscuring of the Catholic idea assumed dangerous proportions, threatening life in two ways: it appeared first of all in the aggressive, heretical form of Hussitism and in the various, heretical (or quasi heretical) forms of apocalypsism, spiritualism and communistic socialism; and it also appeared under the guise of a scarcely perceptible, inner decomposition —in the indifferentism and immorality of Renaissance culture, in the secularisation of curialism, in the dangerous, intra-theological disintegration of what was Catholic in Occamism, and, most decisively, in the a-dogmatic and anti-dogmatic relativism of humanist, enlightened education and theology.

And yet it is precisely here that the mysterious element in the subsequent Reformation schism becomes evident. The Church was still the dominant power of the time, the acknowledged guardian and leader, the moulder, so men thought, of both public and private life. Proof of this can be adduced from many sides. The Christian faith was still the central point of all life, and it was taught and dispensed by the priests of the Roman pope; in science, theology, philosophy, law, as in social life, including the administration of justice, and charitable activity, the leadership of the clergy was not seriously called in question. Even the life of the state seemed conceivable only on a foundation of Church order.

And it is not as if this dominance was purely exterior. Precisely in this does the incomparably provocative and alluring paradox of the period fully disclose itself. We can sense this if we contrast the deep, truly evangelical, Church piety, the religious Church art of the years from 1500 to 1520, with the almost instantaneous defection of such wide circles to Luther.

At the same time we must interpret that proposition about the still unbroken dominance of the Roman Church over life in a very restricted sense, if we wish to avoid reaching an enormously false conclusion. In fact, fundamentally, the papal church was no longer the ruler and guide. Hussitism had torn away an entire country, Bohemia, from the western Church community and from the empire. But the decisive factor was that the visible and invisible foundations of life, out of which this dominance of the Church had first grown, had altered most radically. A breaking away from the Church on a gigantic scale, in part visible, in greater part invisible, had taken place; the power of the tradition of the Church as a demand for, and affirmation of, unquestioning obedience to the Church, had been essentially weakened.

Great revolutions are possible only where serious vacuums have formed within a dominant way of life. The vacuums suck alien, hostile forces in from outside, and these rush with elemental power into that which has become empty. The façade still stands, asserting its rights; but because it is itself in the wrong, and has become too superficial, the alien forces advance of themselves. Then there arises that apparently inexplicable, and yet basically natural process of the victory of new ideas over ancient, established power.

. . . . Amongst the general causes we list, as always, the destruction of one's own substance by oneself, through the consumption of capital, instead of increasing one's substance and living upon the interest from capital. For example, spiritual capital was used up through the exaggerated use of spiritual weapons. This was one of the furthest-reaching causes, and one which had been longest at work in preparation. Here one must take account of the total process, extending over centuries, of the struggle between papacy and empire, with its excommunications, its antipopes and its large-scale invective. At the beginning of the preparation for the coming religious-ecclesiastical revolution stands the damage to the irreplaceable, religious, mystical aura which surrounded the pope as a completely other-worldly power. With every step into the sphere of politics, especially with every victorious step, the pope more and more became one ruler amongst many others. The twelfth and thirteenth centuries, too, contributed to this development, even although the life of faith was still advancing, and the purely spiritual substance of the hierarchy was still strong—as a result, maybe, of the mighty warnings uttered by St Bernard and St Francis. But then came Boniface VIII, Philip the Fair and the shattering incident of Anagni [the humiliation of Pope Boniface, 1303], after which, to all outward appearance, there remained in the most power-conscious of all popes, no trace of any likeness to God. Europe was left only with the profound experience that papal power, even in spiritual things, had very narrow limits. Then came the undignified haggling between Philip the Fair and Clement V—pope turned French court bishop and finally, Avignon, the emperor Louis the Bavarian [anti-papal sponsor of Occam] and then the schism [1378–1417].

And we must not forget that not only the wholesale application of the highest spiritual punishments automatically diminished their effectiveness but that in the midst of a ceaselessly growing, extraordinarily rich self-awareness on the part of national states, provinces, and of the middle-class laity, Rome always linked very real political and economic demands with spiritual punishments. If the papacy, by an interdict on entire countries, could simply write them off . . . , then, whether this was formally justified or not, the situation had become quite impossible, so that the deepest, invisible foundation of faith, which presented Church and papacy as divine things, was severely threatened and dangerously weakened. Contemporaries knew well that in reality the papacy was identified with these things. The man, harshly affected by some punishment, distinguished between a secular and a dogmatic position, and yet did not distinguish. The wrath of the stricken was directed against individual popes, but very easily against the papacy as well.

In accordance with the universal character of the Church these developments applied almost equally to all of Europe. The Reformation, however, arose in Germany. Why?

The problem is very complicated and must, therefore, be approached from different angles. A provisional answer, leaving many elements (chiefly Luther) out of account, would run something like this: in Germany in the Catholic period there was never sufficient national fulfilment within the Church. What we mean is this: in Spain, France and England a present, although dangerous (cf. England) remedy against the common threat of an explosion in Church stability and European unity had been provided in time by the formation, with papal approval and within the unity of the Church, of national Churches, allowing considerable satisfaction of national interests within the Church. In these countries the explosive force was paralysed by this satisfaction, but the Germans were not satisfied and so the tendency towards rebellion in all the movements we have mentioned became, for the most part, concentrated in Germany. Because in Germany national interests had not been sufficiently satisfied by Rome there resulted a twofold intensification of the danger, making it easier for the breach to take place there than elsewhere. On the other hand, the political development in the kingdoms to the west made possible the political form of the Church just mentioned.

Certainly, in accordance with the basic law of all development, including the preliminary stages of all revolutions, the far-reaching disintegration mentioned above was in many ways still latent. Many of the faithful were close to the point where any further step was bound to lead them away from the foundation of the Church, to separate them from it in fact, but they had no idea that this was so. The period was uniformly Catholic, and yet that unity was threatened at its foundations. It was precisely this interior, unconscious disintegration that characterised the situation; and it was precisely this circumstance which made the attack, when launched with such force by Luther, such a destructive blow.

A bitter proof of the correctness of this thesis is to be found in the incomprehensibly rapid change in attitude to the Church, the clergy, the mass and ceremonies, amongst large groups in all classes of society. The special value formerly—in spite of every protest—conceded everywhere as a matter of course to the sacral priesthood with all its radiance, collapsed, in many places overnight. One day the great patrician families of Nuremberg were calmly donating new, wonderful, costly altars and numerous splendid statues in honour of the saints; next day they were dragging out of the cloister the child whom they had dedicated to the life of perfection as a nun under the seal of the threefold vows of the Church—rescuing her from the net of godless human ordinances, from the sacrilege of papistical idolatory. This is a saddening, insoluble riddle. But here too we come to know what a spiritual façade without adequate substance, and what the sudden process of spiritual crystallisation or spiritual collapse mean. The attitude of respect collapsed all the sooner on account of its having been retained in spite of all, simply from habit, without reflection or deeper motivation, and not really possessed. Spiritual possession presupposes increase. In the widest circles of the faithful who were absolutely loyal to the Church, this increase was out of the question. The spiritual riches of the gospel and the liturgy were unknown to many loyal members of the Church. And . . . this was true not least of the uneducated masses who enjoyed insufficient religious care. . . .

* * * * *

One has only to consider side by side, the indicated 'necessity' of the Reformation and the mystery of its advent, in order to raise the question: Why had this condition of coexistence and confrontation not already been resolved at the end of the fifteenth century by the outbreak of a reformation?

This question seeks to uncover the positive strength of the Reformation. And that was Luther. In spite of the absolute rule of the Church over life, in spite of flourishing, pure, Christian piety, the

Reformation was prepared for within the Church by the latent inner disintegration we have mentioned. But it only became possible through the Reformer himself. . . .

LAYING THE FOUNDATION

In great measure the German Reformation is Martin Luther. Luther, that is to say, forms a great part of German history during the Reformation period. His importance demands, therefore, that any historical study of the period provide a thorough, detailed exposition of Luther.

Martin Luther expressed very few views to which we do not find parallels in earlier theologians and reformers. None the less Luther is something new—an original phenomenon of creative quality and power. He is a proof of the great mystery of all life, that the whole is essentially more than the sum of all the parts, in this case, than the sum of all of the separate ideas. Luther was certainly also the spark that lit the heap of powder that had long been piling up—but he is much more.

It seems easy to describe this man. His day-to-day life, outward and inward, is exposed to the clear light of day, as it were, in a great mass of his own sayings, and a colossal number of reports concerning him. His interior life . . . was not exempt, for the amazing richness of his literary works—few of which should be described as 'books'—is one great confession of his agitated soul.

However, Luther's unique intellectual and spiritual endowment, the transformation of nature which he underwent, his unrestrained impetus of will and of feeling in love and hate, his tendency to emotion and experience, added to his very early self-consciousness and resultant sense of mission on the largest scale, his revelling in paradoxes allied to a perceptible deficiency in theological and conceptual precision, his sometimes complete massing together of feeling and experience on the occasion of sudden oppressive sorrow or suddenly liberating fresh insight, and finally his utterly amazing eloquence, which became more and more vivid as its assault upon mind and ear climbed relentlessly towards its climax, flooding the reader or hearer with elemental power, all of these things, on the one hand, led Luther of necessity to those exaggerated superlatives which fill his works from beginning to end, and on the other, opened the way to far-reaching vacillations that develop into plain contradiction.

All of these circumstances . . . show how difficult it must be to pick out from Luther's statements, from time to time, the thing that was decisive for him, when seen as a whole.

The older Luther became, the less fitted was his mind—and even less his emotions—to reproduce faithfully what he had experienced and believed in his Catholic days. After long interior preparation his mind rapidly changed, and in his imagination popery became constructed as one great evil. We have to see, to feel, the prophetic impulse through which he identified the essence of Catholicism with the corrupt condition of the Church at the time. Clear or even calm tones are hardly ever heard in all his thousand mentions of the pope's Church. His attitude to the papacy had turned to one-sided hatred. He lived and moved and had his being in this hatred. His judgments proceeded from it; he talked, wrote and acted in terms of it every day. At the beginning of the parliament of Augsburg in 1530 he seemed to show some appreciation, but this did not last.

How could Luther have described his own past but from this point of view? It had been his own papistical period. He, too, had been involved in these things. And so he perpetrated objective falsification through the power of deep conviction.

Having taken full account of these facts, we see how cautious we must be in our evaluation of Luther's retrospective judgments, even the most renowned of all—the preface to the first volume of his collected works of 1545, which contains the magnificent dramatic description of his reformation experience in the tower.

Luther's works are full of such reminiscences—consider for example his literary utterances, the table talk with his close adherents in particular. It is these very reminiscences, animated by seething fury against the papacy and Catholicism in general, and perpetuated by Melanchthon [humanist and chief early Lutheran, 1497–1560] and others of the first generation, that have created the notorious Luther legend, through which Protestants down to very recent times . . . saw the Catholicism of those days.

It was from this first Luther legend that Reformed polemic, as well as the Catholic reaction to it, acquired its churlish tone throughout the centuries; and for the same cause, for 400 years right down to the present day, historical study of the Reformation has been largely unable, on either side, to arrive at accepted conclusions. Here as everywhere, bilateral confessionalism, i.e., a one-sided attitude of antagonism, has proved its fundamental fruitlessness.

*   *   *   *   *

On the other hand, it is not only rigidity of belief—preconceived sympathy for the hero of the Reformation or hatred of the disrupter of Church unity and a condemned arch-heretic—that must bear the blame for the split in the interpretation of Luther. Proof of this is supplied by the variety of interpretation put forward by Protestants, who are not all of one mind in an enthusiastic estimate of Luther, but represent a great wealth of mutually contradictory views of the Reformer.

Luther is an ocean of powers, impulses, perceptions and experiences. His eloquent power of imagery is incomparable, as is his power of pathos. The richness of his utterances is almost entirely the result of *ad hoc* decisions arising out of totally different situations, the utterances of one subjectively inclined and insufficiently controlled by a system. He himself saw and admitted the Vulcanlike quality of his work. He maintained that he was not one of the allegedly great minds, who are able to exhaust the meaning of scripture at one glance, without having toiled, resisted temptation and gained experience, who are in fact nonentities: in contrast to these, he had developed through writing and teaching.

*   *   *   *   *

Fundamentally, Luther worked entirely from experience. Self-confidence, sense of mission, arrogance, peremptoriness, strength of will—all at the level of genius—all compelled the situation of the moment to take on, for him, the character of crisis. Thus the unsurpassable superlatives, which are used as though unique, vary with the object of the different experiences. Exclusive superlatives like 'never', 'nothing', 'all', etc., become for him such a commonplace of polemical propaganda, that they flow from his pen at times completely and obviously misplaced.

People have, none the less, made a valiant effort to see Luther as a systematiser. Luther did not think of himself in that light. He thought that his own books, stimulated by outward events that were governed by absolutely no regular order, formed a rather coarse and disordered chaos. They were, he said in 1545, 'much too wordy, and becoming wordier—nothing but a forest, a chaos of words'; and in 1530 that they were: 'sword, fire and earthquake; stormy and bellicose; the work of a rude forester breaking new ground'. His most systematic work was his book on the non-free will, written in 1525. He never successfully completed his plans (*c.* 1530) for a complete dogmatic treatise on justification.

Even the admirable analyses of Karl Holl have not put a stop to attempts to see Luther as a systematiser. Anyone who wants to do this must first dry him out in a retort; and that is the very thing most vigorously resisted by this full-blooded son of the Thuringian soil. It is true that now we are far more skilled in such cold-blooded operations than men were in the days of Melanchthon, and a far greater richness is left intact. Nevertheless the result is essentially the same —Luther's explosive power and life force are reduced.

If we accept Holl's definition of a systematiser as 'a man who is capable of viewing mighty configurations of ideas as a whole', then indeed we can say without hesitation that Luther was such a man; for his whole strength, which was also his weakness, consisted in his ability to focus all of the many and deep problems of the doctrine of redemption at a single point. . . . We used the term 'viewing'. This is most appropriate in respect of Luther's intellectual and spiritual works. We could express the situation negatively also: in his conceptual thinking, Luther lacked any element of intellectualism. At all events, such a quality did not in the least affect the dominance and intensity of his intuitive and emotional primary experience. Obviously we must not judge what is characteristic and unusual in Luther from those passages in which the new religious sentiment, the very ambiguous, living religious testimony, is still overlaid by the old terminology, those passages, that is, wherein Luther still seems to be speaking the language of [late medieval] nominalist scholasticism, whereas this language is no longer a true vehicle for his thought. The efficacy of Luther's thought lay precisely in its not being pure thought, but belonging most emphatically to the domain of the heart, the feelings, the soul. Whoever doubts the experiential character of Luther's fundamental utterances will never be able to do him justice.

*   *   *   *   *

As a rule, however, one gives the word 'systematiser' a rather wider connotation. We expect a systematiser not only to have a vision of the whole context but also to define every detail clearly, to be able to elaborate the context, to express the interrelation and superordination of the parts, and to resolve whatever tensions there may be. Luther did not do these things; and it was necessary that these capacities should be lacking, for his power could never have existed alongside systematisation. He had to break through all boundaries.

But his words were not spent in a thin flow of idle rhetoric. On the contrary, he possessed, too, a quite unusual power of concentration.

He felt the irresistible need to reduce everything to a few basic doctrines, to a single point. This power and this need he possessed, however, not as a disciplined thinker but as a *doctor hyperbolicus*. He knew
the scholastic distinctions, but had no time for them. His theological
concepts, much as he tried in his early days to define them sharply, are
blatantly ambiguous. They display the manysidedness of new life.

Those who deny these things might care to answer this question:
how else could it have been possible for Luther, using largely the same
words, to link his central experience—which turned the fear of hell
into his gate of paradise—to such different concepts as that of man's
atonement (to Staupitz, 1518), and the justice of God? He was able to
do this because he did not think theologically, but felt and preached in
a religious and prophetic manner.

The intermingling and the ambiguity of his theological concepts is
most apparent when we try to define and distinguish the important
complex of concepts comprising the *iudicium Dei*, the *iustitia Dei*,
iustificatio, timor Dei [God's judgment, God's justice, justification, fear
of God] and *assurance of salvation*. There are passages which demand
and require this. But there are also significant passages where the concepts intermingle. Then everything coalesces: fear of God, anxiety
about election, humility, self-abasement and faith, justice—human and
divine. On this basis alone it became possible for a single word to alter
the whole face of the Bible for him, whether for good (the account of
1545) or for ill (on Ps 77:55; 1513–15).

In great measure German mysticism, with its more spiritual but less
defined terminology, helped Luther to clothe his religious experience
in words. The fact that Luther was so fond of replacing the abstract
formulae of late scholasticism with the wealth of words and images
provided by New Testament preaching, is one explanation of the
mystery of his profoundly Christian effectiveness. But he neglected far
too much to make precise definitions and distinctions. Instead, he
indulged in amplification and emotive utterance.

Luther is the antithesis of correct measure. He represents absence of
measure and formlessness. Just as his monastic controversies, in spite
of all allusive, even fundamental, theological and scholastic concepts,
were indeed in great measure a chaotic emergence of life, drawing from
this their endless fresh power, and thus resisting all external influences,
so this power manifested itself as a tempestuous stream that scarcely
acknowledged any banks. Luther produced formulae that abhorred
measured tones as weakness, that knew no systematic construction,
that were unable to grasp exterior objective values calmly and clearly;

but the effectiveness of these formulae lay precisely in the immoderation of this turbulent stream.

All this was an expression of Luther's nature: subjective, sentimental, eruptive, the spontaneous expression of the spiritual collision taking place at that time.

Not only did Luther love superlatives: he raised them to the level of paradox. He loved the paradox—more than this, it was the life's blood of his theology. There is nothing astonishing about this statement: it touches the foundation of Luther's disposition. His love of paradox is not an overflow from an accidental mood, not even simply his basic mental and spiritual attitude. It is part and parcel of the core of his theology, of his *theologia crucis*, i.e., of a theology in which contradiction itself appears as the very sign of truth. The accursed criminal on the gallows, forsaken by God, is the Son of God.

In understanding Luther it is of prime importance that we make this quite clear, and do not block the way of access to the underlying depths by a too hasty refutation. The contradiction of paradox became Luther's form of creative expression. He took full advantage of this, for in the paradox lay inexhaustible depths of dark creativity; it provided a multitude of lines of thought and justified them all. But he had to carry the burden of the paradox as well: oppressive inner contradiction on the one hand, as well as the watering down and the coarsening of his ideas by mutually opposed followers and imitators, some of whom ended up by destroying what was best in the substance of his thought. Out of the fulness of Luther later ages have separated out a series of decisive or practical formulae in terms of which they have represented his ideas and doctrines of faith in schoolmasterly fashion, with more or less feeling and enthusiasm for this great man of God; and in this way they have made their own lives fruitful. Formally, the same process has been at work in Catholic theology, especially since the Reformation, during which period, with the help of defensive and rational propositional scholasticism, catechesis and edifying literature have transformed the fulness of religious prophetic preaching into a dry intellectual presentation of concepts. One of the judgments, if not the chief judgment, this makes possible, allowing us to go beyond customary superficial comment, is that his religious and theological ideas contain contradiction—consciously, deliberately and in logical consequence of his basic attitude. With Luther the Catholic synthesis of the organic *complexio oppositorum* was supplanted by a harsh contradiction, in the sense of sheer impossibility. Its richness is not the fruitful unity in tension of Yes and Yes, but the oppressive juxtaposition and intermingling of Yes and No. Sinner—just man: both are real and remain simultaneously within a single soul and persist emphatically right to the bitter end. This juxtaposition is not achieved, however, through a higher synthesis or through irenic harmonisation but through a stubborn 'at the same time'. The interior contradiction holds no terror for Luther. Indeed, the divine mysteries of the cross are necessarily a stumbling-block to human reason. Their truth is illumined by their impossibility. Luther comes very close to the *credo quia absurdum* [I believe because it is absurd]. In his doctrine of election and in the presentation of his redemptive faith he revels in this very kind of contradiction. A thing is absolute certainty, because it is faith. But the certainty of election consists in the sinner's uncertainty whether—intrinsically a sinner now and always—he can give up sin, that is avoid being forced into destruction, and be one of the elect.

'In the Epistle to the Romans St Paul wishes to destroy all the wisdom and righteousness of the earthly man, and, in place of it, to stress and exalt sin. How such contradictions will work out, and with what reason they are entitled to exist, we will see in the life to come. But here we must insist that this is just—for faith is addressed to the incomprehensible' (*Lecture on Romans*, 1515–16).

The model, the foundation and justification of these tense paradoxes, lies in the God-man, Jesus Christ, and in his life; and Christians in their turn are true copies of him. His very first lectures on the psalms illustrated the fundamental law of paradox: 'Hence Christ is at once accursed and blessed, at once living and dead, at once suffering and triumphant, so that in him all evil may be consumed and through him all good be offered.'

*   *   *   *   *

THE BEGINNINGS OF LUTHERANISM

The year 1517 saw the Turks conquer Egypt, and the end of the fifth Lateran Council. This council was thoroughly papal, but it heard loud complaints against the evil state of the Church in head and members. At the council on 23 May took place the great creation of cardinals which was to give the Church the particular composition with which it was to face the Reformation. Election was governed by personal, family, economic and political motives. The scene was dominated by the Renaissance princes of the Church. Beside them stood a few influential representatives of the coming Catholic reform: Adrian of Utrecht—

Charles V's tutor—the great Dominican theologian, Cajetan, and Campeggio the diplomat. In that year Cochlaeus, who after Eck was to be the most powerful Catholic theological protagonist in the German Church's defensive war against Luther, was ordained priest in Rome, and began to write. Cardinal Ximenes, reformer of Church and state, who prepared the way for the coming Catholicism of the Counter Reformation in Spain, died. His sovereign, Charles I of Spain, unambiguously registered his application to his grandfather Maximilian for the office of holy Roman emperor. Hutten published Lorenzo Valla's proof that the Donation of Constantine—one of the foundations of medieval papal power—was a forgery. Part two of the *Letters of Obscure Men* appeared, heightening national feeling and greatly intensifying the urge to revolution. In Mainz the *Reichstag* echoed with complaints against abuses in Church and state, and revealed anxiety at the rise of the common people and the knights. The duke of Gueldres openly waged a war of pillage throughout the whole of Holland. In Louvain Erasmus was enjoying the height of his fame. In 1516 he had produced his edition of the Greek New Testament. 'People are in expectation of something great, and all eyes are being turned more and more towards Erasmus: he will be the man' (Huizinga). In that year Hans Sachs proclaimed a new era; and in a letter to Leo X Erasmus announced the dawn of the golden age.

But it was left to Luther to uncover the true face of the age. In March of that year he had completed his commentary on Galatians. In September in a disputation he launched a strong attack upon scholasticism. Then on 30 October the lightning struck; at the age of thirty-four Martin Luther, already the undisputed leader of the new university of Wittenberg, published there his ninety-five theses on the efficacy of indulgences.

In 1505 Pope Julius II (d. 1513) had begun the rebuilding of St Peter's in Rome, under the direction of Bramantes. In the Middle Ages it had been common practice to finance public works, especially the building of churches, by the issuing of indulgences. Following this custom, Pope Julius II proclaimed a jubilee indulgence in 1507, to raise funds for this new project. The indulgence was renewed by his successor Leo X. To gain this indulgence the usual conditions had to be fulfilled: the performance of some good work, in this case, as often, the giving of alms. In addition, the preachers of the indulgence were given special powers in administering the sacrament of penance. By these powers they were able to absolve in confession those who sought a certificate of absolution from sins normally reserved to the pope. This relieved them of the necessity of travelling to Rome. It was necessary also to pay a prescribed sum of money which was adjusted to the economic and social status of the penitent. It was taken for granted that absolution from these, as from any sins, required genuine repentance also; and indeed, this condition was explicitly demanded in every certificate of indulgence.

A just verdict upon the whole indulgence controversy of 1517, and hence an intelligent interpretation of the existent problems, depends upon an intelligent distinction between theory and practice, or better, between pure theology, on the one hand, and the popular practice of the Church, on the other. We include in the Church's practice, however, that debased form of theology which prevailed in the formulae and in the whole style of the curial and episcopal chancelleries, and in the majority of pulpits.

All through the later Middle Ages the antithesis of these two factors developed until, on the eve of the Reformation, it had become a basic feature of the whole theological situation. The correct theological theoretical exposition of the distinction between mortal and venial sins was less important than the casuistic and juridical discussion of questions about man's dues in the sight of God. Men were more interested to know how far they could go in a particular case without falling into sin, or what they had to do to be rid of some sin, or to help the holy souls, or to avoid the pains of purgatory themselves. The central thought of the worthless servant, still alive obviously in theological circles—although misinterpreted by Occamism—the servant who was still worthless even after he had performed all his duties, was utterly suppressed, for practice was too strongly guided by those other categories which have been mentioned.

Nor can we speak about indulgences if we do not know what they are. Many have forgotten this simple fact. If we are to take up complaint against the abuses of the system of indulgences, we must know where the substance ends and the accretions begin. A good example had already been set by vigorous contemporary opponents of these abuses—Wimpfeling, Archbishop Fisher of Rochester, Cochlaeus, Ulrich Kraft (professor of law then parish priest in Ulm 1501–16), the Dominican, Peter of Luxemburg who preached: 'He who would gain an indulgence must be in a state of faith and of love'.

An indulgence is the remission of the temporal punishment due to sin, never of the guilt of sin itself. This remission is worked out either on earth or in purgatory. It depends upon the idea of vicarious satisfaction. One of its essential presuppositions is, therefore, that of the Church as the mystical body of the Lord with Christ as head, of the communion of saints.

The application of indulgences to the faithful departed presented special problems, and, according to the common theological view at the beginning of the sixteenth century, was effected only by way of intercession, not by an act of papal jurisdiction. Very few theologians (e.g., two very different men, Eck and the Dominican John Faber) supported the view that there could be an unconditionally certain application. The view found its supporters rather amongst those who held the more rough and ready practical theory of the chancelleries, and amongst the preachers of indulgences. We should note, however, that even this theory cannot be summarily rejected out of hand.

According to the view held in those days, that which was able to bring aid to the souls in purgatory was nothing other than the condition laid down for every indulgence, that is the performance of some good deed, in the end some kind of sacrifice or prayer performed by one member of the mystical body, and which, according to St Paul, is able to benefit other members. An obvious presupposition is that the mystical body, the Church, is the appointed organ whereby the Lord himself exercises his care. That is to say, the Church, within the framework of its priestly power of the keys, is able to apply the abundant merits of Christ and his saints. In the last analysis the sale of certificates of indulgence (not of absolution) was such a sacrifice. In itself this sale was by no means 'the extreme of materialisation, for the departed has no share in the process through some form of contrition or sacrifice'. The article in the apostles' creed about the communion of saints completely contradicts such materialism. To be logical, objections like that just quoted would have to attack this article itself.

The case of the sale of certificates of absolution is simpler. Because such a thing obviously does not in any way make easier or replace unavoidable repentance, it is nothing but the granting of a privilege by the pope or his representative, for which one must pay a tax.

In reality neither indulgences nor even less, remission of sins, were being sold by the Church.

In itself the performance of some material action in return for spiritual grace was perfectly legitimate. It is true that this was a departure from early Christian practice and ideas. But it was no Roman invention. It was in line, rather, with a Celtic and Teutonic attitude, as is demonstrated by the evolution of western medieval penitential discipline. It represented a coarsening of Christian ideals, but not their denial. The danger of denial first emerged when indulgences began to threaten real moral and Christian earnestness.

This came about. There were two principal causes. First: the mitigation of strict ancient Christian penitential practice through indulgences led, like every mitigation, to the demand for ever greater privileges. The curia gave in to these demands; and thus arose the second cause: indulgences moved from the sphere of the simple performance of some monetary sacrifice, and led to a fatal development of curial fiscalism, to unchristian secularisation. Both of these elements in turn were closely linked with specifically late medieval piety, to the extent that this was connected with pilgrimages and relics. The immoderate multiplication of indulgences and the fiscal function they were made to serve, allied with the dangerous externalisation of late medieval piety, largely emptied the profound idea behind indulgences of all religious content, in many cases turning it into something quite unchristian.

For the present a single indication of what is meant will suffice. A result of the colossal spread of indulgences was that the notion of punishment to be paid by penance completely dominated the Christian mind at that time. No matter how legitimately this notion can be integrated in theology, the centre of gravity was in fact pushed well out on to the periphera. The more correct theological stress on repentance and love, set forth in the edifying literature of the times, was severely suppressed. Life and theory went two different ways.

Danger became reality when correct, reticent theology was ousted in practice by the rough and ready theory of the chancelleries and the indulgence preachers. At the close of the Middle Ages the extravagances of indulgences merge with excessive curialism, one-sidedly aimed at temporal power.

These abuses had indeed reached dangerous proportions. It is true that the theory of indulgences has always remained correct. The tendencies mentioned provide no justification at all for the assertion that Catholic theology in those days developed some sort of extra sacrament of indulgence. Any such seriously meant assertion rests upon utter confusion.

At no time did the Church ever promise remission without contrition or repentance. During the schism of the west there were dissolute deceivers who did promise such a thing. They did this in the same way as they forged papal bulls and sold them—as swindlers. They did it in crass defiance of all the Church's teaching. And it is illuminating to see that such swindling was possible within the milieu of the unscrupulous fiscalism of Boniface IX [1389–1404] and his like. Anything beyond that, however, by way of earlier rumour or recent statement rests upon ignorance or distortion such as may be found in low works like the *Pfaffenspiegel* and other anti-Christian manuals of freemasons and communists. In spite of his petty scholastic style, the painstakingly exact proofs of Nicholas Paulus are absolutely correct. This applies also to the arguments put forward from the Catholic side in the indulgence controversy of 1517.

This, however, is far from concluding the verdict. Now we are only beginning to form a true evaluation. The question turns not upon the correct interpretation of the words, viewed abstractly, but upon the interpretation actually put upon those words, and upon the direction in which they developed with dialectical necessity. Even the theories of Tetzel [indulgence-seller and principal target of the 95 theses] can be proved correct; but the practice he represented and which the Church approved had become largely unchristian. It is impossible to prove that his extreme view, that an indulgence can be applied with certainty to a particular soul, in every case contradicts Christian doctrine, and so is essentially false. But if it is suggested that this application is possible by a sinner having no repentance, that someone in a state of enmity with God, merely by paying the money, can interfere in the secret judgments of the divine majesty, this is the reversal of all that is Christian; and anyone with the least Christian sensitivity is at once aware of danger. The minimising of repentance, which blatantly appeared in the gaining of an indulgence on behalf of a departed soul, gave its stamp to the rest of the practice of the professional indulgence pedlars, no matter how correct the theory underlying that practice. The goal of those who commissioned such preachers was business. To gain their ends they offered to the public—in perfectly good faith—a gloriously easier way to assurance of salvation.

The ambiguous terminology in use for indulgence material was well suited to such purposes. This had evolved in association with the tendency to ever more abundant granting of indulgences and its fiscal exploitation since the time of Boniface IX. The deliberate reticence of Cardinal Nicholas of Cusa over the preaching of the jubilee indulgence of 1450 made little impression. The desired unctuous exaggeration of the advertised indulgence graces won the day. Complete remission of all punishment and guilt was perfectly in order, for repentance and confession were presupposed. But it was so easy for it to seem that the remission of sins was included in the gaining of the indulgence, especially if the preaching of indulgences laid stress upon the sale of the indulgence rather than upon the need for penitence. When the jubilee indulgence was preached as 'the greatest grace and reconciliation of the human race with God', the result depended entirely upon whether or not the preaching and the hearing was done in a spirit of Christian penitence. The people in those days were as little educated theologically as they are today, and as little accustomed to logical hairsplitting. They saw things in broad outline, and the danger of coarsening of ideas was very real. As can be shown, in Germany at the beginning of the sixteenth century there existed a perfectly correct exposition of the doctrine of indulgences, appreciated by a few educated people; but this was no match for the more magnificent and noisy competition of the preaching of indulgences to the accompaniment of bell-ringing, solemn processions, erection of crosses, papal bulls and innumerable extravagant sermons.

The full disintegrating power of the abuse of indulgences was revealed in that affair which became the occasion of Luther's first public appearance.

In 1513 the twenty-three-year-old Albrecht of Brandenburg, youngest brother of the prince elector Joachim, was elected archbishop of the important diocese of Magdeburg by the cathedral chapter. (Albrecht's predecessor had been a Saxon, who also occupied the see of Mainz.) It was an old tradition that the same young man be installed as administrator of the collegiate church in Halberstadt. Finally, in 1514, Albrecht was elected by the cathedral chapter of Mainz to be archbishop of this diocese also, and prince elector. He had undertaken to support the collegiate prebend at his own expense. . . . Mainz was in need of cutting down its expenditure. Within the space of ten years the archepiscopal see had thrice fallen vacant, and each time the confirmation dues to Rome for the see and the pallium had amounted to 14,000 ducats.

Now Albrecht had to apply to the pope not only for confirmation of his election to Mainz but also for permission to occupy this see while retaining that of Magdeburg and the administration of Haberstadt. Such an accumulation of benefices was unheard of, in Germany at least, and was in fact forbidden by canon law. But Leo X was not going to be hindered too much by canon law when political and financial advantage was at stake. With his decisive connivance the ambassadors from Brandenburg were granted confirmation on payment of an additional 10,000 ducats. Moreover it was the curia who made this proposal acceptable to the ambassadors, for they suggested a method by which Albrecht might raise all or part of the sum to be paid. They would

make over to the archbishop of Mainz the sale of the St Peter's indulgence in the archdiocese of Mainz and in the Brandenburg territories, allowing him a half share in the proceeds. The contract was
perfect; a deal was made with the Fuggers who, in return for a share
in the income from the indulgence, advanced the archbishop 29,000
Rhenish guilders—and the whole shameful business was complete.

That this let loose the Reformation storm is highly symbolic and an
expression of historical retribution, for all the corruption in the Church
of that time had its chief cause in the fiscalism of the curia, which was
rotten with simony. In the case just mentioned, the curia, contrary to
canon law, in return for cash, and in the hope of gaining political
advantage, were allowing a young, worldly man to hold an irresponsible accumulation of benefices. In so doing they turned indulgences
into a means of exchange in big business. The executive organ of this
business carried on between the custodian of the merits won by
Christ's blood and a worldly prince of the Church was a bank. Corruption could scarcely have been more blatantly expressed. We are struck
with amazement to discover that Catholic theologians are still so hide-
bound by formalism that they can discuss whether or not this affair
was simony according to the strict letter of canon law. Even to raise
such a question is to create religious confusion. Anyone can see that
the whole affair is utterly at war with the Spirit of Christ.

As a result of various delays, it turned out that the preaching of the
indulgence, taken over by the prince elector of Mainz, did not start
until the beginning of 1517. For the most part the monetary yield was
little enough.

The indulgence preachers of the elector of Mainz based their sermons upon his *instructio summaria*.

This short guide provides an exact illustration of what has just been
said about the abuses of the indulgence system. Its theory can be
justified; but the tendency has to be sharply rejected, for, by the use of
pious formulae, it was rapidly turning the indulgence sermon into
sheer commercial advertising. Money, which was of secondary importance, became the central thing; the atmosphere of the sale-room
prevailed everywhere; there were pompous and solemn openings, and
then bargain clearances at the end.

The Dominican, Tetzel, subcommissar general of the archbishop of
Mainz, faithfully followed out the spirit of this instruction. There is
no doubt that he taught:

> As soon as your money clinks in the bowl
> Out of purgatory jumps the soul.

Admittedly it is also certain that he never claimed that an indulgence could expiate future sins. This calumny was first set going by Luther in his pamphlet *Against Hans Worst* in 1541.

Tetzel was very well paid; but he cannot be charged with any serious misdemeanours. He was not one of those indulgence preachers of whom Eck complained that they paid their mistresses with certificates of indulgence and confession. But he was one of those, pilloried by Emser, for whom repentance and contrition had become eclipsed by money. In fact, for the sake of financial gain he stressed in a dangerous way the mitigation of the demands of the gospel of redemption.

In 1516 Aleander [humanist and papal representative] gave the warning that many people in Germany were merely waiting for the right man to show them how to defy Rome. Obviously when Luther heard of the traffic in indulgences he would be goaded to the limit.

When preaching in Jüterborg, Tetzel was inundated with people from the neighbouring town of Wittenberg in the electorate of Saxony where, because of political and fiscal enmity with Brandenburg, the indulgence was not permitted to be preached. Luther came up against the matter in the confessional. He got to know about the *instructio summaria*. What a contrast he saw to the terrible struggle against sin and hell, which he had endured in the monastery, when he summoned all his strength to escape from the wrath of God. Tetzel lived in a world where a simple monetary transaction could buy 'unheard of and abundant graces'. We must carefully reflect on the tension between these two worlds before we are able correctly to assess the part played in Luther's development by opposition to the preaching of indulgences —an opposition not so important in itself.

It is impossible to understand the true nature of Luther's battles, of his theses and his answers in the period between 1516 and 1519, unless we are thoroughly conversant with the mighty formative process which Luther had passed through in the preceding decade. In method and substance Luther had moved far away from the establishment. However we assess him, he had constructed a new world. He had discovered this world in the greatest possible isolation from the disturbing and interfering public. In 1517, when he encountered indulgences, that is a scholastic theory expounded and actualised in an explicitly curialist and secular form, he was meeting a completely strange world. He had opposed it in theory, but he had never known its authentic existence. His theses on indulgences and the appended refutation by Eck are proof of this: 'this is Aristotelian science, not theology'.

Luther's reaction was to produce his well-known ninety-five theses in Latin 'on the power of indulgences'. Following the custom of the age, he fixed these to the door of the castle chapel, and challenged the scholars to a disputation. Without any dramatic design on Luther's part this took place on 31 October, the vigil of the patronal feast of the collegiate church of All Saints in Wittenberg, in which the prince elector kept his famous collection of relics, to which an indulgence of a million years was attached. Luther's aim was not to reach the common people, otherwise he would have written his theses in German. At the same time his aim was not simply to pose prudent questions. When producing these theses Luther was animated even more strongly by the conscious mood in which he had addressed his disputation theses against scholasticism in September of the same year. 'I do not want anyone to think that I want to whisper these things in a corner, even if they do despise our university'. The most we can say is that here and there they were perhaps deliberately exaggerated and to that extent 'somewhat obscure and enigmatic, as is the custom'. For this reason Luther tried later, in a letter, to keep himself in good standing with the pope.

For Luther, however, superlatives and exaggeration were not exceptions but his normal mode of thought and speech. It is true that he was still unwilling to condemn indulgences out of hand (thesis 71). In 1518 (sermon on *Indulgence and Grace*) he allows some justification to indulgences: '. . . therefore we ought not to object to indulgences, nor yet ought we to recommend them to anyone'. None the less the theses were a real attack; and not just upon the abuses of indulgence preaching. The attack was already levelled at the heart of the power which offered the indulgence.

In his last autobiographical sketch of 1545 Luther did not want to admit this; but he contradicts himself. His reminiscence allows no reality to the earlier reservations in the theses; he gives the impression simply that he had trampled on indulgences. On 1 November 1527 he celebrated the jubilee with 'a really special drink'. If, as he maintained in 1545, his only concern had been to uphold the true opinion of the pope on indulgences against the hucksters, he would hardly have been able to let loose such a diatribe against the wealth of the pope, nor ask why the pope did not simply empty purgatory on the spot. Without realising it, Luther admits this himself in his reminiscence. He asserts that until the Leipzig disputation of 1519 he had been guided by the authority of the pope. At the same time he says that even at that time (1517–19) he no longer acknowledged the divine right of the pope.

Dr John Eck, the theologian from Ingolstadt, who entered the arena as soon as Luther made his public appearance, was perfectly correct in seeing the attack upon the papacy as the quintessence of the indulgence theses. Although the fear of economic damage to the curia might be the first sign of sensitivity to Luther's enmity, his attack was clearly directed against the essential structure of the visible Church, especially against the pope (theses 25 and 27). From various angles a one-sided tendency towards the general priesthood was adumbrated (theses 37 and 90).

Once again the mainspring of criticism was the overstressed separation of the divine from the allegedly purely human, a separation which we must take as Luther's central conception, and which . . . shall prove to be decisive for the whole process of the Reformation. In this case it appears principally as the abrupt exclusion of the power of the keys from the other-worldly sphere (theses 5, 6, 8, 20, 21, 22, 34, 38). The papal canon is applicable only to the living, and does not reach beyond the grave. It is not the pope but God, who remits sin. The pope simply declares that God has remitted it (theses 10, 11, 13).

When Luther complains (theses 81 ff.) that the indulgence pedlars make it very difficult for a competent theologian to defend the authority of the pope against the telling objections of the laity, his arguments do not thereby become any less damaging. Luther's eager desire for attack is all too evident. All too gladly does he appeal to the disaffection of the laity. He smells out the possibilities lurking in this situation. If these rambling objections of the laity were to be suppressed by force and not resolved in a reasonable way, then such action would give the Church and the pope over as a prey to ridicule (thesis 90). The voice of absolute authority had had its day; the laity were on the verge of revolution: Luther became their prophet.

In reality the theses, at the deepest level, were aimed at the people. Luther states this forcibly and unambiguously in his letter to Albrecht of Mainz in December 1517. His aim, he says, is pastoral. He is affected 'not so much by the shouting of the indulgence preachers— which I have not heard—as by the false notion which the simple, poor, coarse people create out of it. They believe that having bought a certificate of indulgence their eternal bliss is assured. . . . But no man can be assured of his salvation by the action of any bishop, for he is not assured thereof even by the infused grace of God. The apostle demands that we work out our salvation in fear and trembling. . . . Why then are the people being relieved of fear and given assurance by these false fables and promises of forgiveness? . . . For it is asserted that by the grace of indulgence men are being reconciled to God'.

That is to say: the theses on indulgences are an expression of
Luther's theory of the uncertainty of salvation, of his theology of the
cross (theses 1, 63, 64, 68). This is most clearly expressed in the great
prelude to the theses: 'When our Lord Jesus Christ said "Do penance",
he wanted us to make our whole life a penance. And so the Christian
life is not peace, peace, but the cross and yet again the cross. It is a
walking with Christ through suffering, death and hell. Thus the
Christian puts his trust more in reaching heaven through many trials
than through easy security' (theses 1, and 92–5). It is the 'wholesome
pain which it is more just for man to choose than reject' (sermon on
the indulgences, 1518). Comfort is death, hardship salvation (theses
63 f.). Comfort and ease are embodied in the indiscriminately dispensed and highly over-rated indulgences. By these the majority of the
people are deceived. They learn 'to fear punishment rather than sin'.

To sum up: the dangerous accessory which had been blown up into
the essential thing was peevishly rejected in its lesser significance, and
instead, true penitence, love, God's word and God's grace were placed
at the centre (theses 53, 55, 62).

. . . Luther's theological development towards the Reformation
revolution was decisively advanced by a fundamentally non-Catholic
Occamism [a doctrine of divine transcendence and the separation
rather than the integration of the realms of man and God], which had
taken root within the Church. Now we discover that the foundation
too of the public Reformer was decisively occasioned by a non-Catholic
realisation of Catholic principles, by the fiscalised practice of indulgence. Both stimuli had a continuous effect upon him. The resultant
was his unhappy confusion of extreme scholastic views and false practices in the Church with the Church itself and its genuine doctrine.
And this confusion decisively influenced Luther's entire life's work.

All that we have so far heard about the indulgence theses might well
have remained within the realm of theology and its controversies. It
only became epoch making because Luther went beyond theological
circles, and raised an echo throughout the nation. That is to say: the
world-historical situation, especially in Germany, was such that the cry
of this monk harmonised with what part of the nation were consciously
expecting, and the bulk of the nation were sullenly and inarticulately
expecting. They expected that this call would set off a cataclysmic,
European, popular movement, especially in Germany, a movement that
would press on towards the light. In short, they expected the interests
of this monk, through the spiritual sensitivity and power that mark a

great historical movement, without more ado to become the interest of great sections of the people. The nation's response turned Luther into a Reformer.

In an almost enigmatic way the theses raged through Germany. How much more comprehensive was the external form of the excitement, how much more directly did interest touch existence, than did the heavy-going controversies of Erasmus with the theologians and the whole allegedly antiquated system of piety! Even Luther himself seems to have felt some displeasure at the unexpected commotion. Was he being led into some evil temptation? Humility struggled with a sense of mission: 'If you want to start something up with me, then do it yourself, and preserve me from letting my own wisdom take over.'

It was not the fault of theology and of dogma if to some extent the nation replied in an elementary way to this theological document. This was caused, rather by the oppression laid upon Germany by the intensification of 'papal power in secular affairs', and by curial fiscalism. Without the *Gravamina of the German nation* the nation would not have answered that first call of Luther's, Luther would not have become a reformer, and the Reformation itself would not have happened.

Suggestions for Further Reading

BOEHMER, HEINRICH, *The Road to Reformation*. Philadelphia: Muhlenberg Press, 1946.

DICKENS, A. G., *The English Reformation*. New York: Schocken Books, 1964.

DICKENS, A. G., *Reformation and Society in Sixteenth Century Europe*. London: Thames and Hudson, 1966.

ELTON, G. R., *Reformation Europe 1517–1559*. London: Collins, 1963.

ERIKSON, ERIC, *Young Man Luther*. New York: W. W. Norton and Company, Inc., 1958.

FEBVRE, LUCIEN, *Martin Luther: A Destiny*. New York: E. P. Dutton & Co., 1929.

GRIMM, H. J., *The Reformation Era*, 2nd ed. New York: Macmillan, 1965.

HARBISON, E. H., *The Age of Reformation*. Ithaca, N.Y.: Cornell University Press, 1955.

JEDIN, HUBERT, *A History of the Council of Trent*, 2 vols. St. Louis: B. Herder Book Co., 1957–61.

WILLIAMS, GEORGE H., *The Radical Reformation*. Philadelphia: Westminster Press, 1962.

SIR GEORGE CLARK

Faith and Politics in the Wars of Religion

‿§¿‿ From the mid-sixteenth to the mid-seventeenth
century, Europe was consumed by a series of wars between
the great powers, fought for mastery, wealth, and power but
greatly affected—in their intensity, in the alliance of contending camps, and sometimes in cause and inspiration—by
religious commitment. This was the plan of no one man or
group of men; no one wanted this wealthy, expanding,
highly cultured society to waste so much of its human and
material resources in seemingly endless conflicts exacerbated by and sometimes dedicated to hair-splitting differences between Catholic and Protestant doctrine. But though
unplanned it happened, and it is a sorry spectacle, and a
salutary lesson to us.

Here was a society whose finest minds had preached
peace, justice, and freedom; and whose political leaders
worked at violence, pillage, and oppression. And the finest
minds became distraught by the violence, frightened by
tyranny, corrupted by the demands and rewards of power,
and joined in the fray. The enlightened message of the early
sixteenth-century humanists gave way to the fanaticism and
hatred of the partisans of the Wars of Religion, advocating
the enslavement, persecution, and destruction of sectarian
and national enemies. How lucky we are that the terror of
nuclear weaponry has restrained us from turning the ideo-

FROM Sir George Clark, *Early Modern Europe from
about 1450 to about 1720* (New York: Oxford University Press,
Galaxy Books, 1960), pp. 70–72, 80–88, 121–152.

logical and political animosities of the cold-war era into another devastating anti-human War of Religion.

Those who wish to consider the unthinkable and contemplate the risks of nuclear war in the interests of American versus Soviet power, or liberal versus communist varieties of democracy should ponder the descent of Europe, from 1550 to 1650, into the maelstrom of hatred and despair. Only the underdeveloped character of their weaponry saved the Europeans then from complete self-destruction. Only the limitations of their technology precluded a terrible and total retribution upon king and lord, upon Catholic priest and Protestant minister, for their unpardonable and almost incredible follies.

The major reason for studying the faith and politics of this fatal age can be found in Lord Acton's dictum: Never, in historical thinking, debase the moral currency. We must look upon the moral sordidness of the era and draw what lessons we can from it. There are other, secondary reasons for studying this era: it was the time of European statebuilding and the development of many of the characteristic stratagems, mechanisms, and assumptions of international relations. (It may indeed be asked whether this persiflage of international diplomacy is still of any positive value to us.) It was the era when the religious divisions of Europe were firmed up, frequently for causes that had nothing to do with popular confessional commitment. Bohemia, for example, was Protestant long before Luther but, in consequence of Habsburg armies and Jesuit inquisitors, ended up within the Catholic camp.

To provide a clear and succinct view of political and ecclesiastical history during the sixteenth and seventeenth centuries is a formidable task. The following discussion by Sir George Clark, one of Britain's most distinguished historians of this century, is a remarkable achievement. Clark himself is obviously a liberal, rationalistic humanist. He apparently finds much of what he describes absurd, outrageous, distasteful. Yet he unquestionably believes in the validity and value of the national state, and probably only a historian who retains this attitude, derived from nineteenth-century liberalism, could bring himself to attempt the overview that Clark here achieves.

Four years after the beginning of his first controversy, Luther had
become the leader of a movement in which one of the motive forces
was German national feeling. He had been driven step by step to take
up the position which has ever since been the Protestant position. Since
Luther was almost as difficult to deal with, either in practical affairs or
in intellectual argument, as anyone who ever lived, this does not mean
that any notable body of people ever exactly accepted any one of his
varying formulations of his doctrines; but millions have followed him
in fervently believing many things, especially that a man can be justified to God by faith but not by works; that all believers are priests,
and so that the laity should receive the communion in both kinds; that
priests should be allowed to marry; that private masses should be done
away with; that the pope is Antichrist. These views he spread broad-
cast in pamphlets written with a mastery of German idiom which had
never been equalled; and from his writings and the legends of his sayings his followers formed not only their creed but also their image of
their leader—of his joviality, his love of music, his courage, his coarseness, his deep earnestness. He was condemned as a heretic, but he
burnt the papal bulls. He was outlawed by the diet, but his elector,
though he never became a Lutheran, hid and protected him. In his
hiding-place he began to translate the Bible into German, and the prose
of this translation set the standard by which German became a single
literary language.

It was not only in language that Luther left legacies to all Germany;
but his religious revolt at once led to conflict and disruption in social
and political life. No sooner was he at the head of a movement than it
became the reason or the pretext for disorders. A turbulent knight, who
had a private war against one of the prince-bishops, took to theological
controversy and gathered about him both armed bandits and venomous
pamphleteers. The peasants of south-west Germany rose against their
masters, burning and destroying. Luther fulminated against them, calling on the authorities to slay; but his own defiance had done something
to liberate theirs. He had shaken some of the beliefs on which the social
order rested. For him marriage was no longer a sacrament. That might
mean much or it might mean little in practice. Luther himself condoned
the bigamy of one Protestant prince. In western Germany there were
fanatical extremists who did not stop short of holding their wives as
well as their property in common. They seized the episcopal city of
Munster and held it as a communist republic for sixteen months,

until the stern punishment of the authorities overtook them. Meanwhile one prince after another was declaring himself a convert to the new opinions, seizing church property and demolishing ecclesiastical jurisdiction.

*   *   *   *   *

It was a necessary consequence of the old unity of western civilization that, from its beginning, Lutheranism attracted adherents outside Germany. National churches, more or less on the Lutheran model, were established in Sweden and Denmark. In other countries there were Lutherans, but they were only one sect among others, for the Lutheran crisis had revealed and released a number of divergent types of anti-Roman belief. Among these the most important, if only because it alone became the official religion of sizeable states, was Calvinism. John Calvin was almost as different from Luther in disposition and upbringing as it was possible for a highly educated man to be. He was a Frenchman, a classical scholar, trained to the law. He organized the Church in the little city-state of Geneva as a model of what the Church in his view should be; it exercised undisputed power over the civil government of that republic, and it was widely imitated abroad. The great instrument of Calvin's power was his book *Institutio Christianae Religionis* (Instruction in the Christian Religion), which he published in 1539. There was nothing fundamentally new in this book. Protestantism was already formed before Calvin wrote. His work was to define and systematize where there was so much confusion, and to work out a plan for church government and for the Church's place in the world. His method was intellectual; he used argument and invective, writing excellent Latin with a classical simplicity, dropping all the jargon and formalities of the schoolmen. There is nothing occasional or ephemeral in his book, and nothing mean or scurrilous. He relied on the Scriptures, which, he held, are known by faith, and not by argument, to be the word of God. Thus the printing-press made possible a new authoritarianism, and, except in a polemic against the bold heretics who had already challenged the doctrine of the Trinity, Calvin scarcely applied his critical powers to the Bible. To the history of Christianity he applied it to some purpose. He held that the test of the true Church was not continuity through tradition handed on by persons, but purity of doctrine. In the 'medium saeculum' [middle age] of Pope Leo I, of Gregory the Great, and St. Bernard, that is from the fifth century to the twelfth, he saw a corrupted faith, and so, from a new point of view, he strengthened the tendency to regard the Middle Ages as a

period of darkness. His view of the relations between the religion of
Jesus Christ and apostolic Christianity and the Christianity of the
early Fathers, his account of creeds and dogmas, his judgements on
papal claims and Roman practices, were all worked out by acute historical criticism; but in another field his doctrine was anti-historical, for
he held that doctrine as contained in the Scriptures was fixed and final,
overriding all previous knowledge and all knowledge from other
sources. He had no patience with idle curiosity, nor much with scientific
curiosity. He did indeed admit that scientific knowledge must be re-
spected, as when he wrote that, although God gave the rainbow to Noah
for a sign, there were rainbows before Noah, since the rainbow is only
a reflection of the solar rays on the opposite clouds. But such exceptions
did not trouble his conviction that he was teaching religious certainties.
He condemned what the Lutherans condemned. In intellectual matters
he simplified and straightened out what they had put forward tentatively and obscurely. The central belief of his followers was predestina-
tion, the idea that each man was predestined to salvation or to eternal
punishment. If this belief narrowed their sympathies, it also fortified
their will. They submitted to a severe system of discipline. Calvin's
programme for church government gave them a fighting organization
in which the ministers, who were not priests but primarily teachers of
the Word, were supported by assemblies of believing laymen.

The tendency to define, and to fight for the principles once defined,
appeared on the Catholic side almost simultaneously with its appearance
in Calvinism. In the days of the German negotiations and expedients
about Lutheranism, there were ambiguities and uncertainties in some of
the Catholic doctrines that Luther impugned. There were openings for
concessions from the Catholic side which did not certainly involve a
departure from the orthodox tradition. In Austria the cup was offered
to the laity with papal approval; perhaps priests might marry; at any
rate the papacy might agree to the demands of the German princes and
burghers, which the emperor supported, for a council to discuss the
whole matter of reform. Reform indeed had . . . begun in Germany
before the revolution, and in the fifteen-twenties it began in Italy. There
too religious orders were reformed; new orders were founded, and also
new charitable institutions. Influential ecclesiastics worked for religious
renewal in a spirit of enlightenment if not of compromise. Appropri-
ately enough the spirit of militant and uncompromisingly orthodox
reform came from Spain.

Among Calvin's contemporaries at the university of Paris was a dis-
abled Spanish officer, Ignatius Loyola, who had been born a gentleman

of one of the Basque provinces adjoining France on the Bay of Biscay. After his wound he had gone through an experience of religious conversion, and now he brought the disciplined zeal of the Spanish army to the aid of the Church in its danger. At the age of thirty-seven or thereabouts he sat among the boys and youths of the Paris lecture-rooms, taking a course in theology. He made the pilgrimage to Jerusalem. He had visions, but they were not of the kind that brings illumination to others. Ignatius did not excel as a writer or a thinker; but he was a great leader of men. In his book of *Spiritual Exercises* he provided a manual not to convince men's intellects but to subdue their whole personalities to obedience and endurance. Eight times he was charged with heresy; but he defeated his accusers. He inspired first one disciple and then another with the will to convert the heathen and to confute the heretic. With his soldier's eye he saw that the way to reorganize the Catholic front was to strengthen the papacy. Before Calvin went to Geneva, Ignatius founded the Society of Jesus. There were years of conflict before the Jesuits, with Ignatius as their general, received their final autocratic constitution under papal auspices; but their historic influence was immediate. In 1545 the general council was at last assembled at the town of Trent in the Tyrol, conveniently between Germany and Italy. The emperor wished it to begin with the reform of the abuses of the Church; but the pope decided that it should first clear up the uncertainties of doctrine. In the next year, the year of Luther's death, the Jesuits were given the commission of providing the theologians who were to advise the papal representatives in the council. The work of the council was impeded for years by long interruptions and by much resistance from other schools of thought and from governments; but it was already certain that, both in Germany and outside, religious militancy would not be found only on the Protestant side. The Roman Church was not yet centralized for defence; but it had gained efficient mobile forces.

The council, before it finally separated in 1563, did two things. It defined belief in such a way that there was no loophole for misunderstanding or concession in the matters where Lutherans or Calvinists or other innovators had taken up new positions. It regulated the outward and practical affairs of the Church in such a way that the inveterate abuses were gradually overcome. The full programme of reform could not be enforced without the consent and help of the states, and some of them resisted. France never accepted the decrees of the council officially before the Revolution. But, however the states hung back, there were ardent reformers among the bishops and clergy, and before long the Roman Church had a good right to consider itself reformed.

From this time until the present day western Christendom has been divided among churches and sects. The religious settlement that was made in Germany by the peace of Augsburg [1555] is commonly summed up in the formula *cuius regio, eius religio*—'whose the region is, his also shall be the religion' or 'he who rules the region may dictate its religion'. This formula may be given a far wider application: it describes the state of things all over Europe throughout the sixteenth century and in most parts of it until well on in the eighteenth. There were Protestants, like Henry IV of France and Augustus the Strong of Saxony and Poland, who changed their religion in order to rule over Catholic countries. There were Catholics like James II of England who failed to maintain this authority over Protestant peoples; but these were exceptions that proved the rule. Every strong government, whether Catholic or Protestant, tried to enforce religious uniformity. Where there was no strong government there was religious dissidence; but where there were strong powers at a lower level than that of the territorial state, they determined the religion of those whom they controlled. In many places, from France to Poland and Transylvania, landowners set up a local 'seigniorial protestantism', whether of a Lutheran or a Calvinistic tinge.

In a sense there was nothing new in this. Christianity had been spread long before by missionaries who converted emperors or kings with the certainty that their subjects would conform. The Church had been reluctant to countenance forced conversions, and it never admitted any right of the state to interfere between the individual and his God; but, where men were not free, this could have only a doubtful effect. The break-up of ecclesiastical unity in conflict, and the mutual estrangement of consciences, led many men to think of belief as the individual concern of the believer; but even so the new Churches, and even the smallest and most eccentric sects, were held together by other ties besides those of creed and practice. Each of them appealed most to some special psychological type of person—Calvinism, for instance, to men with something of Calvin in them; but few individuals had the chance of gravitating to the body that would best have fitted their idiosyncrasies. After the first missionary phase, membership was mainly inherited. Like the society in which they originated, the confessions were based on the family: they were clans, making a wider or narrower use of adoption. Every religious group has, besides its creed and its church order, boundaries which are related to the boundaries of some other social group. Its place in the world, especially its position below or beside or against the state, must affect those boundaries. Its common life creates common *mores*, manners, and even mannerisms in other matters outside the religious sphere. Its own members will see more clearly than anyone else the religious element in its life; others will see more clearly than they the social and the external. Religious organizations are not more closely intertwined with social groupings than religious with secular motives; and so every religious movement has some economic or social, as well as some intellectual, antecedents and accompaniments, all of which are more easily visible from outside than from within. In recent times it has been shown in much detail that Protestantism developed readily among those who were impatient of the old economic order, like some of the commercial men in town and country, or economically at a disadvantage, like the craftsmen of towns during industrial depressions, and that Catholic conservatism meant the preservation of church lands as well as orthodox beliefs. So it was bound to be; but it remains none the less true that the glories and miseries of religious strife in the sixteenth century drew their intensity from spiritual good and spiritual evil.

Persuasion and compulsion divided Christianity; the divisions, intensified by robbery and bloodshed, were perpetuated by habits and loyalties. There were always conversions from one confession to another. The converts sometimes modified the beliefs of their new associates; but many of them, in their loneliness, were more exclusive in their new beliefs than those whom they joined, and their secession was apt to harden the rigidity of those whom they deserted. There were always men of wide sympathy and imagination who hoped and schemed for the reunion of some greater or smaller number of the divided Churches. Most of these irenic endeavours were limited to the unpromising fields of intellectual tenets or constitutional machinery, and throughout the period with which we are concerned they yielded no positive results. There were changes in religious allegiances through the conversions of princes, or the local failures or successes of policy; but in their main lines the divisions which began in the sixteenth century have lasted down to the present time and have been complicated by fresh disagreements.

*   *   *   *   *

For almost exactly a century [(1559–1659) after the beginnings of the Reformation] there followed wars and revolutions in which there was never a genuine and general peace. In the political sphere their greatest result was that Spain lost its ascendancy both in Europe and overseas. Mercifully for the survival of western civilization, the pressure of the

Turks was relaxed. The peace of Le Cateau-Cambrésis [1559, ending the Habsburg-Valois wars] put an end to the active alliance with France which had almost brought them into the European system, and there were signs that all was not well with their empire. One sultan was deposed and another was murdered; the others, and their viziers, were mediocrities or worse; the court became more and more corrupt; the outlying pashas disregarded the central power. The discipline of the army was impaired, and the janissaries became a hereditary caste with other interests outside their proper military business. Before long the French, by means of their commerce and through acting as protectors of its Christian subjects, began to acquire influence within the empire itself. For the present, however, the main fabric was unshaken. The dynasty maintained itself; Constantinople was unapproachable and safe; no territory worth mentioning was lost in the wars.

There was indeed one very famous encounter, the battle of Lepanto. In 1570 the Turks planned an attack on Cyprus, and, to save it, the pope and Spain made an alliance with the Venetians. In 1571 the attack began. The principal fortress of the island surrendered and its garrison was treacherously massacred. Then the allied fleet put out from Messina, with contingents from Malta and nine Italian states. At Lepanto they destroyed the Turkish fleet, and won the most unqualified victory of the Christian arms for nearly 600 years. It proved that, once they could combine, the Christian states were a match for the Turks, at least by sea. That was a great thing; but that was all. The victory was not followed up. The alliance fell apart. Cyprus was lost. In 1580 the Spaniards made a truce of long duration with the Turks. The position in the Mediterranean remained for more than a century substantially what it had been before, with the Christians predominant to the west of the Sicilian narrows, and the Turks to the east, where by degrees they tightened their hold.

On land there were frontier wars, but nothing decisive happened in Europe. In the late sixteenth century the fighting was on the whole favourable to the Habsburgs, who took advantage of a diversion in the Turkish rear brought about by the revival of Persia under its great ruler Shah Abbas. In 1606 the Turks made a treaty of peace with the emperor, and for the first time they negotiated the terms instead of dictating them. For more than half a century the emperors had paid tribute to the Turks, and now they bought it off with a lump sum; but they won back no territory, and it was another fifty years before they had enough quiet at home to conduct any serious military operations on their eastern frontier. In 1620–1 the Turks were at war with Poland, but this was a mere episode, and for more than twenty years after that they had no trouble from any of their Christian neighbours. They were left at liberty to extinguish the Persian revival.

In the quarrels which prevented the European states from combining against the Turks, religion and politics were more closely connected than at any other time, both in the internal affairs of the states and in their mutual relations. It was, indeed, impossible to distinguish domestic from international affairs, for the religious parties were bound together by loyalties which transcended national boundaries. They took sides in political and constitutional conflicts, and tried to succour their friends in other countries with the resources of their states. So intense was this militancy that it threatened to undo the consolidation of some of the strongest states. It broke out as soon as the peace of 1559 set Frenchmen and Spaniards free from their absorption in the struggle for Italy. The great survivors from the crises of the early sixteenth century died within a few years of one another, Ignatius Loyola in 1556, Calvin and the Emperor Ferdinand in 1564. The men who were now in office and in power had grown up after the religious schism began; they no longer tried to restore the old unity by compromises, but took their positions on one side or the other of the dividing lines for granted. Having inherited the new religious enmities along with the old dynastic and constitutional feuds, they sharpened contention wherever they found it.

The year of the treaty of Le Cateau-Cambrésis saw the foundation of the academy at Geneva, a university on a new model, to which ministers and laymen came from all over Europe to learn the fighting faith of Calvin. When the men who were trained at Geneva returned to their homes they nowhere set up institutions exactly on the Genevan plan; but everywhere they did set up organizations of their own, and throughout Europe Calvinism became a unified political and intellectual force. The final sessions of the Council of Trent marked the same stage on the Catholic side. It was natural that the Catholics, once the first confusion of their losses was over, should win some of them back. In Germany they regained here a building, there a convent; there were legal decisions by which property or privileges were restored. It was often necessary to apply or interpret the peace of Augsburg, for there were still princes, including prince-bishops, who turned Protestant; but the peace was meant to keep things as they were in 1559, and therefore it forbade any further secularizations of ecclesiastical property. In Germany the Catholics lost no more ground, either literally or metaphorically. The conquests of Lutheranism ended with the first generation.

The Jesuits, who gained control of the university of Ingolstadt in 1563, began to make themselves useful to the Catholic princes and to make use of them. Soon there was an open Catholic counter-offensive; but it lacked leaders. For many years none of the emperors took a decided line and none of them was willing to use force for the recovery of ecclesiastical rights. The Habsburg possessions were for the time being divided, since two younger branches had been provided with appanages after the death of Ferdinand; this and the feeble character of his successors made the imperial authority less effective than it had been during his lifetime. Thus, although the Catholics organized, converted, restated their claims, the religious peace of Augsburg, which satisfied neither sort of extremists, was stable enough to prevent a renewal of general bloodshed and confusion in Germany for more than sixty years.

During this period of two generations the full force of the great antagonisms was not felt in Germany, or to the eastward. Now and again an emperor or a German prince would take a hand in the ecclesiastical and political strife of a neighbouring country, perhaps as a mediator, perhaps even by sending or leading troops to the help of some belligerent; but not as a principal fully committed to the contest. For Germany it was a long period of neutrality, and incubation. The theatres of war were in the west. In France and the Netherlands the religious strife blazed up and rekindled both old constitutional disputes and the old rivalry of the French and Spanish crowns. During the wars between them each had repressed the heretics in its own dominions. In the Netherlands many of the people, especially the townspeople, had been disgusted by the severity of this persecution, some from mere human kindness, some because they were impressed by the doctrines of the sufferers, or by their patience. The government had not, however, stayed its hand for any reason of policy. In France, on occasion, the persecution had been suspended in order to preserve unity for the purposes of the war. No sooner was the war over than the French Calvinists held their first national synod. As it happened the French monarchy, under a succession of unprincipled and incapable kings, did more to divide the nation than to unite it. Calvinism passed from the seigneurial to the political level. The great lords who took it up, some of them in all sincerity, alternated between factious intrigue and a national policy. National policy meant an aristocratic constitutional programme of government in co-operation with the estates.

Across the frontier to the north there were dissatisfied magnates who wanted to increase their own influence in affairs by a similar programme, and some of them wanted to put an end to religious persecution. They looked for foreign allies against their master Philip II of Spain. From Germany they got some little help from time to time; but to Frenchmen, of one religion or the other, in power or aspiring to it, they could offer an inducement that might purchase more powerful aid. The only point where France could hope to damage Spain strategically was in the Netherlands, so threateningly near to Paris that it seemed a French national need to push back the frontier there. There was no chance of setting up a French party in Spain itself; Spain was so united that France could gain no leverage by playing on religious or constitutional opposition. King Philip II indeed substantially reduced the constitutional liberties of Castile and Aragon, and did nothing to conciliate the discontents of Catalonia; but his opponents, or rather victims, had no body of friends abroad. In France, on the other hand, Spain was able, in the name of Catholic militancy, to collect a party and divide the nation. The first leader in this collaboration with the strongest and most Catholic of all states was the duke of Guise, the lucky general who had captured Metz and Calais. He was a person of no small international consequence: the family of which he was the head had connexions ramifying as far as Scotland. These were some of the elements of the situation in which there began a series of civil wars, simultaneous and inextricably involved together, in France and the Netherlands, in all of which, directly or indirectly, Spain took part.

These wars were cruel and destructive. One after another the leaders on both sides were assassinated. In the Netherlands the duke of Alva enforced military rule with a severity that had never been known before in a rich and highly civilized country. In France Guise touched a new depth of savagery in the massacre of St. Bartholomew. After years of misery the chaos changed into coherent warfare, in which the states kept order at home and waged orderly hostilities against one another: the civil wars became international wars, and in 1598, when France and Spain again made peace, the political, social, and economic map of the region between the Pyrenees and the German frontiers had been redrawn.

In France the constitutional results were decisive. The aristocratic programme of limited monarchy and reliance on the states-general had failed, and so had the alliance of the Guises with the democracies of Paris and other cities. For the future nothing was possible except a strong and centralized monarchy. After 1614 the states-general never met again until the French Revolution began in 1789. The royal officials overcame, one by one, all the local, regional, feudal institutions which had hampered their activities. The only check came from the law-courts, which were manned by a largely hereditary body, with a corporate feeling and not lacking in professional ability.

The religious settlement was a combination of absolute monarchy with toleration protected by special guarantees. France was mainly Catholic, and there could be no future for a régime which did not recognize this fact. The final victor in the civil wars, King Henry IV, began life as a Huguenot, but he was the embodiment of the national spirit which survived the ruin of the two extreme religious parties. He became a Catholic, and sincerely, and he bought off his opponents at whatever price was necessary. Although they had no chance of fulfilling their original hopes of imposing their belief, the Huguenots were still strong enough to ask a high price. In the year when he made peace with Spain, Henry granted them the Edict of Nantes. By this he gave them freedom of conscience, that is freedom from inquisition, and the right to maintain churches in all places where they had them already. They were to be admitted to all offices and to all schools and colleges. They were to be given political control over many towns, one of which was the strongly fortified trading port of La Rochelle; but they had to give up their provincial assemblies and all alliances or negotiations with foreign powers.

In spite of all the confusion, this was one of the great periods of French literature. In the first half of the sixteenth century the most original French writer was Rabelais, a doctor and a priest, a contemporary of Calvin and Loyola at the university of Paris, who fought some of the battles of the Renaissance with an overwhelming uproariousness, and left behind him stores of vitality which writers have drawn upon ever since. During the worst of the warfare there came the poetry of Ronsard, a Catholic soldier and a companion of the tragic Mary Queen of Scots, a poet of roses and nightingales and of French country scenes. Literature in general became more polished, and this is true of political literature. The civil wars turned on questions of authority and resistance, of constitutional right and the relations of Church and State. The main arguments had been stated in the Middle Ages and restated in the early days of the Protestant Reformation; but some of the French pamphlets and treatises gave them classical expression. Catholics and Calvinists in turn, when they were in opposition, claimed the right to resist on religious grounds and so maintained that government ought to rest on the consent, or at least respect the rights, of the governed. The book which in the end held the field, as Henry IV did in action, was a new statement of the case for authority. It was written by Jean Bodin, a lawyer who, like the king, had once been a Huguenot, but who now formulated the doctrine of sovereignty, the doctrine that there ought to be one supreme will in every state, to which all other wills are subject. France, like Spain, had now become a state to which this doctrine seemed obviously appropriate, and neither of them now fitted the older interpretation of the nature of the state, according to which no authority was unlimited, and due subjection to one authority was compatible with some subjection to others.

In the Netherlands the dissatisfaction of the magnates proved to be the prelude to a revolution in which Calvinism and constitutionalism were intertwined with a nationalist element. From time to time the revolutionary party were helped in their civil war by the French and also by the English, who were jealous lest the French might become dangerously strong in that quarter. There was a brief period in which all the Netherlands were united in resistance: a great leader, William the Silent, persuaded them to combine for constitutional government and religious toleration. In the end, however, a dexterous governor regained a foothold from which he renewed the war. The end of it was that the Spaniards retained their hold only on the ten southerly provinces, corresponding very roughly to the modern Belgium, including what had been the richest and most populous parts. Here the Spaniards had to renounce their schemes of modernized and centralized administration. The old prosperity of this region was gone, for many reasons, but most of all because their opponents shut up the port of Antwerp. None the less, although this truncated state, which remained Spanish all through the seventeenth century, was repeatedly a theatre of war, the court of the governors, the palaces of the nobility, and the public and private buildings of the rich burgesses had a characteristic art of their own. It combined the old Flemish warmth and vitality with the proud display of the reformed Catholic Church. Its greatest figure was the painter Rubens.

The other seven provinces, of which the chief was the maritime trading province of Holland, the western centre of shipping and of the Baltic corn-trade, became a new state, a federal republic. This was not the first new unit to be added to the European system, for in the time of Charles the Bold [Duke of Burgundy, 1467–1477] the Swiss cantons had thrown off their old allegiances; but Switzerland was content with safety behind its mountains, and the Dutch republic was the first new state to play an active part in international politics. Although its population can scarcely have numbered more than two and a half millions, its commercial wealth enabled it to build up a navy and to hire substantial numbers of foreign troops. After the struggle for independence had gone on for more than thirty years with the aid of allies, at last none of these was willing to fight on, but the republic was strong enough to stand alone. It began to attack the Spaniards where they were most vulnerable, in their colonies and sea-communications. The Spaniards saw that only a respite could save them from disaster, and in 1609 they agreed to a Twelve Years Truce mediated by the French. They meant to resume hostilities when they were ready, and so they neither recognized the republic as *de jure* independent nor explicitly conceded its right to trade in the East Indies. The truce gave the new state its opportunity. Its East India Company, imitating the Portuguese methods and improving on them, did business all over the east, and especially in the Malay Archipelago. A few years after the truce they had the nucleus of an empire, with a capital, Batavia in Java, and a governor-general. They excluded other European nations from these waters. The trading families, growing in wealth, became a gifted and cultivated governing class, and during the truce the republic immediately established itself as a model of cleanliness and welfare. Classical learning, science, poetry, and architecture flourished there, and above all painting.

The republic shut out the Catholics and some of the Protestant dissenters from full citizenship. They might not hold office. The letter of the law denied them freedom of worship, but they were allowed to buy off the magistrates, so that this was the first populous and developed western state where the sects enjoyed a large measure of toleration, and its example offered Europe an important lesson. These unprivileged religious minorities had little or no share in political power and responsibility, and only imperfect contact with the main streams of education and social life. They had their limitations and their eccentricities; but their freedom to experiment in religious ideas and practices enabled them to awaken receptive minds outside them, and they stimulated creative thought. The municipalities admitted, or sometimes even welcomed, religious refugees from all over Europe: Jews from Spain and Portugal, independents from England, French Huguenots, and, later, Czechs. They helped to stimulate the inquiring, inventive, adaptable spirit of enterprise. In economic affairs both the native and the immigrant dissenters were prominent. While the great monarchies tried to organize their resources in uniformity and system, this federal republic drew its strength from variety and intellectual freedom.

Another European power came into the arena at the same time as the Dutch and partly for the same reasons. Except for brief intervals of friendship with France, England had oscillated between isolation from continental affairs and alliance with the Habsburgs, whose Netherlands were the great market for English wool and cloth. Twice the English royal family, the Tudors, had come into the Habsburg marriage-combinations. On the second occasion the queen, Mary, was married to Philip II of Spain himself, and he reigned jointly with her for four years. This personal union was ended by Mary's death [1558], and her successor Queen Elizabeth would not renew it. She was indeed, at times in spite of herself, the representative of new and revolutionary elements in England which could not exist in the old intimacy with the Habsburgs. During the price-revolution [the accelerating inflation of the later sixteenth century] England grew in wealth and population, and in spite of upheavals of popular unrest the governing class grew stronger. The Tudors worked with it by means of parliamentary legislation and aristocratic local administration; through this co-operation King Henry VIII [1509–1547], and the ministers of his young son Edward VI [1547–1553], carried out great ecclesiastical changes. They confiscated much church property; they assumed even greater authority over church-government than the kings of France and Spain; they closed the monasteries and the chantries. Each stage of these changes was linked by attraction or repulsion with continental Protestantism and war and diplomacy. The reign of Philip and Mary brought a partial reaction, but Elizabeth established a national Church which the papacy could not countenance. The religious settlement was ambiguous, but it was definitive. Continental Protestantism of every colour was kept at arm's length; dissent was punished; but a new nationalism was founded on hostility to Rome.

The same dynasty made great advances towards ending the gravest weakness of England, the Scottish problem. The smaller, poorer, and less settled kingdom of Scotland had naturally been for centuries a potential or actual ally of England's continental enemies and therefore had an old tradition of alliance with France. As it chanced a Scottish king contracted a French marriage during the brief period of the ascendancy of the house of Guise, and so it was that when Queen Elizabeth drew away from friendship with the Habsburgs the Scottish crown was held by Mary, the daughter of a Guise princess, a member of the family which rose and fell with international Catholic militancy under the aegis of Spain. She was faced by rebellious nobles and Calvinistic reformers, and, when she fled from them to England the hopes of the English Catholic peers could not but be centred on her. Conspiracy followed conspiracy, and at last she was executed. This brought open war between England and Spain. The English had been sending aid to the

Dutch for fifteen years already, at first informally and then by assuming an open protectorate over the nascent state. They were no more willing to see the French as masters there than the Spaniards. With the Dutch as allies they withstood the first shock of Spanish attack, and the defeat of the Spanish armada in 1588 was one of the proudest feats in English history. For the remaining years of Queen Elizabeth's reign the fortunes of the war, in alliance with the other enemies of Spain all over the world, swayed to and fro, but the glory of that deliverance was never forgotten. It was not followed by a revival of all the arts. In painting and architecture the Reformation had destroyed so much that it took long to repair the damage, but English literature broke into full flower. The instruments had been tuned by courtly and learned poets of the previous generations; now the supreme players took them up. Shakespeare came to London in the year before the Armada. All through the orchestration of his versatility there sounds his pride and joy in the greatness of England.

This greatness lay not only in glory but in common sense. The Elizabethan statesmen kept in sight the need to settle their problems, and in nothing were they more sagacious than in the matter of Scotland. Mary Queen of Scots had Tudor blood, and they handled the thorny Scottish problem so well that when Queen Elizabeth died [1603] she was peacefully succeeded by Mary's son, James. For the first time one king ruled from the Shetlands to the Scillies. To be sure, it was only a personal union. James failed to complete it by a union of states, because it was still a union of heads and not of hearts; but Great Britain, with a population of more than five millions and another million in turbulent Ireland, was now one unit in international affairs. Five years before the Dutch Twelve Years Truce, James made peace with Spain, and his peoples were able to thrive and to quarrel among themselves in full security.

When the French, the English, and the Dutch had successively made their peace, Spain was still the strongest power in Europe. All through the reign of Philip II, who died in 1598, she was so strong that he was believed, with more justice than his father [Emperor Charles V], to be aiming at a 'universal monarchy'. It was only because his many preoccupations in all the continents made it impossible for him to meet them one at a time that each of these three powers had grown in strength. The Dutch made good their first patch of territory in the year after Lepanto; eighteen years later Philip lost his last chance of mastering them by dispatching an army to intervene in the French civil wars. And in spite of all his losses he had made enormous acquisitions. In 1578 the young king of Portugal was fighting in North Africa against the Moors. At the battle of Alkazar-el-Kebir he was defeated and killed. His successor was his great-uncle, an aged and infirm ecclesiastic, during whose reign of two years half a dozen claimants had their eyes on the succession. One of them was Philip II, and the army, under Alva, which enforced his claim won him two dazzling prizes at a stroke. For the first and only time since the Roman empire, the Iberian peninsula was united, and this personal union, greater in itself than the union of Great Britain, carried with it the union of all the European possessions in Africa, Asia, and America. Spanish civilization rose to its summits. Cervantes, who was wounded at Lepanto, wrote *Don Quixote* to be read in every country of the world. El Greco's genius fused together the solemnity of Byzantium, the pictorial glow of Venice, and the vision of the Spanish mystics. After him came Velasquez, the painters' painter, to commemorate the dignity and courtesy of courtiers and campaigners. There was no decadence in these fields until far on in the seventeenth century; but the future was insecure. Portugal was not assimilated; neither was Catalonia. In social and economic matters there were ominous deficiencies. Spain was rich from the treasure of the Indies, but she had no sufficient industry of her own. She depended on foreign manufactures, shipping, and commerce. While the perpetual drain of warfare overstrained her finances, population began to decline and, especially in the south, lands went out of cultivation for lack of hands. Peace with France, England, and the Netherlands gave an opportunity for reform, and it was well understood that the need was pressing.

It was at best an uneasy peace; the old forces of disunity still heaved below the surface; but the next great outbreak left all these countries outside its range at first, and brought war in the region which had for so long been immune, Germany and some of the lands to the eastward. A good many German princes had been improving their administration by imitating French or Burgundian or Austrian arrangements. Each of the religious parties had become more capable of fighting and more determined to press its claims. At the end of the sixteenth century and in the early seventeenth the two junior Habsburg lines died out, and the inheritance was reunited. The emperor of the moment was out of his mind, and his successor was both elderly and ineffective, but behind the two stood their heir, Ferdinand, a pupil of the Ingolstadt Jesuits. Another of their pupils, a capable military organizer, succeeded to the duchy of Bavaria, Austria's western neighbour. On the Protestant side down to this time all the leading princes had been Lutherans, and so content with the peace of Augsburg which gave a place in the world to Lutheranism but not to any other Protestant creed. Now the Elector Palatine* became a Calvinist, so that a leader was available who, like all Calvinists, brought religion into politics, and who was in a position great enough to raise his German quarrels to the level of international affairs.

At the time of the Dutch Twelve Years Truce and for some years after, it looked as if there would be a European war over a German question, because Protestant and Catholic claimants disputed the inheritance of the Catholic Duke of Jülich and Cleves. His possessions about the lower Rhine were as important strategically as they are in our own day, but Henry IV of France, when he was about to begin hostilities, was assassinated. All the parties accepted a compromise by partition, so that the crisis came in 1618 in another storm-centre.

North-west from Vienna and open on that side, but shut off from Germany and Poland by its mountains, was the kingdom of Bohemia, the country of the Czechs, to which Silesia and Lusatia, across the mountains, also belonged. According to the more or less accepted constitutional law it was an elective kingdom, and, after the battle of Mohacs [1526], Ferdinand I [emperor, 1558–1564] had been elected there, as in Hungary. In Bohemia the religious position was even more confused than in Germany: there were not only Lutherans but also considerable remnants of older national sects, strong in seigniorial support, which traced back their origin to the schism of John Hus in the early fifteenth century. Here the Habsburgs tried to preserve the Roman authority by generous concessions; but heresy spread continually and at last the attempts of Ferdinand II [Emperor, 1619–1637] to enforce ecclesiastical rights led to a revolution. The leaders of the opposition tried to murder his representatives in Prague, and this was the signal for a rising not only all over Bohemia but in Austria as well.

Ferdinand was almost without an army. The rebels got troops together and appeared before Vienna. They hoped for foreign aid, and they offered their crown to the Calvinist Elector Palatine, Frederick. He, among various high connexions, counted King James I of England as his father-in-law; but James was not to be drawn into this ill-considered adventure. The only foreign prince who intervened was the

* The other electors had territorial titles, 'Elector of Saxony' and so on; the Elector Palatine was so called because his remote predecessors had held a court office (*Palatium* being the Latin for a palace), and his dominions were named from his office, the Upper Palatinate, the Lower Palatinate, &c.

Calvinist Gabriel Bethlen, prince of Transylvania, who in the end gained nothing for his allies but added some Hungarian counties to his own dominions. Ferdinand did not take long to recover his position. He made sure of Maximilian of Bavaria and the other Catholic princes, and he bought off the Lutherans by surrendering Lusatia to their leader, the elector of Saxony. Then his general, the Netherlander Tilly, routed Frederick at the White Mountain before Prague.

The Bohemian episode lasted a bare three years. Afterwards, at his leisure, Ferdinand extinguished the political liberties of the country, and stamped out all forms of belief except the Catholic. During the next 200 years Czech culture was put down; German landowners and officials depressed the Czechs to the status of a subject nationality whose language and traditions sank into obscurity. In Germany, however, the Bohemian episode left a legacy of strife. Ferdinand, who had become emperor, caused Frederick's electoral rank to be transferred to the younger branch of his family in the person of Maximilian of Bavaria. This drastic action made many of the princes apprehensive for their 'German liberties'. They feared that the Habsburgs would use their growing power to turn the imperial dignity into a real monarchy. The fugitive Frederick was a symbol, and from time to time one enemy of the Habsburgs or another took up his cause. All this was the more dangerous because in 1621 the Twelve Years Truce ran out, and the Dutch and Spaniards fought again on sea and land.

The fears and ambitions of some of the princes of north-west Germany led them to invite Christian IV of Denmark, a warlike prince who had German possessions, to invade north Germany. The emperor defeated them by the help of a new man, Wallenstein, who used a great fortune, made from the confiscated estates of the Bohemian rebels, to collect a cosmopolitan mercenary army stronger than any that any German prince or emperor had ever commanded. Wallenstein established the emperor's power on the shores of the Baltic, or rather his own power, for political allegiance meant little to him. Even before the Danes had withdrawn from the war, Ferdinand rashly revoked his guarantee of the *status quo* to the Protestants. This, and his new strength on the Baltic, brought a very formidable antagonist against him. . . . Sweden had recently gained great power round the Baltic coasts. Her king, Gustavus Adolphus, was a great soldier, a reformer of armament and tactics; he was also a Protestant leader, and a statesman, well served by able ministers. Some of the German princes, including the electors of Saxony and Brandenburg, found him an uncomfortable ally. His schemes might well be inimical to their liberties, and they had, after all, a genuine regard for the empire so long as it left them at ease. Gustavus won a succession of lightning victories: then he was killed in battle. The dubious electors drew away from the Swedes; but there were still minor princes who kept the field with them. The emperor detected Wallenstein in treasonable designs and had him murdered; but his army was loyal and it became the standing army of Habsburg Austria, a new great power. The Spanish ally gave effective military help. In 1635 the emperor abandoned his attempt to recover the Catholic losses, and so conciliated most of his German opponents. He had reached an unquestionable primacy in Germany. Only two minor German states were still in arms against him. But it was still thirteen years before Germany was pacified, and they were years of still greater destruction and suffering.

The reason was that the Danish and Swedish episodes had given time for the most persistent of all the enemies of the Habsburgs to collect its strength and to choose its ground to attack. France in the early seventeenth century was gaining energy as quickly as Spain was losing it. Henry IV had begun the erection of an efficient monarchy. His death caused an interruption, but the work was taken up again with relentless determination by a minister, the Cardinal de Richelieu. Richelieu found the French nobility dissatisfied and unmanageable, from the magnates who were almost the equals of kings down to the country landowners whom the price-revolution had ruined. Some of them still stood up for the militant faith of Calvin, and when France fought a short war against Charles I of England, the son of James, it called out the old combination of Huguenot nobles with a foreign enemy. Richelieu ended this. He deprived the Huguenots of their guarantees, leaving them their toleration but without the means to defend it. He tamed the whole nobility, making them into obedient subjects, some of them ornamental and others useful, especially in the army. All this was not achieved without many acts little fitting the character of a churchman; but Richelieu was not entirely out of touch with a strong religious movement which began under Henry IV and continued throughout his own time. It owed much to the founders of new orders in Italy, much to the Spanish and something to the German mystics; but it bore the stamp of the French mind. St. Francis de Sales, the most cultivated of devotional writers, and St. Vincent de Paul, the most effective of philanthropic organizers, were both essentially French. They had a confident touch like that of the new French literature, the silken verse and the rapier prose, which gathered European influence in those years. The movement in literature was consciously national. The men of letters were gathered under the cardinal's protection in the French Academy: every polite accomplishment advanced the prestige of France.

It was only slowly and gradually that this strength became effective in international relations, but the way was made ready for it by well-informed and rationally-conducted diplomacy. First France mediated between Sweden and Poland in the peace-negotiations which set Gustavus Adolphus free for his German enterprise. After his death French subsidies kept the Swedish army in pay. Then Richelieu made a fresh alliance with the Dutch and declared war against Spain. By this time the German princes were so much weakened that Germany became a theatre of international war, as Italy and France had been in their turns in the sixteenth century. The rivalry between the two strongest powers in Europe overshadowed and absorbed the lesser conflicts, and the German questions were only settled when the power of Spain was brought low. Before Richelieu died in 1642 the French had conquered Alsace, Catalonia had rebelled and the Portuguese had begun a long war to recover their independence at home and in the colonies. In the year after he died a French general won a decisive victory over the once invincible Spanish army. This battle of Rocroi proved to all the world that the ascendancy of Spain was ending. She had failed to take her chance of recuperating after the wars of Philip II. Five years later she withdrew from the German fighting and Germany had peace.

Looking back on all this German fighting since the Bohemian revolution of 1618 historians gave it the name of the Thirty Years War, a by-word in aftertimes for cruelty and misery. Two things have fixed attention on the recorded horrors of this time. Firstly there was the feeling that much of the misery had been inflicted on Germany by foreign invaders, and this feeling grew stronger in the nineteenth century when a united German nation, strong in military power, was able to wage its wars abroad and to keep the German soil inviolate. But it is an anachronism to allot praise or blame to the soldiers and statesmen of the seventeenth century in proportion as they furthered or hindered the rise of a national spirit and national cohesion in Germany. There was indeed . . . loyalty to the emperor and the empire; but loyalty in those days was as authentic when its object was dynastic or religious as when it was national, and no one thought it morally reprehensible to call in foreign aid for his church or his dynasty. The second reason which has blackened the name of the Thirty Years War is that its total effects are thought to have been injurious to Germany and advantageous to almost all the neighbouring states. Here again it was the abstract Germany of subsequent national sentiment which suffered more than actual groupings of Germans; if this abstract element is omitted, and if exaggerations are pruned away, the Thirty Years War will be seen not as unique but as typical of the wars of the sixteenth and seventeenth centuries.

Considerable German provinces, though remaining constitutionally within the empire, passed to sovereigns whose main territories were outside it. France was confirmed in the possession of Metz, Toul, Verdun, and Alsace. In all these places her lordships fell short of sovereignty, and in Alsace they were so ill-defined that they left obvious openings for future disputes. Sweden took some ports and some strips of territory along the Baltic coasts, and two bishoprics on the estuary of the Weser, though not the great port of Bremen. Thus the kings of Sweden and France now became, like the kings of Denmark and Spain, nominally members of the empire. The Austrian Habsburgs already had possessions outside it in Hungary; the elector of Brandenburg had recently become duke of Prussia, in Poland; the Bavarian house had supplied prince-bishops to Liége since 1581, so that most of the leading states of Germany had interests outside it. In due course this process went still farther when the electors of Saxony became kings of Poland, and the electors of Hanover became kings of England. The emperors, having lost so much in the west, naturally paid more attention to their affairs in Hungary and Bohemia, the more so since in that quarter they had gained so much that they were on balance stronger than before. Theirs was the only one among the greater German dynasties which lost any of its lands. Saxony, Bavaria, Brandenburg all gained. The German liberties were now secure, and if this meant that the empire as such could never become a strong and consolidated state, it also meant that the religious settlement of 1555 was reaffirmed and its benefits were extended to Calvinist princes. The emperors had to reckon with a group of strong neighbours, each with his territorial aspirations; but, although these might lawfully make alliances with foreign powers, they did not aspire to be more than states within the empire. Their rise had simplified the map of Germany and removed some of the impediments to good government.

The political fragmentation of Germany stood in the way of economic unity, but the absorption of some small territories by the greater states made this somewhat less irksome. No noticeable economic loss ensued from the Swedish occupation of the mouths of the Oder and the banks of the Weser. The mouth of a still greater German river, the Rhine, had never been German; but it belonged to men who made their livelihood by trading with Germany. No scientific estimate has ever been made of the economic ravages of the war. Some places were devastated and some were depopulated for a time; but the people were not all slaughtered; some of them merely shifted to safer places. The war may perhaps justly be blamed for the failure of such tardy efforts as German princes made to join in the colonial trade; but Sweden and Denmark also fared badly in that field. It is hard to separate the economic results of the war from the other changes of the time. The shifting of the trade-routes had already drawn trade away from the south German cities; the rise of the Dutch republic and of Sweden had done the same for those of the north; but the shifting of routes, while it depressed some parts of Germany, brought prosperity to others. The great days of Hamburg began.

The sphere in which the war certainly left deep wounds behind it was that of the mind. The Protestant universities lost many of their foreign students and much of their excellence. Literature had no great names to show; and from the early years of the war there were complaints of the infiltration of French literary influences. But even in the sphere of the mind it was more in national feeling than in absolute merit that decline could be noticed. There were gains to set against the losses. The great musical history of Saxony began, and the first German opera was performed when Wallenstein was operating towards the Baltic. Within a generation of the end of the war there were men in the German courts and cities who were famous all over Europe as scholars and thinkers. The name of Magdeburg is remembered for its sack when Tilly took it in 1631; but in 1652 its burgomaster was one of the most distinguished living physicists. At the episcopal court of Mainz Leibniz was soon to display his almost universal genius. In one respect indeed the war cleared the way for developments which, while they were beneficial in some ways and harmful in others, at least fostered the specifically German types of government and character. Except in some minor states the towns declined and the assemblies of estates declined with them. The populace, including the educated townsmen, subsided, so Leibniz complained, into indifference to questions of creed, politics, and morals. But the rulers came to a *modus vivendi* with the nobility. There were no more robber-barons. In the great corn-producing area, for instance, the landlords gave up their political rights and their voice in taxation in virtual exchange for greater rights over the serfs on their farms. The princes were thus able to finance larger and better armies, and to promote a policy of economic welfare by means of an authoritarian bureaucracy. The universities became training-schools for administrators.

Many of the evils which afflicted Germany during the Thirty Years
War were as great or greater in other countries. Bohemia and the Spanish Netherlands were perhaps those which suffered altogether the most.
Probably the only country in which the universities did not to some
extent decline was the Dutch republic, which was not a theatre of war,
and whose tolerance attracted students and men of letters from every
quarter. In Great Britain there were twenty years of civil war and revolution which, although they kept the country out of European embroil-
ments, were connected with the German war both by diplomacy and by
'ideologies'. The union of England and Scotland sharpened the antagonisms within each country, as such unions sometimes do. In this case
the most obstinate antagonisms were religious, and the Puritan opposition in England now had Scottish allies, just as the episcopalian minority
in Scotland, which included the king, now had strong English backing.
This issue became fused with a constitutional struggle between the
Crown and some elements of the English governing classes. King
Charles I was defeated, deposed, and executed. The victorious parties
formed a united republic of England, Scotland, and Ireland; but it was
troubled by sporadic risings of democratic elements hitherto outside the
governing classes and not concerned with public affairs. This whirl of
ideas and action ended with a restored but constitutional monarchy,
holding England and Scotland once more only in personal union, and
leaving each to its own separate religious tenor. In the end the crisis
cleared the way, as in Germany, for new methods of government well
suited to the island peoples; but the arts and letters had been badly
injured, and their recovery after the restoration was curiously parallel
to the German recovery: science and music flourished especially; in
literature and manners there was a strong French influence. This French
leaven, indeed, was working in every country from Poland to Sicily.

In after years the Congress of Westphalia came to be reckoned as
the first in the series of European diplomatic congresses and conferences
in which the peace-settlements and other great international agreements
were negotiated. For the first time there was an assemblage of ambassadors and ministers comparable in power and dignity with the ecclesiastical councils, but its members were representatives of states. It showed
how far the sovereign states had consolidated their system. One sign
was the insignificance of the ecclesiastical diplomacy. Although ecclesiastical principalities were annexed or dismembered by the secular
states, the pope, whose predecessors had claimed supremacy over kings
and republics, could only protest. Another sign was the maturity and
completeness of the international law embodied in the treaties. During

the previous hundred years international lawyers, working on the basis of Roman jurisprudence, had made notable progress. The most famous of them, Hugo Grotius, published his masterpiece, a treatise on the law of war and peace, in 1625. He was a poet, a very learned scholar, a theologian, a historian, a practising lawyer, and a diplomatist. His active career was unhappy: he was a prominent member of a party in his native country, Holland, which tried to press religious tolerance and provincial autonomy further than the more Calvinistic and anti-Spanish military leaders would allow. When his party fell he had to spend many years in exile. He wrote this great book in Paris in Richelieu's day, and afterwards he served the Swedes as an ambassador. Thus, though he wrote it to point out ways of ending what seemed to him the growing inhumanity of wars, he wrote with the hard facts of the times before his eyes. He accepted the sovereign independence of each state as the initial postulate from which international organization must start. He treated the law of war, the reasonable regulation of its conduct, and the rights and wrongs of resorting to it, as part of a wider law which also covers the peaceful relations of states, their contracts with one another and with their subjects, their rights to territory, and all their other activities which can be brought within a legal framework. He died while the Westphalian Congress was sitting, and his book still gives us a programme and an inspiration in the light of which that Congress, in spite of all its shortcomings and failures, is seen to have done something for justice and for peace.

It was, however, only to Germany, Sweden, and the Dutch republic that the Congress gave peace. France and Spain still fought on for eleven bloody years. When Spain, isolated and doomed as a great power, at last gave in to the French demands for frontier provinces in the Netherlands and along the Pyrenees, she gained no respite. The Portuguese still waged their war of independence with French support; and there was no interval of stability for Europe between the end of Spanish ascendancy and the beginning of the exorbitant power of France. Although they were continuous, however, the wars which raged round these two dominations were different in so many ways, and were fought in such different atmospheres, that it is not absurd to regard the humbling of Spain as the end of an age. [see p. 252 in this volume] Fundamentally it had come about because the rest of western Europe had grown in wealth and energy so as to overtake the lead which Spain had gained in the conquering days of colonial discovery and Catholic revival. As the price-revolution and the growth of population continued, her rivals had established their own colonial empires. The French now had Canada and its fur-trade; the English had settled on the eastern shore of North America and in the West Indies; the Dutch were their neighbours in both these regions, and were fighting the Portuguese in Brazil. Spanish trade was harassed and interrupted; indeed the economy of the New World was passing into the control of the smugglers and buccaneers of the new colonizing nations. But about the middle of the seventeenth century all this began to change. The price-revolution slowed down and ended: in most of Europe the general level of prices stood still or began to fall. The flow of emigrants ran more thinly. Instead of expansion there was soon more of organization within the limits which had been reached. And these changes corresponded in some way to great changes in men's minds. Religion and politics were no longer locked together so that every incident in one had its counterpart in the other. A new page of history was being written.

Suggestions for Further Reading

CLARK, G. N., *The Seventeenth Century*, 2nd ed. Oxford: Clarendon Press, 1947.

ELLIOTT, J. H., *Europe Divided, 1559–1589*. New York: Harper & Row, 1968.

GEYL, PIETER, *The Netherlands in the Seventeenth Century*, 2 vols., rev. ed. New York: Barnes & Noble, 1961–1964.

HOLBORN, HAJO, *A History of Modern Germany*, Vol. I. New York: Alfred A. Knopf, 1959.

KOENIGSBERGER, H. G., *The Habsburgs in Europe 1516–1660*. Ithaca, N.Y.: Cornell University Press, 1970.

MATTINGLY, GARRETT, *The Armada*. Boston: Houghton Mifflin, 1959.

NEALE, J. E., *The Age of Catherine de Medici*. London: Jonathan Cape Ltd., 1943.

STEINBERG, S. H., *The Thirty Years' War and the Conflict for European Hegemony 1600–1660*. New York: W. W. Norton, 1966.

THOMPSON, J. W., *The Wars of Religion in France*. Chicago: University of Chicago Press, 1909.

WEDGWOOD, C. V., *The Thirty Years' War*. Garden City, N.Y.: Doubleday, 1968.

HERBERT BUTTERFIELD

The Scientific Revolution

◆§◆ The past quarter-century has witnessed a great increase in the systematic historical investigation of Oriental, African, and Middle Eastern civilizations. The more we know about other civilizations the better we can define by comparison that distinctive nature of Western civilization which made possible the world hegemony it began to move toward in the sixteenth century, a hegemony that was clearly attained by the end of the nineteenth century and that just as clearly has begun to dissolve in our time.

The comparative study of civilizations provides plausible evidence that there is nothing particularly unique about Western achievement in either public administration and law or in art, literature, and music, for certainly the attainment of the Oriental cultures was very high in these areas of human endeavor. The distinctive achievement of Western civilization—its prize possession that non-Western societies have sought to import in the twentieth century—is modern science and its attendant technology. It was Europe's understanding and control of the material world that ultimately made possible unparalleled industrial progress, a hitherto-unknown high standard of living for the masses, and the military technology that gained for the West its now-vanishing imperial suzerainty over all other civilizations. Thus in the last twenty-five years scholars have begun to see that to understand Europe's unique destiny required a detailed knowledge of the rise and develop-

FROM Herbert Butterfield, *The Origins of Modern Science* (New York: The Macmillan Company, 1951), pp. 42–87.

ment of modern science, so that a new distinct branch of historical investigation, the history of science, has appeared to pursue this research, with a growing number of chairs and institutes in major universities. The historian of science has to master the concepts of modern physics, chemistry, biology, and mathematics; at the same time, he must be sensitive to the causes and process of general social and intellectual change. Very few scholars as yet can command this rare combination because of the traditional but unfortunate cleavage between humanities and sciences in our universities. But a small group of scholars of unusual learning and perception has emerged and begun the extremely difficult task of placing the development of the physical and biological sciences in the context of European history.

The first great obstacle the historian of science faces is the prevailing doubt among philosophers of science on the exact nature of what is generally termed "modern science." What is the distinctive quality of modern science that separates this body of thought from the cosmology and theories of nature that prevailed in the ancient and medieval worlds? It cannot be simply the observation of the physical world and the belief that our senses import to us the existence of a real objective world outside our minds. For whereas Plato and his long line of disciples down into the thirteenth century believed only in the reality of ideas and dismissed the world of sense experience as transient and insignificant, the other mastermind of Greek thought, Aristotle, regarded the physical world as real and permanent and pursued the careful observation of natural phenomena. Aristotelianism enjoyed a tremendous revival in twelfth- and thirteenth-century Europe and was regarded as authoritative in the late medieval universities. Yet it was Aristotelianism that the scientific revolution of the late sixteenth and seventeenth centuries had to fight against and overthrow before the "new physics" could be formulated and gain intellectual consensus. Therefore modern science cannot be identified merely with a belief in the reality of the observable natural world.

It has been widely assumed that modern science can be identified with the experimental method, but philosophers have had a very difficult time determining the exact process of reasoning which underlies experimentation. In any case it is a disconcerting fact that the protagonists of the new physics of the early modern period were hesitant and uncertain about the indispensable need for experimentation and were extremely awkward, sloppy, and unsystematic in the actual execution of those experiments they did undertake. The crucial breakthroughs made by Copernicus and Galileo were largely the consequence of intuitive perception and abstract reasoning on the basis of well-known data, and had little or nothing to do with what we would call experimental work. As a matter of fact, the same uncomfortable point can be made about Einstein's revolutionary discoveries in the early twentieth century.

It has sometimes been thought that the predication of general rules or laws of natural phenomena is the foundation of modern science, but this proposition runs contrary to the fact that classical and medieval thinkers were not reluctant to define natural laws and that Aristotle both advocated this and provided many rules for the operation of the physical world. When all other definitions fail, scholars are driven back on the conclusion that it was the expression of natural laws in mathematical form, the positing of the relationships of the physical universe in quantifiable terms, which is the distinctive quality of the new physics of the sixteenth and seventeenth centuries and the basis of modern science. The scientists of the early modern era stated their propositions about nature in mathematical form. These formulae were susceptible to experimental proof and were slowly found to have a practical use in industrial and military technology: this is the great change that occurred in the form of scientific thinking.

It is this view of the nature of modern science which has come to be most widely held among philosophers of science and which has formed the basic assumption for investigation of the scientific revolution of the sixteenth and seventeenth centuries. It is an idea that raises certain problems, because mathematics is an idealized Platonic world of pure thought that does not absolutely and necessarily conform to the actual operation of the physical world. As some twentieth-century physicists have pointed out, there is an "inconstancy" in nature that cannot be perfectly capsulated in a mathematical formula, but at least as regards the breakthrough to the new physics of the sixteenth and seventeenth centuries, the definition of science as the quantifiable formulation of nature is meaningful and significant.

Among several attempts to depict the course of the scientific revolution, the most perceptive and satisfying for the general student of history is the essay published by Herbert Butterfield in 1951, *The Origins of Modern Science*. Butterfield was appointed Regius Professor of Modern History at Cambridge and then Master of Peterhouse College, Cambridge. Although without any professional training in science, he has been able to master the conceptual problems of early modern physics and brings to bear on the scientific revolution an original and subtle mind that has made very important contributions to several aspects of modern European intellectual history.

In his characteristically clear, direct, almost conversational manner, Butterfield is able to get at the heart of the problem of the scientific revolution. He points out that the new physics was in part made possible by mid-sixteenth-century advances in mathematical knowledge; it was a deficiency in mathematics that helps to account for the aborting of the ambitious and promising scientific movement among the Oxford and Paris scholastics of the early fourteenth century. Butterfield suggests that Galileo's achievement has something to do with contemporary improvements in technology and advances in mechanical skill. He delineates the thesis which has been explored in detail in a recent work by the American scholar Thomas Kuhn: scientific revolutions occur when the prevailing theory (what Kuhn calls the intellectual paradigm) significantly fails to relate and explicate the observable data. With his fine insight into the ways of social change, Butterfield emphasizes what may be termed the nonscientific or strictly social foundations of the scientific revolution, namely, the importance of educational institutions and the forms of communication of data and theories. Finally Butterfield takes pains to lay to rest certain dogmas of the late nineteenth-century historical thought, particularly the assumption that Protestantism was necessarily more hospitable to a new view of the universe than Catholicism, and that the scientific movement was somehow allied with a secularist onslaught on faith and mysticism. He shows that it is difficult to generalize about the new scientists' relationship with either of the contending religions of the sixteenth century and that the protagonists of the scientific revolution not only were conventionally devout, but in some instances were actually inspired in their work "by a mystical semi-religious fervor," by a medieval passion to demonstrate the divinely perfect relationship of the heavenly spheres.

As the crucial stage in the grand controversy concerning the Ptolemaic system does not seem to have been treated organically, and is seldom or never envisaged as a whole, it is necessary that we should put together a fairly continuous account of it, so that we may survey the transition as a whole. A bird's-eye view of the field should be of some significance for the student of the scientific revolution in general, especially as the battles come in crescendo and rise to their greatest intensity in this part of the campaign.

It would be wrong to imagine that the publication of Copernicus's great work in 1543 either shook the foundations of European thought straight away or sufficed to accomplish anything like a scientific revolution. Almost a hundred and fifty years were needed before there was achieved a satisfactory combination of ideas—a satisfactory system of the universe—which permitted an explanation of the movement of the earth and the other planets, and provided a framework for further scientific development. Short of this, it was only a generation after the death of Copernicus—only towards the close of the sixteenth century—that the period of crucial transition really opened and the conflict even became intense. And when the great perturbations occurred they were the result of very different considerations—the result of events which would have shaken the older cosmos almost as much if Copernicus had never even written his revolutionary work. Indeed, though the influence of Copernicus was as important as people generally imagine it to have been, this influence resulted not so much from the success of his actual system of the skies, but rather from the stimulus which he gave to men who in reality were producing something very different.

When Copernicus's work first appeared it provoked religious objections, especially on Biblical grounds, and since the Protestants were the party particularly inclined to what was called Bibliolatry, some scathing condemnations very soon appeared from their side—for example, from Luther and Melanchthon personally. One may suspect that unconscious prejudice had some part in this, and that the Aristotelian view of the universe had become entangled with Christianity more closely than necessity dictated; for if the Old Testament talked of God establishing the earth fast, the words were capable of elastic interpretation, and Biblical exegesis in previous centuries had managed to get round worse corners than this. In any case, if the Old Testament was not Copernican, it was very far from being Ptolemaic either. And it gives something of a blow to Aristotle and his immaculate fifth essence, surely, when it says that the heavens shall grow old as a garment, and, talking of God, tells us that the stars and the very heavens themselves are not pure in His sight. The prejudice long remained with the Protestants, and when a few years ago the Cambridge History of Science Committee celebrated in the Senate House the tercentenary of the visit to England of the great Czech educator Comenius or Komensky, the numerous orations overlooked the fact that he was anti-Copernican and that his textbooks, reprinted in successive editions throughout the seventeenth century, were a powerful influence in the Protestant world on the wrong side of the question. On the other hand, Copernicus was a canon in the Roman Catholic Church and high dignitaries of that Church were associated with the publication of his book. The comparatively mild reception which the new view received on this side led only recently to the enunciation of the view that the Roman Catholics, being slow in the uptake, took nearly fifty years to see that Copernicus was bound to lead to Voltaire. The truth was, however, that the question of the movement of the earth reached the stage of genuine conflict only towards the end of the sixteenth century, as I have said. By that time—and for different reasons altogether—the religious difficulties themselves were beginning to appear more serious than before.

Although Copernicus had not stated that the universe was infinite—and had declared this issue to belong rather to the province of the philosopher—he had been compelled, for a reason which we shall have to consider later, to place the fixed stars at what he called an immeasurable distance away. He was quickly interpreted—particularly by some English followers—as having put the case in favour of an infinite universe; and unless they had some non-religious objections Christians could hardly complain of this, or declare it to be impossible, without detracting from the power and glory of God. Unfortunately, however, that *enfant terrible* amongst sixteenth-century Italian speculators, Giordano Bruno, went further and talked of the actual existence of a plurality of worlds. There arose more seriously than ever before the question: Did the human beings in other worlds need redemption? Were there to be so many appearances of Christ, so many incarnations and so many atonements throughout the length and breadth of this infinite universe? That question was much more embarrassing than the purely Biblical issue which was mentioned earlier; and the unbridled speculations of Bruno, who was burned by the Inquisition for a number of heresies in 1600, were a further factor in the intensification of religious fear on the subject of the Copernican system.

Apart from all this, it is remarkable from how many sides and in how many forms one meets the thesis that is familiar also in the writings of Galileo himself—namely, the assertion that it is absurd to suppose that the whole of this new colossal universe was created by God purely for the sake of men, purely to serve the purposes of the earth. The whole outlay seemed to be too extravagant now that things were seen in their true proportions and the object had come to appear so insignificant. At this later stage the resistance to the Copernican hypothesis was common to both Roman Catholics and Protestants, though in England itself it appears to have been less strong than in most other places. The Protestant astronomer, Kepler, persecuted by the Protestant Faculty at Tübingen, actually took refuge with the Jesuits in 1596. Both the Protestant, Kepler, and the Roman Catholic, Galileo, ventured into the realms of theology by addressing their co-religionists and attempting to show them that the Copernican system was consistent with a fair interpretation of the words of Scripture. Galileo made excellent use of St. Augustine, and for a time he received more encouragement in the higher ecclesiastical circles in Rome than from his Aristotelian colleagues in the university of Padua. In the long run it was Protestantism which for semi-technical reasons had an elasticity that enabled it to make alliance with the scientific and the rationalist movements, however. That process in its turn greatly altered the character of Protestantism from the closing years of the seventeenth century, and changed it into the more liberalising movement of modern times.

The religious obstruction could hardly have mattered, however, if it had not been supported partly by scientific reasons and partly by the conservatism of the scientists themselves. It has been pointed out by one student that to a certain degree it was the astrologers who were the more ready to be open-minded on this subject in the sixteenth century. Apart from the difficulties that might be involved in the whole new synthesis which Copernicus had provided (and which [it must be noted] included a quasi-superstitious reliance upon the virtues of circles and the behaviour of spheres as such), there were particular physical objections to the attribution of movement to the earth, whether on the plan put forward by Copernicus or in any other conceivable system. Copernicus, as we have seen, had tried to meet the particular objections in detail, but it will easily be understood that his answers, which we have already noted, were not likely to put the matter beyond controversy.

Copernicus himself had been aware that his hypothesis was open to objection in a way that has not hitherto been mentioned. If the earth moved in a colossal orbit around the sun, then the fixed stars ought to show a slight change of position when observed from opposite sides of the orbit. In fact, there is a change but it is so slight that for three centuries after Copernicus it was not detected, and Copernicus had to explain what then appeared to be a discrepancy by placing the fixed stars so far away that the width of the earth's orbit was only a point in comparison with this distance. If the Ptolemaic theory strained credulity somewhat by making the fixed stars move at so great a pace in their diurnal rotation, Copernicus strained credulity in those days by what seemed a corresponding extravagance—he put the fixed stars at what men thought to be a fabulous distance away. He even robbed his system of some of its economy and its symmetry; for after all the beautiful spacing between the sun and the successive planets he found himself obliged to put a prodigal wilderness of empty space between the outermost planet, Saturn, and the fixed stars. The situation was even more paradoxical than this. When Galileo first used a telescope, one of his initial surprises was to learn that the fixed stars now appeared to be smaller than they had seemed to the naked eye; they showed themselves, he said, as mere pin-points of light. Owing to a kind of blur the fixed stars appear to be bigger than they really ought to appear to the naked eye, and Copernicus, living before that optical illusion had been clarified, was bound to be under certain misapprehensions on this subject. Even before his time some of the fixed stars had seemed to strain credulity when the attempt had been made to calculate their size on the basis of their apparent magnitude. His removal of them to a distance almost immeasurably farther away (while their apparent magnitude remained the same, of course, to the terrestrial observer) made it necessary to regard them as immensely bigger still, and strained a credulity which had been stretched over-far already.

Beyond this there was the famous objection that if the world were rushing from west to east a stone dropped from the top of a tower ought to be left behind, falling therefore well to the west of the tower. The famous Danish astronomer, Tycho Brahé, took this argument seriously, however absurd it might appear to us, and he introduced the new argument that a cannon-ball ought to carry much farther one way than the other, supposing the earth to be in motion. This argument had a novel flavour that made it particularly fashionable in the succeeding period.

In the meantime, however, certain other important things had been happening, and as a result of these it gradually became clear that great changes would have to take place in astronomy—that, indeed, the older theories were unworkable, whether the Copernican hypothesis should happen to be true or not. One of these was the appearance of a new star in 1572—an event which one historian of science appears to me to be correct in describing as a greater shock to European thought than the publication of the Copernican hypothesis itself. This star is said to have been brighter in the sky than anything except the sun, the moon and Venus—visible even in daylight sometimes—and it shone through the whole of the year 1573, only disappearing early in 1574. If it was a new star it contradicted the old view that the sublime heavens knew neither change nor generation nor corruption, and people even reminded themselves that God had ceased the work of creation on the seventh day. Attempts were made to show that the star existed only in the sublunary region, and even Galileo later thought it necessary to expose the inaccurate observations which were selected from the mass of available data to support this view. After all, Copernicus had only put forward an alternative theory of the skies which he claimed to be superior to the ancient one—now men were meeting inconvenient facts which sooner or later they would have to stop denying.

In 1577 a new comet appeared, and even some people who disbelieved the Copernican theory had to admit that it belonged to the upper skies, not to the sublunary regions—the more accurate observations which were now being made had altered the situation in regard to the observation of the whereabouts of comets. As this one cut a path straight through what were supposed to be the impenetrable crystal spheres that formed the skies, it encouraged the view that spheres did not actually exist as part of the machinery of the heavens; Tycho Brahé, conservative though he was in other respects, declared his disbelief in the reality of these orbs. In the last quarter of the sixteenth century Giordano Bruno, whom I have already mentioned, pictured the planets and stars floating in empty space, though it now became more difficult than ever to say why they moved and how they were kept in their regular paths. Also the Aristotelian theory that comets were formed out of mere exhalations from the earth, which ignited in the sphere of fire—all within the sublunary realm—was now contradicted. And those who did not wish to fly in the face of actual evidence began to modify the Aristotelian theory in detail—one man would say that the upper heavens were not unchangeable and uncorruptible; another would say that the very atmosphere extended throughout the upper skies, enabling the exhalations from the earth to rise and ignite even in the regions far above the moon. Quite apart from any attack which Copernicus had made upon the system, the foundations of the Ptolemaic universe were beginning to shake.

It is particularly towards the end of the sixteenth century that we can recognise the extraordinary intermediate situation which existed—we can see the people themselves already becoming conscious of the transitional stage which astronomical science had reached. In 1589 one writer, Magini, said that there was a great demand for a new hypothesis which would supersede the Ptolemaic one and yet not be so absurd as the Copernican. Another writer, Mæstlin, said that better observations were needed than either those of Ptolemy or those of Copernicus, and that the time had come for "the radical renovation of astronomy". People even put forward the view that one should drop all hypotheses and set out simply to assemble a collection of more accurate observations. Tycho Brahé replied to this that it was impossible to sit down just to observe without the guidance of any hypothesis at all.

Yet that radical renovation of astronomy which Mæstlin required was being carried out precisely in the closing years of the sixteenth century; and Tycho Brahé was its first leader, becoming important not for his hypotheses but precisely because of what has been called the "chaos" of observations that he left behind for his successors. We have seen that in the last quarter of the sixteenth century he achieved practically all that in fact was achieved, if not all that was possible, in the way of pre-telescopic observation. He greatly improved the instruments and the accuracy of observation. He followed the planets throughout the whole of their courses, instead of merely trying to pick them out at special points in their orbits. We have noticed also his anti-Copernican fervour, and in one respect his actual systematising was important, though his theories were not justified by events; and when he had made his observations he did not follow them up with any development of them since he was not a remarkable mathematician. He

attempted, however, to establish a compromise between the Ptolemaic
and the Copernican systems—some of the planets moving around the
sun, but then the sun and its planetary system moving in a great sweep
around the motionless earth. This is a further illustration of the intermediate and transitional character of this period, for his compromise
gained a certain following, he complained later that other men pre-
tended to be the inventors of it, and after a certain period in the seventeenth century this system secured the adhesion of those who still
refused to believe in the actual movement of the earth. He was not
quite so original as he imagined, and his compromise system has a
history which goes back to much earlier times.

Still more significant was the fact that the chaos of data collected
and recorded by Tycho Brahé came into the hands of a man who had
been his assistant for a time, Johann Kepler, the pupil of the very
person, Mæstlin, who had demanded a renovation of astronomy.
Kepler, therefore, emerges not merely as an isolated genius, but as a
product of that whole movement of renovation which was taking place
at the end of the sixteenth century. He had the advantage over Tycho
Brahé in that he was a great mathematician, and he could profit from
considerable advances that had taken place in mathematics during the
sixteenth century. There was one further factor which curiously assisted that renovation of astronomy which we are examining at the
moment, and it was a factor of special importance if the world was
to get rid of the crystal spheres and see the planets merely floating in
empty space. An Englishman, William Gilbert, published a famous
book on the magnet in 1600 and laid himself open to the gibes of Sir
Francis Bacon for being one of those people so taken up with their pet
subject of research that they could only see the whole universe transposed into the terms of it. Having made a spherical magnet called a
terrella, and having found that it revolved when placed in a magnetic
field, he decided that the whole earth was a magnet, that gravity was a
form of magnetic attraction, and that the principles of the magnet
accounted for the workings of the Copernican system as a whole.
Kepler and Galileo were both influenced by this view, and with Kepler
it became an integral part of his system, a basis for a doctrine of
almost universal gravitation. William Gilbert provided intermediate
assistance therefore—brought a gleam of light—when the Aristotelian
cosmos was breaking down and the heavenly bodies would otherwise
have been left drifting blindly in empty space.

With all these developments behind him, therefore, the famous
Kepler in the first thirty years of the seventeenth century "reduced to
order the chaos of data" left by Tycho Brahé, and added to them just

the thing that was needed—mathematical genius. Like Copernicus he created another world-system which, since it did not ultimately prevail, merely remains as a strange monument of colossal intellectual power working on insufficient materials; and even more than Copernicus he was driven by a mystical semi-religious fervour—a passion to uncover the magic of mere numbers and to demonstrate the music of the spheres. In his attempt to disclose mathematical sympathies in the machinery of the skies he tried at one moment to relate the planetary orbits to geometrical figures, and at another moment to make them correspond to musical notes. He was like the child who having picked a mass of wild flowers tries to arrange them into a posy this way, and then tries another way, exploring the possible combinations and harmonies. He has to his credit a collection of discoveries and conclusions —some of them more ingenious than useful—from which we today can pick out three that have a permanent importance in the history of astronomy. Having discovered in the first place that the planets did not move at a uniform speed, he set out to find order somewhere, and came upon the law that if a line were drawn from a given planet to the sun that line would describe equal areas in equal times. At two different points in his calculations it would appear that he made mistakes, but the conclusion was happy for the two errors had the effect of cancelling one another out. Kepler realised that the pace of the planets was affected by their nearness to the sun—a point which encouraged him in his view that the planets were moved by a power actually emitted by the sun.

His achievements would have been impossible without that tremendous improvement in observation which had taken place since the time of Copernicus. He left behind him great masses of papers which help the historian of science to realise better than in the case of his predecessors his actual manner of work and the stages by which he made his discoveries. It was when working on the data left by Tycho Brahé on the subject of the movements of Mars that he found himself faced with the problem of accounting for the extraordinary anomalies in the apparent orbit of this planet. We know how with colossal expenditure of energy he tried one hypothesis after another, and threw them away, until he reached a point where he had a vague knowledge of the shape required, decided that for purposes of calculation an ellipse might give him at any rate approximate results, and then found that an ellipse was right—a conclusion which he assumed then to be true also for the other planets.

Some people have said that Kepler emancipated the world from the myth of circular motion, but this is hardly true, for from the time of the ancient Ptolemy men had realised that the planets themselves did not move in regular circles. Copernicus had been aware that certain combinations of circular motion would provide an elliptical course, and even after Kepler we find people accounting for the new elliptical path of the planets by reference to a mixture of circular movements. The obsession on the subject of circular motion was disappearing at this time, however, for other reasons, and chiefly because the existence of the hard crystal spheres was ceasing to be credible. It had been the spheres, the various inner wheels of the vast celestial machine, that had enjoyed the happiness of circular motion, while the planet, moving by the resultant effect of various compound movements, had been realised all the time to be pursuing a more irregular course. It was the circular motion of the spheres themselves that symbolised the perfection of the skies, while the planet was like the rear lamp of a bicycle—it might be the only thing that could actually be seen from the earth, and it dodged about in an irregular manner; but just as we know that it is really the man on the bicycle who matters, though we see nothing save the red light, so the celestial orbs had formed the essential machinery of the skies, though only the planet that rode on their shoulder was actually visible. Once the crystal spheres were eliminated, the circular motion ceased to be the thing that really mattered—henceforward it was the actual path of the planet itself that fixed one's attention. It was as though the man on the bicycle had been proved not to exist, and the rear lamp, the red light, was discovered to be sailing on its own account in empty space. The world might be rid of the myth of circular motion, but it was faced with more difficult problems than ever with these lamps let loose and no bicycle to attach them to. If the skies were like this, men had to discover why they remained in any order at all—why the universe was not shattered by the senseless onrush and the uncontrollable collidings of countless billiard-balls.

Kepler believed in order and in the harmony of numbers, and it was in his attempt to fasten upon the music of the spheres that he discovered, amongst many other things, that third of his series of planetary laws which was to prove both useful and permanent—namely, the law that the squares of the period of the orbit were proportional to the cubes of their mean distances from the sun. By this time Kepler was not the strange mystic that he had been at first—he was no longer looking for an actual music of the spheres which could be heard by God or man, or which should be loaded with mystical content. The music of the spheres was now nothing more or less to him than mathematics as such—the purely mathematical sympathies that the universe exhibited—so that what concerned him was merely to drive ahead, for ever eliciting mathematical proportions in the heavens. In fact, we may say that this worship of numerical patterns, of mathematical relations as such, took the place of the older attempt, that was still visible in Galileo, to transpose the skies into terms of circles and spheres, and become the foundation of a new kind of astronomy. It is in this particular sense that Kepler can most properly be described as having provided an improvement upon the old superstition which had hankered only after circular motion. Furthermore, by the same route, Kepler became the apostle of a mechanistic system—the first one of the seventeenth-century kind—realising that he was aspiring to turn the universe into pure clockwork, and believing that this was the highest thing he could do to glorify God. It will be necessary to glance at the Keplerian system as a whole when we come to the problem of gravitation at a later stage of the story. We must note that, of course, Kepler believed in the motion of the earth, and showed that if this supposition were accepted the movement conformed to the laws which he had discovered for the planets in general.

Besides Kepler's three planetary laws, one final addition was being made in this period to the collection of material that spelt the doom of Ptolemy and Aristotle. In 1609 Galileo, having heard of the discovery of the telescope in Holland, created a telescope for himself, though not before an actual sample of the Dutch instrument had appeared in Venice. Instantly the sky was filled with new things and the conservative view of the heavenly bodies became more completely untenable than ever. Two items were of particular importance. First, the discovery of the satellites of Jupiter provided a picture of what might be described as a sort of miniature solar system in itself. Those who had argued that the moon obviously goes round the earth, *ergo* in a regular heaven the celestial bodies must move about the same centre, were now confronted with the fact that Jupiter had its own moons, which revolved around it, while both Jupiter and its attendants certainly moved together either around the sun as the Copernicans said, or around the earth according to the system of Ptolemy. Something besides the earth could be shown to operate therefore as the center of motions taking place in the sky. Secondly, the sunspots now became visible and if Galileo's observations of them were correct they destroyed the basis for the view that the heavens were immaculate and unchanging. Galileo set out to demonstrate that the spots were, so to speak, part of the sun, actually revolving with it, though the Aristotelians tried to argue that they were an intervening cloud, and that some of Galileo's discoveries were really the result of flaws in the lenses of his telescope. Galileo was seriously provoked by these taunts and at this point of the story the whole controversy with the Aristotelians flared up to an unprecedented degree of intensity, not only because the situation was ripe for it, but because Galileo, goaded to scorn by university colleagues and monks, turned his attention from questions of mechanics to the larger problem of the Aristotelian issue in general. He ranged over the whole field of that controversy, bringing to it an amazing polemical imagination, which goaded the enemy in turn.

His intervention was particularly important because the point had been reached at which there was bound to be a complete impasse unless the new astronomy could be married somehow to the new science of dynamics. The Aristotelian cosmos might be jeopardised, and indeed was doomed to destruction by the recent astronomical disclosures; yet these facts did not in the least help the enquirers over the original hurdle—did not show them how to square the movement of the earth itself with the principles of Aristotelian mechanics or how to account for the motions in the sky. Copernicus had taken one course in treating the earth as virtually a celestial body in the Aristotelian sense—a perfect sphere governed by the laws which operated in the higher reaches of the skies. Galileo complemented this by taking now the opposite course—rather treating the heavenly bodies as terrestrial ones, regarding the planets as subject to the very laws which applied to balls sliding down inclined planes. There was something in all this which tended to the reduction of the whole universe to uniform physical laws, and it is clear that the world was coming to be more ready to admit such a view.

After his construction of a telescope in 1609 and the disturbing phenomena which were revealed immediately afterwards in the skies, Galileo's relations with the Peripatetics—the worshippers of Aristotle —at the university of Padua became intensely bitter. Though for a time he met with support and encouragement in high places, and even in Rome itself, the intensified controversy led to the condemnation of the Copernican hypothesis by the Congregation of the Index in 1616. This did not prevent Galileo from producing in the years 1625–29 the series of Dialogues on *The Two Principal World-Systems* which he designed to stand as his *magnum opus* and which were to lead to his condemnation. This book traversed the whole range of anti-Aristotelian argument, not merely in the realm of astronomy, but in the field of mechanics, as though seeking to codify the entire case against the adherents of the ancient system. It stands as a testimony to the fact that it was vain to attack the Aristotelian teaching merely at a single point—vain to attempt in one corner of the field to reinterpret motion by the theory of impetus as the Parisian scholastics had done—which was only like filling the gap in one jigsaw puzzle with a piece out of a different jigsaw puzzle altogether. What was needed was a large-scale change of design—the substitution of one highly dovetailed system for another—and in a sense it appeared to be the case that the whole Aristotelian synthesis had to be overturned at once. And that is why Galileo is so important; for, at the strategic moment, he took the lead in a policy of simultaneous attack on the whole front.

The work in question was written in Italian and addressed to a public somewhat wider than the realm of learning—wider than that university world which Galileo had set out to attack. Its argument was conducted much more in the language of ordinary conversation, much more in terms of general discourse, than the present-day reader would expect—the *Dialogues* themselves are remarkable for their literary skill and polemical scorn. Galileo paid little attention to Kepler's astronomical discoveries—remaining more Copernican in his general views, more content to discuss purely circular motion in the skies, than the modern reader would expect to be the case. He has been regarded as unfair because he talked only of two principal world-systems, those of Ptolemy and Copernicus, leaving the new systems of Tycho Brahé and Johann Kepler entirely out of account. In his mechanics he was a little less original than most people imagine, since, apart from the older teachers of the impetus-theory, he had had more immediate precursors, who had begun to develop the more modern views concerning the flight of projectiles, the law of inertia and the behaviour of falling bodies. He was not original when he showed that clouds and air and everything on the earth—including falling bodies—naturally moved round with the rotating earth, as part of the same mechanical system, and in their relations with one another were unaffected by the movement, so that like the objects in the cabin of a moving ship, they might appear motionless to anybody moving with them. His system of mechanics did not quite come out clear and clean, did not even quite explicitly reach the modern law of inertia, since even here he had not quite disentangled himself from obsessions concerning circular motion. It was chiefly in his mechanics, however, that Galileo made his contributions to the solution of the problem of the skies, and here he came so near to the mark that his successors had only to continue their work on the same lines and future scientists were able to read back into his writings the views which in fact were only perfected later. Galileo's kind of mechanics had a strategic place in the story, for they had to be married to the astronomy of Kepler before the new scientific order was established. And the new dynamics themselves could not be developed merely out of a study of terrestrial motion. Galileo is important because he began to develop them with reference to the behaviour of the heavenly bodies too.

At the end of everything Galileo failed to clinch his argument—he did not exactly prove the rotation of the earth—and in the resulting situation a reader either could adopt his whole way of looking at things or could reject it *in toto*—it was a question of entering into the whole realm of thought into which he had transposed the question. It was true that the genuinely scientific mind could hardly resist the case as a whole, or refuse to enter into the new way of envisaging the matter; but when Galileo's mouthpiece was charged in the *Dialogues* with having failed to prove his case—having done nothing more than explain away the ideas that made the movement of the earth seem impossible—he seemed prepared to admit that he had not demonstrated the actual movement, and at the end of Book III he brought out his secret weapon—he declared that he had an argument which would really clinch the matter. We know that Galileo attached a crucial importance to this argument, which appears in the fourth book, and, in fact, he thought of taking the title of the whole work from this particular part of it. His argument was that the tides demonstrated the movement of the earth. He made a long examination of them and said that they were caused, so to speak, by the shaking of the vessel which contained them. This seemed to contradict his former argument that everything on the earth moved with the earth, and was as unaffected by the movement as the candle in the cabin of a moving ship. It was the combination of motions, however—the daily rotation together with the annual movement, and the accompanying strains and changes of pace—which produced the jerks, he said, and therefore set the tides in motion. Nothing can better show the transitional stage of the question even now than the fact that Galileo's capital proof of the motion of the earth was a great mistake and did nothing to bring the solution of the question nearer.

Aristotelian physics were clearly breaking down, and the Ptolemaic system was split from top to bottom. But not till the time of Newton did the satisfactory alternative system appear; and though the more modern of the scientists tended to believe in the movement of the earth from this time, the general tendency from about 1630 seems to have been to adopt the compromise system of Tycho Brahé. In 1672 a writer could say that the student of the heavens had four different world-

systems from which to choose, and there were men who even talked
of seven. Even at this later date an enquirer could still come forward
—as Galileo had done—and claim that at last he had discovered the
capital argument. The long existence of this dubious, intermediate
situation brings the importance of Sir Isaac Newton into still stronger
relief. We can better understand also, if we cannot condone, the treatment which Galileo had to suffer from the Church for a presumption
which in his dialogues on *The Two Principal World-Systems* he had
certainly displayed in more ways than one.

It is not always realised to what a degree the sciences in the middle
ages were a matter for what we today would describe as literary transmission, and came into European history as a heritage from ancient
Greece and imperial Rome. Nobody can examine the actual state of
scientific knowledge in, say, the tenth century A.D. without realising
what had been lost both in scholarship and in technique—indeed, in
civilisation as a whole—since the days of ancient Athens and ancient
Alexandria, or even since the time when St. Augustine flourished.
Nobody who has any picture of Europe as it emerged from the dark
ages, or any impression of our Anglo-Saxon fore-fathers one or two
centuries before the Norman Conquest, will imagine that the world
was then in a condition to discover by its own enquiries and experiments the scientific knowledge which Athens and Alexandria had attained at a time when their civilisation was at its peak. Actual contact
with the science of the ancient world had to be re-established by the
unearthing of texts and manuscripts, or by the acquisition of translations and commentaries from peoples like the Arabs or the subjects of
the Byzantine Empire, who already possessed, or had never lost, the
contact. That process of recovery reached its climax and came to full
consciousness in the period of what we call the Renaissance. It would
have taken many hundreds of years more if the middle ages had had,
so to speak, to find the same things out for themselves—to re-create
so much of the development of science by independent enquiry and
unaided research.

All this helps to explain why so much of the history of medieval
thought rests on a framework of dates which are really dates in the
literary transmission of ancient science and scholarship. Historians find
it of primary importance to discover at what date such and such a work
of Aristotle was rediscovered in western Europe; or when this or that
scientific treatise became available through an Arabian translation, and
—better still—when western Europe was able to acquire the authentic
text in the original Greek. The process was not stopped by any reluc-

tance on the part of Catholic Europe to learn from the infidel Arabians or the Byzantine schismatics or even the pagan Greeks. Nor is it known that there was any opportunity which the middle ages missed—any great store of science that they turned their backs upon because it was tainted with paganism or infidelity. Because the intelligentsia in the middle ages was a clerical one and the intellectual leadership was religious in character, such natural science as existed was the more likely to keep the subordinate place it had always had in a larger philosophical system—what we call "natural scientists" could hardly be said to have existed then, in any significant sense of the term. Because the purely literary transmission was so important, that thing which we call science and which might rather be called natural philosophy was first and foremost a series of ancient texts upon which one commentary after another would be compiled often by people writing, so to speak, at a desk. If even at the Renaissance philology was considered the queen of the sciences, this was because the man who was master of the classical languages did in fact hold the key position. We can still read the letters of humanists who cursed their fate because they had to ruin their style by translating works of physics from the Greek.

So in the middle ages men found themselves endowed with an explanation of the physical universe and the workings of nature which had fallen upon them out of the blue, and which they had taken over full-grown and ready-made. And they were infinitely more the slaves of that intellectual system than if they had actually invented it themselves, developing it out of their own original researches and their own wrestlings with truth. There even seems to have been a perceptible hurdle here and there where there was a gap in the transmission—where patches of ancient scholarship were undiscovered. We have already noticed, for example, certain tendencies in fourteenth-century Paris which are considered to have been nipped in the bud because of a deficiency in mathematics—a deficiency somewhat rectified by a further recovery of ancient texts in the period of the Renaissance. Under such conditions the chief opening for independent thought—the chief controversies in the sixteenth century even—occurred at those places where the ancient writers were found to have differed from one another. And though in the latter middle ages there were men who were doing experiments and pushing back the frontiers of thought, they were, for the most part, like the theorists of the impetus, only playing on the margin of that Aristotelian system which in the year 1500 must have appeared at least as valid to a rational thinker as it could have done fifteen hundred years before. Though there were men in the later middle ages who were carefully observing nature, and improving greatly in the accuracy of their observations, these tended to compile encyclopædias of purely descriptive matter. When there was anything that needed to be explained these men would not elicit their theories from the observations themselves—they would still draw on that whole system of explanation which had been provided for them by the ancient philosophy. Sir Francis Bacon, early in the seventeenth century, complained of this divorce between observation and explanation, and it was part of his purpose to show how the latter ought to arise out of the former.

So far as one can see, the mathematics of ancient Alexandria, acquired at the time of the Renaissance, and the works of Archimedes, made generally available in translation in 1543, represent the last pocket of the science of antiquity which was recovered in time to be an ingredient or a factor in the formation of our modern science. As we have already seen, this was a body of knowledge which, so far as one can judge, it was necessary to recover before all the components of the scientific movement could be assembled together and the autonomous efforts of scientific enquirers—of a new crowd of pioneers in research —could properly be put into gear. And it is remarkable how quickly things began to move once all the ingredients, so to speak, had at last been collected together. Early in the seventeenth century, as we have already seen, the ancient explanation of the universe—the framework of existing science—was palpably breaking down. There was beginning to emerge what contemporaries clearly recognised as a scientific revolution, and what to us is the dawn of modern science.

Now, if we are seeking to understand this birth of modern science we must not imagine that everything is explained by the resort to an experimental mode of procedure, or even that experiments were any great novelty. It was commonly argued, even by the enemies of the Aristotelian system, that that system itself could never have been founded except on the footing of observations and experiments—a reminder necessary perhaps in the case of those university teachers of the sixteenth and seventeenth centuries who still clung to the old routine and went on commentating too much in what we might call a "literary" manner upon the works of the ancient writers. We may be surprised to note, however, that in one of the dialogues of Galileo, it is Simplicius, the spokesman of the Aristotelians—the butt of the whole piece—who defends the experimental method of Aristotle against what is described as the mathematical method of Galileo. And elsewhere it is the man speaking as the mouthpiece of Galileo himself who says that though Aristotle only gives reasoning to prove that such and such a thing must be the case, still this is only Aristotle's way of demonstrating the thesis—the actual discovery of it must have been the result of experiment. We have already seen how the medical students and the medical university of Padua were ahead of most other people in their regard for experiment, and the most remarkable result of the experimental method that we have met with so far in these lectures is William Harvey's treatise on the circulation of the blood. Yet it was not in the biological sciences that the Aristotelian way of attacking the problem was to receive its spectacular overthrow. It was not there that the scientific revolution found its centre or its pivot—on the contrary, we shall have to study later the effects of the scientific revolution as they come by reflection, so to speak (and at a second remove), upon the biological and other sciences. What is more remarkable still is the fact that the science in which experiment reigned supreme—the science which was centered in laboratories even before the beginning of modern times—was remarkably slow, if not the slowest of all, in reaching its modern form. It was long before alchemy became chemistry, and chemistry itself became in the full sense of the word quantitative in its method, instead of being qualitative, after the manner of ancient science.

It may be interesting in this connection to glance at what perhaps is the most famous experiment of the scientific revolution—what an historian of science declared in 1923 to be "one of the outstanding achievements of scientific history". It comes from the vague story of a disciple and a somewhat romantic biographer of Galileo, who said that his teacher had dropped two bodies of different weights from the tower of Pisa to prove that Aristotle was wrong in his view that they would fall at paces proportional to their weights. Later historians of science filled in the details, so that in a work published in 1918 the final precision was attained, and we learn how this martyr of science climbed the leaning tower of Pisa with a one-hundred-pound cannon ball under one arm and a one-pound ball under the other. Even Dr. Singer repeated the story in 1941 in his history of science, where he calls it "the most famous of experiments" and attributes it to the year 1591. None of the vast crowd who are supposed to have observed the experiment gave any evidence on behalf of it—though, as we shall see, there was a particular reason why they should have done so if they had actually been witnesses—and the writings of Galileo gave no confirmation of the story. On the contrary, the writings of Galileo showed that he had tried the experiment several times in his youth with the opposite result

—he said in one of his juvenile works that he had tested the matter on many occasions from a high tower and that in his experience a lump of lead would very soon leave a lump of wood behind. The supposed experiment had actually been tried by another scientist, Simon Stevin of Bruges, and was recorded in a book published in 1605. Stevin, however, dropped balls of lead only from a height of thirty feet, and, considering how little was known in those days about the effects of such things as air-resistance, the Aristotelians were perhaps not unreasonable in saying that the result was not conclusive—you needed to try the experiment from a great height.

Galileo, who in his youth indulged in curious speculations concerning the behaviour of falling bodies, ought to have been in a position to appreciate that argument; for, again in one of his early works, he had even insisted that it was useless to drop bodies from the top of a tower —the height would need to be doubled before it was possible to form a proper judgment, he said. To crown the comedy, it was an Aristotelian, Coresio, who in 1612 claimed that previous experiments had been carried out from too low an altitude. In a work published in that year he described how he had improved on all previous attempts—he had not merely dropped bodies from a high window, he had gone to the very top of the tower of Pisa. The larger body had fallen more quickly than the smaller one on this occasion, and the experiment, he claimed, had proved Aristotle to have been right all the time. Coresio's work was published in Florence, and it does not appear that either Galileo or anybody else challenged the truth of the assertion, though the date is long after that of the alleged incident in the life of Galileo.

In reality, the predecessors of Galileo had for some time been gradually approaching the settlement of the problem on different lines altogether. At first they had moved timidly and had argued that different weights of the same substance would fall simultaneously, though there might be a difference in pace, they said, if the comparison were between different substances altogether. Galileo, in fact, uses the argument employed by his predecessors—they had reasoned that two tiles each weighing a pound and dropped at the same moment would fall to the ground at precisely the same time. Fastened together, end to end, they would still descend at the pace at which they had fallen when dropped merely side by side. And if one were fastened on the top of the other, still it would not press down more heavily than before, and therefore it would do nothing to press its lower partner to fall any more quickly either. In other words, the predecessors of Galileo had reasoned their way to the answer to this particular problem, and neither they nor

Galileo showed any willingness to alter the conclusion merely because the experimental method had failed to confirm their judgment. In his youth Galileo had held the view for a time that falling bodies did not accelerate—at least, they only accelerated at the beginning of their fall, he said, until they got into proper going form. Even on this point he was not to be put off by mere observation. It was in this connection that he refused to be deterred by the results of an experiment made from a tower, and said that it would be necessary to drop things from twice that height before the experiment could be regarded as decisive. As an appendix to the whole story I may note the existence of a controversy on the question whether Aristotle himself held the views for which this crucial experiment was supposed to have brought him into discredit. The matter is irrelevant, however, as at any rate the Aristotelians of the seventeenth century held these views and accepted the issue as a fair one.

In connection with this and many similar problems, it would be somewhere near the truth if one were to say that for about fifty years there had been considerable comment on what are called the "thought-experiments" of Galileo. In some of his works one can hardly fail to notice the way in which he would assert: "If you were to do this thing, then this other particular thing *would* happen"; and on some occasions it would appear to be the case that he was wrong in his inference—on some occasions nobody stops to worry if one of the parties in the dialogues even makes the point that the experiment has never been tried. It is curious also how often Galileo makes use of these "thought-experiments" in regard to those points of mechanics that affect the question of the rotation of the earth—how often he resorts to them when he is meeting the arguments that were the chief stock-in-trade of the Aristotelians. He discusses what would happen if you were to drop a stone from the top of the mast of a ship (*a*) when the vessel was moving and (*b*) when the vessel was at rest. Much later, in 1641, a considerable sensation was caused by Gassendi, who actually tried the experiment and published the result, which on this occasion confirmed the thesis of Galileo. There was in France a younger contemporary and admirer of Galileo, called Mersenne, who, though a disciple of the great Italian in mechanics, was unable to feel convinced by the arguments which had been put forward in favour of the rotation of the earth. He came across Galileo's "thought-experiments" in this field and on one occasion after another we find him making the significant comment: "Yes, only the experiment has never been tried." As, later, he began to show himself more sympathetic to the Copernican point of view, Mersenne revealed that even now it was a different form of reasoning that appealed to him—a type of argument belonging to a period long before the time of Galileo. He said: "If I could be convinced that God always did things in the shortest and easiest way, then I should certainly have to recognise the fact that the world does move."

The scientific revolution is most significant, and its achievements are the most remarkable, in the fields of astronomy and mechanics. In the former realm the rise of experiment in any ordinary sense of the word can hardly be expected to have had any relevance. In regard to the latter we may recall what we observed when we were dealing with the problem of motion—how it seemed reasonable to say that the great achievement was due to a transposition taking place in the mind of the enquirer himself. Here was a problem which only became manageable when in a certain sense it had been "geometrised", so that motion had come to be envisaged as occurring in the emptiness of Archimedean space. Indeed, the modern law of inertia—the modern picture of bodies continuing their motion in a straight line and away to infinity—was hardly a thing which the human mind would ever reach by an experiment, or by any attempt to make observation more photographic, in any case. It depended on the trick of seeing a purely geometrical body sailing off into a kind of space which was empty and neutral—utterly indifferent to what was happening—like a blank sheet of paper, equally passive whether we draw a vertical or a horizontal line.

In the case of the Aristotelian system the situation had been different—it had always been impossible to forget that certain parts of the universe had a special "pull". There were certain directions which it was fundamental to regard as privileged directions. All lines tended to be attracted to the centre of the earth. Under this system it was not possible to make the required abstraction, and, for example, to draw a simple straight line to represent a body flying off at a tangent—flying off with determination and rectitude into infinite space. It was necessary that the line should curl around to the bottom of the paper, for the very universe was pulling it down, dragging the body all the time towards the centre of the earth. At this point even Galileo was imperfect. He did not attain the full conception of utterly empty, utterly directionless, Euclidian space. That is why he failed to achieve the perfect formulation of the modern law of inertia, for he believed that the law of inertia applied to motion in a circle; and here he was wrong—what we call "inertial motion" must be movement along a straight line. When he talked of a perfectly spherical ball riding off to infinity on a perfectly smooth horizontal plane, he showed his limitations; for he regarded the horizontal plane as being equidistant from the centre of the earth, and pictured it as a plane that actually went round the earth; so that he could seize upon even this as a form of circular motion. In general, he was perhaps a little too "Copernican" even in his mechanics, therefore—a little too ready to regard circular motion as the "natural" kind of motion, the thing which did not require to be explained. In reality, under the terms of the new physics, it was precisely this circular motion which became "violent" motion in the Aristotelian sense of the word. The stone that is swung round in a sling requires a constant force to draw it to the centre, and needs the exertion of violence to keep it in a circular path and prevent it from flying off at a tangent.

The men who succeeded Galileo made a cleaner affair of this business of geometrising a problem, and drew their diagrams in a space more free, more completely empty, and more thoroughly neutral. We can see at times how the new science had to dispose of mental obstructions in the achievement of this task, as when the two vertical sides of a balance were assumed to be parallel and the objection was raised that they must meet at the centre of the earth. It was easy to reply: "Very well, let us leave the center of the earth out of the picture, let us suspend the balance up in the sky, far above the sun itself. Let us take it even an infinite distance away if necessary. Then we can be satisfied that the lines are really parallel." If there was a threat that the diagram should be spoiled by the operation of gravity they would say: "Away with gravity! Let us imagine the body placed in heaven, where there is neither up nor down—where up and down, in fact, are as indifferent as right and left." It was possible to argue: "Surely God can put a body in totally empty space, and we can watch it moving where there is nothing in the universe to attract or repel or in any way interfere with it."

The Aristotelian system had never been conducive to such a policy, which was necessary for the "geometrising" of problems, and which rendered science itself more amenable to a mathematical mode of treatment. It had not even been conducive to such a simple thing as "the parallelogram of forces", though Simon Stevin may not have been absolutely original when he produced this device in the days when Galileo was young. The Aristotelian system had discouraged the idea of the composition of motions, and was uncongenial to any mathematical treatment of the path which a body would follow when one motion happened to be complicated by another. We have seen how, in the case of projectiles, the Peripatetics had been unwilling to consider a mixture of motions, and had preferred to regard the body as driving forwards in a straight line until that motion was spent, and then dropping vertically to the ground. It had been the new school which had begun to curve the corner of the diagram and produced the view that in the mathematical world (which for a time they confused with the real world) the projectile described a parabola. And they worked out by mathematics the angle at which a gun must stand in order to fire the farthest; leaving their conclusion to be tested afterwards by actual experiment. All this helps to explain why Galileo could be in the position of defending what he called the mathematical method even against the experimental system of the better Aristotelians. It helps to explain also why Sir Francis Bacon, for all his love of experiments, was in a certain sense inadequate for the age, and proved to be open to criticism in the seventeenth century because of his deficiency in mathematics. In a certain sense he saw the importance of mathematics—the necessity of making calculations on the results of experiments in physics, for example—and even on one occasion made an emphatic statement in regard to this matter. What he lacked was the geometer's eye, the power to single out those things which could be measured, and to turn a given scientific problem into a question of mathematics.

It was the extension of the new method that was to prove exceptionally important, however. Having conceived of motion in its simplest form—motion as taking place in this empty directionless space where nothing whatever could interfere with it and no resisting medium could put a check on it—the modern school could then reverse the process and collect back the things they had thrown away. Or, rather, we must say, they could draw more and more of these things into their geometrised world and make them amenable to the same kind of mathematical treatment. Things like air-resistance, which had been read out of the diagram at the first stage of the argument, could now be brought back into the picture, but brought back in a different way—no longer despots but subjugated servants. These things themselves were now caught into the mathematical method and turned into problems of geometry, and the same mode of treatment could be applied to the problem of gravity itself. The very method which the new science had adopted was one that directed the mind to more fields of enquiry and suggested new lines of experiment—attracting the student to things that would never have caught the attention of the Aristotelian enquirer. And the new avenues which were opened up in this way, even for experiment, were to carry the natural sciences away from that world of common-sense phenomena and ordinary appearances in which not only the Aristotelians but also the theorists of the impetus had done so much of their thinking. In particular, the mind was to be constantly directed in future to those things—and was to apply itself to those problems—which were amenable to measurement and calculation. Galileo therefore spoke very much to the point when he said that shape, size, quantity and motion were the primary qualities which the scientist should seek to examine when he was enquiring into given bodies. Tastes, colours, sounds and smells were a matter of comparative indifference to him—they would not exist, he asserted, if human beings had not possessed noses and ears, tongues and eyes. In other words, science was to confine its attention to those things which were capable of measurement and calculation. Other objects which might be unamenable to such mathematical treatment in the first instance might still be resolved into their fundamentals. They might be translated or transposed into something else, and so, at a later stage of the argument, might become capable of being measured and weighed in turn.

In any case, it is essential that our interest in the experimental method as such should not cause us to overlook a matter of which the seventeenth century itself was clearly conscious—namely, the importance of mathematics in the developments that were taking place. When the interpretation of the whole scientific revolution is in question, certain facts which seem to have a bearing upon this strike the outsider as peculiarly significant. We have already met with certain important aspirations and developments that belong to the fifteenth and sixteenth centuries—hints of a more modern kind of mechanics for example, foreshadowings of analytical geometry, discussions which seem even to point towards what we call mathematical physics, and even intuitions concerning the value of the purely quantitative method in the natural sciences. We are told, however, that these interesting developments were brought to a halt, apparently because the middle ages lacked the necessary mathematics—the world had to wait until more of the mathematics of the ancient world had been recovered at the Renaissance. It would appear that there can exist a case of what might be called stunted development in the history of science. A movement may be checked, almost before it has cut any ice, if one of the requisite conditions happens to be lacking for the time being. In a similar way, we learn that Kepler's discovery of the laws of planetary motion was made possible only by the fact that he inherited and developed further for himself the study of conic sections, a study in which he excelled all of his contemporaries. And certainly Tycho Brahé's astronomical observations became a revolutionary factor in history only when the mathematical mind of a Kepler had set to work upon that collection of materials. At a later date the same phenomenon recurs and we learn that the problem of gravitation would never have been solved—the whole Newtonian synthesis would never have been achieved—without, first, the analytical geometry of René Descartes and, secondly, the infinitesimal calculus of Newton and Leibnitz. Not only did the science of mathematics make a remarkable development in the seventeenth century, then, but in dynamics and in physics the sciences give the impression that they were pressing upon the frontiers of the mathematics all the time. Without the achievements of the mathematicians the scientific revolution, as we know it, would have been impossible.

It was true in general that where geometrical and mathematical methods could be easily and directly applied—as possibly in optics—there was very considerable development in the seventeenth century. In the period we have now reached—in the age of Galileo—arithmetic and algebra had attained something like their modern external appearance—the Frenchman, François Viète, for example, had established the use of letters to represent numbers; the Fleming, Simon Stevin, was introducing the decimal system for representing fractions; various symbols, now familiar to students, were coming into use between the fifteenth century and the time of Descartes. At the same time aids to mathematical calculation—a matter of importance to students of the heavenly bodies—were being devised, such as John Napier's logarithms, developed between 1595 and 1614, and his devices for simplifying multiplication and division—devices which in the seventeenth century would appear to have had greater renown even than his logarithms. It has been pointed out that as algebra and geometry had developed separately—the former amongst the Hindus and the latter amongst the Greeks—the marriage of the two, "the application of algebraic methods to the geometric field", was "the greatest single step ever made in the progress of the exact sciences". The crucial development here came to its climax in the time of Descartes. Descartes put forward the view that sciences involving order and measure—whether the measure affected numbers, forms, shapes, sounds or other objects —are related to mathematics. "There ought therefore to be a general science—namely, mathematics," he said, "which should explain all that can be known about order and measure, considered independently of any application to a particular subject." Such a science, he asserted, would surpass in utility and importance all the other sciences, which in reality depended upon it. Kepler said that just as the ears are made for sound and the eyes for colours, the mind of man is meant to consider quantity and it wanders in darkness when it leaves the realm of quantitative thought. Galileo said that the book of the universe was written in mathematical language, and its alphabet consisted of triangles, circles and geometrical figures. There is no doubt that in both Kepler and Galileo Platonic and Pythagorean influences played an important part in the story.

If all these things are kept in mind we can see why the resort to experiment in the natural sciences now came to have direction, came at last to be organised to some purpose. For centuries it had been an affair of wild and almost pointless fluttering—a thing in many respects irrelevant to the true progress of understanding—sometimes the most capricious and fantastic part of the scientific programme. There had been men in the middle ages who had said that experiment was the thing that mattered, or had realised that behind the natural philosophy of the Greeks there had been experiment and observation in the first place. But that was not enough, and even in the seventeenth century a man like Sir Francis Bacon, who harped on the need for experiments but had failed to hitch this policy on to that general mathematising mode of procedure which I have described, was early recognised to have missed the point. In the thirteenth century, a writer called Peregrine produced a work on the magnet, and many of his experiments prepared the way for the remarkable book on the magnet produced by William Gilbert in 1600. The chief influence that came from Gilbert's book, however, emerged from his cosmic speculations based on the thesis that the earth was itself a great magnet, and Sir Francis Bacon was ready to seize upon the fact that this was not a hypothesis demonstrated by experiment, the thesis did not arise in the appointed way out of the experiments themselves. Even Leonardo da Vinci had tended to cast around here and there, like a schoolboy interested in everything, and when he drew up a plan of experiments in advance—as in the case of his projected scheme of study on the subject of flying—we can hardly fail to realise that here are experiments, but not the modern experimental method. Neither the medieval period nor the Renaissance was lacking in the ingenuity or the mechanical skill for modern technical achievement, as can be seen from the amazing contrivances they produced even where no urgent utilitarian purpose provided the incentive. Yet it is not until the seventeenth century that the resort to experiments comes to be tamed and harnessed so to speak, and is brought under direction, like a great machine getting into gear.

At this point it is proper to picture Galileo passing his time in a sort of workshop with trained mechanics as his assistants, for ever making things and sometimes carrying out experiments, so that it has been held that in him the mechanic or artisan and the natural philosopher have combined to produce the modern scientist. On all this side, and especially where the sciences of mechanics and hydrostatics are concerned, there is no doubt that Archimedes had a further influence on the course of the scientific revolution, for Archimedes may be regarded as the patron saint of the mechanically minded and of the modern experimenters in physics. It is clear that events in certain technical fields affected the course of things—Galileo speaks of problems arising in the ship building yards at Venice, in connection with artillery or in regard to the pumping of water in mines. It had long been the case that the operations of the metallurgist had played an important part in the history of science. The existence of mechanical objects in the world at large had apparently induced also a sort of specialised interest—an interest in the sheer question of the way in which things worked. Apart from the case of this or that strategic experiment which decides a problem, Galileo gives the impression that from a constant course of experiment he has gained an intimacy with movements and structures—he has watched in action the ways of projectiles, the operation of levers, and the behaviour of balls on inclined planes—has watched these things so long that he knows them, so to speak, from the inside, in the way some men know their dogs. Yet, as we have seen on more than one occasion, we must make many reservations in regard to Galileo as an experimenter. We must beware of imputing his intellectual achievements too definitely to the experimental method itself.

One thing becomes remarkable in the seventeenth century and that is the creation of scientific instruments, especially measuring instruments, and it is hard for us to realise how difficult things must have been in earlier centuries without them. The telescope and the microscope appear at the very beginning of the century—and may have been devised a little earlier—and it is difficult not to regard them as a by-product of the glass- and metal-polishing industries in Holland. The microscope proved to be inadequate, however, for a long time, owing apparently to a defect, not in industrial technique as such but in the actual science of optics. A more powerful single lens was produced, however, in the middle of the century, and much of the important work in the later period was really done with that. Galileo represents an important stage in the development of the thermometer and the pendulum-clock, and the barometer appears in the middle of the century; but for a long time it was possible to detect just the fact that the temperature was changing without having a reliable scale for the actual measurement of temperature. A really accurate thermometer did not exist until the eighteenth century. In the middle of the seventeenth century, again we meet with the momentous discovery of the air-pump, and only after this time do we see the use of the blow-pipe in chemical analysis. Van Helmont in the earlier half of the century studied gases, invented the word gas, and found that different kinds of gases existed—not simply air—but he was greatly handicapped, as he had no means of collecting and isolating a particular gas that he might want to examine. When one considers the richness and the fantastic nature of the objects that littered the laboratory of the alchemist even in the sixteenth century, one may feel that it can hardly have been the lack of industrial technique which delayed the appearance of some of the modern scientific instruments; though it appears that where purity or accuracy was highly necessary, either in the glass or in the metal-work, the technical progress achieved by the seventeenth century is a factor that affects the case. We may gather from repeated statements in books and correspondence, that the experimental method in the first half of the seventeenth century involved a serious financial burden on its practitioners. It also appears that scientific workers were coming closer to one another, communicating their experiments or their problems to one another in informal gatherings, or in correspondence of an international character. Much of the history of science, especially in the first half of the century, rests on the study of this correspondence, which is occasionally very voluminous. Later in the century, the informal gatherings turned into scientific societies—the Royal Society in England, the *Académie des Sciences* in France, and similar bodies earlier still in Italy. These societies helped to bear the expense of experiments. Their publications, and the establishment of a periodical literature, speeded up still more the communication and collation of scientific results. It would seem not to have been until the middle of the century that scientific publications really took the form of the communication of actual experiments. Sometimes, as in the case of Galileo, a point would be demonstrated by reasoning, though possibly it had been discovered in the course of experiment first of all.

It is comparatively easy for people today to accommodate their minds to changes that may take place in upper regions of the different sciences—changes which from year to year may add further weight to the curriculum of the undergraduate student of the subject. It is not clear what the patriarchs of our generation would do, however, if we were faced with such a tearing-up of the roots of science that we had to wipe out as antiquated and useless the primary things said about the universe at the elementary school—had even to invert our attitudes, and deal, for example, with the whole question of local motion by picking up the opposite end of the stick. The early seventeenth century was more conscious than we ourselves (in our capacity as historians) of the revolutionary character of the moment that had now been reached. While everything was in the melting pot—the older order undermined but the new scientific system unachieved—the conflict was bitterly exasperated, men actually calling for a revolution, not merely for an explanation of existing anomalies but for a new science and a new method. Programmes of the revolutionary movement were put forward, and it is clear that some men were highly conscious of the predicament in which the world now found itself. They seemed to be curiously lacking in discernment in one way, however, for they tended to believe that the scientific revolution could be carried out entirely in a single lifetime. It was a case of changing one lantern-slide of the universe for another, in their opinion—establishing a new system to take the place of Aristotle's. Gradually they found that it would need not merely one generation but perhaps two to complete the task. By the close of the seventeenth century they had come to see that they had opened the way to an indefinitely expanding future, and that the sciences were only in their cradle still.

Before the seventeenth century had opened, the general state of knowledge in regard to the physical universe had been conducive to the production of a number of speculative systems; these not founded upon scientific enquiry as a rule, but generally compounded out of ingredients taken from classical antiquity. Already in the sixteenth century, also, attention had been directed to the question of a general scientific method, and in the seventeenth century this problem of method came to be one of the grand preoccupations, not merely of the practising scientist, but, at a higher level, amongst the general thinkers and philosophers. The principal leaders in this seventeenth-century movement were Francis Bacon in the first quarter of the century, who glorified the inductive method and sought to reduce it to a set of regulations; and Descartes, whose work belongs chiefly to the second quarter of the century and who differed from Bacon not only in his glorification of mathematics as the queen of the sciences, but in the emphasis which he placed on a deductive and philosophical mode of reasoning which he claimed to have screwed up to such a degree of tightness that it possessed all the discipline and certainty of mathematical reasoning. In the time of Newton and well into the eighteenth century, there was a grand controversy between an English school, which was popularly identified with the empirical method, and a French school, which glorified Descartes and came to be associated rather with the deductive method. In the middle of the eighteenth century, however, the French, with a charm that we must describe as Mediterranean, not only submitted to the English view of the matter, but in their famous *Encyclopédie* made even too ample a return, placing Bacon on a pedestal higher perhaps than any that had been given him before. It would appear that their excess of graciousness or charity brought some confusion into historical science at a later stage in the story.

Bacon held that if Adam, owing to the Fall, had lost for the human race that domination over the created world which it had originally been designed to possess, still there was a subordinate command over nature, available if men worked sufficiently hard to secure it, and this had been thrown away by human folly. There had been only three short periods of genuine scientific progress throughout the whole course of human history, he said—one in Greek times, one in the Roman period, and the third which was being enjoyed in the seventeenth century. In each of the two ancient periods the era of scientific progress had been confined to two hundred years. The earlier Greek philosophers had set the course of enquiry on the right lines, but Plato and Aristotle had supervened, and they had come to prevail precisely because, being of lighter weight, they had managed to ride much farther down upon the stream of time. They had survived the storms of the Barbarian Invasions, precisely because they had been shallow and buoyant, and Aristotle, in particular, had owed his remarkable sway in the world to the fact that, like the Ottoman sultans, he had pursued the policy of destroying all rivals. As for the scholastics of the middle ages, they had had "subtle and strong capacities, abundance of leisure, and but small variety of reading, their minds being shut up in a few authors"; and therefore they had "with infinite agitation of wit, spun out of a small quantity of matter those laborious webs of learning which are extant in their books". Bacon was impressed by the fact that scientific knowledge had made such extraordinarily little progress since the days of antiquity. He begins by saying that men ought to "throw aside all thought of philosophy, or at least to expect but little and poor fruit from it, until an approved and careful natural and Experimental History be prepared and constructed".

For to what purpose are these brain-creations and idle display of power. . . . All these invented systems of the universe, each according to his own fancy [are] like so many arguments of plays . . . every one philosophises out of the cells of his own imagination, as out of Plato's cave.

He uses the term "history" in the sense that we have in mind when we speak of natural history, and he regards it as comprising a collection of data, the fruits of enquiry.

He believed that many men had been led away by allowing their scientific work to become entangled in a search for final causes, which really belonged rather to philosophy, and which he said corrupted the sciences, except those relating to the intercourse of man with man. In education he thought that scholars were introduced too early to logic and rhetoric, which were the cream of the sciences, since they arranged and methodised the subject-matter of all the others. To apply the juvenile mind to these before it had been confronted with the subject-matter of the other sciences was like painting and measuring the wind, he said—on the one hand it degraded logic into childish sophistry, on the other hand it had the effect of making the more concrete sciences superficial. In his reaction against the older ways of discussing science Bacon carried the attack beyond the bounds of prudence on occasion— denying the value of syllogistic modes of reasoning in a way that the modern philosopher would disapprove of; though the general line of attack was understandable, and very useful in view of the situation of things at that time. Bacon wanted men to close in on nature and get to grips with her, bringing their minds to mix in its actual operations. "The secrets of nature", he said, "betray themselves more readily when tormented by art than when left to their own course." "It is best to consider matter, its conformation, and the changes of that conformation, its own action, and the law of this action in motion." He did not support a dead kind of empiricism; the empirics, he said, were like ants merely heaping up a collection of data. The natural philosophers still generally current in the world, however, were rather like spiders spinning their webs out of their own interior. He thought that the scientists ought to take up an intermediate position, like that of the bees, which extracted matter from the flowers and then re-fashioned it by their own efforts. Existing interpretations of nature, he said, were generally "founded on too narrow a basis of experiment". "In any case", he insisted, "the present method of experiment is blind and stupid"—men did it as though they were schoolboys engaged "as it were in sport". He talked of "desultory, ill-combined experiment". The alchemists, he said, had theoretical preconceptions which hindered them from either carrying out their experiments along useful lines or extracting anything important from their results. Men in general glanced too hastily at the result of an experiment, and then imagined that the rest could be done by sheer contemplation; or they would fly off into the skies with a hasty first impression and attempt to make this square with the vulgar notions already existing in their minds. Even Gilbert working on the magnet had no unity or order in his experiments—the only unity in his treatise lay in the fact that he had been ready to try out anything that there was to try out with a magnet.

Now it was Bacon's firm principle that if men wanted to achieve anything new in the world, it was of no use attempting to reach it on any ancient method—they must realise that new practices and policies would be necessary. He stressed above all the need for the direction of experiments—an end to the mere haphazard experimenting—and he insisted that something far more subtle and far-reaching could be achieved by the proper organisation of experiments. It is quite clear that he realised how science could be brought to a higher power altogether by being transported away from that ordinary world of common-sense phenomena in which so much of the discussion had hitherto been carried on. He insisted on the importance of the actual recording of experiments, a point which, as we have already seen, was now coming to be of some significance. He insisted that experimenters in different fields should get together, because they would knock sparks off one another; and things done in one field would give hints to people working in another field. In this sense he anticipated the point of Professor Whitehead who shows how, precisely in this period, the knowledge of several different branches of science at once might have an enriching effect on each. Also suggestions which are scattered in various parts of Bacon's work seem to have served as an inspiration to some of the men who founded the Royal Society.

It often happens that when the philosopher comes to deal with the position of a man like Bacon in the history of thought, he lays great stress either upon the internal inconsistencies that may exist in the intellectual system in question, or on the actual correctness—from a modern point of view—of the man's conclusions, which in the present case would mean the correctness of Bacon's predictions concerning the character and the method which modern science was going to take upon itself. A modern critic may lay about him right and left on the subject of the philosophy of the nineteenth-century Utilitarians, if that teaching merits the name of philosophy; but the historian who remembers all the inhibitions that restricted parliamentary action at the beginning of the nineteenth century, and who has in mind the vast flood of legislation that began to appear in the second quarter of that century, can hardly help realising that on a lower level altogether—in a subphilosophical field—it required a first-class campaign to get rid of the inhibitions and to persuade people of the commonplace fact that laws could be regarded as mere ministers to ordinary utility, that anachronistic legislation was not a thing to be preserved for semi-mystical reasons. It is at this lower level of analysis—in this sub-philosophical realm—that Bacon is so interesting and so important in history, and we must not ask ourselves: How many people adopted the Baconian system literally and *in toto*? We must not be surprised that even in the seventeenth century it was precisely the people in the same line of thought as Bacon—the logicians —who were the least influenced by his teaching. We must not be disconcerted if even at the very heart of his teaching, where he purported to show exactly how the results of experiments could be turned into generalisations, he was on occasion less original than he intended to be, and on occasion actually mistaken. In the days when the grand campaign against Aristotle was coming to its height he produced a programme and manifesto, and some of the most important things that he said are dead to us but were quivering with life in the seventeenth century, because they were right and so happen to have become commonplace today. He did not produce Baconians taking over his whole system, but rather stimulated people in a piecemeal way—people who apparently did not always even read his works in their entirety. And since authors who merely write about method are liable to mistakes which are avoided by men who are actually engaged in research (for the simple reason that the latter can often hardly help following their noses half the time), it is not surprising if some people thought they were disciples of his method when in reality they were doing something different, something which in many cases would be better still. In his own words, "he rang the bell which called the wits together", and many of his aphorisms—especially where he is diagnosing the causes of common errors in thought—would give both profit and stimulus to students of history today. Paradoxically enough, there is possibly some truth in the view that the Baconian influence has been most direct in some of what might be called the literary sciences.

He has been attacked because there is so much in his writing that savours of the old Aristotle; but that was necessary since his system ranged over all the realms of thought and philosophy. He has been mocked because so many of his beliefs about nature were still medieval —but that was also true of the various scientists of the time. If he believed in the existence of vital spirits in the blood, so did William Harvey himself, as we have seen. If he described inanimate things as having aspirations and disposition, or as being drawn by affection to one another, Robert Boyle, much later in the century, explicitly defended this mode of expression. He has been criticised because when he

collected data he included fables and old wives' tales along with established scientific facts. He instructed scientific workers to examine the
fables, however, and repeatedly he made the point that he expected to
find his data corrected by enquiries that would take place in the future.
When he set out to provide a starting-point for scientific enquiry, and to
assemble his catalogues of known facts, achieved experiments and suggested hypotheses, he made terrible mistakes, for he was writing before
modern physics or chemistry or astronomy or physiology had really
begun to be established. The mistaken science of the past always appears as blind superstition to the future, and Bacon at one point and
another would fail to free himself from existing prejudices or, alter-
natively, to prevent his mind from running to fantastic conjecture.
But he realised the possibility of error in advance, and said that it mattered little if his experiments were wrong, "since it must needs happen
in beginnings". He claimed that at any rate his compendiums were
more useful than the scientific knowledge that had hitherto been available. He constantly reiterated, furthermore, that he put forward hypotheses for people to examine; even if they were wrong they would
be useful, he said. On one occasion he noted that it was too early to
put forward an opinion on a given issue, but he would offer his own
for the time being because it might seem like cowardice if he did not.
On another occasion he said:

I do not pronounce upon anything, I set down and prescribe but
only provisionally . . . I sometimes make attempts at interpretation . . .
[but] what need have I of pride or imposture seeing that I so often
declare that we are not furnished with so much history or experiments
as we want and that without these the interpretation of nature cannot
be accomplished; and that therefore it is enough for me if I set the
thing on foot.

If we look for the root of the error that was in him—the cause that
was perhaps behind the other causes—it lay in his assumption that the
number of phenomena, the number even of possible experiments, was
limited, so that the scientific revolution could be expected to take place
in a decade or two. "The particular phenomena of the arts and sciences
are in reality but as a handful", he once said; "the invention of all
causes and sciences would be the labour of but a few years." He
thought that he could make catalogues of facts, of required experiments and of suggested hypotheses; and while on the one hand he
imagined that the whole renovation of the sciences would be held up
unless he provided this guide-book, he spoke at times as though, once
his compendium had been compiled, the work of science would proceed almost by rule of thumb. Even here he was not so inelastic as

some people have made out, however, and not so blind to the importance of hypotheses. If he thought it his special function to provide the hypotheses, he would add the remark that further ones would suggest themselves to the enquirer as he went along.

He believed that out of experiments one could draw generalisations, and that these generalisations themselves would point the way to further experiments. In a curious but significant way he seems to have foreseen the structure that science was to take in the future. . . . Bacon thought that at the first immediate level the generalisations or axioms which might be drawn out of experiments were too low-grade, too near to concrete facts to be of any great utility. Knowledge is limited if we only know that heat can be produced by mixing sulphuric acid and water; and the knowledge is of little value unless these two substances happen to be at hand. The very highest generalisations of all, however, are out of reach, too near to God and to final causes; they must be left to the philosopher. The intermediate axioms are the ones that are "true, solid and full of life", says Bacon—the rather higher generalisations which can be reached by the method of climbing up to them from below. If one knows that violent molecular motion is the factor that produces heat, one is in possession of a wider form of generalisation and this will greatly increase one's power over nature. Incidentally, Bacon makes the remark that there are some things which have become so familiar or which are accepted so automatically that people take them as self-evident, though they are just the things which are most in need of re-examination. In this connection he specifies the causes of gravity, the rotation of the heavenly bodies, heat, light, density and organic formation. He shows some insight in recognising that the progress of science would consist in the pursuit of enquiries upon lines such as these.

It was on the mathematical side—and particularly, so to speak, on the geometrical side—that Bacon missed the point of that kind of science which was to spring from Galileo. His error ought not to be exaggerated. He says in one place: "The investigation of nature is best conducted when mathematics are applied to physics." He says in another place: "If physics be daily improving, and drawing out new axioms, it will continually be wanting fresh assistance from mathematics." On the other hand, he regarded mathematics merely as the hand maid to physics, and actually complained of the dominion which it was beginning to exercise in that science. It was all very well to do sums on the results of one's experiments, but Bacon specifically disliked Galileo's method of turning the problem of motion, in the way we have seen, into the problem of geometrical bodies moving in geometrical space. Far from wanting to read away the air-resistance, in the way the new school of scientists were doing, he wanted to add other things to the picture—for example, the tensions that were bound to take place within the moving body itself. Far from wanting to abstract and to isolate any aspect of a scientific problem, so that motion could be considered as a line drawn in geometrical space, he longed rather to load all the concreteness back into the problem, to see a picture which included air-resistance and gravity and the internal texture of the body itself. Even in the case of the celestial bodies he deprecated the purely geometrical study of motion and said that the enquirer ought not to overlook the question of the kind of material out of which the planets were manufactured. On the subject of projectiles he declined to accept either Aristotle's theory that the motion was caused by the rush of air, or the impetus-theory which had hitherto been its principal rival. He put forward the hypothesis that motion continued after an impact as a result of the play of the internal forces and stresses which had been put into operation by the shock of the original percussion.

Indeed, it is important in the study of Bacon not merely to know the skeleton of his system, but to observe how he treats the problems in any of the branches of science. And it is not sufficient to note whether he was right or wrong according to the views of the present day. We must know where each particular science stood at the time when he was writing, and exactly how he would play upon the margin of it. There is one field in which this matter may perhaps be usefully discussed at the present moment, since it is connected with problems which we have already traversed in a general way; and that is, the field that relates to the problem of the skies. It is the more interesting from the fact that Bacon is so often summarily dismissed for his anti-Copernican prejudices.

On this subject Bacon begins by saying:

I will myself therefore construct a Theory of the Universe according to the measure of the history, [the established facts,] as yet known to us; keeping my judgment however in all points free, for the time when history, and by means of history, my inductive philosophy shall have been further advanced.

Later he says:

Nevertheless I repeat once more that I do not mean to bind myself to these; for in them as in other things I am certain of my way but not certain of my position. I have introduced them by way of interlude lest it be thought that it is from vacillation of judgment or inability to affirm that I prefer negative questions.

He says that many astronomical systems can be put forward which will cover the phenomena. The Ptolemaic is one, the Copernican is another. Either will account for the observed movements, but Bacon prefers the system of Tycho Brahé, the intermediate system by which some of the planets go round the sun and these all together go round the motionless earth. He regrets, however, that Tycho Brahé had not worked out the mathematics of such a system and shown its operation in detail. "Now it is easy to see", he says, "that both they who think the earth revolves and they who hold the primum mobile and the old construction are about equally and indifferently supported by the phenomena." He prefers, however, the view that the earth is stationary —"for that I now think the truer opinion", he says. Still, he puts the question as one for the reader to answer: Whether there is a system of the universe with a centre, or whether the particular globes of earth and stars are just scattered and dispersed, each, as he says, "on its own roots", or each as "so many islands in an immense sea". Even if the earth revolves it does not necessarily follow that there is no system of the universe, he says; for there are planets that do revolve around the sun. But though the rotation of the earth is an ancient idea, the Copernican view that the sun stands immovable at the centre of the universe is one which Bacon considers to be unprecedented. He is prepared to ask whether there may not be many different centres of the universe, the heavenly bodies being congregated in bundles or groups, so that he can picture them as separate parties of people each doing a separate dance. He addresses himself to the problem we discussed in connection with the modern doctrine of inertia when he says: "Let no one hope to determine the question whether the earth or heaven revolve in the diurnal motion unless he have first comprehended the nature of spontaneous rotation." In one place he makes it clear that he dislikes the movement of the earth because it would leave nature without any quiet, any immobility. Repeatedly he tells us that so far as the mathematical aspect is concerned the Copernican system is satisfactory, but he stumbles at the obstacle which we have seen to be the general difficulty even in the days of Galileo: the Copernican hypothesis has not yet been made to square with what is known of physical science in general. Bacon repeats that the mathematician-astronomers can never solve the problem by themselves. Let the observation of the heavenly bodies proceed—we are all the better if we can get the geometry of the skies correct—and the mathematical side of the work must certainly be dovetailed into the discoveries of physical science. On the mathematical side things are going well at the moment, especially with the new optical instruments; but there must be greater constancy of observation, greater severity of judgment, more witnesses to confirm observations, and each particular fact must be tested in different ways. The real weakness still lies in the physics, however. The enquirer ought to have regard to the actual material the stars are made of, learn about the appetites and behaviour of the stuff itself, which must be fundamentally the same in all regions of the heavens. Bacon declines to accept the view that the heavenly bodies are formed of an immaculate substance free from change and exempt from the ordinary forces of nature. It was heathen arrogance, not the Holy Scripture, he says, which endowed the skies with the prerogative of being corruptible. Also he tells us: "I shall not stand upon that piece of mathematical elegance, the reduction of motions to perfect circles." Dispersed through his work are many references to Galileo's telescopic discoveries. He accepts all the empirical data that these observations provide; but he does not accept Galileo's theories, though he does quote Galileo with approval for the view that the effect of gravity diminishes as one goes farther away from the earth. When he discusses the question of the tides, he says that on the supposition that the movement of the earth causes the tides, certain things will follow—not that he personally holds with Galileo's theory on this subject. His own view is that the farthest skies and stars move rapidly in a perfect circle, but that as we come down nearer to earth the heavenly bodies themselves become more earthy and they move in a more resistant medium. Things becoming more heavy and gross as we approach the mundane region, their motion slows down in proportion as they are nearer to earth and hold a lower place in the skies. What appears to be the motion of the planets in one direction is merely the optical illusion produced by the fact that they are so much behind the highest skies and the farthest stars, they merely represent a lag in that single circular movement which they are all supposed to share. Not only is the pace reduced, but the circular motion is departed from, as one comes lower down in the sky and nearer to the gross and material earth. The total result is to produce in the sky the effect of spirals, and Bacon affects to wonder why the spiral has never been thought of before, since it represents an initial circular motion constantly going off the circle as it descends to more turgid realms. In his view the tides are the last weak effects of the total revolution of the skies around the motionless earth.

That was Bacon's system of the universe, though as we have already seen, it was a mere tentative hypothesis and he did not consider that the time had yet come for the production of a general synthesis. It is clear, however, that from the point of view of that time his work was essentially stimulating—especially in the signs it gave of an extraordinary elasticity of mind—and that many people were influenced by it, though their work might not itself have a Baconian look at the finish—his influence tended to make men better than himself, make them something better than mere Baconians. The numerous translations of his works into French in the first half of the seventeenth century show that he aroused great interest across the Channel.

With René Descartes, who lived from 1596 to 1650, we meet a system of thought much more intensive and concentrated, and much more intricately interlocked. We shall find this man, like Galileo, reappearing in various aspects in the story of the scientific revolution, sprawling over the whole area that is left of the seventeenth century. What requires notice at the moment is merely the short treatise—a thing almost of pamphlet size—entitled *A Discourse on Method*, which is one of the really important books in our intellectual history. To the historian its greatest significance lies, not in its one or two philosophical passages or in the disquisition on mathematics, but in its aspect as just a piece of autobiography. In this aspect it influenced, not merely those who were to become Cartesian in philosophy, but the world in general.

It was written in the vernacular, and Descartes meant to address himself to the natural reason of men whose minds had not been perverted by the traditions of the schools. Those who read the *Discourse on Method*, not profoundly as philosophers but superficially in the way in which people do read books, will understand better than the philosophers ever do the importance and the influence of Descartes in general history. More important perhaps than anything the author intended is the manner in which the book was misunderstood; and Descartes himself complains not only in his letters but in this very book of the way in which he was being misunderstood already. He says in the *Discourse* that when he hears his own views repeated he finds them so changed that he cannot recognise or acknowledge them as his—a remark which must go straight to the heart of every author. He cries out against those people who think that they can master in a day the things which he had taken twelve years to think out. He explains in the *Discourse* how he had come to feel that all the sciences which he had been taught in his youth had really told him nothing— how the various opinions to which men in different parts of the world were attached were so often merely the result of custom and tradition.

The book is vivid as a chapter of autobiography, written by a man who after much travail decided that he must sweep away all ancient opinions and start all his thinking over again.

Bacon had talked of the need of "minds washed clean of opinions", but Descartes went further in his determination to unload himself of all the teaching which had been transmitted from the ancient world, his determination to doubt everything and start naked once again, without any foothold whatever save the consciousness that I who do the doubting must exist—even though I may doubt whether I am doubting. Those who never understood the positive teaching of Descartes, and who could never have risen to his philosophy, appreciated this dramatic rejection of inherited systems and ideas. And though he himself said that the attempt to overthrow all tradition in this way was not a thing to be carried out by any and every man; though he cautioned against any imitation of the sceptics—for, in fact, he was only doubting in order to find a firmer basis for belief or certainty—still the influence of the policy of methodical doubt was in the long run to be most significant on the destructive side and in the realm of general ideas. The misunderstanding of Descartes was made more easy, because, in fact, he did not intend his *Discourse on Method* to be anything more than a mere preface to his real study and survey of the problem of method. The essay was an introduction to three treatises—the *Dioptric*, the *Meteors* and the *Geometry*, and it was the intention of Descartes to develop the idea of his method by illustrating it in action, showing how it operated in concrete cases—that is to say, in different branches of science. It proved to be these three treatises that provided the greater sensation and drew the chief attention at the time; but the world soon gets tired of reading out-of-date science, so that these parts of the work gradually lost their initial importance. The *Discourse on Method*, which is stimulating to read at any time, gradually detached itself from the essays to which it was a mere preface, and came to stand on its own feet.

Descartes believed that the essential capacity to see reason was distributed throughout the human race without any difference of degree, however clouded it might be by prejudice or by the illusions of the imagination. He established what became the great principle of common sense in modern times, for if he insisted on one point more than any other it was in his thesis: "All things which we clearly and distinctly conceive are true." If I say "I think, therefore I am", I am not really deducing anything—I am announcing a kind of intuitive perception of myself, a perception which nothing can get behind. Beyond that, if I say "I have a body", I am liable to be misled by pictures and fogs—the visual imagination is precisely the thing that is unreliable. The people who say "I believe in my body because I can see it clearly, but I cannot see God" were turning a popularised Descartes to the purpose exactly the reverse of what had been intended. In the system of Descartes God was another of those clear ideas that are clearer and more precise in the mind than anything seen by the actual eye. Further-more, everything hung on this existence of a perfect and righteous God. Without Him a man could not trust in anything, could not believe in a geometrical proposition, for He was the guarantee that everything was not an illusion, the senses not a complete hoax, and life not a mere nightmare.

Starting from this point, Descartes was prepared to deduce the whole universe from God, with each step of the argument as clear and certain as a demonstration in geometry. He was determined to have a science as closely knit, as regularly ordered, as any piece of mathe-matics—one which, so far as the material universe is concerned (and excluding the soul and the spiritual side of things), would lay out a perfect piece of mechanism. His vision of a single universal science so unified, so ordered, so interlocked, was perhaps one of his most re-markable contributions to the scientific revolution. Indeed, he carried the unification so far that he said that one single mind ought to work out the whole system—he indulged at one time in the hope that he might carry out the whole scientific revolution himself. When others offered to help him with experiments he was tempted to reply that it would be much better if they would give him money to carry out his own.

The physics of Descartes, therefore, depends in a particular way upon his metaphysics; it provides merely the lower stages in an hier-archical system that definitely reaches back to God. Descartes is pre-pared to work out a whole system of the universe, starting with matter (or with what the philosophers call extension) on the one hand, and movement, purely local motion, on the other. Everything was to be accounted for mathematically, either by configuration or by number. His universe, granting extension and movement in the first place, was so based on law that no matter how many different universes God had created—no matter how different from one another these might be at the start—they were bound, he said, to become like the universe we live in, through the sheer operation of law upon the primary material.

Even if God had created the universe different at the beginning, it would have worked itself round to the system that now exists. Even if He had made the earth a cube, it would have rolled itself into a sphere. Perhaps the most essential law in the physical system of Descartes was the law concerning the invariability in the amount of motion in the universe. Motion depended ultimately on God, and the law concerning the invariability in the amount of motion was a law which followed from the immutability of God. It might be thought that Descartes could have arrived at some such law by observation and experiment, or at least by taking it as a possible hypothesis and discovering that it actually succeeded, actually worked in practice. That would never have been sufficient for him, for it could never have provided that clinching demonstration, that exclusion of alternative possibilities, which it was the purpose of his system to achieve. What he wanted was the certainty of a deductive and quasi-geometrical proof, and he had to carry the question back to God, so that his physics had to depend on his metaphysics. Envisaging the matter with the eye of the geometer, however, and conceiving motion therefore so largely in its kinematic aspect, he laid himself open to the criticism that his system suffered from anæmia in respect of questions relating to dynamics. His law on the subject of the conservation of motion proved unsatisfactory and had to be replaced by the law of the conservation of energy.

He tells us in the *Discourse on Method* that from one or two primary truths that he had established he was able to reason his way by the earth, as well as water, air, fire, minerals, etc. When it came farther than that—to the more detailed operations of nature—he needed experiment to show him in which of the alternative ways that were possible under his system God actually did produce certain effects; or to discover which of the effects—amongst a host of possible alternatives that his philosophy would have allowed or explained—God had actually chosen to produce.

Experiment, therefore, only had a subordinate place in the system of Descartes, and in the latter part of the seventeenth century the famous scientist Huygens, who criticised Bacon for his lack of mathematics, complained that the theories of Descartes were not sufficiently confirmed by experiment. The beauty and the unity of the system of Descartes lay in the fact that on the one hand it started from God and worked downwards by a system of reasoning that was claimed to be watertight; while at the same time it worked upwards from below, drawing generalisations or axioms from the experiments. There are signs, however, that Descartes would use an experiment to confirm a hunch or an hypothesis, but would close down the enquiry very soon —refusing to pursue further observations even when these might have affected the case in a more or less indirect manner. He worried much less about establishing a fact than about its explanation—his point was to show that, supposing this thing was a fact, his system would provide the explanation; and, indeed, this system would have explained the case supposing God at one point or another had taken an alternative course that might have been open to Him. So in his treatise on *Meteors*, which was one of the works attached to his *Discourse on Method*, he was prepared to explain how the clouds could rain blood, as was sometimes alleged, and how lightning could be turned into a stone. In fact, he confessed that he preferred to apply his method to the explanation of what were the ordinarily accepted phenomena, rather than to use experiment in order to find new phenomena, or out-of-the-way occurrences. Many of his accepted "facts," like the ones I have just mentioned, were in reality taken over without examination from scholastic writers. He accepted the idea of the circulation of the blood, but quarrelled with Harvey concerning its cause and concerning the action of the heart. He said that when the blood was drawn into the heart it became so heated that it effervesced, caused the heart to expand, and leaped of its own motion into the arteries. In this case the truth was that he accepted unconsciously and without real examination the scholastic assumption that the heart functioned as the centre of heat.

The men who were influenced by Bacon were chiefly affected by the thesis that experiment was the thing that mattered in the natural sciences. And Robert Boyle, who shows clear marks of that influence, was criticised by Huygens and others for having built so little on the great number of experiments that he recorded. The founders of the Royal Society were under that general influence, and in the early proceedings of the Royal Society there is a rage for experiments, not only of what we should call the scientific kind, but in regard to curiosities and prodigies in nature, or in respect of invention and technological devices—sometimes experiments just to test old wives' tales. In the system of Descartes, however, . . . there is the economy and austerity of a highly concentrated deductive system. By its mechanisation it anticipated the structure that physical science was to assume in the future. But the combination of the mathematical and the experimental method in England was destined to put the natural science of Descartes into the shade before the seventeenth century had expired.

Suggestions for Further Reading

BERNAL, J. D., *Science in History*, 3rd ed. rev., Vols. 1 & 2. Cambridge, Mass.: M.I.T. Press, 1971.

BOAS, MARIE, *The Scientific Renaissance 1450–1630*. New York: Harper & Row, 1962.

BRIGGS, ROBIN, *The Scientific Revolution of the Seventeenth Century*. New York: Harper & Row, 1971.

BURTT, E. A., *The Metaphysical Foundations of Modern Physical Science*. New York: Harcourt, Brace, 1927.

COHEN, I. B., *Birth of a New Physics*. New York: Anchor Books, 1960.

GILLISPIE, C. C., *The Edge of Objectivity*. Princeton, N.J.: Princeton University Press, 1960.

HALL, A. R., *The Scientific Revolution*. London: Longmans, Green and Co., 1962.

KOYRÉ, A., *From the Closed World to the Infinite Universe*. Baltimore, Md.: Johns Hopkins Press, 1957.

KUHN, THOMAS, *The Structure of Scientific Revolutions*. Chicago: University of Chicago Press, 1962.

WHITEHEAD, A. N., *Science and the Modern World*. New York: The Macmillan Company, 1957 (1925).

J. H. ELLIOTT

The Decline of Spain

❮§❯ The central political fact of the late sixteenth and early seventeenth centuries was the decline of Spain and the rise of French power. This change signified far more than the replacement of one hegemony by another. It represented the triumph of the new system of bureaucratic absolutism, for which seventeenth-century French government was the prototype (see p. 298 ff. in this volume), over the older Spanish system of medieval autocracy that operated through the narrow confines of the royal court and household. The Spanish decline and French advance also symptomized the waning of ideological conflict in Europe, a new devotion to secular statecraft and the ideal of raison d'état, and the ultimate failure of the forces of the Counter-Reformation and the Habsburg Spanish-Austrian bloc to overwhelm and extinguish Protestantism. Although the French monarch was Catholic, the king's great minister Cardinal Richelieu placed his duty to the state before his office in the Church and led France against the Habsburg forces in the Thirty Years War. Consequently, the military tide turned against the Counter-Reformation and Habsburg power, and the permanent division of Europe into Protestant and Catholic regions—and the effective ending of the century of ideological warfare—was recognized by the Treaty of Westphalia of 1648.

In 1580 this turn of fortune would have seemed astonishing and marvelous to Europeans of all persuasions, for

FROM J. H. Elliott, *Imperial Spain, 1469–1716* (New York: St. Martin's Press, 1964), pp. 279–284, 303–345, 374–382.

at that time Spain still appeared to be the greatest empire
Western civilization had known since Roman days. The
wealth and efficiency of its government was as yet unparalleled elsewhere in Europe, and the strength and size
of its armies and navy were the comfort and hope of
Catholics and the terror and scourge of Protestants. Even
the Spaniards who lived through the agonizing decades of
their country's defeats, disappointments, and decline had a
hard time believing in the mundane reality of this dismal
experience, and often acted as though it was all an incredible nightmare from which they would suddenly re-
awake to the imperial glories of the mid-sixteenth century.

Nineteenth-century liberal Protestant historians, from
their own standpoint, found it as hard as seventeenth-
century Iberian writers to account for the decline of Spain
from imperial grandeur and European hegemony. They too
treated it as a sort of miraculous event, a just retribution
on the Spanish monarchy for its expulsion of Jews and
Moors and its implacable onslaught on Protestantism.
There were suggestions, too, inspired by modern experiences, of a fatal flaw in the Iberian temperament, some
innate racial defect that made the Spaniards impractical in
war and totally incompetent in the arts of peace and
government.

In the last four decades extensive research has finally
been pursued in the very rich archival material of Habsburg Spain, and the solution to the Spanish enigma has at
last come into focus. The most important work has been
carried out by the eminent Spanish scholar Vincens Vives
and the precocious and brilliant Cambridge University historian J. H. Elliott. It is from Elliott's extremely learned and
wonderfully compassionate and perceptive survey of the
rise and decline of *Imperial Spain*, published in 1964, that
the following selection is taken.

It has long been the fashion to dismiss the power of
Habsburg Spain as merely the consequence of a lucky
accident: the *Reconquista* of the Iberian peninsula from the
Moslems by the Christian aristocracy spilled over into a
conquest of Central and South America, and the transatlantic empire provided the sixteenth-century Spanish
monarchy with the money to pursue its ambitious military

adventures. Elliott shows that this view ignored the real achievement of Habsburg government in Spain. Not more than a quarter of royal income was ever derived from America. The greater part was the result of skillfully harnessing the resources of the kingdom, and to do this the royal government had to overcome the severe obstacles attendant on a multiracial society and intense regionalism. Furthermore, settling and governing the American empire was in itself a monumental political and social task. The third great area of achievement of imperial Spain was in religious mysticism, higher education, and art and literature, where the Spanish record is at least equal to the cultural glories of Elizabethan England.

Sixteenth-century Spain was created by the union of two crowns—the Mediterranean, urbanized, cosmopolitan kingdom of Aragon and the mainly landlocked, medieval, nationalist, and rural kingdom of Castile. The key to sixteenth- and seventeenth-century Spanish history, as seen by Elliott, was the Castilian domination of this union, and the preponderance in the royal government of the aristocratic, fanatical, impractical, mystical Castilian temperament. It was a temperament marked by the "constant dualism between the spirit and the flesh, the dream and the reality," "which co-exist and forever separate." It produced a statesman like Olivares, "whose capacity for conceiving great designs was matched only by his consistent incapacity for carrying them through to a successful conclusion." The Spanish successes of the early sixteenth century appeared to be derived from the military ardor of the Castilian nobility and their religious fanaticism. But the persistence of Castilian leadership in the more complex world of the early seventeenth century, when a reunited France had emerged to realign the balance of power, was the main cause of the Spanish collapse.

❧

During the 1590s there were numerous signs that the Castilian economy was beginning to crack under the relentless strain of Philip II's imperial adventures. The apparently inexhaustible stream of silver from the Indies had tempted the King to embark on vast enterprises which swallowed up his revenues and added to his mountain of debts: the Invincible Armada alone is said to have cost him 10,000,000 ducats, and in the mid-1590s he was probably spending over 12,000,000 ducats a year. How long he could continue to spend on this scale would ultimately be determined by the revenue-yielding capacity of his dominions both at home and overseas, and there is good reason to believe that by the 1590s this capacity was reaching its limits.

Less than a quarter of the King's annual revenues came from remittances of American silver; the rest was borrowed, or was paid for by taxes raised primarily by Castile. By 1590 it had become clear that, in spite of the large increase of 1575 in the figure for the *encabeza-miento*, Castile's traditional sources of revenue were inadequate for the Crown's needs. Neither the *alcabala* nor the ordinary and extraordinary *servicios* were any longer sufficient, and it was found necessary to supplement them from 1590 by a new tax which was to bulk large in the fiscal history of seventeenth-century Castile. This new tax, which was voted by the Cortes, was in effect the excise which Charles V had vainly attempted to introduce in 1538. Called the *millones*, because it was reckoned in millions of ducats rather than in the traditional *maravedís*, it was first fixed at 8,000,000 ducats spread over a period of six years, the method of raising the money being left to the towns. On its prolongation in 1596, however, it was increased by a further 1,300,000 ducats a year to be collected in *sisas* on essential foodstuffs; and in 1600 the original and the supplementary levies were lumped together into a subsidy of 18,000,000 ducats payable over six years. This consolidated tax was levied on essential articles of consumption—notably meat, wine, oil, and vinegar—and its grant was made conditional by the Cortes on its being applied to certain specific purposes: the payment of the royal guard and royal officials, and the upkeep of frontier garrisons and the royal households, with any surplus being devoted to the reduction of royal debts by the redemption of *juros*.

In theory, the *millones* was a much more equitable tax than the *servicios*, from which anyone boasting a privilege of nobility was exempted; but in practice it was a good deal less egalitarian than it appeared, since landowners could supply themselves with most of the dutiable articles from their own estates. Once again, therefore, it was the poor who suffered. Inevitably a tax of this nature pushed up the cost of living in Castile. A tax-reformer in the 1620s calculated that, in a poor man's expenditure of 30 *maravedís* a day 4 *maravedís* went in the *alcabala* and the *millones* alone, but the accuracy of the calculation was contested by his opponents, and at present it remains impossible to assess statistically the impact of taxation on individual Castilians or on the Castilian economy as a whole. What cannot be doubted, however, is the heaviness of Castile's fiscal contributions to the Crown in relation to those of other parts of the Monarchy. The Crown's principal sources of revenue in the late sixteenth century (excluding taxes raised in such territories as Naples and Milan, all of which were by now spent locally) were constituted as follows:

1. *Taxes paid by Castile*

		Ducats p.a.
	Alcabala	2,800,000
	Millones	3,000,000
	Servicios voted by Cortes	400,000
		6,200,000

2. *Dues collected in the Spanish Monarchy by papal concession*

	Cruzada	912,000
	Subsidio	420,000
	Excusado	271,000
		1,603,000

3. American silver   2,000,000

Could Castile continue to bear a burden of this nature without being overtaken by economic disaster? Could America continue to supply this quantity of silver? And, in any event, were even these large sums from the New World and the Old sufficient to pay for Philip II's imperial adventures? These were the questions that pressed themselves with increasing urgency on the Spanish Crown and its bankers during the 1590s.

The last question was the first to be answered—and answered in the most brutal manner. On 29 November 1596 Philip followed his procedure of 1575 and suspended all payments to the bankers. The Crown had gone bankrupt again. On this, as on previous occasions, a compromise was finally reached with the bankers: by the so-called *medio general* of 1597, it was agreed that outstanding debts would be repaid in the form of *juros*, which meant in effect the transformation of a floating into a consolidated debt. But, as in all operations of this sort, there were inevitable casualties, and the most important victims of the bankruptcy proved to be the fairs of Medina del Campo. The fairs, which had recovered from the royal bankruptcy of 1575, and had functioned with considerable regularity since reforms in 1578 and 1583, were now once more interrupted; and when they started operations again in 1598 it soon became clear that their great days were past.

The financial capital of Spain was to shift definitively in the early seventeenth century from Medina to Madrid, and such payments as were made in Medina del Campo during the course of that century were no more than sad reminders of a departed age. The towns of North Castile were fading into history, their streets still walked by the ghosts of Simón Ruiz and his friends—figures from a time when Spain basked in the *largueza* that came from abundance of silver, and when Castile could still provide financiers of its own.

But the bankruptcy of 1596 meant more than the end of northern Castile's financial pre-eminence: it meant also the end of Philip II's imperial dreams. For some time it had been apparent that Spain was losing its battle against the forces of international Protestantism. The first, and most crushing, blow was the defeat of the Invincible Armada in 1588. The enterprise of England had come to mean everything both to Philip and to Spain since the Marquis of Santa Cruz first submitted to the King his proposals for the great design in 1583. To Philip it seemed that an invasion of England, which Santa Cruz believed could be successfully undertaken for the cost of little more than 3,500,000 ducats, offered the best, and perhaps the only, hope of bringing the Dutch to their knees. While the King pored over his plans day after day in the Escorial, and the elaborate preparations moved slowly to their climax, the priests from their pulpits whipped up the nation to a frenzy of patriotic and religious fervour, as they denounced the iniquities of the heretical Queen of England and vividly evoked the glories of Spain's crusading past. "I consider this enterprise the most important undertaken by God's Church for many hundreds of years", wrote the Jesuit Ribadeneyra, the author of a moving exhortation to the soldiers and captains engaged in the expedition. "Every conceivable pretext for a just and holy war is to be found in this campaign. . . . This is a defensive, not an offensive, war: one in which we are defending our sacred religion and our most holy Roman Catholic faith (*fe católica romana*); one in which we are defending the high reputation of our King and lord, and of our nation; defending, too, the land and property of all the kingdoms of Spain, and simultaneously our peace, tranquillity and repose."

Only a few months later Ribadeneyra was writing a mournful letter to "a favourite of His Majesty" (probably Don Juan de Idiáquez), attempting to explain the apparently inexplicable: why God had turned a deaf ear to the prayers and supplications of His pious servants. While Ribadeneyra found sufficient explanation in Spain's sins of omission and commission, and full consolation in the very trials sent by the

Almighty to test His chosen people, the psychological consequences of the disaster were shattering for Castile. For a moment the shock was too great to absorb, and it took time for the nation to realize its full implications. But the unthinking optimism generated by the fantastic achievements of the preceding hundred years seems to have vanished almost overnight. If any one year marks the division between the triumphant Spain of the first two Habsburgs and the defeatist, disillusioned Spain of their successors, that year is 1588.

The material effects of the defeat of the Armada were, however, much less striking. Out of an original total of 130 ships, as many as two-thirds managed to limp home. Moreover, the Spanish fleet not only made up its losses with remarkable speed, but actually became a more formidable fighting force than it had been before. In a letter addressed to Sir Francis Walsingham just after the news of the defeat of the Armada had arrived, the Huguenot commander François de La Noue wrote that Philip II's power was founded on his possession of the Indies, and this in turn depended on his control of the sea. "Spain wanted to take Flanders by way of England, but you will be able to take Spain by way of the Indies. It is there that it must be undermined . . ." But it soon became clear that this was not easily achieved. Hawkins, Drake, and the Earl of Cumberland made daring attacks on Spain's overseas possessions and on its transatlantic shipping; a costly expedition was sent to Lisbon in 1589; but the Spanish coasts could not be effectively blockaded, and year after year the silver fleets—too well defended for a successful frontal attack—came safely home to port. Not only this, but Philip himself was soon strong enough to resume the offensive, and, goaded by the attack of Essex on Cadiz in 1596, sent another Armada against England in the following year, only to see it dispersed by the storms.

Yet, if the contest on the high seas remained undecided, the defeat of the Armada had in other ways tilted the balance of power against Spain. La Noue had said in his letter to Walsingham: "In saving yourselves you will save the rest of us." His prophecy proved correct. Spain's great crusade against the Protestant powers of the north had ended in failure. The news of the defeat of the Armada gave Henry III of France the courage to shake off his humiliating dependence on the Roman Catholic fanatics of the Ligue, and to organize the assassination of the powerful Duke of Guise. This event, and the succession to the French throne of the Protestant Henry of Navarre after Henry III's own assassination seven months later, compelled Alexander Farnese to turn his attention from the Netherlands to France. When he died in

December 1592 he left the Dutch still unconquered, and his two French campaigns of 1590 and 1591 had brought Spain no compensating success.

The conversion of Henry of Navarre to Rome in 1593 effectively destroyed any prospect of a successful Spanish candidacy to the throne of France. It was true that France itself had not gone Protestant, but otherwise Philip's northern policy had failed. The bankruptcy of 1596 set the seal on this failure, and made a return to peace imperative. Painfully aware that his days were numbered, and that his inexperienced son would succeed to an empty treasury, Philip set about reducing Spain's enormous commitments. The first step towards the liquidation of the costly imperialism of the 1580s and early 1590s was the dispatch of the Archduke Albert to the Netherlands. His arrival in 1596 marked the beginning of a new policy towards the Low Countries, which were formally handed over in May 1598 to Albert and to the Infanta Isabella Clara Eugenia, who became his wife. It was true that Albert and Isabella, although nominally sovereign princes, were still closely tied to Spain, and that the Low Countries would revert to Spain after their death, if their marriage proved to be childless. But at least the ties between Spain and the Netherlands had been loosened, and it would consequently be easier for Spain to call a halt to the war in Flanders without excessive loss of prestige.

The old King could not bring himself to make peace with England: this would come only in 1604. But on 2 May 1598 he concluded with Henry IV the treaty of Vervins, which brought the Franco-Spanish war to an end. At the time when he signed the treaty, Philip was reported to be so "withered and feeble" that it was thought impossible for him to live much longer; and he died on 13 September 1598, after months of excruciating illness which he bore with his accustomed fortitude.

*   *   *   *   *

While it was relatively easy to expel the Moriscos from Spain, it was infinitely more difficult to expunge the traces of Moorish civilization from the soil of the peninsula. Moorish ways had profoundly influenced the life of Spanish society, and inevitably the processes involved in Spain's turning its back on Africa were painful and slow. It was something of a revolution when the new houses built in Seville during the course of the sixteenth century began to face outwards on to the street, instead of facing inwards as in Arab days. It was still more of a revolution when women started to appear at the windows, for it was in family life, and especially in the role of women in Spanish society, that Moorish habits were most deeply engrained. The Spanish upper classes had inherited the Moorish custom of keeping their womenfolk secluded, and the women themselves still retained many of their Moorish ways. They crouched on cushions instead of using chairs; in all Spain, except for the north and northwest, they remained semi-veiled, in spite of frequent royal prohibitions; and they had an extraordinary habit, which may perhaps have originated in Africa, of nibbling pieces of glazed pottery—a choice of diet which may account for their notoriously poor complexions. But the strongest reminder of the Moorish past was to be found in the extreme inequality between the sexes, which was much greater than in contemporary northern Europe, and which found its counterpart in extreme male gallantry towards the inferior sex.

Under the combined influence of Europe and America, habits slowly began to alter. The appearance in Seville of wealthy and dissolute creole women from the New World led to a gradual relaxation of manners and morals, and the veil was often retained as a convenient means of concealment instead of as a token of modesty. But, in spite of these changes, the position of the upper class Spanish woman seems to have altered far less between the Middle Ages and the seventeenth century than that of her foreign counterparts. Installed at the centre of the family unit, she remained the repository of traditional ideals and customs, many of which had been acquired from the Moors during the time when they were still the masters of Spain.

The survival of Moorish customs in seventeenth-century Spain vividly illustrates the enormous problems of adaptation which this society was called upon to make, and suggests something of the tensions to which it was subjected. If it tended to veer between two extremes—if, for instance, the extreme doctrine of *limpieza* appeared a natural solution to the problem of alien survivals—this was partly because the problems which faced it were themselves of such an extreme character. Castilian society, as the *arbitristas* never tired of pointing out, was a society based on paradox and contrast. The contrasts were everywhere: Moorish and Christian; devoutness and hypocrisy; fervent professions of faith and exceptional laxity of manners; vast wealth and abject poverty. There was no moderation here, no sense of proportion. The *Memorial de la Política Necesaria y Util Restauración a la República de España* of González de Cellorigo is in practice one long text on the extremes of Spanish life and the paradoxes of its social and economic organization. For González, the greatness and perfection of a state were determined not only by the extent of its possessions, but by a "constant and harmonious" proportion between the different classes of its citizens. By this criterion Spain had reached the apex of its perfection in 1492. After the reigns of Ferdinand and Isabella it "began to decline to our own days", when it seemed to be approaching its nadir. All proportion was now gone, and "our republic has come to be an extreme contrast of rich and poor, and there is no means of adjusting them one to another. Our condition is one in which we have rich who loll at ease, or poor who beg, and we lack people of the middling sort, whom neither wealth nor poverty prevents from pursuing the rightful kind of business enjoined by natural law".

It was precisely this absence of "people of the middling sort", lamented by González de Cellorigo, which tended to differentiate the Spain of Philip III from other contemporary societies in western Europe (and conversely to approximate it to east European societies like Poland). Contrasts between wealth and poverty were not, after all, an exclusively Spanish phenomenon. The return of peace at the beginning of the seventeenth century had everywhere heralded the opening of an age of opulence, characterized in the European capitals by a round of masques and fêtes, by lavish spending on building, costumes, and jewellery, and by a relaxation of moral standards which made courts the symbol of every kind of vice to the puritanically inclined. The uniqueness of Spain lay not so much in this contrast, as in the absence of a middling group of solid, respectable, hard-working *bourgeois* to bridge the gulf between the two extremes. In Spain, these people, as González de Cellorigo appreciated, had committed the great betrayal. They had been enticed away by the false values of a disoriented society—a society of "the bewitched, living outside the natural order of things". The contempt for commerce and manual labour, the lure of easy money from investment in *censos* and *juros*, the universal hunger for titles of nobility and social prestige—all these, when combined with the innumerable practical obstacles in the way of profitable economic enterprise, had persuaded the *bourgeoisie* to abandon its unequal struggle, and throw in its lot with the unproductive upper classes of society.

Lacking a middle class which remained true to its own values, seventeenth-century Castile was sharply divided into the two extremes of the very rich and the very poor. "There are but two families in the world," as Sancho Panza's grandmother used to say, "the haves and the have-nots" (*el tener y el no tener*); and the criterion for distinguishing between them ultimately lay not in their rank or social position, but in whether they had anything to eat. Food, indeed, created new social classifications of its own:

>   Al rico llaman honrado,
>   Porque tiene que comer.

The rich ate, and ate to excess, watched by a thousand hungry eyes as
they consumed their gargantuan meals. The rest of the population
starved. The endless preoccupation with food that characterizes every
Spanish picaresque novel was no more than a faithful reflection of the
overwhelming concern of the mass of the populace, from the impoverished *hidalgo* surreptitiously pocketing crumbs at Court, to the *pícaro*
making a desperate raid on a market stall. "Hermano, este día no es
de aquellos sobre quien tiene jurisdicción la hambre"—"hunger holds
no sway today". But the days on which hunger held no sway were rare
indeed; and the long weeks of emptiness were passed in scheming for
a square meal, which itself would soon be consumed in an orgy of eat-
ing, and then forgotten as the pangs of hunger returned.

The best guarantee of a regular supply of square meals was, by tradition, service in *Iglesia, o mar, o casa real*—Church, sea (trade), or the
royal service (at Court or in the army). By the seventeenth century the
refrain had been narrowed down to *Iglesia, o casa real*. Castilians from
all walks of life had come to look, as a matter of course, to the Church,
Court, and bureaucracy to guarantee them the living which they dis-
dained to earn from more menial occupations, at once despised and
unrewarding.

The Church was both rich and welcoming. Although it suffered from
heavy taxation, it had received over the years enormous gifts of money,
jewels, and real estate. Bishoprics may have had heavy pensions
charges against their revenues, but there were still fat benefices available, like the canonries of Seville, which had risen in value between
the early sixteenth and the early seventeenth centuries from 300 to
2,000 ducats—a sixfold increase which shows that, at least in this
diocese, the revenues of the cathedral chapter had risen faster than
prices. The proliferation of new Religious Orders had opened up the
possibilities of a religious life to large numbers of men and women
whose anxiety for food and shelter tended to exceed their sense of
religious vocation. A total figure of 200,000 regular and secular clergy
has been suggested for the Spain of Philip IV, but there are no reliable
statistics. A contemporary writer, Gil González Dávila, put the number
of Dominicans and Franciscans at 32,000, and according to the Cortes
of 1626 there were some 9,000 religious houses in Castile simply for
men. "I am a priest," wrote González Dávila, "but I confess that there
are more of us than are necessary."

Alongside the Church stood the Court, with its glittering prospects of favour, position, and wealth. The Court of Philip III was very different from that of his father. The age of parsimony was over and the new King "increased the service in his royal palace, and admitted many grandees as gentlemen of his household, departing from the style of his father". The break with the House of Austria's traditional practice of keeping the higher aristocracy away from Court came at a moment when the great Spanish nobles were in urgent need of help. The price rise, taken in conjunction with the general increase in expenditure that was expected of the aristocracy during the sixteenth century, had played havoc with the fortunes of the grandees. Since detailed studies of the higher Spanish aristocratic families do not exist, the changing pattern of their fortunes is still unknown, but a comparison of the annual incomes of thirteen ducal families between the early sixteenth century and 1600 (as given by Lucio Marineo Sículo and Pedro Núñez de Salcedo respectively) gives some picture of what was happening:

TITLE	EARLY 16TH CENTURY (ducats)	1600 (ducats)
Frías (Condestable de Castilla)	60,000	65,000
Medina de Ríoseco (Almirante de Castilla)	50,000	130,000
Alba	50,000	120,000
Infantado	50,000	120,000
Medina Sidonia	55,000	170,000
Béjar	40,000	80,000
Nájera	30,000	55,000
Medinaceli	30,000	60,000
Alburquerque	25,000	50,000
Arcos	25,000	80,000
Maqueda	30,000	50,000
Escalona	60,000	100,000
Sessa	60,000	100,000
	565,000	1,180,000

The figures show that the incomes of these thirteen families had barely doubled over a period when prices quadrupled, and it is not surprising that most of the families were heavily indebted by the end of the sixteenth century. While the entail system saved the great houses from having to sell off their estates, they were compelled to mortgage them in order to pay the interest on their debts. According to one of the Venetian ambassadors at the Court of Philip III, the grandees actually received no more than a fifth of their revenues, since the remaining four-fifths were being used to service their debts. This at least was the lot of the Dukes of Infantado, to judge from the will of the fifth duke,

dated 4 March 1598. He explains his heavy debts by the failure of his
parents to pay him the portion of an elder son, which had obliged him
to mortgage his wealth in order to maintain his household; in addition
he had been indebted by lawsuits, by marriage settlements for his
children, and by the expenditure of over 100,000 ducats on repairs
and improvements to the ducal palace at Guadalajara. The Duke's
successors met the challenge in the same way as other impoverished
aristocrats. They left their 85,000 vassals and their 620 towns and villages to the care of stewards and administrators, and transferred themselves to Madrid. Life at Court might be expensive (indeed, the Duke
of Infantado is said to have spent more than 300,000 ducats in the
course of the King's visit to Valencia in 1599), but the grandees expected to make up for their losses by plundering the royal treasury,
just as their ancestors had plundered it when another favourite ruled
Spain, in the reign of John II.

It was not only the grandees who benefited from the affluence of
a generous King. The Spain of Philip III, like the England of James I,
saw an inflation of honours. During the sixteenth century there had
been a relatively moderate increase in the number of Spanish titles:

	EARLY 16TH CENTURY	1600	
Dukes	17	21	(21 grandees)
Marquises	16	42	(8 grandees)
Counts	44	56	(3 grandees)
	77	119	

In the twenty-three years of his reign, Philip III created three dukes,
thirty marquises, and thirty-three counts. This addition of new titles
played its part in keeping a large share of the national wealth in aristocratic hands, in spite of the relative diminution of the wealth of the
old grandee families. The combined rent-rolls of the artistocracy in the
early sixteenth century totalled some 1,500,000 ducats; by 1630, when
there were 155 titled nobles, their nominal combined incomes exceeded 5,000,000.

Although the real incomes of the nobles were far less than their
nominal incomes, they still contrived to spend on a vast scale. Like the
King, they had found it impossible to adjust their way of life to a new
age in which prices were no longer automatically rising and debts were
gratifyingly reduced by the process of inflation. At a time when less
good money was entering Spain and more was leaving it, the King still
managed to live beyond his means by striking a copper coinage for
domestic use and then manipulating it at times of need; and the nobles,

paying their servants—as the King paid his—in debased *vellón*, followed the ways of their royal master and spent more than they had. Their households grew larger and larger, swollen by the Castilian custom of automatically re-employing all old servants when the mastership of the house changed hands, even if the new master already possessed a large household of his own. Thus the Conde Duque de Olivares had 198 servants, the great Duke of Osuna 300, and, in the later years of the century, the Duke of Medinaceli, heir to an imposing array of estates, no less than 700. Royal pragmatics to limit the number of lackeys and servants were useless, for domestic service was one of the few important industries of Castile, and it obeyed the laws of social custom and economic necessity rather than those of the State. A large household enhanced the standing of its owner; and service in a noble household, even when it entailed being underpaid and underfed, was on the whole to be preferred to no employment at all.

Inevitably, therefore, as grandees and lesser aristocrats drifted to Court, they were followed by thousands who either possessed, or aspired to, a place in their service. At a time when the population of Castile had fallen, that of Madrid continued to grow: from 4,000 in 1530 to 37,000 in 1594, to anything between 70,000 and 100,000 in the reign of Philip IV. The Court acted as a great magnet, drawing to it from all over the country, the rootless, the dishonest, and the ambitious. Recognizing this, the Government ordered the great nobles in 1611 to return to their estates in the hope of clearing the Court of parasites, but the order suffered the fate of most of Lerma's good intentions, and the *arbitristas* continued to fulminate in vain against the unchecked growth of a monstrous capital which was draining away the life-blood of Castile.

Younger sons and impoverished *hidalgos* flocked to the Court in the hope of making or restoring their fortunes—a hope that did not seem unreasonable when a Rodrigo Calderón could acquire the marquisate of Siete Iglesias and an annual income of 200,000 ducats. For the Court had much to offer: not only places in the households of nobles, and even, with luck, in the palace, but places also in the proliferating bureaucracy of the Spanish Monarchy. The only drawback to service as a royal official was that it required a modicum of education; but, over the course of the years, the expansion of the educational establishments of Castile had amply catered for this need. According to one *arbitrista*, Fernández Navarrete, there were thirty-two universities and 4,000 grammar schools in Spain, turning out far more educated, or semi-educated, students and graduates than could ever hope to find employment in the professions. During the sixteenth century there had been a continuous foundation of universities and colleges—twenty-one new universities since 1516, and eighteen new colleges at Salamanca alone. Since the number of applicants for places in the administration far exceeded the number of places available, it became increasingly necessary for colleges to look after their own. Those in the best position to do this were the famous *Colegios Mayores*, like the four at Salamanca—*élite* establishments which had virtually acquired the status of independent republics within the universities. The *Colegios Mayores*, which had originally been intended for the aristocracy of talent, had provided Spain with many of its most distinguished scholars, clerics, and administrators: the *Colegio Mayor* of Cuenca at Salamanca, for example, produced over the space of fifty years six cardinals, twenty archbishops, and eight viceroys. But in the course of time poverty no longer became a necessary condition for entry, and standards slipped. The position of the *Colegios Mayores* was, however, impregnable. Their practice was to maintain at Court former pupils known as *hacedores*—men of rank and influence who would back members of their own colleges for official posts, on the understanding that the colleges would in return reserve places for their own friends and relatives. If no satisfactory position were available at the time, favoured students were installed by the colleges in special hostels, where they could pass the years—sometimes as many as fifteen or twenty—in great comfort, waiting for a desirable post to fall vacant.

Influence, favour, recommendation, were therefore essential passports. The more talented graduates had little hope of employment unless they could find an influential patron, and consequently a great army of students joined the ranks of the unemployed. Yet a degree conferred at least some status, and there was always the possibility of a lucky break: "A man studies and studies, and then with favour and good luck he'll find himself with a staff in his hand or a mitre on his head when he least expects it." Everything, then, conspired to attract the population to the economically unproductive occupations in society. There was always the chance of a sudden piece of good fortune to end the long years of waiting; and anyhow, what alternative was there? "The number of religious, and clergy, and students, has doubled," it was said in 1620, "because they have no other means of living or maintaining themselves." In fact, if Church, Court, and bureaucracy absorbed an excessive proportion of the potentially productive part of the population of Castile, this was not only because of their own innate attractiveness to a society which tended to despise the more menial occupations, but also because they offered almost the only prospects of remunerative employment in an underdeveloped economy.

Most of the *arbitristas* recommended the reduction of schools and convents and the clearing of the Court as the solution to the problem. Yet this was really to mistake the symptoms for the cause. González de Cellorigo was almost alone in appreciating that the fundamental problem lay not so much in heavy spending by Crown and upper classes— since this spending itself created a valuable demand for goods and services—as in the disproportion between expenditure and investment. "Money is not true wealth", he wrote, and his concern was to increase the national wealth by increasing the nation's productive capacity rather than its stock of precious metals. This could only be achieved by investing more money in agricultural and industrial development. At present, surplus wealth was being unproductively invested—"dissipated on thin air—on papers, contracts, *censos*, and letters of exchange, on cash, and silver, and gold—instead of being expended on things that yield profits and attract riches from outside to augment the riches within. And thus there is no money, gold, or silver in Spain because there is so much; and it is not rich, because of all its riches. . . ."

The assumptions of González de Cellorigo about the way in which wealth was being used, or misused, find some confirmation in an inventory of the possessions of a wealthy royal official, Don Alonso Rámirez de Prado, a member of the Council of Castile arrested for corrupt practices in 1607. Besides his house, which he had bought from the Duke of Alba for 44,000 ducats, he possessed the following (figures being given in *escudos*, which consisted at this moment of 400 *maravedís*, against 375 *maravedís* to the ducat):

	ESCUDOS
Silverware	40,000
Jewellery	40,000
Tapestries and hangings	90,000
Letters of exchange	100,000
Juros (in the name of himself and others)	470,000
Real estate	500,000
	1,240,000

Such an inventory gives force to González's constant insistence on the urgent necessity of redeeming *juros* and reducing the enormous burden on Castile of the Crown's debts, which lured away surplus wealth into unproductive channels.

The Castile of González de Cellorigo was thus a society in which both money and labour were misapplied; an unbalanced, top-heavy society, in which, according to González, there were thirty parasites for every one man who did an honest day's work; a society with a false sense of values, which mistook the shadow for substance, and substance for the shadow. That this society should also have produced a brilliant civilization, as rich in cultural achievement as it was poor in economic achievement, was no more than one among its many paradoxes. For the age of a copper coinage was the golden age of Spain.

The country's social and economic organization was by no means unfavourable to artists and writers. Among the upper classes of society there was money with which to assist them, and leisure to enjoy their works. Many nobles prided themselves on their patronage of the arts: the Counts of Gondomar and Olivares built up great libraries; the palaces of the Count of Monterrey and the Marquis of Leganés were famed for their picture galleries. The possibilities of building up collections were greatly enhanced by the frequency of auctions in Madrid, which enabled a connoisseur like Don Juan de Espina to gather together a remarkable collection of curiosities and works of art from the sales of great houses. Espina himself was an eccentric and something of a recluse, but among the upper classes of Madrid many kept open house for poets and painters.

On the whole, the wealth of the aristocracy seems to have been spent more on the patronage of literature and painting than on architecture. In the fifteenth and sixteenth centuries there had been much building of palaces, but in the seventeenth century the Church rather than the aristocracy was responsible for the most impressive edifices—innumerable churches and convents, in which the austerities of Herrera gradually yielded to a more ornate and theatrical style, culminating in the often frenzied convolutions of Churrigueresque baroque.

If the decline in aristocratic building is to some extent an indication of a decline in aristocratic wealth—at least in relation to that of the Church—the grandees still retained enough money to indulge in keen competition for the patronage of authors and artists. This was particularly true in Andalusia, where there was acute rivalry among the three great houses of Guzmán, Afán de Ribera, and Girón, for the patronage and friendship of the most distinguished talents. Moreover, the patronage was often well informed. Don Fernando Afán de Ribera, Duke of Alcalá (1584–1637) was an amateur painter, a great book collector, and a distinguished Latin scholar, who devoted his spare time to the investigation of Castilian antiquities; the Count of Olivares, after leaving

Salamanca University, spent several years at Seville in the company of poets and authors, and tried his own hand at writing verse. When he became the Favourite of Philip IV—himself a great connoisseur, and a patron of art and letters—he made the Court a brilliant literary and artistic centre, famous for the theatrical presentations and literary *fiestas*, in which such names as Lope de Vega and Calderón de la Barca figured prominently among the participants.

The climate was therefore propitious for literary and artistic production, although, as Cervantes was to discover by bitter experience, even genius did not guarantee a regular income. At the same time, the moral and emotional involvement of the intellectuals in the tragic fate of their native land seems to have provided an additional stimulus, giving an extra degree of intensity to their imagination, and diverting it into rewardingly creative channels. This was especially true of Cervantes, whose life—from 1547 to 1616—spans the two ages of imperial triumph and imperial retreat. The crisis of the late sixteenth century cuts through the life of Cervantes as it cuts through the life of Spain, separating the days of heroism from the days of *desengaño*. Somehow Cervantes magically held the balance between optimism and pessimism, enthusiasm and irony, but he illustrates what was to be the most striking characteristic of seventeenth-century literary and artistic production—that deep cleavage between the two worlds of the spirit and the flesh, which co-exist and yet are for ever separate. This constant dualism between the spirit and the flesh, the dream and the reality, belonged very much to seventeenth-century European civilization as a whole, but it seems to have attained an intensity in Spain that it rarely achieved elsewhere. It is apparent in the writings of Calderón and the portraits of Velázquez, and it prompted the bitter satires of Quevedo. "There are many things here that seem to exist and have their being, and yet they are nothing more than a name and an appearance", Quevedo wrote at the end of his life. Yet which was the real and which the illusory in González de Cellorigo's "society of the bewitched, living outside the natural order of things"? Was the reality of Spanish experience to be found in the heroic imperialism of a Charles V or in the humiliating pacifism of Philip III? In the world of Don Quixote, or the world of Sancho Panza? Confused at once by its own past and its own present, the Castile of Philip III—the land of *arbitristas*—sought desperately for an answer.

During the second decade of the seventeenth century it became increasingly obvious that the Government of the Duke of Lerma was living on borrowed time. Both at home and abroad the situation was

deteriorating alarmingly. It was true that the murder of Henry IV in
1610 had opportunely removed any immediate danger of war with
France, and that the double marriage treaty of 1612 between Louis XIII
and the Infanta Ana on the one hand, and between Prince Philip and
Elizabeth of Bourbon on the other, held out hopes of a new and happier
chapter in the history of Franco-Spanish relations. But the *pax his-
panica* never extended into the world overseas. The Dutch had used the
years of peace since 1609 to consolidate and extend their gains in the
Far East at the expense of the Portuguese empire. As the depredations
of the Dutch continued, one minister after another came round to the
view expressed in 1616 by Don Fernando de Carrillo, the President of
the Council of Finance, that "it has been worse than if the war had
gone on". The problem of the Dutch, unsolved and perhaps insoluble,
was to dog the Spain of Philip III and IV as it had dogged that of
Philip II, as if to confirm that the Spanish Monarchy would never
shake itself free of the *damnosa hereditas* of the Netherlands.

At home, both the condition of Castile and the state of the royal
finances gave rise to increasing concern. In spite of the return of peace,
the Crown was still managing to spend some 8,000,000 or even
9,000,000 ducats a year—a figure quite without precedent, complained
Carrillo (not entirely accurately) in 1615. If Philip II had managed to
spend even more in the heyday of the 1590s, he had at least been able
to draw on substantial revenues from the Indies. But in 1615 and again
in 1616 the treasure fleet, which could be relied upon in the early years
of the reign to bring the Crown 2,000,000 ducats a year, brought
scarcely 1,000,000 ducats, and in the closing years of the decade the
figure dropped to well below 1,000,000.

The gradual drying-up of the stream of silver from America—which
is to be explained by the increasing cost of working the mines, by the
growing self-sufficiency of the colonists, by heavier expenditure by the
viceregal governments in the New World, and perhaps by a fall in
world silver prices—made it increasingly urgent to tackle the problem
of financial and economic reform. To the voices of *arbitristas* and of
procuradores of the Castilian Cortes were now added those of the
Crown's financial ministers, urging Lerma to take action. In the early
summer of 1618 he at last bowed before the storm. A special Junta,
known as the *Junta de Reformación*, was created, and the Council of
Castile was ordered to produce a report outlining possible remedies for
Castile's present ills. But the Duke himself, who had sensibly taken
out an insurance policy in the form of a cardinal's hat, was not to
benefit from this belated piece of initiative. On 4 October 1618 he fell

from power as the result of a palace revolution engineered by his own son, the Duke of Uceda, and his disgrace was followed by the arrest, in February 1619, of his henchman Don Rodrigo Calderón, who was later brought to trial on an imposing array of charges.

The Council of Castile duly produced its *consulta* on 1 February 1619. This was not, in fact, as impressive a document as it is sometimes made out to be, and its seven curiously assorted recommendations marked no advance on what the *arbitristas* had been saying for years. The misery and depopulation of Castile were ascribed to "excessive taxes and tributes", and the Council proposed a reduction of taxes and reform of the fiscal system, which would partly be achieved by calling on the other kingdoms of the Monarchy to come to Castile's assistance. The Council also suggested that the King should curb his naturally generous instincts in the bestowal of *mercedes*. The Court should be cleared. New sumptuary decrees should be enforced, to curtail the fashion for expensive foreign luxuries. Deserted regions should be repopulated, and agricultural labourers be encouraged by the grant of special privileges. No more licences should be given for the establishment of new religious foundations. Moreover, the number of existing convents and grammar schools should be reduced and the hundred receiverships set up in 1613 be abolished.

Although these recommendations were curiously vague on exactly those points where it was most necessary to be specific, they were none the less important as representing the first real recognition by Philip III's Government of the gravity of Castile's economic problems. But the régime of the Duke of Uceda was no better equipped to transform policy into action than that of his father, and for two precious years the Council of Castile's proposals were quietly ignored. The days of the régime, however, were numbered. In the summer of 1619 Philip III made a State visit to Portugal, where the Cortes were assembled to take the oath of allegiance to his son. On the return journey he was taken ill, and although his condition improved shortly afterwards— thanks, it was said, to the intercession of St. Isidore, whose remains were placed in his room—it soon became clear that he could not expect to live much longer. Full of contrition for a life which was as blameless as it had been unprofitable, he died at the age of forty-three on 31 March 1621, to be succeeded by his sixteen-year-old son, heir to the wasted estate.

Philip IV differed from his father in being quick-witted, intelligent, and cultivated, but resembled him in his absence of character. Quite without the animation of his younger brother Ferdinand (who, with

singular inappropriateness, had been created Cardinal-Archbishop of
Toledo in 1619 at the grave age of ten), he was inclined by temperament to depend on others who might stiffen his resolution and assist
him in the formidable task of making up his mind. Born to rely on
Favourites, he had already adopted—or, more accurately, been adopted
by—his first and most influential Favourite before he came to the
throne. This was a gentleman of his household, Gaspar de Guzmán,
Count of Olivares. The Count was an Andalusian aristocrat, born in
1587 at Rome, where his father was Spanish ambassador. He was
educated at the University of Salamanca and was intended for a career
in the Church, but the sudden death of his elder brother made him heir
to the family title and estates. Ambitious for office and advancement,
he had to wait until 1615 before Lerma, naturally distrustful of so
strong a personality, gave him office as a gentleman of the chamber
to the young Prince Philip. Once in the royal household, Olivares
worked hard, and eventually with success, to win the favour of the
Prince. In the squalid intrigues of the last years of the reign he threw
in his lot with the Duke of Uceda, and successfully manoeuvred for
the recall to Madrid of his uncle, Don Baltasar de Zúñiga, who had
been acting as ambassador at the Court of the Emperor. Being a man
of ability and influence, Zúñiga would be more useful to his nephew at
the Court of the King of Spain.

As Philip III lay on his death-bed, Zúñiga and Olivares moved fast
to wrest control of the Government from the inept hands of the Duke
of Uceda, and the favour of the new King carried them triumphantly
to success. Until his death in October 1622 Zúñiga was nominally the
first minister of Philip IV. But Zúñiga's ministry was in reality no more
than a screen behind which Olivares groomed himself for the position
of *Privado* that he held for twenty-two years, until his fall from power
in 1643. A restless figure, never fully at ease with others or with himself, Olivares was less one personality than a whole succession of personalities, co-existing, competing and conflicting within a single frame.
By turns ebullient and dejected, humble and arrogant, shrewd and
gullible, impetuous and cautious, he dazzled contemporaries with the
versatility of his performance and bewildered them with his chameleon
changes of mood. Somehow he always seemed larger than lifesize,
bestriding the Court like a colossus, with state papers stuck in his hat
and bulging in his pockets, always in a flurry of activity, surrounded
by scurrying secretaries, ordering, hectoring, cajoling, his voice booming down the corridors of the palace. No man worked harder, or slept

less. With the coming of Olivares, the indolent, easy-going days of the Duke of Lerma were gone for ever, and the stage was set for reform.

Olivares was, by nature and conviction, the heir of the *arbitristas*, determined to undertake with ruthless efficiency the reforms that had been so long delayed. But he was also the heir to another tradition which had found powerful advocates in the Spain of Philip III—the great imperial tradition, which believed firmly in the rightness, and indeed the inevitability, of Spanish, and specifically Castilian, hegemony over the world. Under the government of Lerma this tradition had been muted in the capital of the Monarchy, where the eclipse of the crusading tradition had been curiously symbolized by the displacement in 1617 of St. James from his position as sole patron of Spain. In future the warrior saint was to have a feminine partner in the person of a highly idealized St. Teresa. But just as St. James still had his fervent partisans, so also did the militant tradition of which he was the symbol. The supine policies of the Lerma régime were regarded with anger and contempt by many of its agents, who refused to reconcile themselves to the humiliating pacifism of Philip III's Government. Profiting from the weakness of the régime they despised, these agents—the great Italian proconsuls, like the Count of Fuentes, the Marquis of Bedmar, the Marquis of Villafranca, and the Duke of Osuna (viceroy of Sicily from 1611–16 and of Naples from 1616–20)— conducted over the years a militant and aggressive policy entirely at variance with that of Madrid. Although Osuna was recalled in disgrace in 1620 and later imprisoned on the orders of Zúñiga and Olivares, both ministers, in fact, shared many of his aims and aspirations. They believed, like him, that Spain could remain true to itself only if it remained true to its imperial tradition, and they despised the defeatist policies which had, in their opinion, brought it to its present miserable state.

Olivares therefore combined in himself the quixotic imperialism that belonged to the golden age of Charles V and Philip II, and the practical, down-to-earth approach of the *arbitristas*, for whom windmills remained windmills, whatever was said to the contrary. Throughout his career, the ideal and the practical, the crusading tradition and the reforming tradition, existed uncomfortably side by side, and it was oddly appropriate that the very first month of his ministry, when everything was set for reform, should also see the return of Spain to war. In April 1621 the truce with the Netherlands expired, and was not renewed. Apart from the fact that the triumph of the bellicose Orangist party in the United Provinces in any event made the renewal of the war virtually certain, there were powerful arguments in Madrid as well as in the Hague for allowing the truce to lapse. The Council of Portugal insisted on the irreparable harm done to Portugal's overseas possessions by the Dutch during the years of "peace"; the Council of Finance tried to show that the cost of maintaining a standing army in Flanders in peacetime was not substantially less than in war. It was also argued that if the Dutch were once again engaged at home, they would be able to devote less energy to their pirate ventures, and a world-wide struggle could thus be localized. In addition, certain measures had already been taken which suggested that on this occasion there was a real chance of success against the Dutch. The revolt of the Valtelline in 1618 had provided a pretext for the Duke of Feria, Governor of Milan, to establish Spanish garrisons in this strategic valley linking Milan and Austria; and the revolt of Bohemia in the same year allowed Spain's best commander, Ambrosio Spínola, to occupy the Palatinate and secure control of the Rhine passages. These two actions, undertaken in the last year of the Uceda régime, had enabled Spain to consolidate its hold over the vital "Spanish road", up which men and supplies could be sent from Milan to Flanders.

The successes of the Spanish commanders helped to strengthen the hand of those who wanted a return to belligerent policies, and created a climate in which the renewal of war came almost to be taken for granted. So it was that in the very first month of its existence the new Government found itself committed to the continuation of war in the Netherlands and to the probability of its extension in central Europe. This immediately pushed up the figures for the anticipated expenditure of 1621. For years the Duke of Osuna had been insisting that the preservation of an empire as large and scattered as that of Spain depended on the possession of a first-class fleet. Under the Government of Philip III the Spanish fleet had been scandalously neglected, and ships had been allowed to rot in the dockyards for lack of money. But Olivares seems to have appreciated that a vigorous naval policy was essential for the success of Spanish arms, and by an order of November 1621 the Atlantic fleet was to be increased to a total of forty-six ships, and the sum allocated to its upkeep raised from 500,000 to 1,000,000 ducats a year.

By another royal order of the same month, the expenditure on the Flanders army was raised from 1,500,000 to 3,500,000 ducats a year. The Crown's anticipated annual expenditure was now over 8,000,000 ducats—and its annual deficit in the region of 4,000,000, with revenues being mortgaged for three or four years ahead. Since, as Olivares insisted in a memorandum he wrote at this moment for his royal master, "kings cannot achieve heroic actions without money", the return to war itself gave extra urgency to the programme for reform. This was now begun with considerable vigour. As an earnest of the new ministry's intentions, the long list of royal favours and pensions was slashed, an inquiry was ordered into all ministerial fortunes acquired since 1603, and the hated Rodrigo Calderón was publicly executed. At the same time, new life was breathed into the moribund *Junta de Reformación*, and the fruits of its labours appeared in February 1623 in the publication of a series of twenty-three articles of reform. These were a mixed series of ordinances, which draw their inspiration from the writings of the *arbitristas* and from the Council of Castile's *consulta* of 1619, and were infused by a conviction that morals and economics were inextricably intertwined. There was to be a two-thirds reduction in the number of municipal offices; strict sumptuary laws were to be introduced to regulate the prevalent excesses of dress; measures were to be taken to increase the population; prohibitions were to be imposed on the import of foreign manufactures; and brothels were to be closed. Here at last was that general reform of morals and manners which, it was assumed, would bring about the regeneration of Castile.

Unhappily for Olivares's good intentions, the unexpected visit of the Prince of Wales to Madrid the very next month threw austerity to the winds; the origins of ministerial fortunes proved to be so mysterious that the inquiry had to be abandoned; and the plan for the reduction of municipal offices had to be jettisoned on the insistence of the *procuradores* of the Cortes, who found their municipalities threatened with heavy financial loss. Within three years there was nothing to show for the great reform programme except the modest achievement of the abolition of the ruff. In the face of public inertia, and the covert opposition of Court and bureaucracy, even the reforming energies of an Olivares were doomed to frustration.

But if the reform of morals had to be postponed to a more propitious time, the reform of the finances could not afford to wait. The financial situation confronting Olivares resolved itself essentially into two separate but related problems. The Monarchy had run into trouble in the reign of Philip III primarily because of the exhaustion of Castile, which shouldered the principal burden of the Crown's finances. The exhaustion of Castile, in turn, was principally attributed to the weight of taxation that rested upon it, and bore specially hard on its most productive citizens. Therefore the aim of Olivares's financial policies must first of all be to redistribute more equitably the incidence of Castilian taxation, and then to induce the other provinces of the Monarchy to come to Castile's help, so that the disproportionate burden borne by Castile could itself be lightened.

At the heart of Olivares's plans for Castile was a project for establishing a national banking system—a scheme proposed to Philip II by a Fleming, Peter van Oudegherste as early as 1576, and then intermittently considered during the reign of Philip III. A chain of banks would, it was believed, assist the Crown to reduce its debts, relieve it of dependence on the foreign *asentistas*, and, by placing a ceiling of 5 percent on returns, drive much of the money invested in loan funds into direct investments in a search for higher rewards. This scheme was outlined in a letter sent in October 1622 to the towns represented in the Castilian Cortes, and was coupled with another proposal dear to Olivares's heart—the abolition of the *millones*. Instead of this tax on essential articles of consumption, which hit the poor hardest, and was anyhow increasingly unremunerative and difficult to collect, Olivares proposed that the 15,000 towns and villages of Castile should contribute, in proportion to their size, to the upkeep of an army of 30,000 men.

These projects ran into strong opposition in the Castilian Cortes. The *erarios*, or banks, were generally mistrusted—not without reason— and although there was a general desire to see the last of the *millones*, it proved impossible to agree on an alternative form of taxation. As a result, the banking scheme was abandoned in 1626, and the irreplaceable *millones* survived—to be extended to other commodities, and collected at the rate not of 2,000,000, but 4,000,000 ducats a year. Although Olivares had not yet given up all hope, and indeed made another attempt to abolish the *millones* in 1631, it was clear that powerful vested interests stood in the way of the radical fiscal reforms which he longed to introduce.

The plans for reforms in Castile, however, were only one part of an infinitely more ambitious reform programme for the entire Spanish Monarchy. During recent years, financial ministers and *arbitristas* alike had insisted that it was the duty of the other parts of the Monarchy to come to the relief of an exhausted Castile. But it was difficult to see how this could be achieved so long as the existing constitutional structure of the Monarchy was preserved. The privileges of such kingdoms as Aragon and Valencia were so wide, and their Cortes so powerful, that the chances of introducing a regular system of taxation on a scale approaching that of Castile seemed remote. Fiscal necessity, therefore, now came to reinforce the traditional Castilian nationalist arguments that provincial laws and liberties should be abolished, and the constitutional and fiscal organization of other parts of the Monarchy be brought into conformity with that of Castile.

At a time when statesmen all over Europe were attempting to consolidate their hold over their peoples and exploit national resources more effectively in order to strengthen the power of the State, it was natural that Olivares should see in the "Castilianization" of the Spanish Monarchy the solution to many of his problems. If uniform laws were introduced throughout the Monarchy, the "separation" between the various kingdoms, of which he was always complaining, would disappear, and it would be possible to mobilize effectively the resources of an empire which was potentially the most powerful in the world, but which at present was gravely weakened by its total lack of unity. Olivares thus became a partisan of the traditional "Alba" approach to the question of imperial organization. But at the same time he seems to have had a real understanding of the grievances of the non-Castilian kingdoms, which protested at having to pay heavier taxes to maintain an empire of benefit solely to Castile. It is significant that one of his closest friends and advisers was a political theorist called Álamos de Barrientos, who had also been a friend and disciple of Antonio Pérez. It was, perhaps, under the influence of Álamos and of the political theories of the Pérez school that what otherwise might have been no more than a policy of "Castilianization" at its most crude, was modified in Olivares's thought into a more generous and liberal programme. In a famous memorandum which he presented to Philip IV at the end of 1624, he admitted the many grievances of kingdoms which scarcely ever saw their King and which felt themselves excluded from offices in the empire and in the royal households. He therefore proposed that, while the laws of the various kingdoms should be gradually reduced to conformity with those of Castile, the character of the Monarchy as a whole should be made less exclusively Castilian, by means of more frequent royal visits to the various provinces, and by the employment of more Aragonese, Portuguese or Italians in important offices. If Olivares's Monarchy was therefore to consist of "multa regna, sed una lex", it would also be a truly universal Monarchy, in which the many walls of partition between the "multa regna" would be broken down, while their nationals were employed—irrespective of province of origin—in a genuine co-operative venture, of benefit to all.

Olivares himself realized that this grandiose vision of a unified and integrated Spanish Monarchy could not be achieved in a day, but he saw that it was important to "familiarize" the various provinces with each other as quickly as possible, and to accustom them to the idea of thinking collectively instead of in purely individual terms. This meant, in effect, a reversal of the whole approach to the Monarchy that had been adopted by Charles V and Philip II, and had survived in default of any more positive vision. It seemed to Olivares that the process might start with the establishment of some form of military co-operation between the different provinces. This would not only have the merit of inducing the provinces to think of others besides themselves, but would also help to solve the problems of money and manpower which were at present threatening to overwhelm Castile. The long secret memorandum to the King of 1624 was therefore followed by a shorter memorandum, intended for publication, outlining a scheme to be known as the "Union of Arms". The Union was to be achieved by the creation of a common reserve of 140,000 men to be supplied and maintained by all the States of the Monarchy in fixed proportions:

	PAID MEN
Catalonia	16,000
Aragon	10,000
Valencia	6,000
Castile and the Indies	44,000
Portugal	16,000
Naples	16,000
Sicily	6,000
Milan	8,000
Flanders	12,000
Mediterranean and Atlantic islands	6,000

Any kingdom of the Monarchy which was attacked by the enemy would be immediately assisted by the seventh part of this reserve, or 20,000 infantry and 4,000 cavalry.

There were obvious practical difficulties in the way of this ingenious scheme. The States of the Crown of Aragon, for instance, had extremely rigid laws regulating the recruitment of troops and their use beyond the frontiers. It would not be easy to induce them to set aside these laws for the sake of helping a province like Milan, which was always liable to sudden attack. But the Conde Duque (as Olivares came to be known after being created Duque de Sanlúcar la Mayor in 1625) refused to be daunted. Determined to press forward with a scheme which offered real hope of relief for Castile, he and the King set out at the end of 1625 on a visit to the three States of the Crown of Aragon, whose Cortes were to be presented with the Union of Arms.

The Cortes of Aragon, Valencia, and Catalonia, held during the spring months of 1626, proved to be even more unenthusiastic about the Union of Arms than the Conde Duque had feared. It was twenty years or more since the last Cortes had been held, and in the intervening years grievances had accumulated. Both Valencians and Aragonese objected to the novelty of the subsidy demanded by the King, and were adamant in their refusal to conscript men for foreign service. But the most recalcitrant of the Cortes were those of Catalonia, opened by the King at Barcelona on 28 March. The Catalans at this moment were more than usually touchy and disgruntled. Since the visit of Philip III in 1599 they had suffered a number of experiences which had made them particularly sensitive about the intentions of Castile. During the first decade of the century, the viceroys had shown themselves increasingly incapable of dealing with the bandits who had long troubled the peace of the mountainous frontier region, and who had recently taken to committing daring raids on the outskirts of Barcelona itself. The Government of the Duke of Lerma had shown an almost total lack of interest in the problem of preserving public order in the Principality— so much so, that during the feeble viceroyalty of the Marquis of Almazán from 1611 to 1615, it had seemed for a moment as if Catalonia would succumb to total anarchy. The situation was saved by the arrival in 1616 of a vigorous new viceroy, the Duke of Alburquerque. But Alburquerque and his successor, the Duke of Alcalá, only restored order by contravening the Catalan constitutions. Banditry in its worst form had been suppressed, but national susceptibilities had been gravely hurt in the process. When Alcalá finally left office in 1622 he had alienated every section of the community including the towns—the natural allies of the viceregal administration in its struggle against aristocratic disorder—by his contemptuous attitude to everything Catalan, and his high-handed treatment of the Principality's laws and privileges.

The Conde Duque's schemes therefore seemed to the Catalans to mark a further stage in a long-standing Castilian conspiracy to abolish their liberties, and their behaviour became increasingly unco-operative as the Cortes continued. At a moment when a trade recession in the Mediterranean had sapped the credit and confidence of their merchants, they were not to be tempted by Olivares's plans for the establishment of trading companies, including a Levant Company with its headquarters at Barcelona; and the Conde Duque's pleas for a generous co-operation in the military ventures of the Monarchy fell on deaf ears. The Catalans' prime concern was to secure redress for past grievances and security for the future, and rumours that Olivares's ultimate aim was the establishment of a Monarchy with *un rey, una ley, y una moneda*—one king, one law, one coinage—merely stiffened their determination to resist. Moreover, Olivares was in too much of a hurry, and made the mistake of trying to force the pace in an assembly whose procedural methods made it an infinitely slow-moving body at the best of times. As a result, one obstruction followed another, until the Conde Duque decided that further attempts to extract a subsidy were for the moment doomed to failure. On 4 May, before the Catalans realized what was happening, the King and his party were gone from Barcelona, leaving the Cortes still in session.

On arriving back in Madrid, Olivares professed himself pleased with the results of the King's visit to the Crown of Aragon. He had, it is true, obtained a subsidy of 1,080,000 ducats from the Valencians, which the King accepted as sufficient to maintain 1,000 infantry men for fifteen years. The Aragonese, for their part, had voted double this sum. This meant that, for the first time since the end of Charles V's reign, Aragon and Valencia would be making a regular annual contribution to the Crown's finances. On the other hand, both States had stubbornly refused to allow the conscription of troops for foreign service, so that the Conde Duque's plans for securing military co-operation between the provinces had been frustrated; and Catalonia, the wealthiest of the three States, had voted neither men nor money.

Undeterred by these setbacks, the Conde Duque published in Castile on 25 July 1626 a decree proclaiming the official inauguration of the Union of Arms. This explained that the King had undertaken his arduous journey to the Crown of Aragon in order to secure assistance for Castile, and that, as an earnest of the many benefits to come, the Crown itself would pay one third of Castile's contribution out of its own revenues. On 8 May, two months before the publication of this decree, the Government had suspended all further minting of *vellón* coins for Castile—a somewhat belated action, in view of the fact that, in a country flooded with *vellón* coins, the premium on silver in terms of *vellón* had reached nearly 50 percent. These two measures—the inauguration of the Union of Arms and the suspension of *vellón* minting—seemed to symbolize between them the completion of the first stage of the Conde Duque's reform programme, and to hold out hope of relief for Castile and the restoration of the Castilian economy. They were followed on 31 January 1627, twenty years after the Duke of Lerma's bankruptcy, by a suspension of all payments to the bankers. Olivares hoped by this device to end the Crown's expensive dependence on a small group of Italian financiers—a move for which the times seemed propitious, since he had found a group of Portuguese businessmen both able and willing to undertake some of the Crown's *asientos* at lower rates of interest. With these measures successfully achieved, the King was able to announce to the Council of State in 1627 a long list of successes obtained by his ministry during the first six years of the reign: victories abroad, reforms at home, and a dramatic change for the better in the Monarchy's fortunes. If many of the achievements were illusory, and some of Olivares's most cherished projects had been frustrated, this was not revealed to the world. At least in the Conde Duque's eyes, the reform programme was slowly gathering momentum, and under his leadership the shape of the Monarchy would eventually be transformed.

In spite of the vaunted successes of the new régime, the fact remained that unless really effective measures could be introduced to relieve Castile, the Monarchy as a whole would be confronted with disaster. The Union of Arms in its early stages was not likely to make any very significant contribution to the problem of imperial defence; and although, as a result of remedial measures in America, the treasure fleets were again bringing some 1,500,000 ducats a year, the principal cost of the Crown's expensive policies was still being borne by Castile. In 1627–8 the condition of the Castilian economy suddenly deteriorated. The country found itself faced with a startling rise of prices in *vellón* currency, and the Government was assailed with complaints about the high cost of living. It is probable that the inflation of these years was caused primarily by bad harvests and by the scarcity of foreign goods arising from the partial closing of the frontiers since 1624; but it was exacerbated by the recent monetary policies of the Crown, which between 1621 and 1624 alone had minted nearly 20,000,000 ducats' worth of *vallón* coins. Olivares had hoped to deal with the problem of inflation by relatively painless methods. But drastic action became essential after the failure of an attempt at price-fixing and of an ingenious scheme for the withdrawal of the *vellón* coins in circulation, and on 7 August 1628 the Crown reduced the sale of *vellón* by 50 percent.

The great deflation of 1628 brought heavy losses to private individuals, but instant relief to the royal treasury. Taken in conjunction with the suspension of payments to the *asentistas* in the previous year, it might have served as the starting-point for a sounder financial and economic policy, aimed at clearing the Crown of some of its debts and reducing its annual budgets. In terms of the international situation, the moment was particularly favourable. Hostilities with England had petered out since the failure of the ludicrous English attack on Cadiz in 1625; Habsburg arms were victorious in Germany, and Richelieu was fully occupied with the Huguenots in France. The years 1627–8 probably offered the last real chance for a programme of retrenchment and reform in the Spanish Monarchy.

The chance was tragically missed as the result of a series of unfortunate events in Italy. In December 1627 the Duke of Mantua died. The candidate with the best claim to succeed him was a Frenchman, the Duke of Nevers. A French-controlled Mantua might endanger Spain's hold over north Italy and Milan, and the Spanish governor of Milan, Don Gonzalo de Córdoba, sent his troops into Montferrat in March 1628. Without publicly committing himself, Olivares gave the Governor tacit encouragement by sending him supplies; and, almost before he realized what was happening, he found himself engaged in war with the French in Italy.

The Mantuan War of 1628–31 seems in retrospect the gravest blunder made by Olivares in the field of foreign policy. It rearoused all the old European fears of Spanish aggression, and brought French troops across the Alps in support of their candidate's claim. It failed in its object of keeping a Frenchman off the ducal throne of Mantua, and made it virtually certain that sooner or later France and Spain would again be involved in open war. From this moment, the chances of European peace were sensibly diminished. Although France did not declare war on Spain until 1635, the years between 1628 and 1635 were passed under the lengthening shadow of Franco-Spanish conflict, as Richelieu consolidated his system of European alliances and laid his plans to free France from the long-standing threat of Habsburg encirclement.

The Conde Duque therefore found himself committed to heavy expenditure in Italy, and to further large subsidies to the Emperor, who was shortly to see all his victories of the early 1620s rendered nugatory by the advance of the Swedes. The immediate resources on which Spain could draw for the struggle in Italy and Germany were now slender. The Council of Finance reported in August 1628 that it was 2,000,000 ducats short on the year's provisions, and in the next month disaster came with the capture by Piet Heyn of the Nueva España treasure fleet—the first time that the American silver had fallen into enemy hands. These emergencies made it vital to discover and exploit new sources of revenue, and to mobilize the Monarchy more effectively for war.

For some years it had been obvious to the Conde Duque that the existing administrative system was inadequate for this purpose. The cumbersome machinery of the Councils merely obstructed his designs, and gave excessive powers to men who had no sympathy for his reforming policies. Over the years he had gradually been building up a nucleus of "new" men in whom he could place absolute confidence—men like José González, his secretary, and Jerónimo de Villanueva, the Protonotario of the Council of Aragon. He made some progress in undermining the Councils by appointing his own chosen agents to them, but it became increasingly apparent that the whole conciliar system was so heavily committed to the maintenance of the *status quo* that he could never get from the Councils the swift and effective decisions he so badly needed for the promotion of his policies. He therefore turned more and more to the use of special Juntas, which rapidly proliferated under his Government, and took over from the Councils much of their most important work. This was especially true of the so-called *Junta de Ejecución*, which was set up in 1634 and replaced the Council of State as the effective policy-making body in the Spanish administrative system. Dominated by Olivares himself, and filled with his own friends and servants, the *Junta de Ejecución*, was ideally placed to carry through the Conde Duque's designs for a more intensive exploitation of the resources of the Monarchy.

The new men of the Olivares régime displayed both zeal and ingenuity in their efforts to find new sources of revenue. Since administrative difficulties and the opposition of the Cortes prevented any radical reorganization of the tax system in Castile, it was necessary to devise supplementary means of raising money. The year 1631 saw the introduction of a tax on the first year's income from offices known as the *media anata*, and also of a salt tax, which provoked a rising in Vizcaya. In 1632 the Conde Duque obtained the Pope's consent to a special grant from the clergy, and appropriated a year's income from the Archbishopric of Toledo. He also ordered the collection of a voluntary *donativo* to help save Flanders and Italy, nobles being expected to give 1,500 ducats and *caballeros* 150. In 1635 he confiscated half the yield of all *juros* held by natives, and the entire yield of those belonging to foreigners—a device he continued to employ in succeeding years. In 1637 he imposed a new tax in the form of stamped paper, which became obligatory for all legal and official documents. In the same year he seized 487,000 ducats in American silver, and gave the owners "compensation" in the form of unwanted *juros*; and two years later, ignoring the repercussions on Seville's trade, he appropriated a further 1,000,000 ducats by the same device. He sold Crown rents, titles, and offices, and revived the old feudal obligations of the aristocracy, who found themselves expected to raise and equip infantry companies at their own expense. In consequence, although the nominal distinction between *hidalgos* and *pecheros* remained as strong as ever, the practical distinction tended to disappear, as the aristocracy found itself mulcted of its money by a succession of fiscal expedients from which it could find no way of escape.

In spite of the success of the Conde Duque's efforts to squeeze more money from Castile, he was as well aware as anyone that there was bound to come a moment when Castile would be squeezed dry. This meant that the Union of Arms must be made effective, and in particular that Catalonia and Portugal, which were allegedly the two wealthiest States in the peninsula, must be induced to play a part commensurate with their presumed resources. Both of these States seemed to Olivares dangerously "separated" from the rest of the Monarchy. The Portuguese had stood aloof while Castile prepared relief expeditions in 1634 and 1635 for the recovery of Portugal's own possessions in Brazil, which had been lost to the Dutch since 1630. The Catalans had shown themselves even more unco-operative, for they had again refused to vote a subsidy when the King and Olivares returned to Barcelona in 1632 to continue the interrupted session of the Cortes. Obstructions placed by the city of Barcelona had brought the Cortes to a standstill, for reasons that seemed to Olivares unbearably trivial. It was now thirty-three years since the Catalans had voted their last subsidy to the King, and since then the Principality had been nothing but a source of concern and annoyance to the Spanish Crown. If, as the Conde Duque believed, Catalonia was a rich province with a population of over a million (nearly three times the real figure), then it was high time that it should come to the assistance of Castile and to the rescue of the royal treasury.

Although the Conde Duque squeezed a certain amount of money out of the cities of Lisbon and Barcelona by bullying and blackmail, his real need was for regular financial and military assistance from Catalonia and Portugal. It was difficult to achieve this without reorganizing their Governments, but administrative reform was practically impossible in Catalonia because the constitutions forbade the appointment of Castilians to any offices other than the viceroyalty. There were similar difficulties in Portugal, but slightly more scope for manoeuvre. Under Philip III Portugal had been governed by viceroys, but the system had proved unsatisfactory, and in 1621 the viceroyalty had been replaced by an administration of governors. This, however, had led to constant dissension in Lisbon. In 1634 Olivares found, as he believed, the answer to these difficulties by appointing a member of the royal family, Princess Margaret of Savoy, as Governess of Portugal. The Princess's appointment had the merit of meeting Portuguese complaints about royal neglect, and also made it possible to infiltrate a number of Castilians into the Portuguese administration under the guise of advisers.

The scheme was not a success. The Government in Lisbon turned itself into two rival camps of Castilians and Portuguese, whose constant bickering made effective administration impossible. Moreover, the Lisbon Government's fiscal policies soon ran into trouble. The Princess had been sent to Lisbon with instructions to obtain from the Portuguese a fixed annual levy of 500,000 *cruzados,* to be obtained by the consolidation of existing taxes and the introduction of certain new ones. Although these taxes were to be used to equip expeditions for the recovery of Portugal's overseas territories, this did nothing to reconcile a populace which had always hated the union with Castile; and in 1637 riots broke out in Évora and other towns. Fortunately for the Conde Duque, the riots failed to flare up into nation-wide revolution, in spite of Richelieu's promises of help to the Portuguese. Although the lower clergy enthusiastically supported the rioters, the aristocracy, with the Duke of Braganza at its head, held aloof, and the risings petered out. But the Évora riots were an ominous indication that Portugal might one day attempt to break loose from the Castilian connexion. The upper classes might for the present remain loyal to Madrid, but their loyalty was being subjected to a growing strain. The aristocracy felt itself deprived of offices and honours, and neglected by the King. The commercial classes in Lisbon and the coastal towns were beginning to find that the Union of the Crowns had outlasted its economic value. They had found compensation for the loss of their Far Eastern empire under Philip III by building up for themselves a new sugar empire in Brazil, and by exploiting the resources of Castile's American territories. But in recent years there had been increasing discrimination against Portuguese merchants in the Spanish colonies, and the military and naval power of the King of Spain had proved insufficient to save Brazil from the Dutch. The bonds that tied Portugal to Spain were therefore being dangerously weakened at the very moment when Olivares was bringing Portugal under increasing pressure in order to make it an effective partner in the Union of Arms.

It was, however, in Catalonia, rather than in Portugal, that Olivares first came to grief. The outbreak of war with France in May 1635 greatly enhanced the strategic importance of the Principality of Catalonia, since it guarded the eastern half of Spain's border with the enemy. This made it all the more unfortunate that relations between the Catalans and Madrid were so bad, and that Olivares had failed to obtain a subsidy from the Catalans before the war broke out. He was now in the delicate position of having to fight the war from a disaffected frontier province of whose loyalty he could no longer be entirely sure. At the same time, he needed the assistance of the Catalans to supplement the diminished manpower of Castile, and to contribute to the royal revenues. This was all the more necessary now that the war with France had again increased the Crown's expenditure. For the financial year October 1636 to October 1637, for instance, the Council of Finance had attempted to arrange the following provisions:

	ESCUDOS
For Flanders	4,384,000
For Germany	1,500,000
For Milan	2,500,000
To be provided in Spain	2,000,000
For the fleet	500,000
For the royal households (in the event of a military expedition by the king)	64,000
For ambassadors	150,000

In addition to this, a further 2,000,000 *escudos* were required for the royal households, the ordinary expenses of the fleet, and the frontier garrisons.

These figures provide some indication of why it seemed impossible to Olivares to leave the Catalans alone: unable to raise more than half this sum from his ordinary and extraordinary revenues, he could afford to neglect no opportunity for attempting to extract a few more hundred thousand ducats wherever there seemed the remotest chance of success. Since all direct approaches to the Catalans had proved abortive, he began to toy with ideas of obtaining their assistance by more covert means. In 1637, when French troops crossed the Catalan frontier, the Catalans themselves had been slow in sending help; in 1638, when the town of Fuenterrabía in Guipúzcoa was besieged by the French, Catalonia alone of the States of the Crown of Aragon had refused all military aid. Determined to make the Catalans concern themselves, "as up to now they have apparently not been concerned, with the general affairs of the Monarchy and of these kingdoms", he decided in 1639 that the projected Spanish attack on France should be undertaken from the Catalan border, so that the Catalans would find themselves involved in the war whether they liked it or not.

In the event, it was the French army which entered Catalonia in the early summer of 1639, capturing the frontier fortress of Salses on 19

July. The fall of Salses gave the Conde Duque a useful pretext for pushing the Catalans a little further into the Union of Arms. The Count of Santa Coloma, the native viceroy of Catalonia, was ordered by Madrid to mobilize the Principality for war, so that it could assist the royal army in Rosellón (Roussillon) to recover the captured fortress. During the autumn of 1639 the viceroy and the local ministers did their best to induce the adult male population of Catalonia to turn out for the war, and relentlessly harried the country into sending supplies to the front. For six long months the siege went on, amidst such foul conditions that many troops, both Catalan and non-Catalan, deserted the ranks. Furious at the desertions, Olivares ordered the royal ministers in the Principality to ignore the constitutions of Catalonia whenever the well-being of the army was at stake, on the grounds that the supreme law of defence outweighed all lesser laws. The unconstitutional proceedings of the ministers confirmed Catalan suspicions about the Conde Duque's ultimate intentions, and made the Principality more and more reluctant to co-operate in the Salses campaign. Hatred of Madrid, of the viceroy, and of the viceregal administration mounted throughout Catalonia during the autumn and early winter of 1639, as royal orders became harsher and the country was constantly pressed to provide more men and more supplies for the Salses army. As a result, when the French finally surrendered the fortress on 6 January 1640, the Principality was in a dangerously explosive mood. The aristocracy, who had suffered heavy casualties during the campaign, hated and despised the Count of Santa Coloma for putting the orders of Madrid before the interests of his colleagues and compatriots. Barcelona and the towns had been finally alienated from a Government which had done nothing but attempt to extract money from them over a period of twenty years. The peasantry had suffered severely from the confiscation of their animals and crops. Increasingly, the Principality was listening to the appeals of the clergy to hold fast to its historic liberties, and was finding a responsive leadership in the Catalan *Diputació* headed by a vigorous cleric, Pau Claris, canon of the cathedral chapter of Urgel. By the beginning of 1640, therefore, Olivares, who had won a campaign, was on the point of losing a province—a danger of which he apparently remained unaware. For all his actions at the beginning of 1640 suggest that he believed himself to be close at last to the achievement of one of his most cherished ambitions: the establishment of the Union of Arms.

By 1640 the Conde Duque had come to see the Union of Arms as the best, and perhaps the only, hope for the Monarchy's survival. After early successes in the war with France, of which the most spectacular was the Cardenal Infante's invasion of France from Flanders in 1636, Spain had suffered a number of serious reverses. In 1637 the Dutch recaptured Breda, whose surrender to Spínola in 1625 had been immortalized by Velázquez. In December 1638 Bernard of Weimar took Breisach—a far more serious loss, since it meant that the Spanish road from Milan to Brussels was cut, and that the Spanish armies in the Netherlands could only be reinforced by sea through the English Channel. Then, in October 1639, Admiral Tromp defeated the fleet of Don Antonio de Oquendo at the Battle of the Downs, destroying at a single blow both the navy on which Olivares had expended so much effort, and the chances of sending relief to the Cardenal Infante in the Netherlands. On top of this came the failure of the combined Spanish-Portuguese armada which set out from Lisbon in September 1638 to attempt the reconquest of Brazil. After spending a fruitless year off Bahia, it was brought to battle by a considerably smaller Dutch fleet on 12 January 1640. At the end of four days of inconclusive fighting, its Portuguese commander, the Count of La Torre, abandoned his attempt to attack Pernambuco, and allowed the armada to disperse to the West Indies, leaving the control of the Brazilian seas in the hands of the Dutch.

These reverses filled the Conde Duque with gloom. For years he had been struggling to scrape together men, and money, and ships, and all his efforts seemed doomed to disappointment. He placed much of the blame for these defeats on the inadequacies of the Spanish commanders. Almost from the beginning of his ministry he had been complaining of what he called the *falta de cabezas*—the lack of leaders. It was because of his belief that the Spanish nobility was failing in its duties of leadership that he had sponsored the founding in 1625 of the Colegio Imperial at Madrid, an academy for the sons of nobles run by the Jesuits and designed to provide, in addition to a liberal education, practical instruction in mathematics, the sciences, and the art of war. But the Colegio Imperial failed in its principal aim. No new generation of military commanders appeared to take the place of Spínola and the Duke of Feria, and the higher Castilian aristocracy proved a constant disappointment to the Conde Duque. By 1640 he no longer bothered to conceal his contempt for the grandees, and they in response turned their backs on a Court where nothing awaited them but gibes from the Favourite and endless appeals to their pockets.

The absence of leaders was one of the principal reasons for Olivares's increasing anxiety to obtain a peace settlement. It was particularly with this in mind that he wrote in March 1640 in a memorandum for the King: "God wants us to make peace, for He is depriving us visibly and absolutely of all the means of war." But peace was not easy to obtain. As early as 1629 he had made moves for a truce with the Dutch, and by 1635 he was offering to close the Scheldt and hand over Breda, as long as the Dutch would give back Pernambuco. But the Dutch were adamant in their refusal to surrender their conquests in Brazil, and Olivares in turn could not afford to give up Brazilian territory for fear of the repercussions in Portugal. He had also begun secret negotiations with France almost as soon as the war broke out, but as long as Spain was winning victories he pitched his demands too high, while as soon as Spain began to suffer defeats and he moderated his demands, Richelieu lost interest in the immediate conclusion of a settlement.

Yet if peace was unattainable, it was becoming increasingly difficult to prosecute the war. Castile was by now so denuded of men that the levies were pitiful affairs, and it was becoming quite impossible to keep the armies up to strength. Moreover, the economic position was by now exceptionally grave, for Spain's last real source of economic strength— the trading system between Seville and America—was failing. Olivares's repeated confiscations of silver remittances and his constant interference with the American trade had produced the inevitable result. The merchants had lost confidence; Sevillan shipping was in decay; and although the silver supplies were still coming regularly to the Crown—at least until 1640 when no silver fleet arrived—the whole system of credit and confidence by which Seville had for so long shored up the Spanish Monarchy was gradually crumbling. With Castile exhausted and America failing, the principal foundations of Spanish imperialism over the past hundred years were slowly giving way.

The gravity of the situation inspired Olivares with the boldness of despair. There was still, he believed, hope—not of out-and-out victory, but of a stalemate which would induce a no less exhausted France to come to terms. But this required an unrelenting pressure on the French, such as would only be possible if every part of the Monarchy—Catalonia and Portugal, Flanders, and Peru—joined forces in a supreme co-operative endeavour. The Catalans, for instance, must contribute troops for use in Italy, and they must prepare themselves for a fresh campaign along the French frontier. If the constitutions stood in the way of this, then the constitutions must be changed, and surely there could be no more favorable moment than the present, when a royal army was actually stationed in the Principality. The Conde Duque therefore arranged that the army which had been fighting the Salses campaign should be billeted in Catalonia until the next campaigning season; and under the shadow of the army he planned to hold a new session of the Catalan Cortes, which was to be used solely for the amendment of the more obnoxious constitutions.

The proposed Catalan Cortes of 1640 never met. The Catalan towns and peasantry were hardly in the mood to support the burden of billeting a foreign army, while the troops were in no frame of mind to put up with the second best. During February and March of 1640 troops and civilians clashed in many parts of the Principality, and the Count of Santa Coloma proved quite unequal to the task of keeping order. The Conde Duque responded to the situation as he had responded in the autumn of the previous year—by harsh threats and increasingly imperious orders to the viceroy to see that one of Spain's last remaining veteran armies was properly billeted, at whatever cost to the native population. At the beginning of March, on hearing that the clashes over billeting were continuing, he ordered Santa Coloma to arrest one of the *Diputats*, Francesc de Tamarit, and to have a secret inquiry made into the activities of Claris. But the arrest of Tamarit only made a serious situation worse. The peasantry were banding together against the *tercios*, and the towns and villages of northern Catalonia were in a highly inflammatory mood. At the end of April a royal official was burnt to death at Santa Coloma de Farnés, and the *tercios* were ordered to billet in the town and the surrounding countryside to punish the population for their crime. On reaching Santa Coloma de Farnés they could not be prevented from sacking it and setting it on fire. Their action roused the entire countryside to arms. Encouraged by the Bishop of Gerona's excommunication of the troops, a growing peasant army bore down on the *tercios*, which succeeded in making a skillful retreat towards the safety of the coast with the rebel forces following close on their heels. Finding themselves balked of their prey, the rebels then moved southwards, and on 22 May a group of them made an entry into Barcelona itself, headed straight for the prison, and released the arrested *Diputat*.

It was only when the news of the release of Tamarit reached the Conde Duque that he began to realize that he was faced with open rebellion. Until now he had tended to let himself be guided in his handling of the Principality's affairs by the Protonotario, Jerónimo de Villanueva, a character as antipathetic to the Catalans as they were to him. The Protonotario had encouraged him to believe that his Catalan policies were on the verge of success and that the Principality would shortly become a useful member of the Spanish Monarchy; but now he was suddenly confronted with evidence that the policies were leading to disaster. To some ministers it seemed that the rebels' entry into Barcelona provided Madrid with the necessary pretext for using the army to punish the Principality and to strip it of its obnoxious laws and liberties, but the Conde Duque realized that it was essential to set the problem of Catalonia into the wider context of the affairs of the Monarchy as a whole. He had to think of the repercussions in Aragon, Valencia, and Portugal of a frontal assault on Catalan liberties, and he had to bear in mind the gravity of the military situation in Germany and Italy, the exhaustion of Spain's armies, and the dangers at such a time of holding down a province of the Monarchy by force of arms. Realizing that there could at this stage be no simple and clear-cut solution to the intractable problem of the Catalans, he reversed his policies of the preceding months, and ordered on 27 May that steps should immediately be taken to conciliate and pacify the Catalans before the situation got entirely out of hand.

The Conde Duque's change of policy came too late. The rebellion in Catalonia was rapidly acquiring a momentum of its own, inspired by hatred not only of the troops and the royal officials, but also of the rich and of all those in authority. The rebel bands moved from town to town, stirring up the countryside in their wake. Seeing that his authority was gone and that law and order were everywhere collapsing, the unfortunate Count of Santa Coloma begged the town councillors of Barcelona to close the city gates against the casual labourers who always flocked into the city at the beginning of June to hire themselves out for harvesting. But the councillors were either unable or unwilling to agree; the harvesters made their usual entry; and on Corpus day, 7 June 1640, they inevitably became involved in a brawl. The brawl soon acquired the dimensions of a riot, and within a few hours the mob was hounding down the royal ministers and sacking their houses. The viceroy himself had moved to the dockyards for safety, but a group of rioters forced its way in, and Santa Coloma was caught and struck down as he attempted to escape from his pursuers along the rocky beach.

The murder of Santa Coloma left such authority as remained in Catalonia in the hands of the *Diputació* and of the city councillors and aristocracy of Barcelona. Although they managed to shepherd the rebels out of Barcelona itself, it was impossible to maintain control over a movement which was spreading through the Principality, wreaking vengeance on all those of whom the rebels disapproved. Stunned as he was by the viceroy's murder, Olivares still seems to have hoped that the rebellion could be checked without recourse to arms, but the new viceroy, the Catalan Duke of Cardona, died on 22 July without being able to halt the drift to anarchy. Almost at the same moment the rebels gained control of the vital port of Tortosa. The loss of Tortosa made it finally clear that troops would have to be sent into Catalonia, in spite of the obvious risk of war in a province bordering on France; and Olivares pressed ahead with the formation of an army for use against the rebels.

The Conde Duque believed that the Catalans were still too loyal to call on the French for help, but he underestimated the determination and vigour of Claris, and the hatred of his Government and of Castile which his politics had inspired in every class of Catalan society. Some time before, Claris had already made tentative overtures to the French, and Richelieu, who had shown himself well aware of the possibilities of causing trouble both in Catalonia and Portugal, declared himself ready to offer help. During the autumn of 1640 Claris and Olivares stood face to face, Claris hoping to avoid the necessity of committing the Principality to an open break with Madrid, and Olivares equally hoping to avoid the necessity of using an army against the Catalans. "In the midst of all our troubles," wrote the Conde Duque to the Cardenal Infante in October, "the Catalan is the worst we have ever had, and my heart admits of no consolation that we are entering an action in which, if our army kills, it kills a vassal of His Majesty, and if they kill, they kill a vassal and a soldier. . . . Without reason or occasion they have thrown themseves into as complete a rebellion as Holland. . ."

But worse was to come. The revolt of the Catalans was bound to have its repercussions in Portugal, where there was a growing determination to cut the country's links with Castile. Uneasily aware that he could never be sure of Portugal as long as the Duke of Braganza and the higher Portuguese nobility remained at home, Olivares had ingeniously thought to kill two birds with one stone by ordering the Portuguese nobility to turn out with the army that was to be sent into Catalonia. This order meant that, if Portugal was ever to break free from Castile, it must act quickly before Braganza was out of the country. Plans for a revolution were laid in the autumn of 1640, probably with the connivance of Richelieu, who is believed to have sent funds to the conspirators in Lisbon. On 1 December, while the royal army under the command of the Marquis of los Vélez was gingerly advancing into Catalonia, the Portuguese conspirators put their plan into action. The guards at the royal palace in Lisbon were overwhelmed,

Miguel de Vasconcellos—Olivares's confidant and principal agent in the government of Portugal—was assassinated, and Princess Margaret was escorted to the frontier. Since there were virtually no Castilian troops in Portugal, there was nothing to prevent the rebels from taking over the country, and proclaiming the Duke of Braganza king as John IV.

The news of the Portuguese Revolution, which took a week to reach Madrid, forced Olivares and his colleagues to undertake an urgent reappraisal of their policies. Simultaneous revolts in the east and west of the Spanish peninsula threatened the Monarchy with total disaster. Peace was essential: peace with the Dutch, peace with the Catalans. But although the Conde Duque now offered favourable terms to the Catalans, and the upper classes in Catalonia seemed predisposed to accept them as the army of los Vélez moved closer and closer to Barcelona, the populace was in no mood for surrender. It rioted in Barcelona on 24 December, hunting down "traitors" with a savagery surpassing that of Corpus; and Claris, faced on one side with the fury of the mob, and on the other with the advancing Castilian army, took the only course open to him. On 16 January 1641 he announced that Catalonia had become an independent republic under French protection. Then on 23 January, finding that the French were not satisfied with this, he withdrew his plans for a republican system of government, and formally declared the allegiance of Catalonia to the King of France, "as in the time of Charlemagne, with a contract to observe our constitutions". The French were now prepared to give the Catalans full military support; the French agent, Duplessis Besançon, hastily organized the defence of Barcelona, and on 26 January a combined French and Catalan force met the army of los Vélez on the hill of Montjuich outside the walls of Barcelona. Los Vélez unaccountably gave the order to retreat, and the last chance of bringing the revolt of the Catalans to a speedy end was lost.

In September 1640, before the outbreak of the Portuguese revolt, Olivares had written in a long memorandum: "This year can undoubtedly be considered the most unfortunate that this Monarchy has ever experienced". The defeat of los Vélez at Montjuich set the seal on the disasters of 1640, confirming in the most conclusive manner that there could be no going back on the events of that fatal year. For 1640 had, in fact, marked the dissolution of the economic and political system on which the Monarchy had depended for so long. It had seen the disruption and decline of the Sevillan commercial system which had given the Spanish Crown its silver and its credit; and the disruption

also of the political organization of the Spanish peninsula, inherited
from the Catholic Kings and transmitted unchanged by Philip II to his
descendants. This political disruption was itself the outcome of the
crisis of the reign of Philip III—the crisis of the Atlantic economy as
the New World shrank back into itself, and the crisis of the Castilian
economy, undermined by long years of abuse and by the strain of un-
ending war. In attempting to exploit the resources of the peripheral
provinces of the peninsula, Olivares had simply attempted to redress
the balance that had been tilting more and more against Castile, but he
did it at a moment when the economies of Portugal and Catalonia
were themselves being subjected to growing pressure, and when Castile
no longer had the strength to impose its will by an assertion of military power. As a result, he had imposed an excessive strain on the
fragile constitutional structure of the Spanish Monarchy, and precipitated the very disaster that it was most necessary to avoid.

From the moment of defeat at Montjuich, Olivares knew that the
game was up. He had neither the money nor the men to prosecute effectively the war abroad, while simultaneously attempting to suppress
two revolutions at home. But for all his despair, he was not the man
to surrender without a struggle, and he made superhuman efforts to
gather together fresh armies and to husband the Crown's diminished
resources. The unbroken succession of defeats, however, had gravely
weakened his position, and had given a new boldness to his many
enemies. Throughout Castile he was hated as a tyrant, but the real
danger came less from the populace than from the grandees. In the
summer of 1641 his agents unearthed a conspiracy by two great
Andalusian nobles, the Duke of Medina-Sidonia and the Marquis of
Ayamonte, both of them members of his own family of Guzmán.
Medina-Sidonia was the brother of the new Queen of Portugal, and it
seems that plans were being made not only to remove the Conde Duque
and to restore an aristocratic chamber to the Castilian Cortes, but also
to follow the example of Portugal and turn Andalusia into an independent State.

In spite of the failure of Medina-Sidonia's conspiracy, the nobles
continued to plot. Conditions in Castile were terrible, for in February
1641 the Conde Duque had begun tampering with the coinage, and
vellón prices rose to dizzy heights, with the premium on silver in terms
of *vellón* reaching 200 percent in certain instances before a deflation-
ary decree in September 1642 again brought prices crashing down.
Yet for all the misfortunes both at home and abroad, the King was
still unwilling to part with his Favourite. In April 1642 he and the

Conde Duque left for the front in Aragon, where the army met with no more success than before their arrival. During September French forces completed the conquest of Roussillon by capturing Perpignan, and in October the army commanded by the Conde Duque's cousin and close friend, the Marquis of Leganés, was defeated in its attempts to recapture Lérida. Back in Madrid, the Count of Castrillo, who had been entrusted with the government, was working away to undermine the Conde Duque's influence, and when the King returned to Court at the end of the year it was clear that the Conde Duque's days were numbered. On 17 January 1643 the King at last took the decision that had been so long awaited: Olivares was given leave to retire to his estates, and on 23 January he left for Madrid for exile, never again to return to the capital where he had reigned for twenty-two years. Stunned by his dismissal, he still sought to vindicate his policies, which found an eloquent exposition in a tract entitled the *Nicandro*, written to his instructions and under his inspiration. But nothing now could set the clock back. Exiled farther away, to his sister's palace at Toro, he died on 22 July 1645 under the shadow of madness. So passed the first and the last ruler of Habsburg Spain who had the breadth of vision to devise plans on a grand scale for the future of a world-wide Monarchy: a statesman whose capacity for conceiving great designs was matched only by his consistent incapacity for carrying them through to a successful conclusion.

*   *   *   *   *

It is natural to look back over [the seventeenth] century and wonder where things had gone wrong. Both contemporary and later generations could not fail to be struck by the extraordinary and terrible contrast between the triumphant Spain of Philip II and the broken Spain inherited by Philip V. Was not this a repetition of the fate of Imperial Rome? And could it not be interpreted by the confident rationalists of the eighteenth century as an object lesson in the disastrous consequences of ignorance, superstition, and sloth? To an age which took the idea of progress as its gospel, the Spain which had expelled the Moriscos and allowed itself to fall into the clutches of ignorant monks and priests had condemned itself to disaster before the bar of history.

In retrospect, it would seem that, in analyses of the "decline", too much has been made of what were assumed to be exclusively "Spanish" characteristics. While there *were* profound differences between Spain and other west European nations, springing in particular from the Afro-European character of Spain's geography and civilization, there were also marked similarities, which it is a mistake to underplay. At the end of the sixteenth century there was no particular reason to believe that the future development of the peninsula would diverge so markedly from that of other parts of western Europe as it was later to do. Habsburg Spain had, after all, set the pace for the rest of Europe in the elaboration of new techniques of administration to cope with the problems of governing a world-wide empire. The Spain of Philip II would seem to have had at least as good a chance as the France of Henry III of making the transition to the modern, centralized State.

The failure to make this transition was essentially a seventeenth-century failure, and, above all, a failure of the second half of the century. The economic depression of the earlier and middle years of the century, although exceptionally severe in certain parts of the peninsula, was not unique to Spain. France and England, as well as Spain, were plunged in an economic crisis in the 1620s and a political crisis in the 1640s. The real divergence came only after the middle of the century, when the moment of most acute political crisis had everywhere been passed. It was in the years after 1650 that certain European States seemed to strike out on a new course, building up their power by a more rational exploitation of their economic possibilities and their military and financial resources—and this at a time when the new science and the new philosophy were beginning to teach that man could, after all, shape his own destiny and control his environment.

This moment of exceptionally rapid intellectual and administrative advance in many parts of Europe was, for Spain, the moment of maximum political and intellectual stagnation. Castile in particular failed to respond to the challenge posed by the crisis of the mid-seventeenth century, and relapsed into the inertia of defeat, from which it took the best part of a century to recover. The immediate explanation of this failure is to be found in the disastrous events of the age of Olivares, and notably in the country's defeat in war. The strain of war had precipitated the Conde Duque into constitutional experiments which entailed a radical reorganization of the country's administrative structure, and he lacked both the military and economic resources, and the prestige that would have been conferred by foreign victories, to carry these experiments through to success. The result of his failure was even worse than if the experiments had never been tried. The frictions between the peoples of the peninsula were exacerbated by his efforts; and the extent of the failure effectively discouraged any attempt to repeat the experiment during the half-century when other States were reorganizing their administrative systems, in order to compete more effectively in the international struggle for power.

Yet the fatal over-commitment of Spain to foreign wars at a time when Castile lacked the economic and demographic resources to fight them with success, cannot be simply attributed to the blunders of one man. It reflects, rather, the failure of a generation, and of an entire governing class. Seventeenth-century Castile had become the victim of its own history, desperately attempting to reenact the imperial glories of an earlier age in the belief that this was the sole means of exorcising from the body politic the undoubted ills of the present. That it should have reacted in this way was not inevitable, but it was made the more probable by the very magnitude of the country's triumphs in the preceding era. It was hard to turn one's back on a past studded with so many successes, and it became all the harder when those successes were identified with everything that was most quintessentially Castilian. For had not the successes derived from the military valour of the Castilians and their unswerving devotion to the Church?

It was one of the tragedies of Castile's history that it found itself, by the end of the reign of Philip II, in a position where it seemed that readjustment to the new economic realities could be achieved only at the price of sacrificing its most cherished ideals. However stern the warnings of the *arbitristas*, it was difficult for a society nurtured on war to find a substitute for the glory of battle in the tedious intricacies of mercantile ledgers, or to elevate to a position of pre-eminence the hard manual labour it had been taught to despise. It was no less difficult for it to draw on the ideas and the experiences of foreigners, especially when the foreigners were so often heretics, for Castile's instinctive distrust of the outside world had been amply reinforced by the religious revolutions of sixteenth-century Europe. By a tragic succession of circumstances, the purity of the faith had come to be identified during the reign of Philip II with a fundamental hostility to ideas and values gaining ground in certain parts of contemporary Europe. This identification had led to a partial isolation of Spain from the outer world, which had constricted the nation's development to certain well defined channels, and lessened its capacity to adapt itself to new situations and circumstances through the deployment of new ideas.

Yet the very violence of Spain's response to the religious upheaval of the sixteenth century demands a sympathetic understanding it does not always receive, for Spain was confronted with a problem more complex than that facing any other State in Christendom. It alone was a multi-racial society, in which the inter-penetration of Christian, Jewish and

Moorish beliefs created a constant problem of national and religious identity. To this problem there was no obvious solution. The closing of the frontiers and the insistence on the most rigorous orthodoxy represented a desperate attempt to deal with a problem of unparalleled complexity; and it is hardly surprising if religious uniformity appeared the sole guarantee of national survival for a society characterized by the most extreme racial, political and geographical diversity. The price paid for the adoption of this policy proved in the end to be very high, but it is understandable enough that to contemporaries the cost of *not* adopting it should have seemed even higher.

While the policies adopted by Philip II made the task of his successors incomparably more difficult, they did not make it impossible. Certain aspects of the career of Olivares suggest that there was still room for manoeuvre, and that Castile still retained some freedom of choice. This freedom was lost in the half-century after 1640, partly because of the tragic events of the Olivares era, and partly because of the unredeemed mediocrity of the Castilian ruling class at a moment when the highest gifts of statesmanship were required if the Monarchy were to escape disaster. There was here a failure of individuals, over and above the collective failure of a society so profoundly disillusioned by its unbroken series of reverses that it had lost even the capacity to protest.

The degeneracy of the dynasty played an obvious part in this failure, but there is also a striking contrast in the calibre of the ministers, the viceroys and the officials who ran the Monarchy for Charles V, and those who ran it for Charles II. The over life-size figure of the Conde Duque de Olivares appears in retrospect the last of that heroic line which had shed such lustre on the sixteenth-century Monarchy: such men as the diplomat, poet and commander, Diego Hurtado de Mendoza (1503–75), or Francisco de Toledo (1515–82), the great viceroy of Peru. The insistent references of Olivares to the "lack of leaders" suggests a sudden collapse of the country's ruling class, as the last great generation of Spanish pro-consuls—the generation of the Count of Gondomar (1567–1626)—finally passed away. But a satisfactory explanation of this collapse has yet to be given. Is it to be found in the excessive interbreeding of an exclusive aristocratic caste? Or in the failure of the country's educational system as its mental horizons narrowed, for was not Diego Hurtado de Mendoza as much a product of the "open" Spain of Ferdinand and Isabella as the Duke of Medinaceli was a product of the "closed" Spain of the seventeenth century? The men of the seventeenth century belonged to a society which had lost the strength that comes from dissent, and they lacked the breadth of vision and the strength of character to break with a past that could no longer serve as a reliable guide to the future. Heirs to a society which had over-invested in empire, and surrounded by the increasingly shabby remnants of a dwindling inheritance, they could not bring themselves at the moment of crisis to surrender their memories and alter the antique pattern of their lives. At a time when the face of Europe was altering more rapidly than ever before, the country that had once been its leading power proved to be lacking the essential ingredient for survival—the willingness to change.

The drastic failure of Habsburg Spain to make the vital transition should not, however, be allowed to obscure the extent of its achievement in the days of its greatness. If the failures were very great, so were the successes. For nearly two centuries, Spain had sustained a remarkable creative effort, which added immeasurably to the common stock of European civilization. In the Europe of the mid-seventeenth century the influence of Castilian culture and customs was widespread and fruitful, upheld as it was by all the prestige of an empire whose hollowness was only just becoming apparent to the outside world.

It is all too easy to take for granted what was perhaps the most remarkable of all Spain's achievements—the ability to maintain its control over vast areas of widely scattered territories, at a time when governmental techniques had scarcely advanced beyond the stage of household administration, and when the slowness of communications would seem at first sight to have made long-distance government impossible. While in course of time the failings of the Spanish governmental system made it the laughing stock of the world, no other sixteenth- or seventeenth-century State was faced with so vast a problem of administration, and few succeeded in preserving over so long a period such a high degree of public order in an age when revolts were endemic.

The soldiers, the lawyers, and the administrators who made this achievement possible possessed in full measure the defects generally associated with a conquering race, but the best of them brought to their duties a sense of dedication which sprang from an unquestioning acceptance of the superiority of their society and of the absolute rightness of their cause. Nor did it seem in the sixteenth century as if this confidence was misplaced. Few nations had experienced such spectacular triumphs as the Castile of the Catholic Kings and of Charles V, and Castilians could be pardoned for thinking that they had been singled out for special favours by a God who had chosen them to further His manifold purposes.

It is this supreme self-confidence which gives Castilian civilization of the sixteenth century its particular quality, just as it was the sudden failure of confidence that gave a new, and more poignant, character to

Castilian civilization of the seventeenth. Tremendous challenges faced the sixteenth-century Castilian and he rose to them with a kind of effortless ease which seems in retrospect deeply impressive. He had to explore, colonize, and govern a new world. He had to devise new methods of cartography and navigation—work that was done by such men as Alonso de Santa Cruz, the inventor of spherical maps, and Felipe Guillén, who perfected the compass in 1525. He had to study the natural history of the newly discovered American continent—the achievement of Bernardino de Sahagún, and of botanists like Francisco Hernández and José de Acosta. He had to improve the primitive techniques of mining and metallurgy, and to pioneer, like Pedro de Esquivel, new methods of geodesy. And he had to solve novel problems of political and social organization, and to grapple with the moral questions connected with the establishment of government over uncivilized and pagan races.

This last work, accomplished by the theologians of sixteenth-century Spain, and in particular by the great school of Salamanca led by the Dominican Francisco de Vitoria, illustrates one of the most striking characteristics of the Castile of Charles V and Philip II: the constant and fruitful alliance between theory and practice, between the man of action and the man of learning, which provided intellectuals with a strong incentive to formulate their theories with clarity and precision, and to direct their attention to the pressing problems of the day. The inherent tendency of the Castilian mentality to concern itself with the concrete and practical was thus encouraged by the demand of Castilian society that the scholar and the theologian should contribute to what was regarded as a collective national effort. Yet, at the same time, the need to meet this social demand led to no sacrifice, at least among the better scholars, of their independence of judgment and intellectual integrity. There is something deeply moving about the characteristic forthrightness and independence of the Jesuit Juan de Mariana (1535–1624), still campaigning for constitutionalism in a Castile where constitutionalism was fast dying, and steadfastly refusing to accept anything on trust. "Nos adoramus quod scimus", he wrote to the Archbishop of Granada in 1597, at a time when the discovery of some mysterious lead books in Granada had convinced many of his gullible contemporaries that they had found irrefutable evidence for the doctrine of the Immaculate Conception and for the visit of St. James to Spain. There could have been no better motto for the scholars of the Spanish Renaissance.

Paradoxically, however, alongside this empirical approach, there seems to have existed in many sixteenth-century Castilians a highly developed awareness of another world, beyond that cognizable by the human senses. Saint Teresa of Avila, that most practical of mystics, seemed to be entirely at home in both worlds—worlds that were caught and held in a strange juxtaposition by El Greco when he painted in 1586 the "Burial of the Count of Orgaz". The sombre, withdrawn faces of the witnesses to the miracle are the faces of men who seem only half to belong to the terrestrial world, because they feel themselves simultaneously to be citizens of another.

The mystical movement of the later sixteenth century possessed a degree of intensity which inevitably made it a transient phenomenon: it was all too easy for the mystical to degenerate into the mannered, and for the unpremeditated combination of the natural and the supernatural to degenerate into something that was merely arch. But at moments of apparently excessive strain Castilian art and literature had a capacity for self-revival by drawing fresh inspiration from the springs of popular tradition. The Castile of Cervantes resembled the England of Shakespeare in this ability of its writers and artists to synthesize the traditions of the populace with the aspirations of the educated, in such a way as to produce works of art simultaneously acceptable to both.

To some extent this ability disappeared during the course of the seventeenth century. The *conceptismo* of Quevedo and the *culteranismo* of Góngora were perhaps symptoms of a growing divorce between the culture of Court and country which itself seemed to symbolize a slackening of the previously close-knit texture of Castile's national life. The *arbitristas* with their practical solutions went unheeded by the Court; the universities closed in on themselves; the men of letters and the men of action were drifting apart. One of the most marked intellectual repercussions of this was to be found in the realm of science, more dependent than the arts on a collective effort and a continuing tradition. In the early seventeenth century the continuity had barely been established, and society and the State had lost interest; and Castilian science, as a result, was either extinguished or went underground, to be pursued in secrecy by a few dedicated spirits in a mental climate totally uncongenial to their efforts.

The arts, on the other hand, continued to prosper, enjoying as they did the patronage of the great. Wide as was the gulf between Court and country, it could still be bridged by an artist of the calibre of Velázquez, drawing his inspiration impartially from both. But that fusion of the classical and the popular which had inspired so many of the greatest achievements of the Golden Age, was overlaid in the works of Velázquez by an extra dimension of awareness, peculiarly characteristic of the disillusioned Castile of Philip IV. For Velázquez caught in his paintings the sense of failure, the sudden emptiness of the imperial splendour which had buoyed up Castile for more than a century.

There is no doubt a certain paradox in the fact that the achievement of the two most outstanding creative artists of Castile—Cervantes and Velázquez—was shot through with a deep sense of disillusionment and failure; but the paradox was itself a faithful reflection of the paradox of sixteenth- and seventeenth-century Castile. For here was a country which had climbed to the heights and sunk to the depths; which had achieved everything and lost everything; which had conquered the world only to be vanquished itself. The Spanish achievement of the sixteenth century was essentially the work of Castile, but so also was the Spanish disaster of the seventeenth; and it was Ortega y Gasset who expressed the paradox most clearly when he wrote what may serve as an epitaph on the Spain of the House of Austria: "Castile has made Spain, and Castile has destroyed it."

Suggestions for Further Reading

DAVIES, R. TREVOR, *The Golden Century of Spain*, rev. ed. New York: St. Martin's Press, 1954.

HAMILTON, EARL J., *American Treasure and the Price Revolution in Spain*. New York: Octagon Books, 1965.

HARING, C. H., *The Spanish Empire in America*. New York: Oxford University Press, 1947.

LYNCH, JOHN, *Spain under the Habsburgs*, Vol. I. New York: Oxford University Press, 1964.

MATTINGLY, GARRETT, *The Armada*. Boston: Houghton Mifflin Company, 1959.

MATTINGLY, GARRETT, *Renaissance Diplomacy*. Boston: Houghton Mifflin Company, 1955.

MERRIMAN, ROGER B., *Rise of the Spanish Empire in the Old World and the New*, 4 vols. New York: The Macmillan Company, 1918–31.

ORTIZ, ANTONIO DOMINGUEZ, *The Golden Age of Spain, 1516–1659*. New York: Basic Books, 1971.

PARRY, J. H., *The Age of Reconnaissance*. New York: Praeger Publishers, 1969.

H. R. TREVOR-ROPER

The General Crisis of the Seventeenth Century

~§§~ When some years ago, in the happy times when Harold Macmillan was Prime Minister of England, the Crown (actually the Prime Minister) appointed H. R. Trevor-Roper Regius Professor of Modern History at Oxford (that venerable university's, and perhaps England's, most prestigious history chair), there was much murmuring and not a little indignation among the academic guild of historians. Trevor-Roper, at that time, had a rather limited and mixed record of scholarly accomplishment: a mediocre and at times silly biography of Archbishop Laud; a study of the last days of Hitler which was a fine piece of high journalism; and a thunderous, convincing but overkilling demolition of a thesis propounded by a Marxist historian, Lawrence Stone. In spite of this checkered record before his elevation by the Tories, since then Trevor-Roper has amply demonstrated his worthiness to occupy the exalted Regius chair of history: he has revealed an extraordinary capacity for historical generalization. Not the learned monograph but the synthesizing essay is his forte. A wide knowledge sweeping over countries and time, a keenly perceived general pattern, a delicate and supple style: these are the distinctive qualities of Trevor-Roper as historian, and they are qualities to be admired and prized indeed.

Trevor-Roper's most famous essay, "The General Crisis of the Seventeenth Century," has aroused an extensive and

FROM H. R. Trevor-Roper, *Religion, The Reformation and Social Change* (London: Macmillan & Co. Ltd., 1967), pp. 46–89.

valuable debate and inspired several other historians to re-examine the general pattern of seventeenth-century European government and society. Trevor-Roper begins by noting that in the 1640's and 50's there were revolutions or rebellions in England, France, Spain, Naples, and other countries and hypothesizes that there must be a causal relationship—some general factors that precipitated crisis all over Europe. An American scholar, Roger B. Merriman, had raised the same question in the 1930's, but Trevor-Roper has a provocative thesis to provide an answer to the question.

He contends that the crisis occurred in the relationship between state and society. Put another way, it was the crisis of the early modern bureaucratic—or as he calls it—the Renaissance state. At the end of the fifteenth century, the monarchical states, absorbing the resources of the Church, had expanded their power and wealth at the expense of the autonomous cities of the late Middle Ages whose independence they crushed. Everywhere the same new political structure emerged: absolutist prince, extravagant court, elaborate ministerial bureaucracy. But this court and bureaucracy in the late sixteenth century became overextended and "parasitic" upon society. Thus when the royal governments were faced with the strain of prolonged warfare after 1618 (the outbreak of the Thirty Years War) and the severe, widespread economic depression that set in about the same time, the stability and even the existence of monarchy and its attendant court and bureaucracy was gravely threatened (and in England the monarchy collapsed). The people who rose in rebellion in several countries against the prevailing system can be generally regarded as "puritans" or the "country party." They resented the intolerable imposition of parasitic bureaucracy and wanted rationalization of the political system by administrative reform (reduction of the burden of court and bureacracy upon society) and economic reform (mercantilist direction and stimulation of the economy).

Trevor-Roper's is a brilliant, extremely valuable thesis; it is a concept-pattern or model that does provide meaning to the confused political history of Europe in the early seventeenth century. Some criticisms are that, first, the differences among the rebels of the 1640's and 50's—the English puritan gentry, the nobles of the Fronde in France, and the Catalan and Portuguese quasi-nationalists—remain greater than the similarities. Second, the princes did not rise around 1500 at the sacrifice of the autonomy of the cities; independent cities were few although famous, the cities had been losing their autonomy since the twelfth century, and in any case, this whole urban matter was not very important, because Europe in 1500 was still overwhelmingly a rural society. Third, and perhaps most significant, the main problem with early seventeenth-century royal bureaucracy was not its corrupt and overextended quality; the crux was that political skills and ambitions had greatly outrun the communications and technological system. No matter how moral, industrious, and dedicated the early seventeenth-century bureaucrats, they could not achieve the centralized political system they sought within the prevailing structure of primitive communications and technology. Bureaucracy had to await the communications system provided by nineteenth-century technology—railways, telegraphs, etc.—in order to integrate itself with society and achieve a perpetually functioning equilibrium between its demands and its contributions to public welfare. Finally, the ideology of rebellion in the mid-seventeenth century had more strains to it than Trevor-Roper's model seems to allow: atavistic tribalism, aristocratic revivalism, and democratic millenarianism. This was, after all, more than a political uprising, or a series of uprisings; it was a rebellion against social order itself. In some ways the crisis of the seventeenth century was a struggle for modernity and a political rationalism; in other ways a revolt against reason, a struggle against the tide of modernity.

The middle of the seventeenth century was a period of revolutions in Europe. These revolutions differed from place to place, and if studied separately, seem to rise out of particular, local causes; but if we look at them together they have so many common features that they appear almost as a general revolution. There is the Puritan Revolution in England which fills the twenty years between 1640 and 1660, but whose crisis was between 1648 and 1653. In those years of its crisis there was also the series of revolts known as the Frondes in France, and in 1650 there was a *coup d'état* or palace revolution, which created a new form of government in the United Provinces of the Netherlands. Contemporary with the troubles of England were those of the Spanish empire. In 1640 there was the revolt of Catalonia, which failed, and the revolt of Portugal, which succeeded; in 1641 there was nearly a revolt of Andalusia too; in 1647 there was the revolt of Naples, the revolt of Masaniello. To contemporary observers it seemed that society itself was in crisis, and that this crisis was general in Europe. 'These days are days of shaking . . .' declared an English preacher in 1643, 'and this shaking is universal: the Palatinate, Bohemia, Germania, Catalonia, Portugal, Ireland, England.' The various countries of Europe seemed merely the separate theatres upon which the same great tragedy was being simultaneously, though in different languages and with local variations, played out.

What was the general cause or character of this crisis? Contemporaries, if they looked beyond mere surface parallels, tended to find deep spiritual reasons. That there was a crisis they felt sure. For a generation they had felt it coming. Ever since 1618 at least there had been talk of the dissolution of society, or of the world; and the undefined sense of gloom of which we are constantly aware in those years was justified sometimes by new interpretations of Scripture, sometimes by new phenomena in the skies. With the discovery of new stars, and particularly with the new comet of 1618, science seemed to support the prophets of disaster. So also did history. It was at this time that cyclical theories of history became fashionable and the decline and fall of nations was predicted, not only from Scripture and the stars, but also from the passage of time and the organic processes of decay. Kingdoms, declared a Puritan preacher in 1643, after touching lightly on the corroborative influence of the comet of 1618, last for a maximum period of 500 or 600 years, 'and it is known to all of you how long we have been since the Conquest'. From our rationalist heights we might suppose that the new discoveries of science would tend to discredit the apocalyptic vaticinations of Scripture; but in fact this was not so. It is an interesting but undeniable fact that the most advanced scientists of the early sixteenth century included also the most learned and literal students of biblical mathematics; and in their hands science and religion converged to pinpoint, between 1640 and 1660, the dissolution of society, the end of the world.

This intellectual background is significant because it shows that the crisis of the mid-seventeenth century did not come by surprise, out of sudden accidents: it was deep-seated and anticipated, if only vaguely anticipated, even before the accidents which launched it. No doubt accidents made revolution longer or deeper here, shorter or more superficial there. No doubt, too, the universality of revolution owed something to mere contagion: the fashion of revolution spreads. But even contagion implies receptivity: a healthy or inoculated body does not catch even a prevailing disease. Therefore, though we may observe accidents and fashions, we still have to ask a deeper question. We must ask, what was the general condition of western European society which made it, in the mid-seventeenth century, so universally vulnerable— intellectually as well as physically—to the sudden new epidemic of revolution?

Of course there are some obvious answers. Most obvious of all is the Thirty Years War, which began in 1618, the year of the comet, and was still raging in the 1640s, the years of revolution. The Thirty Years War, in the countries affected by it, undoubtedly prepared the ground for revolution. The burden of war-taxation, or military oppression, or military defeat, precipitated the revolts in Catalonia, Portugal, Naples. The dislocation of trade, which may have been caused by the Thirty Years War, led to unemployment and violence in many manufacturing or commercial countries. The destructive passage or billeting of soldiers led to regular peasant mutinies in Germany and France. One need only look at M. Roupnel's study of Burgundy in those years, or at the reports sent to the chancellor Séguier describing the constant risings of the French peasants under the stress of war-taxation, or at the grim etchings of Callot, to realize that the Thirty Years War was a formidable factor in the making of that discontent which was sometimes mobilized in revolution.

And yet it is not a sufficient explanation. After all, the European wars of 1618–59 were not new phenomena. They were a resumption of the European wars of the sixteenth century, the wars of Charles V against François I and Henri II, of Philip II against Elizabeth and Henri of Navarre and the Prince of Orange. Those sixteenth-century wars had ended with the century, in 1598, in 1604, in 1609: in 1618 and 1621 and 1635 they had been resumed, consciously resumed. Philip IV looked back constantly to the example of Philip II, 'mi abuelo y mi señor' [my grandfather and my master]; Prince Maurice and Prince Frederick Henry to William of Orange, their father; Oliver Cromwell to 'Queen Elizabeth of glorious memory'. Richelieu and Mazarin sought to reverse the verdict of Câteau-Cambrésis in 1559.

And yet, in the sixteenth and seventeenth centuries these wars had led to no such revolutions. Moreover, the seventeenth-century revolutions were sometimes independent of the war. The greatest of those revolutions was in England, which was safely—some said ignominiously—neutral. In the country which suffered most from the war, Germany, there was no revolution.

I have said that the sixteenth-century wars had led to no such revolutions. Of course there had been revolutions in the sixteenth century: famous, spectacular revolutions: the religious revolutions of Reformation and Counter-Reformation. But we cannot say that those revolutions had been caused by those wars. Moreover, those revolutions, however spectacular, had in fact been far less profound than the revolutions of the next century. They had led to no such decisive breach in historical continuity. Beneath the customary wars of Habsburg and Valois, beneath the dramatic changes of the Reformation and Counter-Reformation, the sixteenth century goes on, a continuous, unitary century, and society is much the same at the end of it as at the beginning. Philip II succeeds to Charles V, Granvelle to Granvelle, Queen Elizabeth to Henry VIII, Cecil to Cecil; even in France Henri IV takes up, after a period of disturbance, the mantle of Henri II. Aristocratic, monarchical society is unbroken: it is even confirmed. Speaking generally, we can say that for all the violence of its religious convulsions, the sixteenth century succeeded in absorbing its strains, its thinkers in swallowing their doubts, and at the end of it, kings and philosophers alike felt satisfied with the best of possible worlds.

How different from this is the seventeenth century! For the seventeenth century did not absorb its revolutions. It is not continuous. It is broken in the middle, irreparably broken, and at the end of it, after the revolutions, men can hardly recognize the beginning. Intellectually, politically, morally, we are in a new age, a new climate. It is as if a series of rainstorms has ended in one final thunderstorm which has cleared the air and changed, permanently, the temperature of Europe. From the end of the fifteenth century until the middle of the seventeenth century we have one climate, the climate of the Renaissance; then, in the middle of the seventeenth century, we have the years of change, the years of revolution; and thereafter, for another century and a half, we have another, very different climate, the climate of the Enlightenment.

Thus I do not believe that the seventeenth-century revolutions can be explained merely by the background of war, which had also been the background of the previous, unrevolutionary century. If we are to find an explanation, we must look elsewhere. We must look past the background, into the structure of society. For all revolutions, even though they may be occasioned by external causes, and expressed in intellectual form, are made real and formidable by defects of social structure. A firm, elastic, working structure—like that of England in the nineteenth century—is proof against revolution however epidemic abroad. On the other hand a weak or over-rigid social structure, though it may last long in isolation, will collapse quickly if infected. The universality of revolution in the seventeenth century suggests that the European monarchies, which had been strong enough to absorb so many strains in the previous century, had by now developed serious structural weaknesses: weaknesses which the renewal of general war did not cause, but merely exposed and accentuated.

What were the general, structural weaknesses of the western monarchies? Contemporaries who looked at the revolutions of the seventeenth century saw them as political revolutions: as struggles between the two traditional organs of the ancient 'mixed monarchy'—the Crown and the Estates. Certainly this was the form they took. In Spain, the Crown, having reduced the Cortes of Castile to insignificance, provoked the Catalan revolution by challenging the Cortes of the kingdom of Aragon. In France, after the meeting of the Estates-General in 1614, Richelieu contrived to discontinue them, and they never met again till 1789; the Parlement of Paris struck back in the Fronde, but only to be defeated by Mazarin and reduced to the insignificance which was afterwards so bluntly rubbed in to it by Louis XIV. In Germany the Emperor challenged and reduced the Electoral College, even though the electors, as individual princes, reduced their own diets to insignificance. In England the Parliament challenged and defeated the king. At the same time the kings of Denmark and Sweden, struggling with or within their diets, ended by establishing personal monarchies, while the king of Poland, unable to imitate them, became the puppet of his. Altogether, we may say, the universal casualty of the seventeenth century was that Aristotelean concept, so admired in 1600, so utterly extinct in 1700, 'mixed monarchy'. The position was described summarily by the English political philosopher James Harrington, who, in 1656, diagnosed the general crisis which had produced such violent results in his own country of Oceana. 'What', he asked, 'is become of the Princes of Germany? Blown up. Where are the Estates or the power of the people in France? Blown up. Where is that of the people of Aragon and the rest of the Spanish kingdoms? Blown up. Where is that of the Austrian princes in Switz? Blown up. . . . Nor shall any man show a reason that will be holding in prudence why the people of Oceana have blown up their king, but that their kings did not first blow up them.'

Now there can be no doubt that politically Harrington was right. The struggle was a struggle for power, for survival, between crowns and estates. But when we have said this, have we really answered our questions? If revolution was to break out otherwise than in hopeless rural *jacqueries*, it could be only through the protest of estates, parliaments, cortes, diets; and if it was to be crushed, it could be only through the victory of royal power over such institutions. But to describe the form of a revolution is not to explain its cause, and today we are reluctant to accept constitutional struggles as self-contained or self-explanatory. We look for the forces or interests behind the constitutional claims of either side. What forces, what interests were represented by the revolutionary parties in seventeenth-century Europe —the parties which, though they may not have controlled them (for everyone would agree that there were other forces too), nevertheless gave ultimate social power and significance to the revolts of cortes and diets, estates and parliaments?

Now to this question one answer has already been given and widely accepted. It is the Marxist answer. According to the Marxists, and to some other historians who, though not Marxists, accept their argument, the crisis of the seventeenth century was at bottom a crisis of production, and the motive force behind at least some of the revolutions was the force of the producing *bourgeoisie*, hampered in their economic activity by the obsolete, wasteful, restrictive, but jealously defended productive system of 'feudal' society. According to this view, the crisis of production was general in Europe, but it was only in England that the forces of 'capitalism', thanks to their greater development and their representation in Parliament, were able to triumph. Consequently, while other countries made no immediate advance towards modern capitalism, in England the old structure was shattered and a new form of economic organization was established. Within that organization modern, industrial capitalism could achieve its astonishing results: it was no longer capitalist enterprise 'adapted to a generally feudal framework': it was capitalist enterprise, from its newly won island base, 'transforming the world'.

This Marxist thesis has been advanced by many able writers, but, in spite of their arguments, I do not believe that it has been proved or even that any solid evidence has been adduced to sustain it. It is, of course, easy to show that there were economic changes in the seventeenth century, and that, at least in England, industrial capitalism was more developed in 1700 than in 1600; but to do this is not the same as to show either that the economic changes precipitated the revolutions in Europe, or that English capitalism was directly forwarded by the Puritan 'victory' of 1640–60. These are hypotheses, which may of course be true; but it is equally possible that they are untrue: that problems of production were irrelevant to the seventeenth-century revolutions generally, and that in England capitalist development was independent of the Puritan Revolution, in the sense that it would or could have occurred without that revolution, perhaps even was retarded or interrupted by it. If it is to be shown that the English Puritan Revolution was a successful '*bourgeois* revolution', it is not enough to produce evidence that English capitalism was more advanced in 1700 than in 1600. It must be shown either that the men who made the revolution aimed at such a result, or that those who wished for such a result forwarded the revolution, or that such a result would not have been attained without the revolution. Without such evidence, the thesis remains a mere hypothesis.

Now in fact no advocate of the Marxist theory seems to me to have established any of these necessary links in the argument. Mr Maurice Dobb, whose *Studies in the Development of Capitalism* may be described as the classic textbook of Marxist history, consistently assumes that the English Puritan Revolution was the crucial 'break-through' of modern capitalism. It bears, he says, 'all the marks of the classic *bourgeois* revolution': before it, capitalism is cramped and frustrated, never progressing beyond a certain stage, a parasite confined to the interstices of 'feudal' society; in it, the 'decisive period' of capitalism reaches its 'apex'; after it, the bonds are broken and the parasite becomes the master. Similarly, Mr E. J. Hobsbawm, in his two articles on 'The Crisis of the Seventeenth Century',* consistently maintains the same thesis. 'Had the English Revolution failed', he writes, 'as so many other European revolutions in the seventeenth century failed, it is entirely possible that economic development might have been long retarded.' The results of the Puritan 'victory' were 'portentous': nothing less than the transformation of the world. But it is to be observed that although Mr Dobb assumes this position throughout his book, he nowhere gives any evidence to prove it. As soon as he reaches the 'decisive period' of capitalism, he suddenly becomes vague. 'The lines of this development', we learn, 'are far from clearly drawn'; 'the de-

* In *Past and Present*, no. 5 (May 1954) and no. 6 (Nov. 1954); reprinted in *Crisis in Europe 1560–1660*, ed. Trevor Aston (1965).

tails of this process are far from clear and there is little evidence that bears directly upon it'. In fact, not a single piece of documented evidence is produced for what is throughout assumed to be the crucial event in the whole history of European capitalism. And Mr Hobsbawm is even more summary. He dwells at length upon the economy of Europe at the time of the revolutions. He assumes the 'portentous' importance of the Puritan Revolution in changing the economy. But of the actual connection between the two he says not a word.*

Altogether, it seems to me that the Marxist identification of the seventeenth-century revolutions with 'bourgeois capitalist' revolutions, successful in England, unsuccessful elsewhere, is a mere a priori hypothesis. The Marxists see, as we all see, that, at some time between the discovery of America and the Industrial Revolution, the basis was laid for a new 'capitalist' form of society. Believing, as a matter of doctrine, that such a change cannot be achieved peacefully but requires a violent break-through of a new class, a 'bourgeois revolution', they look for such a revolution. Moreover, seeing that the country which led in this process was England, they look for such a revolution in England. And when they find, exactly half-way between these terminal dates, the violent Puritan Revolution in England, they cry εὕρηκα! Thereupon the other European revolutions fall easily into place as abortive bourgeois revolutions. The hypothesis, once stated, is illustrated by other hypotheses. It has yet to be proved by evidence. And it may be that it rests on entirely false premises. It may be that social changes do not necessarily require violent revolution: that capitalism developed in England (as industrial democracy has done) peacefully,

---

* As far as I can see, Mr Dobb's only arguments of such a connection are the statements (1) that agricultural capitalists supported the Parliament while old-fashioned 'feudal' landlords supported the Crown; (2) that 'those sections of the bourgeoisie that had any roots in industry . . . were wholehearted supporters of the parliamentary cause'; and (3) that the industrial towns, particularly the clothing towns, were radical. None of these statements seems to me sufficient. (1) is incorrect: the only evidence given consists in undocumented statements that Oliver Cromwell was an improving agriculturalist (which is untrue: in fact having—in his own words—'wasted his estate', he had declined from a landlord to a tenant farmer), and that 'Ireton his chief lieutenant was both a country gentleman and a clothier' (for which I know of no evidence at all). In fact some of the most obvious 'improving landlords', like the Earl of Newcastle and the Marquis of Worcester, were royalists. (2) is unsubstantiated and, I believe, incorrect; wherever the industrial bourgeoisie has been studied—as in Yorkshire and Wiltshire—it has been found to be divided in its loyalty. (3) is correct, but inconclusive; the radicalism of workers in a depressed industry may well spring from depression, not from 'capitalist' interest.

and that the violent Puritan Revolution was no more crucial to its history than, say, the fifteenth-century Hussite and Taborite revolutions in Bohemia, to which it bears such obvious resemblances.

If the crisis of the seventeenth century, then, though general in western Europe, is not a merely constitutional crisis, nor a crisis of economic production, what kind of a crisis was it? In this essay I shall suggest that, in so far as it was a general crisis—i.e. ignoring inessential variations from place to place—it was something both wider and vaguer than this: in fact, that it was a crisis in the relations between society and the State. In order to explain this, I shall try to set it against a longer background of time than is sometimes supposed necessary. For general social crises are seldom explicable in terms of mere decades. We would not now seek to explain the communist revolution in Russia against a background merely of the twelve years since 1905, nor the great French Revolution against the background merely of the reign of Louis XVI. For such a purpose we would think it necessary to examine the whole *ancien régime* which came to an end here in 1917, there in 1789. Similarly, if we are to seek an explanation of the general European crisis of the 1640s, we must not confine ourselves to the preceding decade, ascribing all the responsibility (though we must undoubtedly ascribe some) to Archbishop Laud in England or the Count-Duke of Olivares in Spain. We must look, here too, at the whole *ancien régime* which preceded the crisis: the whole form of State and society which we have seen continually expanding, absorbing all shocks, growing more self-assured throughout the sixteenth century, and which, in the mid-seventeenth century, comes to an end: what for convenience we may call the State and society of the European Renaissance.

The Renaissance—how loose and vague is the term! Defining it and dating it has become a major industry among scholars, at international congresses and in learned papers. But let us not be deterred by this. All general terms—'*ancien régime*', 'capitalism', 'the Middle Ages'—are loose and vague; but they are nevertheless serviceable if we use them only generally. And in general terms we know well enough what we mean by the European Renaissance. It is the sudden expansion of our civilization, the excited discovery of world upon world, adventure upon adventure: the progressive enlargement of sensitivity and show which reached its greatest extension in the sixteenth century and which, in the seventeenth century, is no more. Expansion, extension—these are its essential characteristics. For the sixteenth century is not an age of structural change. In technology, in thought, in government, it is the same.

In technology, at least after 1520, there are few significant changes. The expansion of Europe creates greater markets, greater opportunities, but the machinery of production remains basically constant. Similarly, in culture, the great representatives of the European Renaissance are universal, but unsystematic. Leonardo, Montaigne, Cervantes, Shakespeare, take life for granted: they adventure, observe, describe, perhaps mock; but they do not analyse, criticize, question. And in government it is the same too. The political structures of Europe are not changed in the sixteenth century: they are stretched to grasp and hold new empires, sometimes vast new empires, vaster than they can contain for long without internal change. Nevertheless, as yet, there is no such internal change. It is not till the seventeenth century that the structure of government is adjusted to cope with the territorial expansion of the sixteenth, in Spain, in France, in Britain. Until then, the Renaissance State expands continuously without bursting its old envelope. That envelope is the medieval, aristocratic monarchy, the rule of the Christian prince.

It is a fascinating spectacle, the rise of the princes in sixteenth-century Europe. One after another they spring up, first in Italy and Burgundy, then all over Europe. Their dynasties may be old, and yet their character is new: they are more exotic, more highly coloured than their predecessors. They are versatile, cultivated men, sometimes bizarre, even outrageous: they bewilder us by their lavish tastes, their incredible energy, their ruthlessness and *panache*. Even when they are introverted, bigoted, melancholic, it is on a heroic scale: we think of Charles V solemnly conducting his own funeral at Yuste or Philip II methodically condemning millions of future lives to the treadmill of ceaseless prayer for his own soul. Undoubtedly, in the sixteenth century, the princes are everything. They are tyrants over past and future; they change religion and divine truth by their nod, even in their teens; they are priests and popes, they call themselves gods, as well as kings. And yet we should remember, if we are to understand the crisis at the end of their rule, that their power did not rise up out of nothing. Its extraordinary expansion in the early sixteenth century was not *in vacuo*. Europe had to make room for it. The princes rose at the expense of someone or something, and they brought in their train the means of securing their sudden, usurped new power. In fact, they rose at the expense of the older organs of European civilization, the cities; and they brought with them, as the means of conquest, a new political instrument, 'the Renaissance Court'.

Not much has been written about the eclipse of the European cities on the eve of the Renaissance; but it is an important phenomenon. For how can we think of the Middle Ages without thinking of the cities, and yet who thinks of them after 1500? In the Middle Ages the free communes of Flanders and Italy had been the founders of Europe's trade and wealth, the centres of its arts and crafts, the financiers of its popes and kings. The German cities had been the means of colonizing and civilizing the barbarous north, the pagan east of Europe. These cities, moreover, had had their own way of life and had imposed upon Europe some of their own methods of government and standards of value. In its earliest form, the Renaissance itself had been a city phenomenon: it had begun in the cities of Italy, Flanders and south Germany before it was taken over, and changed, by princes and popes. And this early Renaissance had the character of the cities within which it was still contained. Like them it was responsible, orderly, self-controlled. For however great their wealth, however splendid their town halls and hospitals, their churches and squares, there is always, in the cities, a trace of calculation and self-restraint. It is the virtue of civic self-government, however oligarchically controlled: a spirit very different from the outrageous, spendthrift, irresponsible exhibitionism of the princes which was to come.

For between the fifteenth and the sixteenth centuries the princely suitors came, and one after another the cities succumbed. The rich cities of Flanders gave in to the magnificent dukes of Burgundy, the rich cities of Lombardy and Tuscany to the magnificent princes of Italy. The Baltic cities of the Hanse were absorbed by the kings of Poland or Denmark or ruined themselves by vain resistance. Barcelona yielded to the King of Aragon, Marseilles to the King of France. Even those apparent virgins, Genoa and Augsburg, were really 'kept cities', attached by golden strings to the King of Spain and the Emperor. The Doge of Venice himself became a prince, ruling over lesser cities in the *terra ferma*. Only a few, like Geneva, remained obstinate spinsters; and that sour, crabbed city missed the gaiety of the Renaissance. Even the exceptions prove the rule. Accidental princely weakness, or indirect princely patronage, lies behind the new prosperity of Frankfurt, Ragusa, Hamburg, Danzig.

For as a rule surrender was the price of continued prosperity: how else could the cities survive, once the princes had discovered the secret of State? By subduing the Church, extending their jurisdiction, mobilizing the countryside, the princes had created a new apparatus of power, 'the Renaissance State', with which they could tax the wealth of the cities, patronize and extend their trade, take over and develop their art and architecture. If the cities hope to thrive now, it must be by new methods. It must not be through independence: those days are past. It must be through monopoly, as the sole grantees of princely trade in these expanding dominions; as Lisbon and Seville throve on the grants of the kings of Portugal and Spain. Or they might thrive as centres of extravagant princely consumption, as royal capitals. For in some of the old cities the victorious princes would establish their new courts: courts which sucked up the wealth of the whole country and rained it down on the city of their residence. Essentially the sixteenth century is an age not of cities but of courts: of capitals made splendid less by trade than by government. It was not as industrial or commercial cities, but as courts, that Brussels, Paris, Rome, Madrid, Naples, Prague achieve their splendour in the sixteenth century. And the brilliance of these courts is not the discreet, complacent self-advertisement of great merchants out of their calculated profits: it is the carefree magnificence of kings and courtiers, who do not need to count because they do not have to earn.

Of course the cities wriggled at first. Ghent resisted its Burgundian dukes. The old cities of Spain struck back against their foreign king. Florence sought to throw out the Medici. Genoa and Augsburg surrendered only after doubt and strife. But in the end each in turn was overpowered, subdued, and then—if lucky—rewarded with the golden shower which fell not from trade, or at least not directly from trade, but from the Court. And with the cities the old city culture was transformed too. Erasmus, preaching peace and civic justice and denouncing the heedless wars and wasteful magnificence of princes, is a true figure of the first, the city Renaissance, cultivated, pious, rational; but he is swept up in the princely embrace and made a mascot of royal courts, until he flees to die in a free city on the Rhine. Sir Thomas More, whose Utopia was a league of virtuous, independent cities, is captured and broken by the splendid, cannibal Court of Henry VIII. Soon after 1500 the age of independent city culture is over. So is the age of careful accountancy. We are in the age of the Field of Cloth-of-Gold, of heroic conquests and impossible visions and successive state bankruptcies: the age of Columbus and Cortés, of Leonardo da Vinci and St Francis Xavier, each, in his way, like Marlowe's hero, still climbing after knowledge infinite, or, like Don Quixote, pursuing unattainable mirages, heedless of mortal limitations. It is the age, also, whose fashionable handbooks were no longer civic or clerical, but were called *The Courtier*,

The Governour, The Prince, The Institution of a Christian Prince, The Mirror (or *the Horologe*) *of Princes.*

How was this miracle possible? When we look back at that age, with its incredible audacities, its contemptuous magnificence in speculation and spending, we are amazed that it lasted so long. Why did not European civilization burst in the sixteenth century? And yet not only did it not burst, it continued to expand, absorbing all the time the most fearful strains. The Turks in the east wrenched away the outposts of Europe; Christendom was split asunder by religious revolution and constant war; and yet at the end of the century the kings were more spendthrift, their courts more magnificent than ever. The Court of Spain, once so simple, had been changed to a Burgundian pattern; the Court of England, once so provincial, had become, under Queen Elizabeth, the most elaborate in Europe; and the princes of Italy and Germany, with palaces and libraries, picture-galleries and *Wunderkammer*, philosophers, fools and astrologers, strove to hold their own. As the century wore on, social conscience dwindled, for social change seemed impossibly remote. Was ever an architect more effortlessly aristocratic than Palladio, or a poet than Shakespeare, or a painter than Rubens?

How indeed was it possible? One answer is obvious. The sixteenth century was an age of economic expansion. It was the century when, for the first time, Europe was living on Asia, Africa and America. But there was also another reason. The reason why this expansion was always under the princes, not at their expense, why the princes were always carried upwards, not thrown aside by it, was that the princes had allies who secured their power and kept them firmly in place. For the princes could never have built up their power alone. Whatever weaknesses in society gave them their opportunity, they owed their permanence to the machinery of government which they had created or improved, and to the vested interests which that machinery fostered. This machinery, the means and result of princely triumph, is the Renaissance State, and it is to this that we must now turn: for it was the Renaissance State which, in so much of Europe, first broke or corroded the old power of the cities and then, in its turn, in the seventeenth century, faced its own crisis and dissolved.

We often speak of the Renaissance State. How can we define it? When we come down to facts, we find that it is, at bottom, a great and expanding bureaucracy, a huge system of administrative centralization, staffed by an ever-growing multitude of 'courtiers' or 'officers'. The 'officers' are familiar enough to us as a social type. We think of the great Tudor

ministers in England, Cardinal Wolsey, Thomas Cromwell, the two
Cecils; or of the *letrados* of Spain, Cardinal Ximénez, the two Granvelles,
Francisco de los Cobos, António Pérez; and we see ther common character: they are formidable administrators, Machiavellian diplomats, cultivated patrons of art and letters, magnificent builders of palaces and
colleges, greedy collectors of statues and pictures, books and bindings.
For of course these men, as royal servants, imitated their masters, in
lavishness as in other matters. But what is significant about the sixteenth
century is not merely the magnificence of these great 'officers', it is the
number——the ever-growing number—of lesser officers who also, on
their lesser scale, accepted the standards and copied the tastes of their
masters. For all through the century the number of officers was growing.
Princes needed them, more and more, to staff their councils and courts,
their new special or permanent tribunals which were the means of governing new territories and centralizing the government of old. It was
for this reason that the Renaissance princes and ther great ministers
founded all those schools and colleges. For it was not merely to produce
scholars, or to advance learning or science, that old colleges were re-
organized or new founded by Cardinal Ximénez or Cardinal Wolsey,
by Henry VIII of England or John III of Portugal, or François I of
France. The new learning, it is notorious, grew up outside the colleges
and universities, not in them. The function of the new foundations was
to satisfy the royal demand for officers—officers to man the new royal
bureaucracies—and, at the same time, the public demand for office:
office which was the means to wealth and power and the gratification
of lavish, competitive tastes.

Thus the power of the Renaissance princes was not princely power
only: it was also the power of thousands of 'officers' who also, like their
masters, had extravagant tastes and, somehow, the means of gratifying
them. And how in fact were they gratified? Did the princes themselves
pay their officers enough to sustain such a life? Certainly not. Had that
been so, ruin would have come quicker: Cobos and Granvelle alone
would have brought Charles V to bankruptcy long before 1556, and
Henry VIII would have had to dissolve the monasteries fifteen years
earlier to sustain the economic burden of Cardinal Wolsey. The fact is,
only a fraction of the cost of the royal bureaucracy fell directly on the
Crown: three-quarters of it fell, directly or indirectly, on the country.

Yes, three-quarters: at least three-quarters. For throughout Europe, at
this time, the salaries paid to officers of State were small, customary
payments whose real value dwindled in times of inflation; the bulk of
an officer's gains came from private opportunities to which public office

merely opened the door. 'For the profits of these two great offices, the Chancellor and the Treasurer', wrote an English bishop, 'certainly they were very small if you look to the ancient fees and allowances; for princes heretofore did tie themselves to give but little, that so their officers and servants might more depend upon them for their rewards.' What Bishop Goodman said of Jacobean England was true of every European country. Instances could be multiplied indefinitely. Every officer, at every Court, in every country, lived by the same system. He was paid a trivial 'fee' or salary and, for the rest, made what he could in the field which his office had opened to him. Some of these profits were regarded as perfectly legitimate, for no man could be expected to live on his 'fee' alone: it was taken for granted that he would charge a reasonable sum for audiences, favours, signatures, that he would exploit his office to make good bargains, that he would invest public money, while in his hands, on his own account. But of course there were other profits which were generally regarded as 'corruption' and therefore improper. Unfortunately the line dividing propriety from impropriety was conventional only: it was therefore invisible, uncertain, floating. It differed from person to person, from place to place. It also differed from time to time. As the sixteenth century passed on, as the cost of living rose, as the pressure of competition sharpened and royal discipline slackened, there was a general decline of standards. The public casuists became more indulgent, the private conscience more elastic, and men began to forget about that conventional, invisible line between 'legitimate profits' and 'corruption'.

Let us consider a few instances which illustrate the system. In England, the Master of the Wards had a 'fee' of £133 p.a., but even Lord Burghley, a conscientious administrator, made 'infinite gains'—at least £2000 p.a.—out of its private opportunities, quite apart from its non-financial advantages. His son did far better. The Lord Treasurer's fee was £365 p.a., but in 1635 even Archbishop Laud, a notable stickler for administrative honesty, reckoned that that great officer had 'honest advantages' for enriching himself to the tune of over £7000 p.a. The archbishop made this calculation because he had been shocked by the much larger sums which recent lord treasurers had been making at the expense of king and subject alike. In 1600 the Lord Chancellor's fee was £500 p.a., but in fact the office was known to be 'better worth than £3000 p.a.'. To Lord Chancellor Ellesmere this did not seem enough, and, like many great men, he sighed that he could not make ends meet. He was thought conscientious: perhaps (like Burghley) he was also hypocritical. At all events, his successors had no such difficulty.

How have the Lord Chancellors lived since [exclaimed Bishop Good-man], how have they flowed with money, and what great purchases have they made, and what profits and advantages have they had by laying their fingers on purchases! For if my Lord desired the land, no man should dare to buy it out of his hands, and he must have it at his own price; for any bribery or corruption, it is hard to prove it: men do not call others to be witnesses at such actions.

All writers of the early seventeenth century agree that the casual profits of office had grown enormously; and these casual profits were multiplied at the expense of the consumer, the country.

Thus each old office granted, each new office created, meant a new burden of the subject. Royal parsimony made little difference. Our Queen Elizabeth, we all know, was judged very parsimonious: far too parsimonious by her own officers. After her death, her parsimony became one of her great retrospective virtues: how favourably it compared with the giddy extravagance of James I, the fiscal exactions of Charles I! But she was not praised for her parsimony in her own time. For what in fact did it mean? 'We have not many precedents of her liberality', says a contemporary, 'nor of any large donatives to particular men. . . . Her rewards consisted chiefly in grants of leases of offices, places of judicature; but for ready money, and in any great sums, she was very sparing.' In other words, she gave to her courtiers not cash but the right to exploit their fellow subjects: to Sir Walter Ralegh the right to despoil the bishops of Bath and Wells and Salisbury and to interpose his pocket between the producer and consumer of tin; to the Earl of Essex the right to lease the monopoly of sweet wines to merchants who would recoup themselves by raising the cost to the consumer. Thanks to these invisible *douceurs* she contrived, at the same time, to keep her taxes low and her officers sweet.

Whether they kept taxes low or not, all European sovereigns did likewise. They had no alternative. They had not the ready money, and so, if they were to gratify their servants, reward their favourites, service their loans, they had to raise it at a discount or pay excessively in kind. They leased Crown lands at a quarter (or less) of their true value in order that 'officers' or 'courtiers' could live, as lessees, on the difference. They granted monopolies which brought in to the Crown less than a quarter of what they cost the subject. They collected irrational old taxes, or even irrational new taxes, by imposing, fourfold, irrational burdens on the tax-payers. The King of France obliged his peasants to buy even more salt than they needed, in order to raise his yield from the *gabelle* [salt tax]. We all know what a burden wardship and purveyance became in the reigns of Queen Elizabeth and King James. Both visibly cost the subject four times what they brought to the Crown. Invisibly—that is, beyond that invisible line—they cost far more.

Nor was it only the Crown which acted thus. The practice was universal. Great men rewarded their clients in exactly the same way. It was thus that those great empires of personal patronage were built up which at times threatened to disrupt the whole system of monarchy. In France, it was through his 'clients'—that is, 'le grand nombre d'officiers que son crédit avoit introduit dans les principales charges du royaume'—that the Duke of Guise was able to make royal government impossible, to control the Estates-General of France, and nearly place his own dynasty on the throne of the Valois. It was to prevent the recurrence of such a portent that Henri IV afterwards, by the institution of the *Paulette*, made offices hereditary, subject to an annual payment to the Crown. This did not cure the social fact, but it cured the aristocratic abuse of it. In Elizabethan England the Earl of Leicester similarly built up a great system of patronage, 'Leicester's Commonwealth', which rivalled Lord Burghley's *regnum Cecilianum*. Queen Elizabeth managed to control Leicester, but not his stepson, the heir to his ambitions, the Earl of Essex. Essex, for a moment, looked like the Guise of England. Like Guise, he had to be removed, surgically. Later the Duke of Buckingham would build up, by royal permission, a similar empire of patronage. He would be removed surgically too.

The Church, in this respect, was similar to the State: it was, after all, by now a department of State, and it must be seen, sociologically, as an element in the bureaucratic structure. Originally an attempt had been made to separate it from that structure. The Reformation movement, Catholic as well as Protestant, was in many respects a revolt against the papal 'Court'—using the word 'Court', as I always do, in the widest sense—that is, not merely a national revolt against a foreign Church, but a social revolt against the indecent, costly and infinitely multiplied personnel, mainly of the regular orders, which had overgrown the working episcopal and parish structure. We only have to read the history of the Council of Trent to see this: the exclusion of the Protestants from that assembly merely shows that, socially, Catholic demands were identical. Protestant societies, by revolution, disembarrassed themselves of much of the papal Court. But even Protestant princes, as princes, preferred to take over, rather than to destroy the bureaucracy of the Church. Catholic princes went further: they accepted both the existing clerical structure and the positive increase which was entailed upon it by the Counter-Revolution. For although, in one sense, the Counter-

Revolution may have been a movement of moral and spiritual reform, structurally it was an aggravation of the bureaucracy. However, the princes found that it paid them to accept this aggravation, for in return for their allegiance it was placed under their control, and became at once an extended field of patronage and a social palliative. The Catholic princes had vast clerical patronage for laymen as well as clergy: the Church absorbed the potential critics: and the new or strengthened religious orders, by evangelization, reconciled society to the burden which they imposed upon it. Thus the Catholic princes of the Counter-Reformation were generally able to stifle the forces of change to which Protestant princes found themselves more nakedly exposed, and it became a truism, and perhaps a truth, that popery was the sole internal preservative of monarchy. But even in Protestant monarchies, the bureaucratic pressure of the Church was felt and resented. The Church, it was said, was burdened with absentee clergy, tithe-eating laity, a swollen number of ecclesiastical officers, and parasitic lessees who lived happily on 'beneficial leases' of Church lands. For Church lands, like Crown lands, were regularly leased at absurd under-rents. It was not only the State: the whole of society was top-heavy.

Moreover, and increasingly as the seventeenth century succeeded to the sixteenth, this multiplication of ever more costly offices outran the needs of State. Originally the need had created the officers; now the officers created the need. All bureaucracies tend to expand. By the process known to us as Parkinson's Law, office-holders tend to create yet more offices beneath them in order to swell their own importance or provide for their friends and kinsmen. But whereas today such inflation is curbed by the needs of the Treasury, in the sixteenth century the needs of the Treasury positively encouraged it. For offices, in the sixteenth century, were not granted freely: they were sold, and—at least in the beginning—the purchase-price went to the Crown. If the Crown could sell more and more offices at higher and higher prices, leaving the officers to be paid by the country, this was an indirect, if also a cumbrous and exasperating, way of taxing the country. Consequently, princes were easily tempted to create new offices, and to profit by the competition which forced up the price. As for the purchaser, having paid a high price, he naturally sought to raise his profits still higher, in order to recoup himself, with a decent margin, for his outlay: a decent margin with which an ambitious man might hope, in the end, to build a house like Hatfield or Knole, entertain royalty to feasts costing thousands, retain and reward an army of clients, plant exotic gardens and collect *objets d'art* and pictures.

So 'the Renaissance State' consisted, at bottom, of an ever-expanding bureaucracy which, though at first a working bureaucracy, had by the end of the sixteenth century become a parasitic bureaucracy; and this ever-expanding bureaucracy was sustained on an equally expanding margin of 'waste': waste which lay between the taxes imposed on the subject and the revenue collected by the Crown. Since the Crown could not afford an absolute loss of revenue, it is clear that this expansion of the waste had to be at the expense of society. It is equally clear that it could be borne only if society itself were expanding in wealth and numbers. Fortunately, in the sixteenth century, the European economy was expanding. The trade of Asia, the bullion of Africa and America, was driving the European machine. This expansion may have been uneven; there may have been strains and casualties; but they were the strains of growth, which could be absorbed, individual casualties which could be overlooked. Occasional state bankruptcies clear off old debts: they do not necessarily affect new prosperity. War increases consumption: it does not necessarily consume the sources of wealth. A booming economy can carry many anomalies, many abuses. It could even carry—providing it went on booming—the incredibly wasteful, ornamental, parasitic Renaissance court and Churches.

Provided it went on booming . . . But how long would it boom? Already, by 1590, the cracks are beginning to appear. The strains of the last years of Philip II's wars release everywhere a growing volume of complaint: complaint which is not directed against constitutional faults —against the despotism of kings or the claims of estates—but against this or that aspect or consequence of the growth and cost of a parasitic bureaucracy. For of course, although war has not created the problem, war aggravates it: the more the costs of government are raised, the more the government resorts to those now traditional financial expedients— creation and sale of new offices; sale or long lease, at under-values, of Crown or Church lands; creation of monopolies; raising of 'feudal' taxes: expedients which, on the one hand, multiply the already over-grown bureaucracy and thus the cost to the country, and, on the other hand, further impoverish the Crown.

But if the strains are already obvious in the 1590s, they are, as yet, not fatal: for peace comes first. A few opportune deaths—Philip II in 1598, Queen Elizabeth in 1603—hasten the process, and throughout Europe war after war is wound up. And then, with peace, what relief! The overstrained system is suddenly relaxed, and an era of pleasure and renewed extravagance follows. Was there ever an era of such lavishness as the time between the end of Philip II's wars and the outbreak of the

Thirty Years War, the time when the world was ruled, or at least enjoyed, by Philip III and the Duke of Lerma in Spain, James I and the
Duke of Buckingham in England, 'The Archdukes' in Flanders, Henri IV
and Marie de Médicis in France? It is a world of giddy expenditure,
splendid building, gigantic feasts and lavish, evanescent shows. Rubens,
when he came to the Duke of Buckingham's England, marvelled at such
unexpected magnificence 'in a place so remote from Italian elegance'. No
nation in the world, said a contemporary Englishman, spent as much as
we did in building. We built houses, said another, thinking of Hatfield
and Audley End, 'like Nebuchadnezzar's'. All 'the old good rules of
economy', said a third, had gone packing. But the Spanish ambassador,
reporting to his king these costly Jacobean festivals, would only say that
no doubt they would seem very impressive 'to anyone who had not seen
the grandeur and state with which we do such things in Spain'—as well
he might, in the days when the Duke of Lerma, the courtier of the almost bankrupt King of Spain, went forth to meet his future queen with
34,000 ducats' worth of jewels on his person, and another 72,000 ducats'
worth carried behind him.

Such is the character of the Renaissance courts in their last Indian
summer after the close of the sixteenth century. And even this, of
course, is only the conspicuous, still sunlit tip of the iceberg whose sides
are hidden from us by intervening oblivion and whose greater base was
always, even at the time, submerged. How, we may ask, could it go on?
Even in the 1590s, even a far less expensive, more efficient bureaucracy
had been saved only by peace: how could this much more outrageous
system survive if the long prosperity of the sixteenth century, or the
saving peace of the seventeenth, should fail?

In fact, in the 1620s they both failed at once. In 1618 a political crisis
in Prague had set the European powers in motion, and by 1621 the wars
of Philip II had been resumed, bringing in their train new taxes, new
offices, new exactions. Meanwhile the European economy, already
strained to the limit by the habits of peacetime boom, was suddenly
struck by a great depression, the universal 'decay of trade' of 1620.
Moreover, in those twenty years, a new attitude of mind had been
created: created by disgust at that gilded merry-go-round which cost
society so much more than society was willing to bear. It was an attitude of hatred: hatred of 'the Court' and its courtiers, hatred of princely
follies and bureaucratic corruption, hatred of the Renaissance itself: in
short, Puritanism.

In England we naturally think of our own form of Puritanism: extreme Protestantism, the continuation, to unbearable lengths, of the

half-completed sixteenth-century Reformation. But let us not be deceived by mere local forms. This reaction against the Renaissance courts and their whole culture and morality was not confined to any one country or religion. Like the thesis, the antithesis also is general. In England there is an Anglican Puritanism, a 'Puritanism of the Right'. What greater enemy had English Puritanism, as we know it, than Archbishop Laud, the all-powerful prelate who drove it to America till it returned to destroy him? And yet he too illustrates this same reaction. Did English Puritans denounce 'the unloveliness of lovelocks', gay clothes, the drinking of toasts? The archbishop forbade long hair in Oxford, reformed clerical dress, waged war on ale-houses. In Roman Catholic countries it was the same. Did the English Puritans first denounce, then close the London theatres? In Spain—even the Spain of Lope de Vega —*pragmática* after *pragmática* denounced stage plays. In France the Jansenist Pascal disliked them hardly less. In Bavaria there was a Catholic prudery, and a police enforcement of it, as disagreeable as the worst form of English Puritanism. There was the same war against luxury too. In 1624 Philip IV of Spain cut down his household, published sumptuary laws, and banished the ruff—that symbol of sartorial magnificence—from Spain by decree, from Europe by example. In France Cardinal Richelieu was doing likewise. It was a sudden war, almost a crusade, against the old Renaissance extravagance. In Flanders Rubens would find himself surviving his old Court patrons and would turn to country landscapes. Literature reflects the same change. Of Castiglione's famous manual, *The Courtier*, at least sixty editions or translations were published between 1528 and 1619; after the latter date, for a whole century, none.

In the 1620s Puritanism—this general mood of Puritanism—triumphs in Europe. Those years, we may say, mark the end of the Renaissance. The playtime is over. The sense of social responsibility, which had held its place within the Renaissance courts of the sixteenth century—we think of the paternalism of the Tudors, the 'collectivism' of Philip II— had been driven out in the early seventeenth century, and now it had returned, and with a vengeance. War and depression had made the change emphatic, even startling. We look at the world in one year, and there we see Lerma and Buckingham and Marie de Médicis. We look again, and they have all gone. Lerma has fallen and saved himself by becoming a Roman cardinal; Buckingham is assassinated; Marie de Médicis has fled abroad. In their stead we find grimmer, greater, more resolute figures: the Count-Duke of Olivares, whose swollen, glowering face almost bursts from Velázquez's canvases; Strafford and Laud, that

relentless pair, the prophets of Thorough in Church and State; Cardinal
Richelieu, the iron-willed invalid who ruled and remade France. In literature too it is the same. The fashion has changed. After Shakespeare,
Cervantes, Montaigne, those universal spirits, with their scepticism,
their acceptance of the world as it is, we are suddenly in a new age: an
age here of ideological revolt, Milton's 'jubilee and resurrection of
Church and State', there of conservative pessimism, cynicism and dis-
illusion, of John Donne and Sir Thomas Browne, of Quevedo and the
Spanish Baroque: for the baroque age, as Mr Gerald Brenan says, '—
one cannot say it too often—was a tight, contracted age, turned in on
itself and lacking self-confidence and faith in the future'.

Such was the mood of general, non-doctrinal, moral Puritanism
which, in the 1620s, launched its attack—here from within, there from
without—on the Renaissance courts. There are differences of incidence,
of course, differences of personality from place to place, and these differences could be crucial—who can say what would have happened if
Archbishop Laud had really been, as Sir Thomas Roe thought, 'the
Richelieu of England'? There were also differences in society itself. But
if we look closely we see that the burden on society is the same even
if the shoulders which creak under it are different. For instance, in
England the cost of the Court fell most heavily on the gentry: they were
the tax-paying class: wardships, purveyance and all the indirect taxes
which were multiplied by the early Stuarts fell heaviest on them. On the
other hand in France the *noblesse* was exempt from taxation, and the
taille and *gabelle*, which were multiplied by the early Bourbons, fell
heaviest on the peasants. No doubt English landlords could pass some
of their burdens on to their tenants. No doubt impoverishment of
French peasants diminished the rents of their landlords. But the difference is still significant. It was a commonplace in England, where 'the
asinine peasants of France', with their 'wooden shoes and canvas
breeches', were regularly contrasted with our own, more prosperous
yeomen. It is illustrated by the ultimate result: in England, when revolution came, it was a great revolution, controlled by the gentry; in
France, there were, every year for the same twenty years, revolts—little
but serious revolts—of the peasants. Nevertheless, if the rebels were different, the general grievance against which they rebelled—the character and cost of the State—was the same.

For wherever we look, this is the burden of all complaints. From 1620
to 1640 this is the cry of the country, the problem of the courts. We
can hear the cry from the back benches of the English parliaments in
the 1620s. We can see the problem in Bacon's great essays, written be-

tween 1620 and 1625, on 'Sedition and Troubles' and 'The True Greatness of Kingdoms'. We hear the cry in Spain in the protests of the
Cortes, see the problem in the pamphlets of the *arbitristas* [reform-
minded economists]: Sancho de Moncada's *Restauración Política de España;* in Fernández Navarrete's *Conservación de monarquías* with its
wonderful analysis of the social ills of Spain, and in Olivares's long
memorandum to Philip IV, outlining his new programme for the country, all written in the critical years 1619–21. We see it in France, above
all, in the *Testament politique* of Richelieu, written in 1629 and the
early 1630s, the period when governments everywhere were facing
these problems, or trying to face them, before it was too late. And these
demands, these problems, are not constitutional, they are not concerned
with monarchy or republic, Crown or Parliament. Nor are they economic: they are not concerned with methods of production. Essentially
they are demands for emancipation from the burden of centralization;
for reduction of fees; reduction of useless, expensive offices, including
—even in Spain—clerical offices; abolition of the sale of offices ('for
whosoever doth farm or buy offices doth bind himself to be an extor-
tioner', and 'they which buy dear must sell dear'); abolition of heredity
of offices; abolition of those wasteful, indirect taxes which yield so little
to the Crown but on whose superabundant 'waste' the ever-expanding
fringe of the Court is fed.

Thus the tension between Court and country grew, and the 'revolutionary situation' of the 1620s and 1630s developed. But revolutionary
situations do not necessarily lead to revolutions—nor (we may add) are
violent revolutions necessary in order to create new forms of production or society. Society is an organic body, far tougher, far more resil-
ient, than its morbid anatomists often suppose. The frontiers between
opposing classes are always confused by a complex tissue of interests.
Office-holders and *bourgeoisie,* consumers and producers, tax-gatherers
and tax-payers are not neatly distinguishable classes. On the contrary,
men who think of themselves as 'country' at one moment often discover
that they are 'Court' at another, and such discoveries may lead to un-
predictable apostasy. For this reason, social tensions seldom if ever
lead to a clean split: rather they lead to an untidy inward crumbling
whose stages are determined not by the original social tensions but by
intervening political events and political errors. Therefore, if we are to
carry this study further, from revolutionary situation to revolution, we
must take account of these intervening events and errors: events and
errors which, by definition, must vary from place to place, and whose

variation will explain, in part, the difference between the revolutions in those different places.

Perhaps we can see the problem best if we consider the means of avoiding revolution. If the Renaissance courts were to survive, it was clear that at least one of two things must be done. On the one hand the parasitic bureaucracies must be cut down; on the other hand the working bureaucracy must be related to the economic capacity of the country. The first programme was one of administrative, the second of economic reform. The first was easy enough to define—any country gentleman could put it in two words—but difficult to carry out: it meant the reduction of a parasitic, but living and powerful class; and although this can be done without revolution, as it was done in nineteenth-century England—one only has to read the *Extraordinary Black Book* of 1831 to see the huge parasitic fringe which had grown again around the eighteenth-century Court—it is at best a delicate and difficult operation. The second was far more difficult to define: it meant the discovery, or rediscovery, of an economic system. Nevertheless, such a definition was not beyond the wit of seventeenth-century thinkers, and in fact several thinkers did point out, clearly enough, the kind of economic system which was required.

What was that system? It was not a 'capitalist' system—or at least, if it was capitalist, there was nothing new about it. It did not entail revolution or a change in method of production or in the class structure. Nor was it advocated by revolutionary thinkers: in general, those who advocated it were conservative men who wished for little or no political change. And in fact the economic programme which they advocated, though applied to modern conditions, looked back for its example. For what they advocated was simply the application to the new, centralized monarchies of the old, well-tried policy of the medieval communes which those monarchies had eclipsed: mercantilism.

For what had been the policy of the medieval cities? It had been a policy of national economy—within the limits of the city-state. The city had seen itself at once as a political and as an economic unit. Its legislation had been based on its trading requirements. It had controlled the price of food and labour, limited imports in the interest of its own manufactures, encouraged the essential methods of trade—fishing and shipbuilding, freedom from internal tolls—invested its profits not in conspicuous waste or pursuit of glory, or wars merely of plunder, but in the rational conquest of markets and the needs of national economy: in technical education, municipal betterment, poor relief. In short, the city had recognized that its life must be related to its means of livelihood.

In the sixteenth-century eclipse of the cities, in their transformation into overgrown, overpopulated capitals, centres merely of exchange and consumption, much of this old civic wisdom had been forgotten. Now in the seventeenth-century eclipse of the spendthrift Renaissance Courts, it was being remembered. The economists wished to go farther: to reapply it.

Of course, they would reapply it in changed circumstances, to different national forms. The princes, it was agreed, had done their work: it could not be reversed. The new nation-states had come to stay. But, said the reformers, having come, let them now apply to their different conditions the old good rules of the cities. Let them not merely pare down the parasitic fringe that had grown around them, but also relate their power, in a positive sense, to economic aims. Let them favour a gospel of work instead of aristocratic, or pseudo-aristocratic *hidalguía*. Let them protect industry, guarantee food-supplies, remove internal tolls, develop productive wealth. Let them rationalize finance and bring down the apparatus of Church and State to a juster proportion. To reverse the Parkinson's Law of bureaucracy, let them reduce the hatcheries which turned out the superfluous bureaucrats: grammar schools in England, colleges in France, monasteries and theological seminaries in Spain. Instead, let them build up local elementary education: skilled workers at the base of society now seemed more important than those unemployable university graduates, hungry for office, whom the new Renaissance foundations were turning out. 'Of grammar-schools', declared that great intellectual, Sir Francis Bacon, 'there are too many': many a good ploughboy was spoiled to make a bad scholar; and he and his followers advocated a change in the type of education or the diversion of funds to elementary schools. Of colleges, declared the founder of the French Academy, Cardinal Richelieu, there are too many: the commerce of letters, if unchecked, would banish absolutely that of merchandise 'which crowns states with riches' and ruin agriculture 'the true nursing-mother of peoples'. Of monasteries, declared the Catholic Council of Castile in 1619, there are too many, and it prayed that the Pope be asked to authorize their reduction, for although the monastic state is no doubt, for the individual, the most perfect, 'for the public it is very damaging and prejudicial'. Monasteries, protested the Cortes of Castile, have outgrown the needs of religion: they now contain persons 'rather fleeing from necessity to the delights of indolence than moved by devotion'. So, in country after country, the protest was raised. It was the backswing of the great educational impulse of the Renaissance and Reformation, the great religious impulse of the Counter-Reformation.

To cut down the oppressive, costly sinecures of Church and State, and to revert, *mutatis mutandis*, to the old mercantilist policy of the cities, based on the economic interest of society—such were the two essential methods of avoiding revolution in the seventeenth century. How far were either of them adopted in the states of western Europe? The answer, I think, is instructive. If we look at those states in turn, we may see, in the extent to which either or both of these policies were adopted or rejected, some partial explanation of the different forms which the general crisis took in each of them.

In Spain neither policy was adopted. It was not for lack of warning. The Cortes of Castile, the Council of State, the *arbitristas*, individual statesmen continually pressed both for reduction of officers and clergy and for a mercantilist policy. In 1619 Philip III was urged to abolish, as a burden to society, the hundred *receptores* newly created six years earlier, even though that should mean repaying the price at which they had bought their offices. In the same year the greatest of Spanish ambassadors, Gondomar, whose letters show him to have been a consistent mercantilist, wrote that Church and Commonwealth were both endangered by the multiplication of clergy 'since the shepherds now outnumber the sheep'; and he added that the same was true in the State, where 'ministers of justice, *escribanos*, *comisarios* and *alguaciles*' were multiplying fast, but there was no increase of 'ploughmen, ships or trade'. Two years later, under the pressure of economic crisis and the renewal of war, it seemed that something would at last be done. The reign of Philip IV began [1621] with the famous *capítulos de reformación*. The number of royal officers was fixed by law. Next year the king declared that since an excessive number of offices is pernicious in the State ('most of them being sold, and the officers having to make up the price they have paid'), and since a great number of *escribanos* is prejudicial to society ('and the number at present is excessive, and grows daily') the number of *alguaciles*, *procuradores*, and *escribanos* in Castile must be reduced to one-third, and recruitment must be discouraged by various means. For a moment, it seemed that the problem was to be faced. The leaders of the war-party themselves, implicitly, recognized the cause of Spain's weakness. The purpose of *las Pazes*—the successive treaties of peace in 1598, 1604, 1609—they said, had been to repair the strength of Spain; but in fact peace had strengthened the mercantilist Dutch and only weakened bureaucratic Spain. Now war was necessary to redress the balance; but even to make war the structure of society must be reformed; the bureaucratic state had failed alike as a system of peace and as a system of war.

So spoke the reformers of the 1620s. But their voice was soon stifled, for there was no social or institutional force behind them to make their protest effective. The Castilian middle class was weak and penetrated by office-holders; the power of the old Cortes towns had been suppressed in their last rising against the Burgundian State a century before; and the Cortes of Castile was now an aristocratic body which hardly sought to do more than demur. Besides, war, which exposed the economic weakness of the bureaucratic system, equally prevented any reform of that system. A few reforms were attempted, or at least enacted on paper; but the mood soon changed. The need for immediate funds caused the government to exploit the existing machinery, not to reform it for the sake of future efficiency. So all the projects of the reformers were soon forgotten, and in 1646 the Cortes of Castile would draw attention to their failure. In spite of all those protests and those efforts, offices had not diminished during the war: they had multiplied. Instead of one president and three councillors of the Treasury, there were now three presidents and eleven councillors; instead of three *contadores* and a *fiscal*, there were now fourteen *contadores*; instead of four councillors at war there were now more than forty; and all these, salaried or unsalaried (for their salaries, their 'fees', were anyway trifles), had entertainment, expenses, lodgings, privileges and perquisites at the expense of the subject. The weight of this burden might have been redistributed a little within the country, but it had certainly not been reduced. Nor had the Spanish economy been enabled to bear it. For meanwhile the national wealth of Spain had not increased: it had diminished. The voices of the mercantilists were stifled. The trade of Spain was taken over almost entirely by foreigners. The vitality of the country was crushed beneath the dead weight of an unreformed *ancien régime*. It was not till the next century that a new generation of *arbitristas*—philosophers inspired by English and French examples—would again have the strength and spirit to urge on a new dynasty the same reforms which had clearly but vainly been demanded in the days of Philip III and Philip IV.

Very different was the position in the emancipated northern Netherlands. For the northern Netherlands was the first European country to reject the Renaissance Court, and the Court they rejected was their own Court, the greatest, most lavish Court of all, the Burgundian Court which, with the abdication of Charles V, had moved and made itself so fatally permanent in Spain. The revolt of the Netherlands in the sixteenth century was not, of course, a direct revolt of society against the Court. That is not how revolutions break out. But in the course of the long struggle the Court itself, in those provinces which freed themselves, was a casualty. There the whole apparatus of the Burgundian Court simply dissolved under the stress of war. So did the Burgundian Church, that huge, corrupt department of State which Philip II unskilfully sought to reform and whose abuses the great patrons of revolt, in the beginning, were seeking to preserve. Whatever the causes or motives of the revolution, the United Provinces emerged from it incidentally disembarrassed of that top-heavy system whose pressure, a generation later, would create a revolutionary situation in other countries. Consequently, in those provinces, there was no such revolutionary situation. The new Court of the Princes of Orange might develop some of the characteristics of the old Court of the dukes of Burgundy, but only some: and as it started lean, it could better afford a little additional fat. There were crises no doubt in seventeenth-century Holland—the crises of 1618, of 1650, of 1672: but they were political crises, comparable with our crisis not of 1640 but of 1688; and they were surgically solved for the same reason: the social problem was no longer acute: the top-heavy apparatus of the State had been purged: society beneath was sound.

Moreover, if accident rather than design had rid the United Provinces of the Renaissance State, policy had also achieved there the other, economic reform of which I have written. It was not that there was a *bourgeois* or 'capitalist' revolution in Holland. Dutch industry was relatively insignificant. But the new rulers of Holland, seeking the means of guarding their hard-won freedom, set out to imitate the fortune and the methods of those older mercantile communities which had preserved their independence through centuries by rationally combining commercial wealth and maritime power. By adopting the techniques of Italy, welcoming the *émigré* experts of Antwerp, and following the old good rules of Venetian policy, Amsterdam became, in the seventeenth century, the new Venice of the north. The economic originality of seventeenth-century Holland consisted in showing that, even after the victory and reign of the Renaissance princes, whom they alone had driven out, the mercantilism of the cities was not dead: it could be revived.

Midway between completely unreformed Spain and completely reformed Holland lies what is perhaps the most interesting of all examples, Bourbon France. For France, in the seventeenth century, was certainly not immune from the general crisis, and in the Frondes it had a revolution, if a relatively small revolution. The result was, as in Spain, a victory for the monarchy. Triumphant over its critics and adversaries, the monarchy of the *ancien régime* survived in France, and survived for another century and a half. On the other hand the French monarchy of Louis XIV was not like the Spanish monarchy of Philip IV and Charles V. It was not economically parasitic. Industry, commerce, science flourished and grew in France, in spite of the 'failure' of the '*bourgeois* revolution', no less than in England, in spite of its 'success'. To all appearances, in 1670, in the age of Colbert, absolutism and the *ancien régime* were perfectly compatible with commercial and industrial growth and power.

And indeed, why not? For what had hindered such growth in the past, what had caused the crisis in society, was not the form of government, but its abuses; and though these abuses might be removed by revolution, or might fall as incidental casualties of a revolution, their removal did not necessarily require revolution. There was always the way of reform. It is not necessary to burn down the house in order to have roast pig. And although France (like Holland) had had a fire in the sixteenth century, in which some of its burden of waste matter had been incidentally consumed, it did also, in the years thereafter, achieve some measure of reform. The fire, indeed, had prepared the ground. The French civil wars of the sixteenth century, if they had done much harm, had also done some good. They had burnt up the over-grown patronage of the great nobles and reduced the patronage of the Court to the patronage of the king. Henri IV, like the Prince of Orange, like Charles II of England after him, found himself at his accession disembarrassed of much ancient parasitism: he could therefore afford to indulge a little new. And on this basis, this *tabula partim rasa*, he was able to achieve certain administrative changes. The *Paulette*, the law of 1604 which systematized the sale of offices, did at least regulate the abuses which it has often, and wrongly, been accused of creating. Sully, by his *économies royales*, did keep down the waste around the throne. And Richelieu, in the 1630s not only meditated a complete mercantilist policy for France: he also, even in the midst of war, succeeded—as Laud and Olivares, whether in peace or war, did not—in regulating that most expensive, most uncontrollable of all departments, the royal household. Thanks to these changes, the *ancien régime* in France was repaired and strengthened. The changes may not have been radical, but they were enough—at least for the time being.

Of course the French solution was not permanent. The advantage of the French government, in the early seventeenth century, was simply that it had shed some of its burdens: it was less encumbered than the Spanish by the inheritance of the past. In the course of time the old weight would soon be resumed: the later reign of Louis XIV would be

notorious for its plethora of offices and benefices, multiplied deliberately in order to be sold. And even in the earlier years, the pressure of
war had the same effect. Again and again, as in Spain, there were demands that the venality of office be reformed or abolished; again and
again the government considered such reform; but in the end, on each
occasion, the French monarchy, like the Spanish, faced with the demands of war, postponed its projects and instead of reforming, positively strengthened the system. Richelieu at first, like Olivares in Spain,
sought to combine war and reform, but in the end (again like Olivares)
sacrificed reform to war. Marillac would have sacrificed war to reform.
By the end of the seventeenth century, Louis XIV would be financing
his wars by massive creations of useless offices. But at the beginning of
the century the position was different. Richelieu and Mazarin no doubt
had other advantages in their successful struggle to maintain the French
ancien régime in the era of the Huguenot revolt and the Frondes. They
had an army absolutely under royal control; they had taxes whose increase fell not on gentry, assembled and vocal in Parliament, but on
scattered, inarticulate peasants; and they had their own political genius.
But they had also an apparatus of state which had already undergone
some salutary reform: a State which, in the mind of Richelieu and in
the hands of his disciple Colbert, could become a mercantilist State,
rationally organized for both profit and power.

Finally there is England. In England the Crown had not the same
political power as in France or Spain, and the taxes fell on the gentry,
powerful in their counties and in Parliament. In England therefore, it
was doubly important that the problem be faced and solved. How far
was it in fact faced? To answer this question let us look in turn at the
two sides of the problem, administrative and economic.

In the sixteenth century the apparatus of the English State had
neither suffered nor benefited from any such destructive accident as had
befallen Holland or France. The Renaissance Court of the Tudors,
whose parsimony under Elizabeth had been so unreal and whose magnificence and ceremony had so impressed foreign visitors, survived intact into the new century, when its cost and show were magnified beyond all measure by King James and his favourites. Already in 1604,
Francis Bacon warned the new king of the danger. The Court, he said,
was like a nettle: its root, the Crown itself, was 'without venom or ma-
lignity', but it sustained leaves 'venomous and stinging where they
touch'. Two years later, King James' greatest minister, Robert Cecil,
Earl of Salisbury, apprehended revolution against the same burden of
the Court; and in 1608, on becoming Lord Treasurer, he applied all his

energies to a large and imaginative solution of the whole problem. He sought to rationalize the farming of taxes and the leasing of Crown lands, to reform the royal household, liberate agriculture from feudal restrictions and abolish archaic dues in exchange for other forms of income whose full yield, or something like it, instead of a mere fraction, would come to the Crown. In 1610 Salisbury staked his political career on this great programme of reorganization. But he failed to carry it through. The 'courtiers', the 'officers' who lived on the 'waste', mobilized opposition, and the king, listening to them, and thinking 'not what he got but what he might get' out of the old, wasteful, irritant sources of revenue, refused to surrender them. Within two years of his failure, Salisbury died, out of favour with the king, completely unlamented, even insulted by the whole Court which he had sought to reform and, by reform, to save.

After Salisbury, other reformers occasionally took up the cause. The most brilliant was Francis Bacon. He had been an enemy of Salisbury, but once Salisbury was dead he sang the same tune. He diagnosed the evil—no man, perhaps, diagnosed it so completely in all its forms and ultimate consequences—but he could do nothing to cure it except by royal permission, which was refused, and he was overthrown. After his fall, in the years of the great depression, even the Court took alarm, and a new reformer seemed to have obtained that permission. This was Lionel Cranfield, Earl of Middlesex, who set out to carry through some at least of Salisbury's proposals. But permission, if granted, was soon, and conspicuously withdrawn. Cranfield, like Bacon, was ruined by Court faction, led from above by the royal favourite, the Duke of Buckingham, the universal manager and profiteer of all those marketable offices, benefices, sinecures, monopolies, patents, perquisites and titles which together constituted the nourishment of the Court. Thus when Buckingham was murdered and Strafford and Laud, the 'Puritans of the right', came to power, they inherited from him an utterly unreformed Court.

Did they do anything to reform it? Ostensibly they did. 'The face of the court', as Mrs Hutchinson wrote, 'was changed.' King Charles was outwardly frugal compared with his father: but such frugality, as we have seen in the case of Queen Elizabeth, was relatively insignificant. Laud and Strafford waged war on the corruption of the Court, whenever they perceived it; but they left the basic system untouched. Whenever we study that system we find that, in their time, its cost had not been reduced: it had grown. The greatest of Court feasts in Buckingham's days had been his own entertainment of the king in 1626, which had cost £4000; the Earl of Newcastle, in 1634, went up to £15,000. An office which was sold for £5000 in 1624 fetched £15,000 in 1640. Ward-ships, which had brought in £25,000 to the Crown when Salisbury had sought to abolish them in 1610, were made to yield £95,000 in 1640. And the proportion that ran to waste was no smaller. For every £100 which reached the Crown, at least £400 was taken from the subject. As Clarendon says, 'The envy and reproach came to the King, the profit to other men.'

Thus in 1640 the English Court, like the Spanish, was still unre-formed. But what of the English economy? Here the parallel no longer holds. For in England there was not that absolute divorce between Crown and *arbitristas* that was so obvious in Spain. The early Stuart governments did not ignore matters of trade. They listened to the City of London. By their financial methods, whether deliberately or not, they encouraged the formation of capital, its investment in industry. There were limits, of course, to what they did. They did not satisfy the sys-tematic mercantilist theorists. They paid less attention to the base of society than to its summit. Nevertheless, in many respects, they fa-voured or at least allowed a mercantilist policy. They sought to natural-ize industrial processes; they sought to protect supplies of essential raw-materials; they sought to monopolize the herring-fisheries; they protected navigation; they preferred peace abroad and looked to their moat. The years of their rule saw the growth of English capitalism, sponsored by them, on a scale unknown before. Unfortunately such growth entailed dislocation, claimed victims; and when political crisis increased the dislocation and multiplied the victims, the stiff and weak-ened structure of government could no longer contain the mutinous forces which it had provoked.

For in 1640 the leaders of the Long Parliament did not seek—they did not need to seek—to reverse the economic policy of the Crown. They sought one thing only: to repair the administration. The Earl of Bedford as Lord Treasurer, John Pym as Chancellor of the Exchequer, intended to resume the frustrated work of Salisbury: to abolish mo-nopolies, wardships, prerogative taxes, cut down the 'waste', and estab-lish the Stuart Court on a more rational, less costly basis. Having done this, they would have continued the mercantilist policy of the Crown, perhaps extending it by redistribution of resources, and rationalization of labour, at the base of society. They would have done for the English monarchy what Colbert would do for the French. All they required was that the English monarchy, like the French, would allow them to do it.

For, of course, monarchy itself was no obstacle. It is absurd to say that such a policy was impossible without revolution. It was no more

impossible in 1641 than it had been in the days of Salisbury and Cranfield. We cannot assume that merely human obstacles—the irresponsibility of a Buckingham or a Charles I, the reckless obscurantism of a
Strafford—are inherent historical necessities. But in fact these human
obstacles did intervene. Had James I or Charles I had the intelligence of
Queen Elizabeth or the docility of Louis XIII, the English *ancien régime*
might have adapted itself to the new circumstances as peacefully in the
seventeenth century as it would in the nineteenth. It was because they
had neither, because their Court was never reformed, because they defended it, in its old form, to the last, because it remained, administra-
tively and economically as well as aesthetically, 'the last Renaissance
Court in Europe', that it ran into ultimate disaster: that the rational
reformers were swept aside, that more radical men came forward and
mobilized yet more radical passions than even they could control, and
that in the end, amid the sacking of palaces, the shivering of statues
and stained-glass windows, the screech of saws in ruined organ-lofts,
this last of the great Renaissance Courts was mopped up, the royal
aesthete was murdered, his splendid pictures were knocked down and
sold, even the soaring gothic cathedrals were offered up for scrap.

So, in the 1640s, in war and revolution, the most obstinate and yet,
given the political structure of England, the frailest of the Renaissance
monarchies went down. It did not go down before a new '*bourgeois*
revolution'. It did not even go down before an old 'mercantilist revolution'. Its enemies were not the '*bourgeoisie*'—that *bourgeoisie* who, as
a Puritan preacher complained, 'for a little trading and profit' would
have had Christ, the Puritan soldiers, crucified and 'this great Barabbas
at Windsor', the king, set free. Nor were they the mercantilists. The
ablest politicians among the Puritan rebels did indeed, once the republic
was set up, adopt an aggressive mercantilist policy; but in this they
simply resumed the old policy of the Crown and, on that account, were
promptly attacked and overthrown by the same enemies, who accused
them of betraying the revolution.* No, the triumphant enemies of the
English Court were simply 'the country': that indeterminate, unpolitical,
but highly sensitive miscellany of men who had mutinied not against
the monarchy (they had long clung to monarchist beliefs), nor against
economic archaism (it was they who were the archaists), but against the

---

* Those who regard the whole revolution as a *bourgeois* revolution on the
strength of the mercantile policy of the Rump between 1651 and 1653 might
well reflect (*a*) that this policy, of peace with Spain, navigation acts, and rivalry with Holland over fishery and trade, had been the policy of Charles I
in the 1630s, and (*b*) that it was repudiated, emphatically and effectively, by
those who had brought the revolution to a 'successful' issue—the Puritan
army—and only revived at the Restoration of the monarchy.

vast, oppressive, ever-extending apparatus of parasitic bureaucracy which had grown up around the throne and above the economy of England. These men were not politicians or economists, and when the Court had foundered under their blows, they soon found that they could neither govern nor prosper. In the end they abdicated. The old dynasty was restored, its new mercantilist policy resumed. But the restoration was not complete. The old abuses, which had already dissolved in war and revolution, were not restored, and, having gone, were easily legislated out of existence. In 1661 Salisbury's 'Great Contract', Bedford's excise, were at last achieved. The old prerogative courts—whose offence had been not so much their policy as their existence—were not revived. Charles II began his reign free at last from the inherited lumber of the Renaissance Court.

Such, as it seems to me, was 'the general crisis of the seventeenth century'. It was a crisis not of the constitution nor of the system of production, but of the State, or rather, of the relation of the State to society. Different countries found their way out of that crisis in different ways. In Spain the *ancien régime* survived: but it survived only as a disastrous, immobile burden on an impoverished country. Elsewhere, in Holland, France and England, the crisis marked the end of an era: the jettison of a top-heavy superstructure, the return to responsible, mercantilist policy. For by the seventeenth century the Renaissance Courts had grown so great, had consumed so much in 'waste', and had sent their multiplying suckers so deep into the body of society, that they could flourish only for a limited time, and in a time, too, of expanding general prosperity. When that prosperity failed, the monstrous parasite was bound to falter. In this sense, the depression of the 1620s is perhaps no less important, as a historical turning-point, than the depression of 1929: though itself only a temporary economic failure, it marked a lasting political change.

At all events, the princely Courts recognized it as their crisis. Some of them sought to reform themselves, to take physic and reduce their bulk. Their doctors pointed the way: it was then that the old city-states, and particularly Venice, though now in decadence, became the admired model, first of Holland, then of England. And yet, asked the patient, was such reform possible, or even safe? Could a monarchy really be adapted to a pattern which so far had been dangerously republican? Is any political operation more difficult than the self-reduction of an established, powerful, privileged bureaucracy? In fact, the change was nowhere achieved without something of revolution. If it was limited in France, and Holland, that was partly because some of the combustible rubbish had already, in a previous revolution, been consumed. It was also because there had been some partial reform. In England there had been no such previous revolution, no such partial reform. There was also, under the early Stuarts, a fatal lack of political skill: instead of the genius of Richelieu, the suppleness of Mazarin, there was the irresponsibility of Buckingham, the violence of Strafford, the undeviating universal pedantry of Laud. In England, therefore, the storm of the mid-century, which blew throughout Europe, struck the most brittle, most overgrown, most rigid Court of all and brought it violently down.

Suggestions for Further Reading

ASHTON, ROBERT, *The Crown and the Money Market*. Oxford: Clarendon Press, 1960.

ASTON, TREVOR H., ed., *Crisis in Europe 1560–1660*. New York: Basic Books, 1965.

BRIDENBAUGH, CARL, *Vexed and Troubled Englishmen, 1590–1642*. New York: Oxford University Press, 1968.

ELLIOTT, J. H., *The Revolt of the Catalans*. London: Cambridge University Press, 1963.

ELTON, G. R., *The Tudor Revolution in Government*. London: Cambridge University Press, 1962.

FRIEDRICH, C. J., AND C. BLITZER, *The Age of Power*. Ithaca, N.Y.: Cornell University Press, 1957.

GEYL, PIETER, *The Revolt of the Netherlands*, 2nd ed. New York: Barnes & Noble, 1958.

HILL, CHRISTOPHER, *The Century of Revolution*. Edinburgh: Thomas Nelson & Sons, 1961.

HURSTFIELD, JOEL, *The Queen's Wards*. Cambridge, Mass.: Harvard University Press, 1958.

OGG, DAVID, *Europe in the Seventeenth Century*, 8th ed. rev. New York: Collier Books, 1962.

SUPPLE, BARRY, *Commercial Crisis and Change in England*. Cambridge: Cambridge University Press, 1959.

SWART, K. W., *The Sale of Offices in the Seventeenth Century*. The Hague: Nijhoff, 1949.

HANS ROSENBERG

Absolute Monarchy and Its Legacy

◆§§◆ The sixteenth century opened as a new dawn in European history, with promise, hope, and great expectations in almost every phase of social life. An intellectual and artistic renaissance, the enrichment and purification of religious experience, unprecedented economic boom, and the vast potential promised by the discovery of the new world—these happy developments roused the anticipation of contemporary observers for the inauguration of a golden age of mankind, and twentieth-century historians have almost unanimously taken up this theme and depicted the first three decades of the sixteenth century as the great turning point in the development of Western civilization, the beginning of the modern era.

It is only in the historical literature of the last two decades that historians have begun to be equally sensitive to the anguish and despair which prevailed in western Europe only a century after the supposed inauguration of this golden age. Only very recently have scholars clearly perceived the tragic disappointment of the high hopes of the generation of 1500 and come to speak of "the crisis of the seventeenth century." The fifty years after 1600 were in fact an era marked by savage warfare, civil war, class conflict, economic depression, and mean and debilitating struggles over abstruse points of theology, to the credit of no church or sect (see Selections 4 and 7 in this Volume).

FROM Hans Rosenberg, *Bureaucracy, Aristocracy and Autocracy; The Prussian Experience, 1660–1815* (Cambridge, Mass.: Harvard University Press, 1958), pp. 1–25.

How did Europe come upon the hard times of the early seventeenth century after the high hopes of the early 1500's? No historian has yet provided a full and certain answer to this question; indeed, historians were for a long time so blinded by the vision of the new dawn of 1500 that they could not even conceptualize this problem. The number of important historical studies on the period 1450 to 1550 is much greater than the significant interpretations of the following hundred years, and the dimensions of the crisis of the late sixteenth and early seventeenth centuries is only now coming into sharp focus.

It is clear that at least two things went wrong and aborted the golden age of early modern society. The prosperity of the early sixteenth century began to peter out in subsequent decades and widespread economic stagnation set in, marked by the slowdown of industrial growth, trade dislocations, and tight credit. The cause of this depression seems to lie in the technological backwardness of the European economy. The growth of population and urbanization and an increase in the means of industrial productivity were not accompanied by any marked change in European transportation and communications technology. Therefore, while the European economy by 1550 was on the verge of developing the factory system, industrial capitalism, and a high-consumption economy, it failed to make this breakthrough because of the severe check placed on economic growth by the persistence of preindustrial, underdeveloped transportation and communications facilities. The European economy by 1550 was in the position of a high-powered dynamo operating through power lines that could take only a low voltage current. The result was to be endemic depression and a very low level of economic growth until the technological revolution of the eighteenth century.

These economic problems had far-reaching social consequences. They frustrated and demoralized the bourgeoisie, sapped their energies and drained off their political ambitions, and left power in the hands of the old elite of king, court, and aristocracy. This old ruling group was revitalized and given a renewed importance in European life by the wars and civil wars that were largely engendered by confessional conflict in the hundred years after 1550. How the enrichening and deepening of religious experience by the reform movements of the early sixteenth century was slowly debased into armed conflict between ideological camps is a sad story whose outlines are not yet entirely clear to historians in spite of the hundreds of volumes written on the Protestant and Catholic reformations. Scholars have been more concerned with laying partisan blame than with discovering the reasons for the corruption of idealism and the hardening of faith into hatred. Lucien Febvre, Joseph Lortz, and Sir George Clark have perhaps made the most serious and illuminating inquiries into these disillusioning and disheartening events.

It is against this background of economic failure and ideological wars and in response to the misery and confusion they engendered that the political system historians have chosen to call "absolute monarchy" took hold in European life in the later sixteenth and early seventeenth centuries. The prototype and most effective instance of this governmental and social system was created in France, where it enabled the seventeenth-century kings to harness the resources and control the society of the wealthiest and most populous country in Europe, and to begin their assent to hegemony in the balance of power conflict before 1650. Absolutism, moreover, became the fashion everywhere and shaped the course of European history until the closing decades of the eighteenth century. After all the achievements in trade and finance, humanism, religious thought, and overseas exploration of the sixteenth century, the dominant force and most imposing legacy of the early modern era turned out to be absolute monarchy, which harnessed these other trends in its own interest.

It is commonly said that England alone during the seventeenth century remained outside this triumph of absolutist government. But a closer and more realistic consideration of the actual political and social system signified by the term indicates that this is not the case. Although in somewhat different proportions than in France, the same political and social ingredients can be found at work in late seventeenth- and eighteenth-century England after the failure of the radical gentry and bourgeoisie in the English civil war of the 1640's and 50's to withstand the advancing tide of absolutism.

Identification of the nature of early modern absolutism was achieved in the 1940's and 50's by the careful research of several scholars, among them Roland Mousnier in France, Otto Hintze in Germany, and Hans Rosenberg in the United States. The following essay by Rosenberg, which comprises the first chapter of his study of the development of absolutism in late seventeenth- and eighteenth-century Prussia, offers the clearest and most succinct analysis of the development and nature of early modern absolute monarchy. Rosenberg shows that in the absolutist system the king's claim to unchecked authority by no means meant unlimited personal power in practice. Absolutism was a complex system involving the subtle interaction and balancing of royal autocracy, oligarchical bureaucracy, and an aggressive and revivified aristocracy that staffed the bureaucratic and military establishments and in a subtle way limited and even controlled monarchy. During the sixteenth and seventeenth centuries, Rosenberg says, "dynastic absolutism was superseded by bureaucratic absolutism before the absolute state itself was seriously challenged by modern liberalism." "The principal political result was the subtle conversion of bureaucratized monarchical autocracy into government by an oligarchical bureaucracy, self-willed, yet representative of the refashioned privileged classes." In the preceding selection in this volume, H. R. Trevor-Roper examines the crisis experienced—and to a considerable degree precipitated—by early seventeenth-century monarchical bureaucratic government, a crisis out of which emerged the more fully articulated absolutist system Rosenberg describes.

Although Rosenberg does not discuss the English situation in the seventeenth century, his model can be used to show that by the early eighteenth century the difference between the two sides of the Channel was not, as has been so often said, that France was despotic and England free and liberal; but rather that in France the king retained a very strong position against the bureaucracy and aristocracy, whereas in England the king lost his autocratic position and the aristocracy and its bureaucratic oligarchy dominated the government and controlled society in its own interest.

Rosenberg concludes his essay by suggesting the bitter legacy of early modern absolutism for twentieth-century Germany. In Prussia the peculiar balance of autocracy, aristocracy, and bureaucracy, which had its prototype in early seventeenth-century France, was perpetuated into the nineteenth century, and when in the 1920's the old authoritarian leadership at last found itself losing its position to democratic liberalism, it sought to salvage its archaic status through a fatal alliance with the totalitarian Nazi movement. Rosenberg personally witnessed and experienced the results of this long-range heritage of early seventeenth-century government and society. As a brilliant young German liberal scholar, he had to take refuge in the United States from Nazism in the 1930's. He is now professor of history at the University of California at Berkeley. His study of the rise of the Prussian state is widely regarded as a masterpiece of political sociology, and the following introductory essay on bureaucratic absolutism a contribution of the first importance to understanding the political and social structure of early modern Europe.

All the states of the contemporary world, despite enormous differences in the moral, legal, and material basis of their authority and in the function, efficiency, control, and responsibility of governmental action, form part of a single political order. Everywhere government has developed into a big business because of the growing complexity of social life and the multiplying effect of the extension of the state's regulative functions. Everywhere government engages in service-extracting and service-rendering activities on a large scale. Everywhere the supreme power to restrain or to aid individuals and groups has become concentrated in huge and vulnerable organizations. For good or for evil, an essential part of the present structure of governance consists of its far-flung system of professionalized administration and its hierarchy of appointed officials upon whom society is thoroughly dependent. Whether we live under the most totalitarian despotism or in the most liberal democracy, we are governed to a considerable extent by a bureaucracy of some kind. This condition represents the convergence of a great number of social movements.

Bureaucratic public administration in the modern sense is based on general rules and prescribed routines of organized behavior: on a methodical division of the integrated activities of continuously operating offices, on clearly defined spheres of competence, and a precise enumeration of official responsibilities and prerogatives. Thus, in principle, nothing is left to chance and personal caprice. Everybody in the hierarchy has his allotted place, and no one is irreplaceable. In the past two centuries, this impersonal method of minutely calculated government management by a standing army of accountable salaried employees has acquired world-wide significance.

In the free societies of our time, nonbureaucratic forms of administration remain important. Even the totalitarian dictatorships make substantial use of nonprofessional agents for policy enforcement, although here bureaucracy is the intolerant and vindictive master of the government. Under fully developed totalitarianism all social activity, including the private life of the individual itself, is the object of public administration. As summed up by Mussolini: "All in the State; nothing outside the State; nothing against the State."

The totalitarian system has produced two novel kinds of professional "public service": the ruling party bureaucracy and the permanent secret police force. They are postdemocratic because they presuppose the ascent of the democratic ideal, officially proclaim its superiority over all competing creeds, and masquerade as the vanguard of "real democracy," of a progressive "people's democracy." They become barbarous when they make organized lawlessness, brute force, and irrationality parts of "normal" government.

The modern bureaucratic state is a social invention of Western Europe, China's early civil service notwithstanding. Aside from its administrative system, nothing so clearly differentiates the modern state from its predecessor as the legitimate monopoly of physical coercion, the vast extent of the central power, and the distinction between public and private pursuits, interests, rights, and obligations.

Incipient, though largely ephemeral, features of this new type of state evolved during the half millennium of inconclusive struggle which marked the transition from feudal to bureaucratic forms of political organization. Genuine bureaucratic elements and some seemingly "modern" characteristics of governmental administration crystallized within the Occidental feudal monarchies, after they had appeared and receded in the Byzantine and Saracen polities.

The emergence of nuclei of a literate class of appointed professional administrators accompanied the rise of centralized institutions. Most notable was the reorganization of royal household government, as

carried out in the kingdom of Sicily under Roger II (1101–1154) and
Frederick II (1208–1250), in the English monarchy after the Norman
Conquest, and in the French royal demesne during the thirteenth and
fourteenth centuries. Social experimentation was instigated to increase
the personal power and profit of forceful and imaginative rulers.

These reforms entailed the establishment of new, central bureaucratic bodies in finance, administration, and justice such as the famous
Exchequer and Chancery in England and the *parlement, chambre des
comptes* and *cour des aides* in France. These innovations were associated with the employment of more efficient methods in the management of the king's estate and the introduction of improved techniques
in revenue administration. On the local level, the growth of the effective power of the reconstructed royal court (*curia regis*), insofar as it
was exercised through centrally controlled professional personnel, was
symbolized by the royal itinerant justices in England and by the *baillis*
and *sénéchaux* of the French king.

As the new administrative departments and field offices were nothing
but special parts of the king's personal organization, so no distinction
was made between household and other officials. The dynastic court
remained the center of initiative and decision. Management of the
ruler's affairs meant administration in and through his household. In
consequence, the rising bureaucrats belonged to the same category of
servitors as the domestic servants. Originally, like the king's cooks,
scullions, grooms, and valets, they were amenable to their master's will
and dependent upon the pleasure of their employer. In fact, however,
they formed a special group within the household staff, distinguished
by their education, special skills, and superior functions.

These clerks, accountants, secretaries, judges, and councilors were
in charge of delegated executive tasks. Whether they sprang from the
ecclesiastical order or from the secular bourgeois, they were men who
had studied in the schools. Through this permanent body of trained
professionals, learning became important for large-scale government.
In contrast to their deceptive legal status as dynastic underlings, these
technicians enjoyed a good deal of discretion in their work and, as a
rule, permanent tenure. Living mainly on fees and other perquisites of
office and securing their jobs through patronage and open or disguised
purchase, they were quick to develop a strong proprietary claim to their
positions.

The reformed system of rulership through personal servants made
the exercise of dynastic authority more effective. But it did not substantially add to the very limited tasks of medieval government. Nor

did it signify, prior to the revival of the late Roman-Byzantine principles of *ius publicum*, a departure from medieval concepts of government.

Some kings and princes grew stronger by effecting a redistribution of existing authority, by compelling the contending magnates to relinquish some of their traditional powers and jurisdictions. But the consequent shift in the relations of might and right affected the location and qualitative utilization rather than the nature and functional extent of governmental power.

The medieval central executive concerned itself only with two major administrative activities. Aside from the dispensation of justice, that is, the income-yielding protection of established rights and privileges in the realm, practical government was preoccupied with securing the prince's claims as a proprietor in accordance with the feudal principle of dynastic ownership in countries. The public role of the rulers was incidental to the employment of their power in the service of personal enrichment and dynastic advantage. And since the proprietary principle centered in land and in legal rights over people living on the land, the drive for greater effectiveness in "public" administration was directed toward tightening the prince's authority in his demesne. To be master in his household; to be free in the selection, promotion, and removal of his officials; and to obtain through them bigger revenues from his estate—these were the dominant objectives of the successful princely reformers.

In their deliberate advancement of dynastic jurisdictions, the progressive princely polities of the twelfth and thirteenth centuries were the precursors of the absolute monarchies. But in all other vital matters the pre-absolutist states retained their medieval character and base. The extent of the central authority in "the State" remained highly limited. The personal qualities of the feudal ruler continued to be of cardinal importance for the effective operation of the government. The modern distinction between private and public life was nonexistent.

The proprietary conception of rulership created an inextricable confusion of public and private affairs. Rights of government were a form of private ownership. "Crown lands" and "the king's estate" were synonymous. There was no differentiation between the king in his private and public capacities. A kingdom, like any estate endowed with elements of governmental authority, was the private concern of its owner. Since "state" and "estate" were identical, "the State" was indistinguishable from the prince and his hereditary personal "patrimony."

It is therefore misleading and lacking in historical perspective to classify the patrimonial bureaucrats of the feudal age and their immediate successors as "public servants" and embryonic "civil servants" in the modern sense. Although they were appointed, professional government executives, it was not their business to act in behalf of the public interest, let alone to equate the public with the general interest. Instead, they were employed to make their master the richest and most powerful man in the country by means of peaceful, routinized exploitation of his private resources and personal prerogatives. This was true even of the Anglo-Norman monarchy, despite England's early centralization of judicial administration on a national scale and her development of a common law.

A number of factors combined to give considerable public significance to the newly created administrative departments and their permanent staffs. Their lucrative activities grew wider in geographic scope. Procedural norms were gradually worked out. Eventually they detached themselves from the court in the narrow sense and partially emancipated themselves from their ruler's personal intervention. Increasingly, too, they tended to employ for their personal ends the authority delegated to them. All these incidents of change were, of course, important to the common weal. The deeds and misdeeds of the practitioners of effective princely government affected the security and welfare of the community at large. These men acquired public power by wielding power over the public. However, this alone was not enough to make them public servants.

In medieval times, the later notion of a public trust, given for a public purpose, gained practical significance and found, to some extent, formal recognition not in the larger principalities and kingdoms but in numerous cities, established as legal associations under a corporate authority and vested with varying rights of self-government. These bodies, acting through the creative leadership of their wealthy patrician governors, devised the rudiments of a modern system of public administration, public taxation, public finance, public credit, public works, and public utilities. Here a managerial personnel arose which, as a group, served the collective ends of their little commonwealths.

Aside from some full-time clerks, accountants, notaries, and the like who formed the tiny body of the permanent municipal bureaucracy, the great bulk of a city's administrative officials consisted of part-time employees, appointed or, now and then, elected, for a definite period of time. Being only semiprofessionals, they were, at the most, semibureaucrats. These men, like the directing and hiring city fathers, did not keep official activity neatly apart from private life. They did not

perform impersonal public functions, for, as a rule, they collected and
appropriated, in part or in whole, a fee for their personalized services.
Their relationship to their local clients was quite similar to the cash
nexus that existed between a handicraftsman and his customers. As the
artisan was paid for his labor or the product of his labor, so the town
functionary was entitled to charge a "just price" for his exertions. But
while the management of urban administration remained semiprivate
in character, its ownership and control had become public.

Abuse and corruption notwithstanding, a reasonably clear line was
drawn between private and public property, private and public buildings, private assets and public funds. The separation of public from
private affairs and the disentanglement of governmental authority from
patrimonial property found particularly noteworthy expression in the
pattern of municipal taxation. The proceeds of direct and indirect taxes,
unlike princely exactions, were devoted to objects of general utility.
They were employed for the construction of town halls, market places,
warehouses, wharves, locks, bridges, canals, fortifications; for the purchase of land and forests by the town; for the pavement of streets and
for assuring the city's water supply.

All this stimulated civic sentiment: loyalty was attached not to a
personal lord, but to a communal entity, founded on association and
voluntary coöperation from below rather than on coercion from above.
Concomitantly, there developed a new set of civic obligations, as epitomized by the collective liability of all burgesses for the debts of their
local *patrie*.

The larger polities of the later Middle Ages were not rebuilt in the
image of the pioneering municipalities. Nonetheless, these town governments produced some of the tools and, unwittingly, adumbrated
some of the modern ideas of public need and public service which the
thoroughly bureaucratized absolute monarchies applied in their practice
of public administration at a later period and in perverted form.

The extension of real royal power was not a continuous process in
western Europe and southern Italy. It was followed by a secular trend
of retrogression. The impetus to renewed and, this time, more decisive
growth came a few centuries later, under the aegis of dynastic absolutism. Meanwhile, the Magna Charta, the great palladium of the
"feudal reaction," indicated at an early date how evanescent were many
of the princely gains. A massive resistance movement against royal
encroachments checked the stabilization of an independent monarchical
authority which had been sustained by the formation of a civil bureaucracy. But the "feudal reaction" was progressive as well as reactionary.
It made possible the triumph of medieval constitutionalism. Thus came

into being a new, transitional type of state, in which the Estates
(*Stände*) were the cobearers of the central power. This *Ständestaat*, as
the Germans call it, was no longer really feudal and not yet really
bureaucratic, but betwixt and between.

After the thirteenth century, the course of administrative bureaucrat-
ization did not halt. There were marked increases in the number and
variety of administrative tasks. These were undertaken either by professionals or by "gentlemen" amateurs. For instance, the status and
mobility of the labor force and the fixing of maximum wages on a vast
territorial scale became objects of central government regulation and
supervision. In the English and French monarchies this expansion of
state activity was precipitated by the Black Death of the mid-four-
teenth century. Similar policies, likewise attendant to the sharp decline
of population and the sudden rise of acute labor shortage, were
adopted in the Prussian state of the Order of the Teutonic Knights
during the fifteenth century.

Bureaucratic officialdom itself continued to increase in numbers,
especially in France, but at the same time its political and social position changed. Its members ceased to function as mere instruments of
the ruler's will. Slowly and imperceptibly, government by the king in
person had begun to shade into government under the king exercised
in his name. In fact, "royal household servants," capitalizing on the
procedures and strong traditions of corporate action which they had
evolved, were the first effectively to limit princely caprice. The bureaucratic "routine, devised to restrain the aristocracy, grew into a check on
the arbitrary power of the Crown."

Quite often, and mainly because of the heavy influx of incompetents,
this transformation was associated with a lowering of the bureaucracy's
professional quality. Most of its members developed, in law or in fact,
into owners of government offices. They regarded the authority delegated to them as their heritable freehold. They replenished their ranks,
in accordance with the ancient practices of all privileged groups, largely
by coöptation, which in practice meant by nepotism and favoritism.
Such patronage kept in active government a string of self-perpetuating
family dynasties, assuring managerial continuity. Though this official
oligarchy developed rules and habits of professional conduct upon its
own terms, it exerted its energies, above all, to affirm the time-honored
rights and customs of the aristocratic power elites, to which it belonged.

Many of the patrimonial dignitaries were noble dilettantes who had
snatched up valuable posts as profits arising out of their superior social

status. Others, not blessed with high-born ancestors, had found it worth their while to exchange a bag of money for a leisurely place of public distinction. Frequently, these noble placemen and plutocratic social climbers served as members of advisory councils, administrative boards, or collegiate courts of law. If so, they shared their responsibilities with colleagues who, whatever the modes of their appointment, possessed specialized skills, and who did the actual work. The experts were chiefly "hired Doctors" and trained jurists. They took charge of the day-to-day business of central and regional government as a running concern.

Concurrently, the notables, comprising the ecclesiastical magnates, the seignioral lay aristocracy and the patrician governors of the chartered towns, pressed forward their interests and views in defense of their special liberties and immunities. They managed to impose restraints upon both the prince and his councilors and executives. The organizational result of this extremely complicated, unresolved contest for supremacy was the gradual reconstruction of the central government on the basis of institutions, representative of the ruling groups, which were identical with the most affluent and most privileged elements of society. Thus, a sort of co-regency developed among the prince, the government bureaucrats, and the notables. Politically, the latter were constituted as the Estates of the realm. Since these associations of local rulers were often divided by intergroup as well as intragroup quarrels, they held only an unstable share in the exercise of the central authority. In numerous instances, however, they succeeded in formally restricting the freedom of the prince to choose "his" servants as he wished. Time and again, they wavered between organized coöperation and passive or active resistance. Their chief weapons were the techniques of political barter and contract which had developed within the feudal system. But when confronted with acute crises and sharp conflicts over the interpretation of customary law, the estates did not shun the use of violence.

In essence, then, the *Ständestaat* was a corporate-aristocratic form of superficially centralized territorial rulership in which the elite of the patrimonial bureaucracy and the notables were the decisive forces. Both central and local government management were the preserve of a hereditary, pluralistic oligarchy which did not have, however, the character of a rigorously closed corporation. The princely ruler, himself regarded as a superior estate, was a *primus inter pares*. Such a federative government of ill-defined though constitutionally limited and divided powers was the typical basis of statehood throughout

Europe from the thirteenth to the fifteenth centuries. Only the political
tyrannies of the Italian Renaissance stood apart. Against this background monarchical absolutism arose during the period from the late
fifteenth to the late seventeenth centuries.

The whittling away of the powers of the assemblies of estates
ushered in a new era in the history of the ownership, control, and
management of the means of political domination. The emergence of
centralizing authoritarianism found conspicuous expression in the
partial or total eclipse, as organs of government, of the Spanish *cortes*,
the French *états*, the south Italian *parliamenti*, the German and Austrian *Stände*, and the Russian *zemskii sobor*. Their decline was both
the cause and the effect of the establishment of a princely monopoly
over the central power in the state.

Through this momentous usurpation of preponderant influence,
backed up by superior military force, the *Ständestaat* gave way to an
absolute state in the sense that the legal authority of the prince was
released from the restraints which natural law, rivaling jurisdictions,
old-standing customs, and the special liberties of the ruling groups had
imposed upon him. In real life, unchecked authority did not mean
unlimited power, and the claim to omnipotence was scarcely more than
wishful thinking. But despite its pretentious legal façade, at the prime
of its development the absolute monarchy was an exacting fiscal and
military police state. In accord with the revised ideas of Roman imperial absolutism, the exclusive right to make policy and law and to
direct enforcement at will was concentrated in a single individual. The
newly proclaimed "sovereignty" of the state was embodied in the person of the monarch.

In politics and governmental administration the abandonment of the
proprietary conception of rulership was extremely slow. The differentiation between kingship as a public trust and a personal status advanced faster in theory than in practice. Wherever princely despotism
did become the legitimate government, the identification of the dynastic interest with *raison d'état* and *salus publica* was the official
mainspring of political integration. In consequence, obedience to the
monarch and his appointed designees supplanted, in principle, voluntary coöperation by the old co-owners of public jurisdictions. Even
the hitherto independent few—the hopes and desires of the many
hardly mattered—were now expected to bow their heads and to take
orders.

The rise of centralized domination under the leadership of autocrats,
whether kings, princes, prime ministers, or political cardinals, wrought
profound changes in the functions of the central government; in the

methods of political and administrative management; in the recruitment and behavior of men in authority; and in the conception of the
rights and duties of officeholding.

Absolutism also altered the nature of political power. The new state
rulers were not content to add to their "patrimony" the traditional
jurisdictions of the estates and to absorb most of their functions. They
also built a new bureaucratic empire. They raised sizable permanent
armies, imposed ever larger taxes, multiplied fiscal exactions. They
extended and intensified the regulative and administrative intervention
of the dynastic government into the sphere of private rights and local
home rule. And they made a place for the Crown as a strong commercial competitor and monopolist in production and distribution.

Thus, the makers of the absolute monarchy did not merely learn to
handle old institutions in a new way. They also invented novel and
more effective instruments of compulsion. By constructing a large-
scale apparatus of finance, administration, and military might operated
by a class of appointed career executives accountable to them, they
became the founders of a thoroughly bureaucratized state wtih many
strikingly "modern" features. The great political entrepreneurs had the
wit to realize that "a bureaucratized autocracy is a perfected autocracy."

An aggressive, methodical, and often oppressive machine of hier-
archical state management by dictation and subordination came to
prevail over the less elaborate, more slovenly, and infinitely more
personal medieval contrivances. Dynastic absolutism itself was only a
passing historic phenomenon. But it gave birth to an administrative
system which survived to enter the common heritage of contemporary
civilization.

The growth of the power of the central authority meant the growth
of the power of the executive bureaucracy. Everywhere throughout the
formative stage, new, removable bureaucrats and not the "old" patrimonial officials and notables were in the lead. The *nouveaux arrivés*
challenged the diehard notion that the privileged should continue to
derive the right to govern by inheritance or purchase without special
training and without devoting their energies to it exclusively. The
power of the monarch to nominate officers at his discretion, uncon-
firmed by the estates and in violation of ancient usage, and to regulate
the functions and status of the incumbents as he saw fit, deeply
affected both the practice and theory of government.

The crown's arrogated power to appoint and to remove at will made
possible the resurgence and rapid expansion of autocratic personnel
administration. The rise of absolutism furnished an important basis for

gaining authority, income, wealth, external dignity, social honors, and for the extraction of deference from the lower orders. It raised a dependent parvenu elite of commissioned government managers to a position of functional superiority in the polity.

Henceforth, centrally directed executive government was far more ramified than in medieval times. Impersonal relations were to prevail over personal ties, since administrative *étatisme* was growing into a big business. Its operators originated as "dynastic servants." But unlike the professional officials in the feudal states, they were, a few relics of the past notwithstanding, clearly separated from the princely household.

The new bureaucrats were not modern civil servants, but their forerunners. They were dynastic rather than public servants. They served the welfare of the government of the autocratic prince, not that of the governed. The well-being of the subjects was not an end in itself but a means to bolster the position of the government. Nowhere in Europe did the conversion of dynastic bureaucrats into public agents present itself as a serious issue before the end of the eighteenth century. Only thereafter did allegiance to the king-employer as a person or to the crown as the institutional embodiment of authority or to the aristocratic few begin to merge into loyalty to the abstract ideas of the State or of popular sovereignty.

Government bureaucracy and civil service are not synonymous terms or identical concepts. The modern civil service is a special type of responsible bureaucracy. It deserves its name only if it equates the public interest with the general welfare. In reality, during the nineteenth century the evolving civil service elites of the European world showed a strong propensity toward attaching themselves to the interests and ideals of limited groups rather than to "the people" and egalitarian conceptions of civic right and political liberty. The tardy adjustment demonstrated how great was the vitality of the ancient aristocratic societies.

The New Monarchy, as it is sometimes called, modified but did not destroy the confused mass of jurisdictions which had been transmitted from the past. It merely made a start in disengaging public prerogatives from the law of private property, from vested family interests, and from the grip of the possessors of legal, social, and political privilege. The new bureaucrats epitomized this trend which in medieval times had been noticeable only in the cities.

France, the most populous political unit of Europe in the sixteenth and seventeenth centuries, was then the chief model of the absolute monarchy. Here law and political theory drew a sharp distinction between the numerous patrimonial officials, the strongly entrenched *officiers*, and the rising small body of absolutist bureaucrats, the *commissaires*. All the modernized states of Europe, in their own peculiar and fleeting ways, developed striking analogies to this dual personnel pattern which reflected two antagonistic principles of officeholding and the coëxistence of two distinct managerial hierarchies.

The *officiers*, as defined and protected by French law, gave concrete expression to the close association of public authority with rights of private ownership, which the feudal state had passed on to its successors. The *officiers* were holders of administrative and judicial jobs whose appointment had legally to be approved by the crown. Actually, in the course of the fourteenth and fifteenth centuries, when the French *Ständestaat* was built, the purchase of offices was common enough to reduce royal confirmation to a formality. Through this practice the buyer gained a personal proprietary title to a particular *charge* or *fónction*.

Sale of offices on a large scale was peculiar to France. There it grew rapidly during the dislocating price revolution of the sixteenth and early seventeenth centuries. Fiscal expediency accounted for this further growth which was to prove a blight to the public and disastrous to the long-term interests of the "sovereign" monarch striving for supreme mastery. The financial straits of the crown coincided with a strong craving for public distinction. This demand came not from the increasingly impoverished class of noble landed *rentiers*, but from socially ambitious families who had made fortunes in trade, in finance, or in the legal profession. As in the immediately preceding centuries, officeholding was one of the chief means by which men from the middle ranks of society entered the old upper class. All over Europe, the expansion of acquisitive business enterprise gave a fresh impetus to social mobility and to the amalgamation of private and public activity.

The *Paulette* of 1640, named after the secretary of state Paulet, provided a firm legal foundation for the perpetuation of venal authority and the sanctity of commercialized government administration in France. The office was made transferable at the will of the incumbent who in return for this right was obligated to pay an annual fee to the crown. In theory and practice, the office was recognized as a regularly established public function as well as an object of private ownership. It was distinct from an "ordinary" capital investment, since it was a springboard of legal privilege, a secure base of personal power, and often also a means of acquiring prestige titles and noble status. The income derived from it was not so much in wages and allowances as in fees and perquisites. The *officier* owned his post and appendant rights almost like a piece of real estate which he had either bought with hard cash or inherited or acquired as a dowry. He was the "old" bureaucrat and hence a semi-autonomous, virtually irremovable and largely unaccountable functionary with strong regional and local attachments.

The *commissaire* appeared in the sixteenth century as an irregular and more carefully selected representative of the king. He differed fundamentally from the *officier*, with regard to both legal status and political function. The *commissaire* was the new bureaucrat, the official champion of monarchical centralization, and a salaried subordinate, although his emoluments were seldom confined to a fixed stipend. He was a "permanent probationer," subservient to the wishes of his ruler. Entrusted with a revocable *commission*, he was subject to specific instructions regulating his functions and duties, to disciplinary controls, to sudden transfer or dismissal. He was the creature but also the maker and chief direct beneficiary of the absolute form of government.

The concept of the *commissaire* was distinct from that of the *officier*. Historic reality, however, was less precise and more perplexing. Actually the two categories shaded into each other, and sometimes the lines of demarcation became hopelessly blurred. Everywhere a more or less substantial percentage of the rising *commissaires* was originally recruited from the ranks of the old official hierarchy. They were then, literally speaking, "commissioned officers."

From the outset, the power elite of "commissars" was built up, like their age-old competitors, on gradations of rank and permeated with hierarchical conceptions. Their initial political status was that of a mere transmission belt. They were commissioned by the monarch to ensure his sovereignty by curbing or destroying the powers of the traditional leadership groups in general and by working out a *modus vivendi* with the corporate organizations of the *officiers* in particular. They had to make a place for themselves in a neatly stratified and predominantly noncompetitive society, founded on status, unequal rights, class privileges, and the persistent aristocratic conviction "that the inequalities which distinguish one body of men from another are of essential and permanent importance." In such a social order, the commissars, loosely scraped together from heterogeneous strata, could not relax until they, too, had arrived.

The long and bitter struggle of these interlopers for dominance in the management of public administration, for political leadership, and for recognition as a superior status group was concentrated on two fronts. They could not attain their ends without putting into their place the old political and executive elites and without effecting their own emancipation from monarchical autocracy.

Nowhere in Europe under the absolutist Old Regime were the new administrative bureaucracy and the time-honored bodies of aristocratic rulership implacable enemies. The upper brackets of the commissar class found their social identity in close interaction with those very forces who as independent *seigneurs* or as semi-independent *officiers* had heretofore owned the means of government and administration. The commissars gained an assured social position and extended their power by infiltration and limited amalgamation, chieflly through holding interlocking positions. Thus they developed into a social elite which was not merely a self-perpetuating official aristocracy but also a highly prominent segment of the nobility and of the plutocracy. Thus they fortified themselves as a political hierarchy. As a group, they grew almost independent of effective royal control in the exercise of delegated administrative and judicial tasks. But in addition, and whether or not they came from the new or the old bureaucracies, the top executives, and sometimes even strategically placed subaltern officials, eventually managed to capture the lion's share in the central power of political decision.

This whole process was accompanied by the regrouping of all the competing governing elites. The principal political result was the subtle conversion of bureaucratized monarchical autocracy into government by an oligarchical bureaucracy, self-willed, yet representative of the refashioned privileged classes. Everywhere, earlier or later, dynastic absolutism was superseded by bureaucratic absolutism before the absolute state itself was seriously challenged by modern liberalism.

The transition to the more advanced stage in the evolution of the Old Regime began to be quite conspicuous in France in the late days of Louis XIV, in Russia under the successors of Peter I, and in the monarchy of the Austrian Habsburgs during the reign of Maria Theresa. In Prussia this development did not become clearly discernible before the latter part of the eighteenth century. The main reason for this delay was not so much the fact that the Hohenzollerns were relative latecomers in practicing political integration by coercion, but rather the accident that here princely leadership was nominal only from 1688 to 1713. At the helm of the Prussian absolute state, prior to the French Revolution, stood three men who for long periods ruled autocratically in person: the Elector Frederick William, later called the Great Elector (1640–1688), King Frederick William I (1713–1740), and Frederick II, better known as Frederick the Great (1740–1786).

In substance, but on a grander scale and with the aid of perfected methods, the commissars played a social and political role which closely resembled that of their far distant professional forebears. The bureaucratic managers of the reformed feudal monarchies had supplied the initial kernel of the growing body of patrimonial officials. And the elite of this old hierarchy had succeeded in trimming the discretionary powers of the prince, but had been forced to share the spoils of victory with the large landowners and the urban patricians.

So enormous was the influence of the historic heritage that the absolute dynastic state turned out to be merely another phase in the history of the inveterate struggle for the abridgment of royal prerogatives. As for the social forces in the state, the "modern Old Regimes" were indeed not more than a variation of the aristocratic monarchy, a monarchy dominated by aristocratic power groups of bureaucrats and notables. Related by direct descent to the *Ständestaaten* and the feudal polities, the absolute monarchies retained certain traits of their predecessors. At the same time, however, they were far more centralized and bureaucratized, more active and more strictly utilitarian, more machine-like, more authoritarian, and more efficient in the use of material resources and in the direction and coördination of human energy.

* * * * *

In the course of her growth as an absolute state Prussia acquired certain traits which, by entering into a peculiar synthesis, gave her a rather singular complexion. The rigorously autocratic practice of "cabinet government," as worked out by Frederick William I and Frederick II; the blending of civil and military administration and personnel; the excessive militarization of social life; and the emergence of "Prussian Puritanism," allied with the political docility and social quietism of orthodox Lutheranism, were deviations from general European trends. They prefigured the far graver detachment from the West, as it developed in the nineteenth century: the alienation from the Western ways of public life and the prevailing frame of values of Western social and political thought. This separation was symbolized, above all, by the prolonged concentration of political leadership in the irresponsible central executive, the adoration of state power, and the far-reaching political and intellectual influence of the irrational teachings of German Romanticism.

Yet, in the basic direction of development under the Old Regime, Hohenzollern Prussia moved in harmony with the other absolute polities of Europe.

* * * * *

At the dawn of the nineteenth century the harshness and soullessness of the Prussian system began to give way to a softer and more benignant pattern of authoritarian rule. The administrative servants of the crown finally succeeded in curtailing the arbitrary powers of the king and in making him the political prisoner of the ruling class. In helping themselves, they also helped, to some extent, the Prussian people. But in the midst of this freedom-loving revulsion of "idealistic" bureaucrats moving against the moribund state of Frederick II, there appeared an ominous new trend: the flight into a world of dangerous illusions and misconceptions and the immoderate use of high-sounding words.

In practicing the vices of self-glorification and group arrogance, the Prussian bureaucracy was not unique in the nineteenth century. To be sure, its pretensions and its extravagant hierarchism were often harmless and simply amusing. But in posing as the practical incarnation of the social and political teachings of German Idealism; in operating behind a metaphysical smoke screen; in persuading many that public administration was "the" government, bureaucracy "the" State, authority liberty, and privilege equality of opportunity, the Prusso-German bureaucracy made indeed a special place for itself among the governmental services of the European world.

Because of their aristocratic-oligarchic traditions and of their strong vested interests everywhere, it has not been easy, in more recent generations, to turn the bureaucratic manipulators of unaccountable upper class government into public servants, representative of the freely expressed will of "the people" who make up the State. No nation can rightfully claim that it has completed this transformation of masters into agents. In the large European states, the failure to effect this change and the bleak impact of this failure have been greatest in modern Germany, aside from Russia.

The Hohenzollerns and their partners in the seventeenth and eighteenth centuries unintentionally laid the groundwork for the later conquest of Germany by Prussia. Bismarck, a conservative squire and a statesman of moderation and reasonableness, accomplished this feat by developing into a *Herrenmensch* with democratic gloves and by posing as a German nationalist. His bold, dynamic leadership helped to release forces beyond his control. But, typically enough, Bismarck was also, as were almost all Prussian ministers and imperial chancellors, a select bureaucrat promoted to high political office. From its inception until 1918, except for a few months in 1848, the Prussian state was governed by "impartial" career bureaucrats, "nonpolitical" army officers, and landed Junkers. Though members of self-assertive groups, they held the honest conviction that men of their kind were destined to be for all time the natural guardians of the general interest.

In the course of the development of German conservatism from the war dictator Ludendorff to Hugenberg, these habits of mind, deeply rooted, as they were, in the Old Regime, had catastrophical repercussions. The increasingly frantic determination to assure against all odds the subjection of the governed to the will of a privileged minority accelerated not only the transformation of "aristocratic" into "plebeian conservatism," it also made many members of the old authoritarian leadership groups lose their heads. Thus, toward the bitter end and at a colossal cost to themselves and to millions of innocent people, they set out to salvage their political fortune and traditional social position in alliance with the totalitarian Nazi movement.

Suggestions for Further Reading

ASTON, TREVOR H., ed., *Crisis in Europe, 1560–1660*. New York: Basic Books, 1965.

BURCKHARDT, C. J., *Richelieu: His Rise to Power*. New York: Oxford University Press, 1940.

CHURCH, W. F., *Constitutional Thought in Sixteenth-Century France*. Cambridge, Mass.: Harvard University Press; London: H. Milford, Oxford University Press, 1941.

ERGANG, R. R., *The Potsdam Führer*. New York: Columbia University Press, 1941.

FIGGIS, J. N., *The Divine Rights of Kings*. New York: Harper and Brothers, 1952.

FRIEDRICH, C. J., *The Age of the Baroque, 1610–1660*. New York: Harper and Brothers, 1952.

MEINEKE, FRIEDRICH, *Machiavellism, The Doctrine of Raison d'État and its Place in Modern History*, trans. Douglas Scott. New Haven, Conn.: Yale University Press, 1957.

MOUSNIER, ROLAND, "The Exponents and Critics of Absolutism," in *The New Cambridge Modern History*, Vol. IV. London: Cambridge University Press, 1970.

RANUM, OREST, *Richelieu and the Councillors of Louis XIII: A Study of the Secretaries of State and Superintendents of Finance in the Ministry of Richelieu, 1635–1642*. Oxford: The Clarendon Press, 1963.

STONE, LAWRENCE, *The Crisis of the Aristocracy, 1558–1641*. Oxford: The Clarendon Press, 1965.

TREASURE, GEOFFREY, *Seventeenth Century France*. New York: Anchor Books, 1967.